The True Life
of
Johann Sebastian Bach

The True Life of Johann Sebastian Bach

Klaus Eidam

Translated by Hoyt Rogers

BASIC BOOKS

A Member of the Perseus Books Group

CONTENTS

Translator's Note ∼ IX
Introduction ∼ XI
A Note in Passing ∼ XV

The True Life of Johann Sebastian Bach ∼ 1

Works Cited ∼ *373*
Notes ∼ *377*
Index ∼ *397*

The True Life of Johann Sebastian Bach

COURT COMPOSER
TO THE KING OF POLAND
AND ELECTOR OF SAXONY
COURT MUSIC DIRECTOR
TO THE PRINCE OF ANHALT-CÖTHEN
AND THE DUKE OF WEISSENFELS
&
DIRECTOR MUSICES &
SCHOOL CHOIRMASTER OF
THE ST. THOMAS SCHOOL
LEIPZIG

TRANSLATOR'S NOTE

My main objective has been to reproduce the content, style, and tone of Klaus Eidam's biography of Bach as faithfully as possible. In some places the editors at Basic Books have insisted on minor emendations, with a view to making the narrative more accessible to the general reader. In the same spirit they have asked me to render specialized terms such as *Kapellmeister, Cantor,* and *Rektor* by approximating them in ordinary English rather than merely transliterating the German. It must be pointed out, however, that there are no precise equivalents of these words. The *Kapellmeister* ("music director") directed the small musical ensemble or band (*Kapelle*) that was a common feature of Bach's time. The *Cantor* ("choirmaster") was primarily a teacher, not a choir director in the modern sense. Instead of resorting to "rector," I have translated *Rektor* as "headmaster." The editors also requested me to approximate the titles of all Bach's works (including cantatas), at least when they appear in the text for the first time. In these and other cases, wherever they considered it necessary, the English and German are given side by side; they have determined which language should take precedence, when to use italics or quotation marks, and the like. In general, throughout the book they have systematically applied their standards for punctuation, capitalization, etc., rather than my own. During our cordial collaboration in the final stage of this project, William Morrison demonstrated both his extraordinary precision and his editorial acumen.

A recognized Bach scholar, David Schulenberg of the University of Notre Dame, has double-checked my manuscript to assure that it reflects current usage in the fields of musicology, theology, and seventeenth-century history. I am indebted to him as well for some helpful suggestions about syntax and phraseology. It goes without saying that we have both been concerned exclusively with points of translation; Klaus Eidam's research and conclusions are entirely his own. The author himself has kindly answered a number of my questions and has formally approved my translation of his book.

In the course of my labors, I have found one work invaluable above all others—*The New Bach Reader: A Life of Johann Sebastian Bach in Letters and Documents.* The original version was published decades ago by Hans T. David and Arthur Mendel; it has recently been revised and updated by Christoph Wolff. My loyal friends in Munich, the renowned translator Friedhelm Kemp and his multilingual wife, Cornelia Kemp, provided me with apt solutions to some of the thornier problems I encountered. I owe profound thanks to them and to my parents, Eleanor and Theodore Boone, who supported my efforts with their usual patience and grace, and to whom this translation is dedicated.

—*Hoyt Rogers*

INTRODUCTION

To honor the master,
To teach his heralds

Among the many little-known German musicians, Johann Sebastian Bach is undoubtedly the most famous. We know that
Beethoven said of him: "He should have been called 'ocean' instead
of 'brook' [*Bach* in German]." There are theologians who would like
to acknowledge him as the fifth evangelist, and Albert Schweitzer
described him as the "climax and end of Baroque music." From
these few comments, we can already gather that he is in fact barely
known—a fate he shares with most composers of his rank.

Many people still think of Mozart as "German music's genius
of light and life," who guiltlessly ended up in an indigent's grave
because of his frivolous wife; of Beethoven as "the Titan stricken
with deafness"; of Haydn as the good-natured "Papa" with a pig-
tail—a "classic" of course, but really of the second order. The
image of Schubert as a winsome Romantic, the image of Schumann as a brooding creator of "reveries," are slowly beginning to
change only now. Just as many the legends of the saints have superseded their reality, so these portrayals, remote from all factuality,
appear to be invincible, and even today clichés triumph over knowledge again and again.

No musicologist forgets to mention that Mendelssohn-Bartholdy was of Jewish origin, but almost none mentions that he was a Christian of deeply held beliefs. Of course we know that Mozart did not look like he does on the wrappers of the Salzburg chocolates, but a man who died so young and who wrote such heavenly music can only have been a radiant youth as long as he lived. Indeed, the observation that he was a human being too, and for his contemporaries sometimes a rather difficult one, is still regarded by many people as a personal offense. And occasionally such clichés are discarded for no other purpose than to replace them with others that are seldom better grounded but that are usually set forth with more pretense, proclaimed with less modesty, and adjusted with more complacency to current needs.

Johann Sebastian Bach has often proved to be an exceptionally suitable object for such endeavors. Friedrich Smend, who wanted to canonize him through and through, and Walter Vetter, who strove to secularize him completely, are but two examples among many. Bach literature is incalculably vast, yet the number of more or less serious Bach biographies is fairly limited.

When I say "more or less serious," that is putting it kindly: Bach spent twenty-seven years—the principal period of his life and creativity—in Leipzig, yet it is doubtful whether any of his biographers since Philipp Spitta—that is, for the last 120 or more years—has ever taken a look at the Leipzig city council records again. What Spitta did not read, none of his successors was able to copy down from him. At least in the last thirty or forty years, these fundamentally important sources for Bach's life story and circumstances have—demonstrably—never been reexamined. It is indisputable that Bach researchers have shown themselves to be interested in this man's life only in the most superficial manner.

He crossed my path three times before he came to accompany me through ten years of my existence. The first was during my piano lessons, when I struggled with his two- and three-part inventions as a ten- or eleven-year-old. They appeared just as simple as they were difficult in fact, but the more trouble they gave me the more I was drawn to them. Then his D Minor Toccata in the film *The Immortal Heart*—at the movies!—struck me like a thunderbolt. The film was about the fate of Peter Henlein, the inventor of the pocket watch, and later I made my own film about his life for television. But the deeper motivation was that the D Minor Toccata that introduced the film had affected me as profoundly as Ravel's *Boléro*—in quite a different country and at quite a different time—had affected the young Leonard Bernstein. Because of this toccata, I absolutely had to learn to play the organ, and by age fifteen I actually was able to sit at the organ and play the toccata from memory. I did not stop with that piece: From there I branched out into earlier and associated domains of organ literature. I had an uphill battle with *The Well-Tempered Clavier*. When I attended a performance of Bach's D Minor Concerto for Three Harpsichords, I was so carried away that I bought the score and wrote a piano arrangement of it for myself. And at some point, in the middle of the war, I went to Leipzig for the first time and found my way, as though by instinct, to that church where the great choirmaster *(Cantor)* of St. Thomas had worked. Standing full of awe near his memorial plaque at the front of the nave, I gazed up at the organ. So it was here that the master of all masters had stood Sunday after Sunday, and until the end of his life, Sunday after Sunday, had gladdened his congregation with the most magnificent church music the world has ever known.

Naturally I knew that the organ was no longer the same that Bach had played. The one up there was built according to Karl Straube's intentions, though I could not grasp how an organ at which Bach had sat could ever have been replaced by another. After all, I too only knew his music. I did not realize that the cliché of him I carried in my heart was worth exactly as much as the Salzburg Mozart chocolates: What was transfigured by the foil wrapping there was obscured by a halo here.

My third encounter took place decades later, when I had long since distanced myself from the organ as thoroughly as Offenbach had distanced himself from the synagogue: I had become a playwright. In addition, the up-and-coming medium of television had me in its claws, especially television for children and young people.

In my eternal search for material, one day I came across a record jacket that sketched the circumstances of Bach's life at the time he wrote the D Minor Toccata. Bach's adventures as a young man in Arnstadt gelled into a film for television that belonged to the programming schedule year after year from then on. Then a renowned Hungarian film director saw it. She insisted on filming the script all over again. And in Hungary as well the film became such a success (in prime time) that it had to be repeated many times. It was even featured on a talk show because viewers had asked whether the events it depicted were true to life or merely the author's fantasies. A musicologist was brought on, who of course could only confirm the veracity of the script.

Why make anything up? When you can establish how the facts are interconnected, life is hardly to be outdone by fantasy. Over the following decade, as I became more and more familiar with Bach's life—supposedly spent in such quiet, orderly, and modest routines—I was deeply shaken by the great storms in his biography. And very soon I was obliged to ascertain that the towering monument that had been erected to him from so many sides consisted mainly of papier-mâché, finished with plaster for better conservation. But inside its hollow interior I found something far more remarkable than all the panegyrics:

The true life of Johann Sebastian Bach.

A NOTE IN PASSING

My acquaintance with the biographers of Johann Sebastian Bach began over a quarter of a century ago and intensified when East German Television hired me to write a series about his life: The four episodes were shown throughout the world in 1985–1986.

Though at first I had closely dealt only with Bach's Arnstadt period, I then started to study musicology publications more thoroughly, attending a few conventions of Bach specialists as well. But I felt increasingly uncertain. Not only did constantly recurring biographical details and judgments amaze me, but as I tried to profit from the findings of musicology, I felt obliged to take issue with them. I began to search for sources that none of these scholars had ever studied and to seek connections where they had settled for bare facts.

As a result, my image of Bach started changing in many and far-reaching ways. But the attempt to explain the reasons for this change landed me in a complicated situation: If I were to describe Bach's life accordingly, in a version that was simply different from the others—that is, just as I had found it to be—then the relevant experts could maintain that I had gotten it all completely wrong whereas their accounts were based on "proven scholarly findings." To which I would naturally have to reply that in honest scholarship, honestly speaking, nothing should be considered absolutely proven.

But I have not encountered this attitude often. So I have had no other recourse than to contrast the rediscovered realities with the time-honored portrayals, if only to quell the suspicion that I was not aware of them. Unfortunately, with this approach it was not always possible to avoid polemics, since new discoveries inevitably contradict the previous conceptions.

My biography will take issue mainly with the works of the following authors:

Philipp Spitta, music historian, university professor, and secretary of the Royal Academy of Arts in Berlin. He hailed from a respected family of theologians: His brother Friedrich was a much-revered professor of theology, and songs by his father and grandfather are still included in the Lutheran hymnbook to this day. The two volumes of his magnum opus, *Johann Sebastian Bach*, appeared in 1873 and 1892. They display such comprehensive, detailed research and exposition of the sources that his work may be considered the basis of the entire field of Bach literature. Almost all later accounts build upon his writings and for the most part adopt his opinions. Many subsequent authors leave us with the impression that if Spitta did not cite something, then they have not bothered to read it.

Charles Sanford Terry, an English biographer, also builds upon Spitta in his lovingly composed life story *Johann Sebastian Bach* and departs from his theologically determined perspectives in only a few evaluations here and there. Above all he concerns himself with the places where Bach lived (in part he even photographed them himself). His book, written in a popular style, contributed significantly to shaping the commonly held view of Bach.

Albert Schweitzer wrote his extensive work *Johann Sebastian Bach, the Poet-Musician* (1904)—as he did his books on Kant's philosophy of religion, the Holy Communion, and the history of research on Jesus' life—before his thirtieth year, as an independent lecturer (with a doctorate in philosophy and a licentiate in theology) and then as director of the Theological Institute of the Kaiser Wilhelm University in Strassburg. This was before he became the great world-renowned humanist and jungle doctor. His voluminous and thoughtful study was long considered, together with Spitta's, as an epoch-making, canonical work of Bach literature. With reverential deference toward Schweitzer's outstanding personality, it was later set aside to some degree. But Bach's life is only superficially described in it: By his own admission, Schweitzer follows Spitta's version to the letter, and unfortunately in many passages his judgments of Bach's behavior in decisive situations as well as his assessments of his music no longer hold up under closer examination. As a music-making theologian (he also wrote a book on the German and French art of organ building) and a pastor's son, Schweitzer, like Spitta, contemplated Bach's work chiefly from a religious perspective. We do not belittle Schweitzer's lifetime achievements when, in the interests of Bach's work and reputation, we point out various mistakes in the work he wrote as a young man almost 100 years ago.

All three of the above-named consider Bach's lifework from the Protestant theological standpoint of the nineteenth century, viewing Bach himself as a composing man of God who found fulfillment in serving his church.

In opposition to that approach, diverse members and allies of the New Leipzig Bach Society, created in 1949, strove to attain a new image of Bach by trying to present his music as a progressive consequence of the German Enlightenment. This idea was propagated officially by the East German government and met with a good measure of approval right away: It sounded scholarly and had a modern touch. Since the New Bach Society conducted itself largely in a nonpolitical manner, it also achieved considerable effect outside East Germany. Writings by Werner Neumann, Walther Siegmund-Schulze, Heinrich Besseler, and others appeared in West German publishing houses as well. Given that the group could not be ignored, its influence is also reflected in the works of Karl Geiringer, Christoph Rueger, Friedemann Otterbach, and others, right up to Peter Schleuning's analysis of the *Art of Fugue* and the biographical study by Martin Geck that appeared in

1993. Occasionally I also mention the commentaries of Christoph Wolff, editor for many years of the *Bach-Jahrbuch* (*Bach Yearbook*).

According to the explanations of all these distinguished musicologists, Johann Sebastian Bach was the last representative of Baroque music, a musician who furthered the Enlightenment through his music. He was a man whose bad temper did him repeated damage. He was a composer who derived his ideas largely from others, who already went into retirement at the age of fifty-two, who toward the end of his life had fallen completely out of fashion, and who was forgotten for almost eighty years after his death. "He does not make a ripple," Albert Schweitzer stated, and—may his admirers forgive me—I am incapable of agreeing with him there.

My concern here, however, is not to engage in a debate with all these musicologists: I simply wish to bring out some neglected aspects of Bach's life. Still, you cannot make an omelette without breaking some eggs. In this regard, Goethe already remarked in 1829:

> World history has to be rewritten from time to time: In our day we can no longer have the slightest doubt about that. Such a need arises not because much that has happened is only discovered afterwards, but because new perspectives open up as the contemporary of an advancing era is led to standpoints from which the past can be surveyed and assessed in a new way.

So let us begin.

1

His life story is generally known: born in Eisenach, orphaned early on, raised in his brother's home in Ohrdruf; attendance at the Latin School in Lüneburg, a brief first stint in Weimar; organist in Arnstadt, then in Mühlhausen; Weimar again; court music director *(Kapellmeister)* in Cöthen; and finally, for twenty-seven years, the great choirmaster of St. Thomas in Leipzig, until the end of his days. "On the whole, life treated him favorably; the difficulties were not more than his genius could surmount," the fundamental Bach biographer Philipp Spitta sums up. And so I had always imagined it too: after a hard-up youth and a few years of travel, Weimar as the first great organ period, Cöthen as a small-town music director's idyll, and the post as choirmaster in Leipzig as the true vocation and fulfillment of his life. As a rule, basic wisdom and knowledge in this world are both amazingly simple and amazingly false—the hues that transfigure the pictures of the saints serve mainly to cover up the holes.

There are a number of such holes in depictions of Johann Sebastian Bach's life. Generally they begin with the family tree. The story goes that in his lifetime the Bachs held virtually all the positions as organists and other musicians in Thuringia. Veit Bach, who had immigrated from Hungary 120 years earlier, had remarkably strong powers of reproduction. Carl Philipp Emanuel Bach recounted to

Johann Nikolaus Forkel that the Bachs got together every year for a big family reunion, and a quodlibet for such an occasion has been preserved from Bach's Arnstadt period. But every year? Later we learn nothing more about such family gatherings, and at Bach's death all the Bachs appear equally indifferent to the event, as though these reunions had never taken place. Where were they then? Karl Geiringer, in his book on the Bach family of musicians, passes over this in silence. Certainly there were some very capable composers among them: Heinrich Bach, his son Johann Christoph, and his son Johann Michael as well; Johann Bernhard Bach, progenitor of the Erfurt Bachs; and Johann Lorenz, great-nephew of old Christoph.

Legend has praised one of the Bachs to the skies in particular: Johann Sebastian's eldest son, Wilhelm Friedemann. But Albert Emil Brachvogel's novel about him is just as broadly fictitious as the Bach novel *Toccata and Fugue* by Hans Franck and Józef Ignacy Kraszewski's novel about Countess Cosel. Poetry has always triumphed over truth: Switzerland owes the worldwide fame of its national hero Wilhelm Tell above all to Friedrich von Schiller, who never laid eyes on Switzerland, whereas the *Chronicon Helveticum* of Aegidius Tschudi that forms the basis of his drama is known to specialists at best and virtually unknown to most literary scholars.

More research is needed, then, on the whereabouts of the Bachs who made music in Thuringia around 1700. Christoph Rueger expresses his surprise that a genius should suddenly have arisen among so many "mediocre" musicians. But Handel and Bruckner lack musical kindred altogether, and mediocrity as the measure of all things is a relative proposition. What seems mediocre or insignificant to posterity often appeared important or even outstanding to contemporaries. Who knows Paer or Kozeluch nowadays, and what opera house still performs Spontini?

Among the Bachs musical talent was apparently hereditary in the widely extended family, and so was the choice of profession. That the sons should become musicians in turn and that the daughters should marry musicians was natural in a world of firmly established social ranks.

2

Martin Geck would have us believe that it was not heredity at all that made Johann Sebastian into a musician like the other Bachs, but rather the artistic atmosphere of the court city Eisenach. It is true that his father, Johann Ambrosius, was not only town musician there but served as court trumpeter as well. Still, there are no grounds for asserting that in those days Eisenach as a city could boast of a distinguished musical standing, much less that it could have exercised a decisive influence in this regard on little Sebastian. Of course music was played in Ambrosius's house, and lots of music was called for in the town of Eisenach, otherwise why have a town musician and his town band? The term itself was not at all belittling as such: Town bands still existed into the first third of the twentieth century; they made music that was not to be sneezed at, and serious musicians issued from their ranks. One of them was Paul Lincke, who is not taken seriously by musicology but whose compositions prevail without it because they combine splendid ideas with the most solid workmanship. Today the Eisenach band would be called the municipal orchestra and Johann Ambrosius Bach the municipal music director. At the time, it was understood that he was not only obliged to look after his two journeymen and two apprentices but also had to arrange for the appearances of the free-lance musicians, the "beer fiddlers."

No doubt as he exercised his calling his art was hardly, to echo Schiller's words, a "high, heavenly goddess," but rather first and foremost a "productive cow, that provided him with butter." "Town band," "journeymen," "apprentices"—all these terms underline the craftsmanly nature of the profession. In that sense musicians resembled the painters of the period, who had to conceive of their art as a craft and adapt themselves to the wishes of their customers. They pursued their art in order to fulfill the needs of their fellow men, just like bakers, cobblers, and tailors. Presumably, an artist who chiefly lived for his own aims would have seemed fairly superfluous not only to his fellow men but also to himself. There was no connoisseurship as yet for the metaphysical meaning of tone clusters, scrap-metal sculptures, and "happenings"; the

3

population was not open-minded enough. The city remunerated its municipal music director very meagerly: Already at eighteen, as an organist in Arnstadt, Johann Sebastian had a better salary than his father. But for both father and son their main income, in Eisenach as later in Leipzig, came from earnings on the side. The position, the title, provided respectability; as for earning a living, the court trumpeter and town musician had to take care of that himself, just as the *director musices* would later have to do in Leipzig.

Spitta and others have voiced their astonishment that the later, so tirelessly active Johann Sebastian should have been the king of hooky players in his Eisenach days. A plausible explanation seemed to fit: The Eisenach school was so bad that the youngster simply was not interested.

Now that is most improbable: Even in the midst of his duties, it is unlikely that Bach's father would have lost track of his youngest son so completely as not to notice his absences from class. It is also unlikely that he would have left it up to a child to decide about the quality of the instruction offered. No, the boy had a very passable voice and musical understanding on top of that; he was merely more useful in the choir than in school. He was supposed to become a musician anyway, not a scholar. So it was quite comprehensible that the youngster, just as farmers' children still did at the beginning of the twentieth century, would have stayed away from school as often as he was needed. Sebastian, the constantly absent pupil, was not an idler. "I had to be hardworking early on," he himself later declared.

Besides, having a truant as his youngest son would not have been compatible with the prestige of the town musician and court trumpeter. He was a highly respected personage. That can be surmised from the fact that Erfurt city councilor Valentin Lämmerhirt had given him his daughter Elisabeth as a wife, so that he was closely connected with city council circles as a son-in-law. And "city council society" counted for something in the strictly divided ranks of the bourgeoisie at that time. A councilor would not have entrusted his daughter to just any musician. Town musician Bach was already a man of standing in his youth, and he doubtless enjoyed a sub-stantially higher reputation with the Eisenach city council than his famous son did later with the three councils in Leipzig.

His house stood either on the Frauenplan or at today's 35 Luther Street. But the address is meaningless. Nowadays those who visit the house on the Frauenplan, which has been set up as a Bach Museum, learn next to nothing about life in Eisenach at the time or about the household into which Johann Sebastian Bach was born.

It was quite a lively home. The children grew up among musi-cians from the very beginning. That the sons would also become musicians was taken for granted. In Bach's childhood the eldest of them was already living elsewhere and holding down a steady job. Sebastian had to sing in the choir as soon as he could sing at all, just like his brother Johann Jacob, who was older by three years. Among children three years is a significant age difference, but Jo-hann Jacob was the closest in age to Sebastian. The parents could hardly pay much individual attention to their children. What with journeymen and apprentices there were a lot of mouths to feed, and there were also many obligations: weddings, christenings, fu-nerals, official celebrations, family festivities, and annual holidays. On such occasions self-respecting people ordered the services of the choir, the town band, or both. And twice a day—at ten in the morning and at five in the afternoon—the court trumpeter had to blow his trumpet abroad from city hall. If no symphony concerts by the town band were scheduled, then there was "useful music" to be made. And nobody should turn up his or her nose at the word "useful." The only really bad music is music that is not used, or worse, that is of no use at all.

The home of town musician Bach was a busy and flourishing place, but destiny struck even before Johann Ambrosius Bach could celebrate his silver anniversary with his wife. On May 2, 1694, he had to bury her, and with her died the soul of the house. The household could not make do without a housewife, and after half a year of mourning Sebastian's father married the twice-widowed, dependable Mrs. Keul from Arnstadt. But his beloved twin brother died in the fall of that same year, and the following February, just nine months after the death of his first wife, Johann Ambrosius was laid to rest alongside both of them. He was only fifty years old.

Sebastian was nine when he lost his mother, and before he turned ten he was an orphan. It was the first heavy blow in his life. His mother's death changed many things; his father's death changed everything. The Eisenach city council turned a cold shoulder to the widow. It terminated all salary payments and denied her the widow's portion, as well as the continued direction of the town band with the journeymen, though all this had been granted by the Arnstadt city council to the twin brother's widow. Thus the whole household had to be disbanded and room made for a successor. The city of Eisenach would soon need another town musician, and as far as we know it was not one of the Bachs.

The now thrice-widowed woman returned to Arnstadt. Their father's house was no more, and Jacob and Sebastian were completely orphaned. That meant they had lost parental care, friends, housing, and familiar surroundings. Of their childhood there was nothing left.

True, there was still an organist named Johann Christoph Bach in Eisenach, but he belonged to the Arnstadt branch, so he was only a distant relative. He himself lived in hard-pressed circumstances, as his petitions to the city council demonstrate (from which biographers have concluded that, because he complained, he must have been a difficult person).

Johann Ambrosius's firstborn, who like the Eisenach organist was named Johann Christoph, took the two youngest children in. He was already twenty-four and recently married; his wife was expecting their first child. On the occasion of his wedding, a note in the church register called him "a young but artful man," suggesting that he had already made a name for himself as an organist. His organ teacher was Johann Pachelbel, still famous to this day, who was then in his eighth year as organist at the Preachers

6

Church in Erfurt after having previously spent a year in Eisenach as court organist.

Christoph stayed with Pachelbel for three years, and then he received a post himself in Erfurt at the St. Thomas Church. After a short interlude in Arnstadt, in 1690 he obtained the position of organist at St. Michael's in Ohrdruf. It was actually linked to a teaching job at the Latin School, but he managed to free himself of that, just as his youngest brother, Sebastian, would later do in Leipzig.

The household was not blessed with riches, and Ohrdruf was considerably smaller than Eisenach (which at about 8,000 inhabitants was not exactly a metropolis). Ohrdruf had little more than a single neighborhood. To be sure, a Count von Hohenlohe resided there: This village of a little over 2,000 inhabitants was a court city. But people did not derive much from that, unlike in Eisenach, where the duke of Saxe-Eisenach wanted to turn his ducal seat into a "small Paris" and lived decidedly beyond his means to maintain his court.

The big brother needed to farm and raise livestock in order to make ends meet as an organist. The most remarkable thing about this court city was not the court but the Latin School, the fame of which is unanimously acknowledged by Bach's biographers. The wider Bach relations sent their sons to Ohrdruf as well, where they found room and board at Christoph's house. (As long as Ambrosius Bach was still living, other Bachs had sent their children to the school in Eisenach, which implies that Eisenach was not too bad either.)

What strikes us is Sebastian's stunning success in Ohrdruf. The youngster who was absent from school so often in Eisenach managed to become fourth in his class in Ohrdruf right away and later first. He was permitted to skip a level and held his own in the next higher level, where the other pupils were two or more years older than he was. It necessarily follows from this that not only was he gifted, but the demands of the school clearly lay far below his aptitude. And his having left the school in order to continue his upper-level education in another school implies that his big brother, and he himself, considered there was more to be learned elsewhere than the Ohrdruf Latin School could offer.

Admittedly, there were other reasons as well. Jacob, the elder of the two, had remained in Christoph's house until he was fourteen (in other words, until his confirmation) and had then begun a musical apprenticeship with his father's successor in Eisenach. (His name has not come down to us, presumably because he never complained.) The brother had a heart for his relatives: Not only did Jacob and Sebastian find accommodations with him, but Christoph also for a time took in another young kinsman, Johann Ernst Bach, who went to school with Sebastian. But Sebastian was by that time fifteen, and Christoph's family had grown considerably in the meantime: He needed space for four children, and so there was simply no more room for his little brother. In the school codex there is a (very messily written) comment regarding Sebastian's departure: *"ob defect. hospitios."* This is interpreted in Bach's obituary as "death of the host"; Charles Sanford Terry amends it with the plural—*"ob defectum hospitiorum"*—and so wipes out the entire family. Yet Christoph Bach survived twenty-one years longer and lived to see his own sons receive the same favors from Sebastian that he had earlier done for his little brother.

In the year 1700 it was simply necessary to find Sebastian another place to stay. After finishing the first form in Ohrdruf, he could have gone on to the university in Erfurt, for example, which his big brother as well as his father had attended; it was his mother's hometown, and Nikolaus Bach was a well-respected university teacher there. College studies were a good qualification for a musical career; Bach later had his own two eldest sons study law, when he could still afford it. Nor was his tender age a deciding factor: A student could enroll in the university at sixteen with no problem (by the same token, pupils could be found at the secondary school in Arnstadt who were already over twenty). But Sebastian did not go the university in Erfurt; instead, he moved much farther away to attend the Latin School in Lüneburg and do the first level once again—without repeating his spectacular success in Ohrdruf, by the way, as far as we know. He had more important things to do.

From that time on, from his arrival in Lüneburg until the end of his life, he would earn his living through music: His music had to support him. There was no money for college studies. That same year Christoph, who was so averse to schoolteaching that he expressly had himself relieved of those duties when he took up his post as organist, had to apply for a position in the Latin School after all. In the church register the words *"optimus artifex"*—"a very good artist"—are written beside his name; but he could not live on that alone, just as Johann Sebastian would never have the necessary money at decisive junctures of his life either. There was not enough for university at the time, there was not enough later to acquire the official position that would have freed him from all troubles and annoyance, and again at the end of his life there was not enough for the printing of his musical legacy or even for his tombstone. "On the whole he led a fortunate life"—easy for Spitta to say from the comfort of a Berlin professor's residence.

When his big brother could no longer make room for him in his home, the circumstances still remained propitious. The assistant headmaster *(Rektor)* of the Ohrdruf Latin School, choirmaster Arnold, had been dismissed in 1687 as *"pestis scholae, scandalium ecclesiae et carcinoma civitatis"*—"a plague for the school, a scandal for the church, and a cancer for the citizenry"—and his successor, choirmaster Elias Herda, was a graduate of the Lüneburg Latin School. He had direct knowledge of the high importance placed on the cultivation of music there; he saw and heard what Sebastian was capable of in that domain. He also knew that there was always an interest in good singers in Lüneburg, so he recommended him—along with Georg Erdmann, his senior by two years—for a *Freistelle,* or "free place," there. It was more than a free place: *Freistelle* meant that tuition, room and board, and even firewood for the winter were free. The pupils also received modest fees for their participation in

9

the *chorus symphoniacus,* or general chorus, and in the more selective matins choir.

It is quite remarkable that Sebastian obtained this free place when he was still fifteen, since it was only to be expected that his beautiful soprano voice would not last much longer. But by this time he had also become a competent instrumentalist. As a child he had already been able to learn how a violin is handled from his father, who besides the trumpet also knew how to play the violin and viola. It is unthinkable that a boy as hungry for knowledge as little Sebastian would merely have stood by and watched him. And his brother had instructed him in keyboard instruments—quite methodically, as we know. When Handel, the same age as Bach, was already standing in for his teacher Zachau in Halle during church services, Sebastian's brother would not even let him touch the organ yet. But Bastian took to playing the clavier very quickly. "Our little Johann Sebastian's love of music was already uncommonly strong at this early age," the obituary tells us. "In no time he had mastered all the pieces his brother had voluntarily given him to learn." And it continues: "But a book that his brother owned, full of clavier pieces by the most famous masters of the time—Froberger, Kerll, Pachelbel—was denied to him, who knows for what reasons, regardless of his pleas. So his zeal to make further progress inspired him with the following innocent deceit. The book was stored in a cabinet whose doors consisted merely of grillwork. Since it was only bound in paper, he was able to reach through the grate with his small hands, roll up the book, and pull it out. Then he would copy it by moonlight, since he did not even have access to light. After six months this musical booty was happily in his hands. He was trying to make use of it, secretly and with extraordinary eagerness, when to his great dismay his brother found out about it, and mercilessly took away the copy he had gone to so much trouble to create. If we imagine a miser whose ship sank on the way to Peru with a cargo of a hundred thousand thalers, we might obtain a vivid idea of our little Johann Sebastian's sorrow over this loss of his. He did not recover the book until after his brother's death."

Geck is of the opinion that this story was made up out of whole cloth, that here "a harmless incident was trumped up into an anecdote"—as though old Bach had told lies to his sons! The truth is that the story is nothing short of a key event for understanding the grandiose, uniquely exceptional nature of Johann Sebastian Bach as a whole.

By this age other musical geniuses—Mozart, Handel, Mendelssohn—had already been composing for quite some time. We have a delightful rondo by Beethoven written when he was fifteen. But Johann Sebastian Bach copies out other composers' pieces. Secretly. At night.

We would have to try imitating him to grasp fully what this involved for an eleven- to thirteen-year-old. Music paper had to be set aside, goose quills had to be cut, and the calendar and weather had to be taken into account. (The moon was not always full enough to shine, and anyway with clouds in the sky it would be too dark.) Children at such an age need their sleep, but he could not doze off. He had to stay awake until everybody else in the house had gone to bed, then arrange his utensils on the windowsill, creep over to the cabinet, and cautiously pull the book out—all without making a peep. And then he had to write and write by a wretched light as long as the moon was favorable. It rose an hour later each day, and he had to wait for the nights when it was at least halfway visible. You can almost write a text with your eyes shut. Even when the lines run together and the letters are blurred, they still remain legible. But notes have to be placed exactly on and between five lines, precisely on top of each other, with their different values, accidentals, and bar lines. Afterward all traces had to be eliminated, the book put back just as carefully as it had been removed. Then he had to get a bit of sleep, since school required daily achievement, and he also had to keep his big brother from noticing his lack of rest.

For a boy who is capable of carrying out something like this for months on end, music must consist of much more than music making. That could be taken for granted ("In no time he had mastered all the pieces"). But at the same time, over and above all that, music was for him—as we shall see later again and again—that continent whose exploration preoccupied him throughout his life no less than the exploration of the Arctic obsessed the great Amundsen.

For the fifteen-year-old, Lüneburg was an absolute stroke of luck. Even more than his lovely voice, his social status made him eligible for a free place in the school and the matins choir, whose members had to be "poor people's children, with nothing in life but good voices." That applied to him just as it did to his fellow pupil Georg Erdmann, two years his senior, and so the two of them set out, once choirmaster Herda of Ohrdruf had made the proper arrangements. They would have to walk more than 200 miles, and this in March, not exactly the most pleasant month for such an extended trek.

They must have spent more than two weeks on the road, and it is safe to assume that they had little money for provisions. But as of Easter, which came early that year, on April 3, 1700, we find them both registered as members of the matins choir in Lüneburg, and so began for Sebastian a period of the richest possible musical education, free from the systematic strictness of his brother's supervision. Other gifted people need a teacher who directs them and guides them, leading them step by step up the *gradus ad Parnassum.* Johann Sebastian Bach needed the possibility of looking about and experimenting. In Lüneburg he had the chance to do both, and he amply took advantage of the opportunity right away.

Bach's time in Lüneburg has never been rightly assessed in terms of his development as a musician. It truly became his musical university, and the relative shortness of his stay is not a significant factor. As his Ohrdruf schooldays demonstrate, Bach possessed an extraordinarily rapid intelligence—well nigh unbelievable when it came to music.

The matins choir had many duties: songs every morning; motets on Saturdays, Sundays, and feast days; and polyphonic music with orchestral accompaniment on the high holy days. In addition, within the framework of the *chorus symphoniacus* there were appear-

12

ances for special occasions such as bridal Masses or weddings, funerals, and street singing. The income was distributed according to
a rigorous pecking order, and the pupils received the least, but it
was money all the same. More important than anything else was
what they performed: so-called figural music, which is to be understood as polyphonic music composed contrapuntally. In contrapuntal composition there is no melody and accompaniment as in
other types of music; rather, each voice serves as an independent
melodic line, and yet the ensemble must also follow all the rules of
harmonic composition. Naturally, participation in music such as
this affords the budding musician a unique training of the ear, and
a precise observation of the strengths and limits of the various
types of voices.

In the matins choir, with its wide-ranging repertoire of contrapuntal music, the young Bach gained dominion over the praxis that
later enabled him to make even his most difficult vocal parts still
singable and to attain the extraordinary without going beyond the
doable. Here he became familiar with an important repertoire of
polyphonic music through practical experience. And what was not
included in the program of choral singing he found in the school
music library.

The school choirmaster, Friedrich Emanuel Praetorius, who
was still active until 1695, had accumulated an extensive music collection, 1,100 items. So the young musician, who in Ohrdruf had
had to try to copy out the compositions that fascinated him by
night, found works here by about 200 composers from the last
150 years, practically a comprehensive survey of the music of his
time. In addition there were the treasures from the archive of the
Church of St. John, particularly the collection of organ compositions by such famous masters as Jan Pieterszoon Sweelinck, Samuel
Scheidt, Heinrich Scheidemann, Johann Jacob Froberger, Johann
Caspar Ferdinand Fischer, Johann Kaspar von Kerll, and such important contemporaries as Dietrich Buxtehude, Johann Pachelbel,
and Nicolaus Bruhns. Scores by the French masters were also there,

and Bach made himself copies (copies again!) of Nicolas de Grigny's *Livre d'orgue,* and of works by Dieupart and Gaspard Le Roux, Louis Marchand, François Couperin, and André Raison. (He would later base his great organ passacaglia on a theme of Raison's.) Italians were found in this collection too—Frescobaldi, Pergolesi—and Dutchmen like Orlando di Lasso.

All that was more for him than mere tonal impressions. It goes without saying that when he read the notes, he heard the tones, without using an instrument. But it is just as obvious that he had learned more from his brother than mere keyboard playing. Undeniably it was combined with thoroughbass, the ability to play harmonically complete keyboard music at sight from only a bass line together with notations for chords indicated by numbers and occasional accidentals written above the bass. The first and foremost prerequisite for this is a complete familiarity with the chords and the connections among them. From there the expanse of harmonic theory opens up all on its own. The young musician, who devoured the treasures of the music archives in Lüneburg, was not simply reading musical literature; he also possessed the keys to its creation. He knew the rules of harmony as well as those of polyphonic composition from daily experience. As an expert he contemplated not only the artworks but also their anatomy.

And did not compose! There are people like Terry who suspect the opposite, but they cannot prove it. The only evidence from that time is Bach's copies of other people's compositions. There is no other well-known composer who began composing through such extensive copying. The others overflowed with ideas; Bach was driven by a thirst for knowledge. Of course it could also be that he made his copies with the accumulation of a usable music stock in mind. But in that case why did he make copies of Couperin's and Dieupart's clavier music? He would never be able to use them in church services. No, what interested him was music in general.

2

THE SCHOOL IN THE OLD ST. MICHAEL'S CLOISTER of Lüneburg was a very diverse institution. The *Freistelle* pupils were the poorest. Then there were the commoners whose fathers could pay the tuition, room, and board and who made up the *chorus symphoniacus*. And then there were the young gentlemen of the nobility, who were grouped together in what was called the Cavaliers Academy and were even served by the others. The Cavaliers Academy was entirely oriented toward refinement of manners, and of course at the time that meant French manners. Even the language they used among themselves was French.

French dancing naturally belonged to the course of instruction as well, for which a French dance master, Thomas de la Selle, was specially hired. Dance cannot be taught without music, and Monsieur de la Selle made it himself on his small violin, called a *pochette* because it could be tucked away in the pocket of a jacket. Thus it was possible to learn the authentic French dance forms from him: courante, gavotte, allemande, sarabande, gigue, bourrée, and minuet. Reason enough for Bach to make friends with him.

Besides, this de la Selle was not only a dance master; he was a true musician who performed in the concerts at the court of Celle, which the duke of Braunschweig-Lüneburg maintained entirely in the chic French fashion. He had married a lady from the French nobility and was just as determined as other German princes (the one at Eisenach, for example) to make his court into a small Versailles. That called for a French orchestra, and the music that it played must likewise be French. Here was yet another opportunity to learn something!

The only problem was that it lay at a certain distance. To be sure, Terry affirms that "the seat of another school," Celle, "neighbored" Lüneburg. Walther Siegmund-Schultze speaks of Celle as a "neighboring music center." Klaus Peter Richter calls Celle "the neighboring town." I could continue. If all these musicologists had deigned to glance at a road atlas, they would have found out that this "neighboring town" was over 55 miles away, and nobody in Heidelberg would seriously talk of "neighboring Stuttgart" or in Halle of "neighboring Dresden." No one in Ingolstadt would even refer to "neighboring Munich," especially if he or she had to go there on foot. Admittedly, when the young Bach went to Celle under Monsieur de la Selle's auspices—and how else should he have gone?—the Frenchman must have taken him along in his coach. But driving on the roads of the time was not much faster, and so each time it was a two days' journey from Lüneburg to Celle. This means that in any case a visit to Celle cost four travel days besides the overnight stays, and something to eat was needed too.

All in all that was an expensive proposition for someone who was still attending school and who received at best 1.5 thalers a month in pocket money. Though time-consuming in any event, the experience was nonetheless rewarding, since in this way Bach became familiar with the French style of music making firsthand.

That style derived from the school of the great Jean-Baptiste Lully, the music master of Louis XIV and founder of the Royal Academy of Music. Monsieur de la Selle had been a pupil of his. Imagine all the things there were to recount on the long trips from Lüneburg to Celle and back! The great Lully had been not only a musician but an actor and dancer, had obtained his own orchestra from the king, had been able to perform his operas throughout the

16

land as theater manager, but above all had molded *the* French style of music, austere in form and rigorous in performance. All of this could be immediately experienced in praxis through the music making of the French orchestra at the court of Celle. And Johann Sebastian Bach never forgot these lessons in the French style his whole life; in the *Art of Fugue* one fugue is still headed *"in stilo francese."*

Some musicologists think that Bach attended the concerts; others even say that he performed in them as a violinist—as though just anyone could play in a French court orchestra without further ado! The truth is that both assertions are equally unlikely: that an impoverished sixteen-year-old grammar school pupil from the Lüneburg Cloister School, a commoner, would have been admitted into court society is just as unbelievable as would be his musical participation in such an event. What was really of the highest interest during these visits to the French orchestra in Celle were the rehearsals, which among colleagues required no special admittance. There the pieces were dismantled, divided into parts, their difficulties worked out, the various passages repeated over and over again, until finally, reassembled anew, they sounded forth as a whole. Neither pieces nor performance techniques could be analyzed more precisely than in the rehearsals. An interested, aspiring young musician could sit in on the rehearsals anytime; it was virtually a point of pride for the musicians to show a young person how professionals carry out their work. The concert itself could be heard after that even from beneath a window and was only a minor concern, just as a gunsmith is always much more interested in taking a shotgun apart and putting it back together again than in shooting it.

But the study of modern French music making was only one of the directions in which the young Bach's zeal for learning moved in Lüneburg, along with figural singing and—after his voice broke—accompanying the choir on the harpsichord, playing the violin in the school orchestra, and rummaging through the two great musical archives. These too were really no more than secondary matters. For a long time now, there had been an instrument that was capable of doing much more than the violin and harpsichord put together: the organ.

Naturally, Bach had already come into contact with the organ in his earliest childhood. It was a matter of course at the time that everyone went to church on Sunday. It can also be taken for granted that the organ must have made a stronger impression on the music-hungry little boy than any sermon. Then he went to live with his brother, who was an organist himself. And though he did not allow Bach to play the organ yet as an eleven-year-old, it does not follow that he never let him get close to the organ. In any case the younger brother was allowed to listen and look. Even that was exciting enough: In this way he already discovered the possibilities that this instrument offered, with its two keyboards, with the pedals as a third, and with the tone colors of its stops. And the young Sebastian Bach would not have been Bach if he had merely been satisfied with the diversity of the organ's tones. He had to ferret out just how all these sounds were produced.

The organ as he knew it was not only a captivating instrument but also a technical marvel. There were the different shapes of the pipes and their highly varied sizes, from the almost 16-foot-tall lowest C to the smallest, no larger than a fingernail. Then there were the connections between the keys and the pipes: the action, composed of rollers and trackers—thin rods that led to the pipe vents by diverse hinges in an absolutely inconceivable tangle. Despite their seemingly endless length and complexity, the keys had to be so well balanced that each of them could be struck with a single finger, playing with the same force.

In addition, such an organ basically harbors several organs. The *Brustwerk,* played from the upper keyboard, had a very different tone from the great organ, or *Hauptwerk,* of the lower keyboard. But couplers made it possible to play on both keyboards at once. There were metal pipes and wooden pipes, pipes open on top and others closed with a lid, and also some that were only half closed. They adopted the most various shapes, and the openings at the mouth of the pipes, the lips, were also highly differentiated. Then there were other pipes, like the *Schalmei* or the oboe, in which the tone was generated by an oscillating reed, and whose bell-like curves gave them the most eccentric of shapes.

How did wide pipes sound or narrow ones, open pipes or lidded ones? There were pipes that sounded a whole octave lower than the notation read, and others one, two, or three octaves higher. Then there were stops that played nothing but the overtones: fifth, third, seventh. In combination there were the mixtures with their peculiar names: cornet, *Scharf,* cymbal, sesquialtera. By themselves they sounded as though they were giving off an array of false tones, but together with the other stops they added splendor and color.

How was all that accomplished; on what basic principle was the device founded; how was its specification attained; how was it tuned and voiced? It was clear that an instrument with this kind of rich potential had to be fascinating right from the start to such a quintessential musician as Johann Sebastian Bach. It was not just any instrument; it was *the* instrument. No other came close to matching his own capacities with the vast extent of its possibilities. There was the range of expressive power—from the greatest tenderness to a thundering fortissimo; the gamut of tone colors, ranging from the chimney flute and dulcian, through the silver tone (which already arose through a combination of the "eight-foot" and "one-foot" stops), to the penetrating brightness of the mixtures. And above all there was the wonderful advantage of a polyphony that did not melt together but could be presented with perfect clarity through the differentiation of the stops. That was something neither the harpsichord nor the violin could do, and to achieve it did not require a chorus or an orchestra: two bellows-pumpers sufficed to place a whole world of sound at his disposal, dependent on his will and skill alone. It was a necessity of nature that he should conquer this instrument, after it had conquered him from the beginning.

And once again he had a stroke of luck in Lüneburg. The experienced and well-known organ builder Johann Balthasar Held came to Lüneburg to renovate the organ in St. Michael's Church. Geiringer (and he is not the only one) informs us that in Sebastian's time the organ was also being worked on in Ohrdruf. When his brother Johann Jacob had already begun playing with the town band, the great organ of St. George's Church in Eisenach was being built, a mighty instrument with fifty-two stops on three manuals. Quite possibly Sebastian may have visited his brother in Eisenach—25 miles is just about the limit for a hardy day's walk, for someone who is good at it—and then it is thoroughly conceivable that the two young musicians would have taken a look at the organ construction: An opportunity like that did not come along every day. In any case Held the organ builder was still working on the organ in Lüneburg until 1707, so there were many chances to observe, ask, and learn.

When Johann Sebastian Bach started out at eighteen as a "music lackey" in Weimar, he was already reputed to be an expert on organ building, and he can only have acquired that knowledge during his time in Lüneburg—not from Held alone, of course, but it was he who had given Bach the key to attaining his goal.

It goes without saying that in Lüneburg he must also have sat down at the organ himself as often as possible. Johann Heinrich Löwe, who had been apprenticed to the great Heinrich Schütz, played in the Church of St. Nicholas. Now he could pass on his experience, opinions, and knowledge to the next generation, to the young Bach. And Georg Böhm, a Thuringian compatriot from very near Ohrdruf, sat at the organ of St. John's Church. He enjoyed an equally fine reputation as a composer and as an organist, and at forty was then at the height of his creative powers.

Geiringer dares to assert that Sebastian never knew Böhm in
20 Lüneburg at all and became familiar with his compositions only through his cousin while in Weimar. But that a young man who was so interested in the organ and everything that had to do with it

should never have gone to see the famous organist of St. John's is completely unbelievable. And why else would he have felt compelled to travel to Hamburg to meet the great Johann Adam Reinken, whose most important pupil, namely, Georg Böhm, lived in Lüneburg? Quite the reverse is true. Löwe could report to him about Schütz, but Schütz was dead. Böhm could tell him about his teacher Reinken, who still held his post in Hamburg. That is why it was clear to such a thorough person as Johann Sebastian Bach that he had to go to Hamburg.

When we speak of the great gifts of Johann Sebastian Bach, we truly need to take our hats off as well to his enterprising spirit and steadfast legs. What a lot of walking this young man did in his early years! When it came to acquiring knowledge, no distance was too far for him and no weather too bad. About 25 miles between Ohrdruf and Eisenach, or a round-trip of 50 miles; a little over 200 miles from Ohrdruf to Lüneburg; a round-trip of about 110 miles in order to get to know the French orchestra in Celle—when seen in that light Hamburg was not so far away after all, only about 40 miles, which could be managed well enough in a four-day round-trip. And Johann Ernst Bach, who had lived with him for a time in his brother's house in Ohrdruf and with whom he had gone to school there, was now studying at the university in Hamburg. So he had a place to spend the night. Then why not go see Reinken, the organist of St. Catharine's Church?

Not only was the elderly Reinken (who was already approaching eighty) worth the trip, but so was the organ he played. "In the church organ of St. Catharine's in Hamburg there are no less than sixteen reed stops. The late Music Director, Mr. J. S. Bach in Leipzig, who once made himself heard for two hours on this 'superb instrument in all its parts,' as he said, could not praise the beauty and variety of tone of these reed stops enough," Jakob Adlung would later write in his *Musica mechanica organoedi.*

From 1702 on, another celebrated organist sat at the organ of St. Nicholas, Vincent Lübeck; he was in his late forties at the time

21

and no less worthy of respect than his colleague Reinken. In addition there was a German opera in Hamburg; Reinken had helped to found it. Its music director was a certain Johann Mattheson, twenty-one or twenty-two years old. And there was another musician who was not much older, a concert organizer who was also gaining notoriety as a composer and who was then on the verge of taking over the Hamburg Opera in its entirety: Reinhard Keiser. A little later he would hire a young man from Halle by the name of George Frideric Handel as a violinist for his orchestra. By the time Lübeck went to Hamburg and Keiser took over the opera there, Bach was no longer in Lüneburg. But even so, the trek on foot to Hamburg was well worth the effort.

Time-consuming trips to Celle and Hamburg; explorations of German, Dutch, French, and Italian music; organ-building studies with master Held; interchanges with the organists Löwe and Böhm; practicing the organ; making music with the matins choir and the *chorus symphoniacus*—it is astounding that free pupil Bach still found time for school at all under the circumstances. But there was also a jam-packed curriculum to be assimilated there.

At its center stood religious studies and the practice of music. The two belonged together; this had been the case in Protestant Lutheran schools since Luther and Melanchthon. Instruction in the true faith and singing were the foundation of the community, and with good reason both had become the centerpiece of the curriculum ever since the Reformation. The religious teaching was naturally orthodox Lutheran and was carried out chiefly through Leonhard Hutter's *Compendium locorum theologicorum*, a theological textbook that was already 100 years old. For simplicity's sake, the pupils in Eisenach had to learn it by heart, but it was also brought to bear in Ohrdruf and Lüneburg. Since the textbook as well as the *Dicta scripturae sacrae* were written in Latin, the importance of Latin as the third major subject inevitably followed.

The fact that instruction in the true creed formed the foundation of Protestant schools had a solid grounding. The Thirty Years' War had ended barely fifty years before, and it had been waged as a bitter war of faith; the Counter-Reformation that preceded it had been designed to abolish Lutheran freedoms. The Wars of Religion had ended with the confirmation of a religious truce in 1552, but the pope had expressly condemned the Peace of Westphalia of 1648. Thus the conflict between Catholicism and Protestantism remained as intense as ever, and to that was added the no less intense conflicts among the Protestants themselves. The Reformers, or Calvinists, stood in opposition to the Lutherans, and in the Lutheran camp itself the Orthodox and the Pietists had been fighting for thirty years by this time. The achievements of Luther's Reformation as well as the purity of its theological dogma had to be preserved.

To Luther's Reformation belonged above all the lively participation of the congregation in the worship service, especially the German hymns that were sung together, and therefore the cultivation of church music. For this reason, the choirmaster in a Lutheran Latin School was the most important man after the headmaster. Only in places where an assistant headmaster was assigned to the headmaster did the choirmaster occasionally occupy third place, though he always remained higher in rank than the nominal third man, the *tertius*. In Ohrdruf the superintendent was the headmaster of the school, the highest clergyman of the town. In Lüneburg the Latin School was housed in a Lutheran cloister.

In Eisenach, as in Ohrdruf and Lüneburg, the religious instruction was Lutheran Orthodox, and Johann Sebastian Bach was familiar with the Lutheran Orthodox dogma from his earliest youth. There is no evidence that he ever distanced himself from that teaching, no matter how many vague suspicions and mere claims have been put forward in this regard by the widest range of people. In any case, in the main subjects of the school—religion, music, and Latin—he encountered no difficulties. In Latin class the Latin classics were also read, which seems like the obvious basis for all instruction in Latin to us today. But then it was not taken for granted at all, nor was instruction in Greek, the other cornerstone

23

of a classical education. Greek was also taught in Lüneburg, along with rhetoric and logic, which were considered indispensable subjects at the time, as well as arithmetic, history, and geography. The natural sciences were still of no interest. For a musician, certain useful analogies could be derived from the basic rules of rhetoric, and mathematics must have afforded a real pleasure to a musical mind that would soon unite the most difficult polyphonic combinations with the most joyous naturalness. But fortunately, the young Bach did not have to spend too much time on school.

He remained in the Lüneburg secondary school for more than two years, from Easter 1700 until summer 1702. He had left the Ohrdruf Latin School as a senior without having taken final exams and could have graduated from Lüneburg with a diploma. But what would it have gotten him? The ensuing university studies were unthinkable, and he surely did not think of pursuing them. He lacked the necessary money, for one, but he had also already saturated himself completely with music in every conceivable way. Since his arrival in Lüneburg and the beginning of his sixteenth year of life, he had made his own way entirely, and he wanted to become a musician. He was familiar with the musical life of Lüneburg, Celle, and Hamburg, and he had thoroughly taken the measure of all the music within his reach; his knowledge of organ building was thorough as well. He knew all about choral singing; he played the organ, the harpsichord, and the violin to perfection. He knew what firstclass musicians like Böhm in Lüneburg, Reinken in Hamburg, and the French orchestra in Celle were currently accomplishing. And he also knew without a shadow of a doubt what he himself was already capable of achieving. Armed with that, he could dare to take up his profession.

So what use were finals in rhetoric, logic, mathematics, geography, and history? He was seventeen years old, an orphan without any means—and he was able to make music, he had to make music, he *wanted* nothing else but to make music.

3

The young man who took to the road again in the summer of 1702 in Lüneburg was rather lonely. Lonely, but undaunted. Life had forced him into solitude from his earliest youth, already in his parents' home, where he was the baby of the family. The only brother who was close to him in age, Johann Jacob, had returned to Eisenach already after only a year in Ohrdruf, and his elder brother, Christoph, more than twice as old as he, had above all been his teacher.

Then he had traveled with his classmate Erdmann to Lüneburg, and both had sung in the matins choir. But Erdmann was keen on his studies, not on music, and Bach himself was much too busy with music to find the time or feel the need to form schoolboy friendships. He had to be not only hardworking from an early age, as he said of himself, but also independent. This independence remained with him throughout his life: He pledged allegiance to no musical school or trend. He was familiar with all of them, of course, and did not cut himself off from them the way mediocre "original geniuses" usually do; he simply did not join them. Even the Mizler Society, which sought to bring together the best composers of the time, had to wait a long time for him to become a member, and his admission (with a portrait and a sample piece) was the end of the matter. Apparently he abstained from the yearly compositions that members were expected to contribute; it is only speculation to assert that he delivered them.

A good many biographers claim that a yearning for his homeland led him back to Thuringia. But where was his home? There had been no room for him in Eisenach and no room for him in Ohrdruf. Besides, if there is one thing that does not ring true in regard to Johann Sebastian Bach, it is sentimentality—especially when it comes to his farewell to Lüneburg and his journey back to Thuringia so soon after the beginning of the new school year. The song "A Stranger I Arrived, and a Stranger I Leave" was composed by Schubert, not Bach.

In search of employment, he had a very practical reason for moving back to Thuringia: There the name Bach commanded respect; it was virtually a professional title, a synonym for "musician." If there was anywhere for a young musician by the name of Bach to find a job, then it was Thuringia. Daily papers and publications for specialists did not yet exist. But communication among people was much better than it is today: What you could not read, you could hear about. A man traveling on foot who paused to rest here and there or look for a place to eat or spend the night could find out a great deal. In addition, Johann Sebastian's interests were very particular. As we know, a year later he was already being consulted as an expert on organ building. He could not have acquired the qualifications for that from master Held alone; familiarity with more than two or three organs would have been necessary for him to draw the proper comparisons.

During a trek of more than 200 miles, and all alone to boot, the traveler passed through many towns, and it would have been very foolish to ignore all the churches and organs along the way, especially since the organists were surely the best source of news about the job vacancies available. And anyway, they were the ones who could converse about music in general.

26   The biographers report that at this time there were openings for three positions as organist in Thuringia. In Eisenach the organist of St. George's, Sebastian's uncle, had died. But his son took up his

place—for 131 years the Bachs would occupy the post of organist there. In Arnstadt they were working on the construction of a new organ for the recently built Church of St. Boniface. And then there was a vacancy in Sangerhausen, where the municipal judge and organist Gottfried Christoph Gräffenhayn had died on July 3 of that year. Sebastian set off in that direction and applied for the job. Most likely, news of the vacancy had already reached him in Lüneburg—why else would he have left school when the academic year had already begun?

In any case he tried out for the post, and his playing made an excellent impression: The gentlemen of the town council wanted to hire him on the spot. But Sangerhausen was anything but a free city; the last word was held by Duke Johann Georg of Saxe-Weissenfels. This Bach seemed too young to him (after all, he had not even graduated from school yet), and he had an older and more experienced musician on tap, one Augustin Kobelius, who furthermore had proved himself as court musician in Weissenfels. So Kobelius obtained the position.

At his point there is a gap in Bach's biography that extends through the entire summer, fall, and winter of 1702 and on into the spring of 1703. Not until Easter of 1703 do we find him again, as court musician to Duke Johann Ernst of Saxe-Weimar. "The circumstances of his transfer from Lüneburg to Weimar are unknown," writes Forkel, Bach's first biographer, who was still able to ask Carl Philipp Emanuel Bach about details. Terry knows better: "Between the Courts of Weimar and Weissenfels there existed a relationship Bach's subsequent career illustrates. Not improbably it was now invoked to mitigate his disappointment at Sangerhausen." But if that were correct, then after having been rejected in Sangerhausen in August, Bach would have arrived in Weimar sooner than April of the subsequent year. Nor should we overestimate the kindness of dukes and their interest in young people.

Be that as it may, he turns up the following year as violinist or violist in Weimar, with the rank of a lackey, to be sure, which was

27

quite the normal position for musicians at princely courts at the time. An organist working as a city employee enjoyed a higher prestige, as the post of municipal judge held by the organist Gräffenhayn in Sangerhausen makes clear. The court musician Kobelius would hardly have applied for the position as organist if it had not been a move up for him. But court musicians did not have such a bad job, and they were not treated like ordinary lackeys. Duke Johann Ernst, younger brother of and cosovereign with Duke Wilhelm Ernst, was a music lover possessed of an acute artistic understanding; both of his sons, Ernst August and Johann Ernst, were equally gifted in music, the younger one extraordinarily so. Moreover, the court organist, Johann Effler, was very much taken up with his duties as secretary in the ducal chancellery, and he was also getting on in years. So here was a chance for Bach to sit at the organ bench occasionally and to continue perfecting his skills in that domain. The elderly Effler would have been a fool to object to that; he could only have welcomed the young man's enthusiastic offer to stand in for him. As for the repertoire of the ducal orchestra, wherever French music was not cultivated the Italians came to the fore, and Vivaldi, Corelli, and Tartini had written very beautiful works for the type of chamber ensemble that the duke was able to afford. Money did not exactly grow on trees at the Red Palace in Weimar, but the young Bach had an assured income, and musically he was not starved by any means.

Spitta, Terry, and others make it sound as though Bach were merely biding his time with the artistically minded Duke Johann Ernst and his two musical sons, eagerly awaiting the moment when the organ in the new church at Arnstadt would be finished at last. There they are doubly mistaken. A musician who entered into the service of a sovereign—and both dukes were the rulers of Saxe-Weimar—could not simply resign from his duties, if the need arose, at his own discretion. That was something Bach would later learn the hard way, precisely in Weimar. Nor was it very likely that Duke Johann Ernst would have remained indifferent to the ques-

28

tion of whether he had one musician more or less in his private ensemble. Rueger claims that Bach played in the third row there, so to speak, but there was no such thing: The organization was a chamber ensemble. The young musician by the name of Bach, equally adept at the violin, viola, harpsichord, and organ and also well versed in theory, was very useful in this small private orchestra, and if the duke let him go again so soon, it was only because he held him in high esteem.

As one of the duke's music lackeys, there was no way that the young Bach could take on the position and then drop it as he saw fit. And the claim that Bach was already counting on the organist post in Arnstadt when he entered the duke's service, sure that he would obtain it, is fully untenable on closer inspection. The organ in the new church, even though it was not yet completed, had already been in use for some time; it was being played by the town organist, Börner. And once this new and (so it seems) carefully built organ was finished, it was really almost a foregone conclusion that Börner would continue on the bench of the new instrument. Interim solutions are usually the start of a permanent arrangement.

Yet in Arnstadt events took a different turn: The interim ended fairly abruptly when the organ reached completion. As it was, the construction of the organ had lasted considerably longer than promised. Certain people who apparently do not understand much about the matter have reproached the organ builder, Gottlieb Wender from Mühlhausen, for dragging his feet. That makes no sense, since the price for such an organ was agreed upon before construction began, and it was up to the organ builder to make do after that with the specified amount. The sooner he finished the construction, the sooner he could start work on the next commission.

But when this point was reached, Börner the organist announced to the town council that he was dissatisfied with the execution of the work: Wender's organ did not play the way it should, and he could not accept the result for final inspection. Wender, 29 who had invested more than the usual amount of time in the project and thus more than the estimated costs, understandably protested. Deacon Fischer from Mühlhausen, who had expressly recommended Wender, was also affected by Börner's objections. It was customary to bring in outside experts to examine new organs, and in this instance, because the matter could not be decided amicably even though the organ had been in use for quite a while, an examiner would certainly be needed and would serve as an arbitrator as well.

The story is odd in many respects. For one thing, the organ had been played for a long time already. For another, in such a delicate case a man of proven experience should have been sought out. Bach of Ohrdruf was famous for his skill as an organist. Another important Bach was active in Meiningen, and other well-known Bachs could be found throughout the land. It was advisable to employ a Bach for the task, since Count von Schwarzburg in the Arnstadt Castle had already thought very highly of the older Bach, the twin brother of Johann Sebastian's father. And what a count had to say in such matters is shown by the Sangerhausen incident, when a duke ruined the young Bach's prospects of employment.

Sebastian was still just a youth; he had just turned nineteen in March and was the youngest of all the Bachs in the region. Yet it must have already become widely recognized that he knew a great deal about organ building, and he could not have gained that reputation merely by conversing with old Effler and playing in the duke's orchestra. Once Held, the organ-building master, had initiated him into the technical secrets of the instrument, he must have continued to explore them, as his numerous examinations of organs in later years demonstrate. Comparisons are a prerequisite for gathering the appropriate knowledge, and Bach cannot have acquired it except by thoroughly looking at and trying out all the organs he could lay his hands on—and that is precisely what people must have noticed.

The other organists stayed wherever they were; Johann Sebastian Bach used his legs and kept his eyes peeled. Throughout his life his thirst for information was enormous; that was part and parcel of his professional thoroughness. Today we would call him a perfectionist, a term we use with a hint of annoyance, as though anyone but a perfectionist could produce something that is flawless.

Since this young Bach was known for his familiarity with all the organs of the area and, despite his age, was already serving as a substitute organist for the dukes of Saxe-Weimar, he was obviously the right man to judge whether Wendel's organ was as good as—or better, or worse than—those of the surrounding area. Besides, he was a Bach, and thus from a tried and true family; and on top of that, in view of his youth, he would not cost too much, an important factor for the municipal coffers. All these were very good reasons to bring him in as an expert adviser and examiner in this difficult case. Occasionally the most important motive cited is that the young Bach was related to the mayor of Arnstadt through his mother. But that would be better understood as an obstacle in this instance: Few things could have carried greater weight against an untoward judgment than the charge of nepotism.

If the position as organist had already been reserved for Bach, as is often claimed, a simple audition would have sufficed to confirm that the young man possessed the necessary aptitude for the post. But he was summoned as an examiner.

That was a first-class diplomatic gambit: It placed the aldermen of Arnstadt under no obligation. If the judgment was not satisfactory or was challenged, for instance, they could blame it on the youth of the examiner, and they were certainly not forced to hire the examiner as organist, especially since he already had a livelihood at court. (In the town council minutes he is designated as "Prince. Sax. Court Organist.") Clearly the council was supremely astute at keeping its distances from the whole affair and could not have covered itself more cleverly. The calculation worked out well financially too: The examiner did in fact agree to accept less than what was normally paid for an inspection.

Wender the organ builder, at forty-eight an experienced master, could not possibly have been satisfied with this solution. What kind of knowledge could a man this young have at his disposal, at the age of only nineteen?

But then came the surprises. When the young man set to work as examiner, he spared the organ builder nothing (and he was well known for that trait until the end of his life); yet he was able to find strong points that others would hardly have noticed. And Wender had indeed done good work. His organ stayed in service for 160 years, until it was rebuilt in 1864 according to contemporary taste, and still today stops sound forth in the organ of St. Boniface at Arnstadt that old Wender built and young Johann Sebastian Bach inspected.

But this young organ examiner from Weimar not only understood an astonishing amount about building an organ; he knew just as much or even more about playing one. He made this new organ sound like no organ that anyone in Arnstadt had ever heard before. The impression made on the city councilors was overwhelming. In addition to engaging him to play for the inauguration of the organ, they immediately offered him the post of organist as well—and at a salary such as no other organist was paid in Arnstadt before or after. Admittedly, they also had to dig somewhat deeper into their pockets because the young man had to give up a respectable position at court. (This demonstrates yet again that Bach definitely did not come to Arnstadt in order to take up a job that was already reserved for him.)

No, he did not settle into a fully feathered nest, nor is it true that he had attained the fulfillment of his wishes, a man of child-like piety serving his church at last, as some biographers would have us believe he had resolved to do already in his fourteenth year of life. The musical opportunities for an organist in worship services are not enormous by any means. Preludes and postludes, liturgy and accompaniment of the congregational singing are recurrent tasks within firmly drawn limits. The congregation does not gather to hear an organ recital, and within the sphere of the church service the most beautiful organ music remains reduced in grandeur and effect.

Bach's duties as organist in Arnstadt were confined to the Sunday worship service from eight to ten, the prayer meeting on Monday, and the early service on Thursday from seven to nine. Idle people might say that he did not have much to do. But we could also say that he had little opportunity to make his mark. In any case, he had a lot of time at his disposal and a good salary on top of that: 50 florins and 30 thalers, considerably more than his father had earned in Eisenach or his brother received in Ohrdruf. Still, objectively considered, as court musician to Duke Johann Ernst he had been able to make more music with a bigger repertoire, above all orchestral music, and the organ was available to him as well.

Yet Arnstadt offered him orchestral music too, in addition to the organ. The count maintained a larger ensemble in his castle than the one in Weimar, twenty-four musicians, and reinforcement from a young man who up to now had played violin at the duke's was too welcome an opportunity for him to pass up. Over and above all that, besides a better income Arnstadt afforded Bach something incomparably more important: independence.

The organ was excellent. Whether it was the very best organ that Bach ever had under his fingers in his whole career, as Besseler claims, is certainly subject to doubt, since later in Weimar he got the chance to have an organ built that was virtually the one of his dreams. Still, the organ here was good, and rather than court secretary Essler, he himself kept the key to it. The town was well disposed toward him; he had been offered the post without his having to apply for it. And to the count the name Bach had a decidedly pleasant ring.

Arnstadt could boast a little over 40,000 inhabitants, three churches, and a secondary school, but it had no choir and thus no figural music. Johann Friedrich Treiber, the headmaster of the school, did occasionally compose something himself (among other works an opera on the benefits of brewing beer), but there was no chorus to sing what he wrote. Here was a chance to build something up! Bach, the new organist in town, had ample experience in the cultivation of school music from Eisenach, Ohrdruf, and Lüneburg. What was taken for granted there and elsewhere had to be possible here too.

The only problem was that he had not lived in Arnstadt long enough. So in this particular case he completely misjudged the headmaster, the secondary school students of Arnstadt, and the possibilities open to him. In Arnstadt the school marched to a different drummer. Headmaster Treiber, a music practitioner, knew very well why he omitted figural music from his pupils' schedule. His school was not the Lüneburg St. Michael's school, where only those students could belong to the chorus "who are well known to their teachers for their outstanding piety, modesty, obedience, and diligence." In Arnstadt that would have produced no school chorus at all. Here was a small city where commerce flourished; there were weavers, tanners, brewers—craftsmen who had done very well for themselves, especially since the town also lay on a good commercial route. The leading citizens sent their sons to the school because they could afford to; for their part the sons, as sons of wealthy (and hence influential) parents, knew what *they* could afford to do. They formed a decidedly unruly gang who were in no hurry to finish their studies. A good many of them were already over twenty and still had no thought of graduating. They preferred to engage in nocturnal caterwauling and other high jinks. The citizens of Arnstadt knew that their students were a menace to society and had best be kept at arm's length.

Bach knew about this too, but it did not scare him. He had learned how to handle a school chorus and wanted to prove it. Indeed, when he set to work he was successful right away; apparently it did not even cost him extraordinary effort. The boys did not sing badly at all. And if the town council had been happy before to hire such a fine organist, now the consistory, the superintendent, and the clergy were very content with the new employee for providing them with decent figural music at long last. Even the students thought it was fun. This young man who had imposed himself on the school almost as a choirmaster was close to them in age, and when they sang in church they could show the town that they were all basically splendid fellows at heart. Their participation furnished them with a certain social standing.

For a year, everything went well. But then the whole business gradually developed two major disadvantages. What began as a lark became an obligation for the students and so an utter nuisance. Moreover, this new organist, who was not even as old as the eldest among them, started mistreating them: He made demands!

For Bach was a true perfectionist, as we can observe from his earliest childhood through the end of his life. When he started something, he pursued it in earnest. At many different times in his life, he displayed a keen sense of humor, but when it came to his music there was no playing around: "Almost" was not good enough, and he could not accept sloppiness of any kind.

That was why he awakened resistance among the members of his choir. For them, singing was above all an entertainment, which they were under no obligation to continue; after all, things had gone well enough without all this singing before. But Bach could not be content with their accomplishments. He wanted to make a better chorus out of them, and since he was dissatisfied with them, they became dissatisfied with him. "Dissatisfied" is the wrong word. They rebelled. Bach was determined to prevail. The students were just as determined not to put up with his demands any longer.

It has come down to us that he dubbed one of the malicious troublemakers, Geyersbach, a "prick bassoonist." That sounds more like a jest than an insult to us today, but when people are seething for a fight, no excuse is too trifling. His singers went on the warpath; there was a regular conspiracy among six senior students: Geyersbach, Schüttewürfel, Trassdorf, Hoffmann, Manebach, and Stützhaus. The six—all Bach's age or older—lay in wait for him in

35

the dark with clubs, intending to use brute force to extract from him a formal apology to Geyersbach for having offended him. In reality of course, they were looking for a pretext to beat him up. (If they had been up to anything less, they would not have needed to waylay him at night.)

It has never dawned on the musicological biographers how life-threatening this situation was. They treat the whole episode as though it were no more than a bagatelle. But when Bach crossed their path—probably with his violin case under his arm after a concert at the count's—it would have been easy for these six twenty-year-old rowdies to make a cripple of him in no time. Musicians are extraordinarily vulnerable. Robert Schumann's career as a pianist was destroyed by a finger that went stiff. One well-aimed blow on the hand with a cudgel, and Bach's life might have taken an entirely different course.

Incidentally, that same year the young Handel fell into a situation that was just as dangerous, when his supposed friend Johann Mattheson drew his sword on him after the premiere of Mattheson's opera *Cleopatra*. If Mattheson had stabbed his rival, all of Handel's compositions would have been lost to the world. But Mattheson's blade broke on a button of Handel's jacket.

No coat button could protect Bach from the clubs of Geyersbach and his gang, so he was out of luck. But no! An ornamental rapier was part of court dress. He drew it and went for his attackers. They had reckoned on his fear, not on his determination—and in the end they ran away.

Bach reported the incident to the authorities that governed him. Riotous assembly, nocturnal assault, disturbing the peace—there were quite a few charges against his attackers, and Bach could expect that here justice would be done. But he was not from Arnstadt, and so he was completely mistaken. His relative the mayor, Martin Feldhaus, steered clear of the matter entirely (which once again shows how little Bach's interests there were fostered through family connections). Expulsion from school for Geyersbach as ringleader and detention hall for the others involved would have been the mildest punishments that might be expected. Yet it went otherwise. The six were sons of respected parents, after all. So as ringleader Geyersbach received nothing more than a simple reprimand "not to endanger his future career," and the rest came away without any punishment at all, since "no atrocity could be proved against them." The only one who was seriously chastised for the assault was Bach the organist, who was enjoined by the consistory "to resume the musical instruction of the students again at once in a more moderate form."

The musicologist Paule du Bouchet relates this story under the title "The Youthful Hothead." Albert Schweitzer also puts all the blame on Bach's shoulders. He writes: "Here no one should speak of the church authorities' incomprehension of the young organist's genius. They were in the right with their complaints. Bach did not know how to deal with the chorus. Thus already in Arnstadt that total lack of organizational capacity is revealed which will make his position so difficult for him later on in Leipzig."

To this we can only reply that in Leipzig two sets of very unkindly disposed authorities—the town council and the consistory—never once reprehended Bach for a lack of organizational capacity in all his twenty-seven years of service there, even though in the last thirteen years of his tenure he did not set foot in the St. Thomas School and managed the choirs in his four churches only through his student deputies, the "prefects." The misrepresentations of Du Bouchet and Schweitzer are thus merely fantasies of the authors, flatly contradicted by the facts.

In Arnstadt Bach could already draw on more than a decade of choral experience, and he had begun working with the chorus on his own initiative. In that light Schweitzer's claim that Bach supposedly "did not know how to deal with the choir" must also be challenged as a negligent comment. It is obvious from the text of the records that the injunction to "resume the instruction in a *more moderate* form" implies that Bach's insistence on quality caused the

37

incident. Subsequently, in Leipzig, a similar trend would become evident: Nothing would be held against him as long he did not bother anyone with his demands for excellence.

If he had been the meekly pious man of the church described by Spitta, Terry, Schweitzer, and others, he would have bowed to the dictates of his clerical superiors. But he was a musician, driven to plumb his art to its depths and remain true to his vocation even under the most adverse circumstances. Instead of employment contracts he needed patrons, but of those he had only one in his whole life, and even that one for less than four years.

He had not allowed Geyersbach and his henchmen to beat him up. As Bach's punishment for this the consistory made an obligation out of something he had never been obliged to do before. That thoroughly changed his relationship with Arnstadt. On August 9, 1703, he had signed his contract, and subsequently he had attempted to foster a figural music in the town. Almost to the day two years later, on August 8, 1705, he was assaulted because of his efforts.

No one can hold it against him that he had no intention of fulfilling the demand imposed on him by the consistory. He had merely placed himself in a hopeless position: He could no longer require standards of quality from his singers. The students had "shown" him. In the future they could determine for themselves how much they wanted to put up with from him, and now they also knew that if they attacked him again they had nothing to fear. And Bach had seen that his clerical superiors not only did not cover him, but they openly stood on the side of his opponents. For him, that was the end of figural music in Arnstadt.

Not a single one of his critics could have produced decent figural music under circumstances such as these. How could they all overlook that simple reality?

But Bach could also get along without figural music as an artistic pursuit. The organ continued to command his attention, and he undoubtedly began something in Arnstadt of which we have had no definite traces until now: He started composing. Naturally there are conjectures that he must have already done so in Lüneburg. But that cannot be proved, and it is not even probable—he was too busy with his studies. When we sum up all the things he was occupied with there from Easter 1700 to summer 1702, we are struck by his unbelievable passion for collecting knowledge. Other composers already overflowed with the urge to create at quite an early age. With Bach we have the impression that he approached the various realms of his art with great circumspection, almost scientifically. Until the eighteenth year of his life, there is no certifiable note by him, at least nothing he deemed worth saving. Not until Arnstadt. Here he wrote his first cantata, when he was still working with the chorus. And from the beginning we have three types of composition that will be characteristic of him. First of all there is a fugue—yes, a fugue right away—which he dedicates to his elder brother with a reverential inscription in Latin. The dedication indicates his respect for and distance from his brother; the composition itself bears witness to the progress in his art made by the former pupil in the meantime.

And then there is the *Capriccio On the Departure of His Much Beloved Brother*, for Jacob had accepted a position in Sweden that would take him all the way to Constantinople—quite a distance. And there are a number of remarkable things about this capriccio. The dedication—in German and Italian, like all other indications in the composition—sounds infinitely more heartfelt than that of the fugue, and the individual sections of the piece do not give the impression that Bach wrote them out in brooding world-weariness. Rather, they seem like a real going-away present. Since Jacob was a wind player and not a harpsichordist, we can assume that Sebastian, when the brothers saw each other once more before Jacob's departure, played his composition for Jacob himself. After all, Eisenach and Arnstadt were only 30 miles from each other. And so the work betrays a little bit about Bach's relations with his family.

Another aspect is absolutely astonishing: In its sections the capriccio is a veritable piece of program music. The introductory

Arioso represents "the blandishments of his friends to dissuade him from his journey"; the Fugato that follows, "a foreboding of various incidents that could befall him abroad"; the Adagissimo, "a general lament by his friends," and the whole ends not simply with an *aria di postiglione* but with a fugue upon it. Here one is tempted to ask, With Bach, how could it be otherwise? But the marvel is twofold: first, how naturally polyphony stood at Bach's disposal and, second, how naturally he used it as a means of expression.

In commenting on this capriccio, musicologists have pointed to parallels with Johann Kuhnau's *Biblical Sonatas*, going so far as to suggest that Bach most likely derived the whole idea from Kuhnau. Superficially considered, that rings true, but Bach never borrowed anything else from Kuhnau, and the only conclusion we can really draw from such claims is that the proponents of the theory have never compared the two compositions. Otherwise they would have noticed right away that by this point the young Bach had long since gone beyond any need to learn from old Kuhnau. (Although Kuhnau was a very interesting man, who was the first to coin the concept of "gallant style," forty years before this catchword comes to the fore in the accounts of Bach's biographers.)

In fact the compositions of Bach and Kuhnau do not match each other in any way, in articulation or structure, technique or treatment. In his *Biblical Sonatas* Kuhnau is concerned with recounting plots; Bach portrays the moods inherent in different situations, which is something quite different. Nor did Bach have the slightest need to take note of Kuhnau in composing his capriccio: He had already become familiar with the possibilities of tone painting and the musical depiction of situations while in Lüneburg, where he made himself copies of Couperin. Kuhnau did not even offer him anything novel. And finally, all these writers are overlooking that Bach was, after all, a musical genius who was always on the trail of new possibilities for his art. That is why it is utterly unlikely that he ever needed to study other people's works in order to arrive at the idea of expressing moods with his music. Mediocre minds may perhaps be obliged to stick to imitation; the more gifted come up with something of their own. And the part writing and harmony here are already all Bach.

A further example of this is the intriguing modulations that occur in this capriccio, especially in the marchlike section. Here again Bach could not have been prompted to such a development by Kuhnau; one searches in vain for parallels in Kuhnau's *Biblical Sonatas*.

Another aspect is equally conspicuous: Despite all the pain of parting, a kindly, mischievous humor underlies the whole. It makes itself felt again in the third occasional composition from this period, a wedding quodlibet that alludes to an occasion when the groom approached his beloved at a kneading trough. From then on this humor of Bach's would flash through his creative work again and again, not only in the *Coffee Cantata* and the *Peasant Cantata* but also in the *Christmas Oratorio* and the *Goldberg Variations*. Even the canon with which he had himself painted in the Haussmann portrait is an amusing notion of that kind. And so these three occasional compositions in Arnstadt are rife with the hallmarks of his future creative activity.

4

Bᴜᴛ ᴡʜᴀᴛ ᴅᴏ ᴡᴇ ᴍᴇᴀɴ by "occasional compositions" anyway? Bach's great contemporary Telemann composed only for the occasions when his music was needed. Handel did the same for by far the greater part of his life. Nothing can be said against occasions from an artistic standpoint; it is a happy period that offers some. Mozart's operas were all commissioned works; he even wrote his Requiem on order. In Bach's case, however, and to an extraordinary degree, we find a curious phenomenon: Besides the many works he had to deliver in fulfillment of his professional duties (and which would have sufficed for a lifework on their own), he composed for his personal satisfaction as well. "Pure research," his superiors could have called it, if the expression had already been current, though of course that was not what it was for him. His great organ compositions belong to this category; the B Minor Mass and the *Art of Fugue* as well. No one had commissioned them, and not many could make use of them. His contemporaries could rightly have asked him whether he had nothing better to do. Luckily for all of us, he did not.

The most popular of all his organ compositions is most likely an occasional work: The D Minor Toccata and the accompanying fugue are supposed to have been composed for use at an organ inspection. Where this took place cannot be determined, but it seems certain that he wrote the work in Arnstadt, at the age of nineteen or twenty. Hermann Keller, the commendable editor of many organ works, was inspired to almost poetic verve in describing it: "[There is] no second example of such a thrilling beginning as the one in this toccata, with its tones in unison that descend like a stroke of lightning, the long rolling thunder of its broken chords for full organ, the tempestuous waves of its triplets." Admittedly, there are other beginnings in Bach's organ works that are no less thrilling. But what Keller describes as the "long rolling thunder of its broken chords" is interesting for two other reasons. The first has to do with organ-building technique. At organ inspections Bach had the habit of checking first to see whether the bellows supplied enough air. That can be tested splendidly with these broken chords that gradually draw from the organ as much air as a player can demand from it with hands and feet. The other side is still more interesting. With his grand arpeggio, the gradual adding of tone on tone, Bach engenders a crescendo possible only through the means available to the organ. Anything similar will be sought in vain in organ literature before the D Minor Toccata; this was Bach's own discovery. At the end of the first arpeggio, seven times as many pipes are sounding as on the initial tone; and by the end of the second arpeggio, nine times as many. To express it in numbers, in view of the disposition of Bach's organ in Arnstadt: Twenty-seven pipes sounded on the initial tone simultaneously, and that number rose in the end to 243—a ninefold increase!

There are still more inventions in this piece, such as the form of the work as a whole. Essentially the designation "toccata *and* fugue" is incorrect, since the fugue is seamlessly integrated with the toccata. That is completely different from the norm among organ masters up to that time, as can be verified by examining the works of Krieger, Kerll, Speth, Froberger, Reinken, Buxtehude, Pachelbel, and Muffat. In their compositions the toccata, if not a short unified piece, is a sequence of independent sections, also fugal; and a fugue as long as Bach's is extremely rare. Among all the Bach researchers, apparently not one has ever noticed that the form of this toccata has no contemporary parallels. Virtually from the beginning the young Bach manifests a firmly defined feeling for musical architecture. It is clearly of no interest to him that others write differently. And above all, from the very start his compositions are infused with a musical breath and a breadth of design that make him unique already at the age of twenty. This will pose considerable difficulties for his short-winded contemporaries, incidentally, as well as for their descendants.

There is yet another interesting thing about this toccata, namely, the fugal theme. It takes the shape that will remain typical of Bach's music over long stretches: an incessant movement of sixteenths, and the constant use of a polyphonic type of melody that incorporates an internal pedal point.

In his book on Bach, Friedemann Otterbach tries to trace this characteristic back to the *style brisé* of early French lute music, but surely it is implausible that Bach would have had to borrow from early French lute music, of all things, for his own personal organ style. In any case the old French organ masters, whose music Bach was able to examine in Lüneburg, never did such a thing. In Couperin, Marchand, Grigny, Dieupart, Roux, and Raison, no such borrowings are found. At no time did Bach shy away from borrowings when the need arose; in improvising they were even a welcome source of inspiration to him. But he did not draw the style of the fugal theme in his D Minor Toccata from any school. As incredible as it may seem to people who would always like to derive everything from something else, he came up with the idea himself.

But we must now take a closer look at the treatment of the theme. After their individual entries, the voices usually continue in relatively free formation; secondary ideas branch out; interludes deviate from the theme. But in the fugue in D minor Bach introduces ever new variants of his fugal theme. And he not only presents the theme but at the same time playfully modifies it, while introducing new ideas at the same time. Here again we must look through the

45

works of his contemporaries: This kind of breathtaking artistry is nowhere to be found. (Yet a renowned scholar designates it as "a fugue that gives the impression of being the *weaker* one.")

Among many other important compositions (for example, the preludes and fugues that Schweitzer lists), there is also that Fantasy in G Major of which Joachim Kaiser gave an analysis as splendid as it was profound in the Bach commemorative year 1985, and of which various people claim that it reflects above all the influence of Dietrich Buxtehude. A thematic development such as Bach displayed there, however, is nowhere to be found in Buxtehude. In contrast, figuration like that in Buxtehude is found in contemporaries of whom we know with certainty that they never visited Buxtehude. And what about the strict five-part writing that occupies the middle of this fantasy? That is also unique: Four-part writing is the norm, since it derives from vocal composition. (Geck claims that three voices are the rule, but he lacks practical experience.) Two-voiced *bicinium* is also customary, as well as the three-voiced trio. But the young Bach experimented with a fifth voice—a difficult task, since in five-voiced composition the third can only be doubled by way of exception. Five-voiced pieces can be found in the old French masters, to be sure, but it is notable that difficult challenges appeal to Bach consistently. For example, he writes a fugue that with its theme introduces the countersubject, the *comes,* at the same time. Fugues attract him above all, and without exception amazingly elaborate ones.

None of this can be explained through Buxtehude's influence, any more than the influence of Georg Böhm can tell us anything about Bach's chorale preludes. That is the case with influences in general. Highly imaginative pieces like those of Buxtehude can also be found in the works of his contemporary Pachelbel, who certainly did not stand under his influence. Both Böhm and Buxtehude handle chorale preludes in the same manner, as does Johann Nicolaus Hanff, who like Böhm and Bach was from Thuringia, though he lived in Königsberg. And the same form of the toccata, as a chain of ideas strung together, is found in both Buxtehude and

Gottlieb Muffat. Yet the latter has nothing whatsoever to do with any of the rest because he was both active in Passau and Vienna and a Catholic. At any rate, in Böhm and Buxtehude we will search in vain for such outbursts of temperament as we encounter in Bach's D Minor Toccata or Fantasy in G Major (and there are more examples). In these works "influence" is completely absent. When we compare Böhm's harmony with that of Bach, it is almost hard to believe that the two were contemporaries.

In fact Bach's Arnstadt pieces are already unprecedented in the architecture and complexity of their compositional technique. Where Bach did follow antecedents, it was not in order to emulate them but to transform them. (When Bertolt Brecht wrote his *Three-Penny Opera*, he did not do so "under the influence" of John Gay any more than Beethoven wrote his *Cockatoo Variations* "under the influence" of Wenzel Müller.)

It is striking how many free organ compositions and how few chorale preludes may be dated to the Arnstadt period. If Bach had been fulfilling his dearest wish when he took up the post as organist in Arnstadt by dedicating his music to his church, then he would have devoted his creative activity chiefly to music that was of use for worship services—as later in Leipzig, where he provided a cantata every Sunday. He was obviously far more absorbed in music for its own sake. Even if we attribute the genesis of his chorale partitas to the Arnstadt period, these sequences of variations are also examples of free organ music. Although Schweitzer asserts that it was formerly the custom to present the individual verses of a hymn by alternating them between the congregation and the organ, if he were right about this, there would be chorale partitas on many more hymn tunes by many more organists. Instead, we also find partitas on songs that are not chorales at all.

In any case, there are two reasons why Bach did not see any need to create a stock of chorale preludes for himself in Arnstadt, the 47 way he later laid up a supply of cantatas in Leipzig. For one thing, he was a superb improviser. So improvising preludes and interludes in church services not only posed no difficulty for him, but he even enjoyed it. For another, his relationship with the ecclesiastical authorities had suffered a painful blow in August 1706. The count's consistory had not stood up for him, and from now on it wanted to impose on him, under frankly impossible terms, the direction of the chorus, a task he had assumed on his own initiative.

Bach, whose biographers unanimously reproach him for his terrible temper, acted here with the greatest composure. He waited more than two months for the authorities to see things in a more sympathetic light. Only then did he apply for a leave of absence for further education, in order to travel to Lübeck and study with the famous Buxtehude.

It was a request for four weeks' leave, and he engaged his cousin Johann Ernst Bach to replace him. Since that meant his duties would be attended to, the leave was approved. He was never again in his life granted such a long leave of absence, nor did he ever take so much time off on his own. Possibly the members of the consistory were trying to show a certain flexibility (in hopes that a slight concession from their side would move him to make concessions too). For his part, Bach might justifiably have been much more demanding, but he was well aware that they would not grant him more than four weeks.

It has been pointed out from all sides that he went beyond the allotted leave to a considerable extent. That is true, but it was not an afterthought: He knew from the start that four weeks would never suffice for his intentions, and there is no way that this could have been unclear to him in advance. He had already walked the distance from Ohrdruf to Lüneburg in March, when the days were longer. He was familiar with the distance from Lüneburg to Hamburg, and thus he also knew that Lübeck was quite a bit further.

In fact the distance is about 250 miles, and even if he had managed 20 miles a day he would have needed all four weeks for the journey there and back alone. But it was late autumn when he set out, the end of October. The days were already very short, and every day they got shorter. Dusk came even earlier under the overcast skies that are the rule at this season. He had to cross the Harz Mountains, extremely inhospitable at this time of year. He had to reckon with storms and rain, sodden paths, weather that no one would keep a dog outside in and that would certainly make eight hours of walking impossible.

That he would travel on foot was taken for granted. He was used to it, he had experience doing it, and for him it was appropriate. He did not need to sit around in inns and wait for the next stagecoach. He was not packed together with unpleasant fellow travelers who would disturb his train of thought, and he could find his accommodations for himself. He was independent. Anyway, the stagecoach hardly made faster progress at the time and was even slower, as it got stuck.

So before his trip started, it was a foregone conclusion that his leave was too short and that he would be unable to stay on schedule. Nor did he want to do so. That his superiors knew his destination and authorized the leave all the same only shows their insufficient knowledge of geography.

It has never occurred to a single one of Bach's biographers that he set out at this time with the firm intention not to keep to the number of weeks allotted him. But here we can also perceive what kind of relationship Bach had with the ecclesiastical authorities in Arnstadt: He did not care what they thought. Just as he was much more preoccupied in Arnstadt with the fugue as an art than with liturgically bound organ music, so he was far more preoccupied in general with furthering his musical education than with his church position. All things considered, it had mainly caused trouble for him.

Perhaps the artistry of Pachelbel—to whom his brother owed so much—would have interested him, but Pachelbel had died in Nuremberg in the spring. Buxtehude, as Bach was well aware since his to visit to Hamburg, enjoyed a splendid reputation for two reasons: his talent and energy as well as the devotion of the Lübeck merchants, who appreciated his projects and achievements. (The same cannot be said later of the citizens of Leipzig with regard to Bach.)

People did not go to the Church of St. Mary only for the worship services; they also went specifically to hear Buxtehude play for them. When the quiet season for church music began with Advent at the end of November, he organized his famous vespers concerts (*Abendmusiken*). So Bach arrived just at the right time to see him, and no one can hold it against him that he did not immediately set off again after his long journey on foot. After all, here he could gain living experience of what a capable musician knew how to make of his church employment.

Buxtehude was sixty-nine years old at the time. In May of the following year he would go on to join his great colleague Pachelbel in eternity. He would gladly have gone into retirement; it had already gotten about that the post of organist at St. Mary's would soon be available. That is why in 1704 the conductor, singer, and composer Johann Mattheson had been there with a friend whom he would have been only too happy to consign to the church position in Lübeck, in order to rid himself of a bothersome rival. He himself was content to perform only on the harpsichord during this visit; the friend he wished to dispense with, a certain George Frideric Handel, showed off his talents on the organ. It was the same year when Mattheson would attack that friend with a sword.

Handel might have let himself be persuaded with regard to the post as organist, for the position was very remunerative and even came with a house. But there was a certain condition that had to be met: Whoever wanted the post had to marry the organist's daughter, as had already been required of Buxtehude in his day. Miss Buxtehude was of impressive girth and also a good nine years older than Handel, who was then only nineteen.

Johann Sebastian Bach, who would have been a more than worthy successor to Buxtehude and would have found in Lübeck an ample response to his art, now received the same offer at the beginning of the new year in 1707. But he too declined, not only because of the considerable difference in age but above all because he had long since found the great love of his life in Arnstadt: his cousin Maria Barbara Bach. She was the daughter of Johann Michael Bach from Gehre, and thus a second cousin; she was older than he was, but only by a year. So in January 1707 he set out for home in the depth of winter, during the shortest days of the year, trudging on frozen paths through slush and snow. The young Bach, as we can see, was as strong as an ox. Moreover, he was not irresponsible, as Spitta and others would have us believe. His musical interests had induced him to plan on exceeding the limits of his leave without the slightest scruple. But he headed back as soon as he had learned what there was to learn, without waiting for better weather in which to travel. (It can also of course be inferred that love may have played a role in this.)

At home the predictable trouble ensued right away: a summons to appear before the consistory for ignoring the dates of his leave, combined of course with the demand that he must now finally resume his work with the secondary school students.

What was expected of him in this regard is revealed in a written complaint by the city council to the consistory. Here we must bear in mind that the Latin School was under the control of the consistory, not the town. In Ohrdruf the ecclesiastical superintendent was simultaneously the headmaster of the school. In Arnstadt the headmaster was Johann Friedrich Treiber, but he was subordinate to superintendent Johann Gottfried Olearius, who certainly did not want to be bothered too much with this part of his official duties. The city council's communication to the consistory of April 16, 1706, states the following with regard to the students: "They have no fear of their teachers, they get into fights in their presence and talk back to them in the most offensive manner. They wear their rapiers not only on the street, but also in the school. They play ball during the church services and instruction periods, and even run wild in unseemly places."

So this was the kind of singers the consistory had to offer. Bach had gathered experience, and he would have had to be a fool to get mixed up with these rowdies a second time. But Schweitzer was not the first to lay the blame for the behavior of his singers on Bach alone. Spitta writes: "In his youthful hotheadedness, he over-looked the fact that despite his eminent gifts, in the end he had to fulfill his duty." Yet working with the chorus did not belong to his duties at all.

Terry claims: "He was a bad disciplinarian, easily provoked to temper, and prone to outbreaks." How he knows that he does not let us in on; he simply affirms it.

Otterbach sums up: "Weaknesses in Bach's conduct of his duties and deficiencies in his character are discernible in these examples." And he even goes on to remark, "However, the Bach literature tends to *gloss over them.*" Apparently all these gentlemen would virtually have jumped at the chance, as good subordinates, to get unnecessarily involved with a gang of louts that all the other teachers could not deal with.

Bach's contract did not oblige him to do so at all, and understandably, he had somewhat different interests. Above all he wanted to make music, music corresponding to his newly won knowledge. Because of that, he began to meddle with the worship service. At first his preludes were too long: He could not play the organ enough to suit him. When he was reprimanded for that, he subsequently made them too short. There are records about these matters too, and it is indicative that it was none other than a student, the leader of the school chorus, who complained about him. It was a fresh opportunity to get back at Bach.

What cannot be perceived in the archives at any point is a human relationship between the clergy and the organist. The subordinate was called to account, and requirements were imposed on him. The relations were not improved by that, of course; these superiors had nothing to offer Bach, and so he turned away from them.

52

In any case he was far more preoccupied with a fundamental musical problem in regard to his compositions. Others had long since come to terms with it, but it still haunted him: It was the question of musical tuning and thus of the possible chords and keys.

Describing the physics of this problem is very complicated. Nowadays an equally "tempered" tuning is the norm. At that time it was theoretically calculated but did not yet exist in practice. Especially for the organ, with its numerous overtone stops, considerable difficulties arose as a result. Bach's own compositions bear witness to that: Their tonic keys stay within the limits of three sharps or flats, from E-flat major to A major, with E major and A-flat major occurring as exceptions. So the quandary was this: If the organ virtually prohibited certain keys because of their impurity of tone, which chords from outside the usual range of harmonic possibilities were possible all the same?

There are a half dozen organ chorales from Bach's Arnstadt period that reflect this problem. In that respect it should be noted that at the time the hymns actually were sung somewhat differently than they would be today. The organ inserted interludes between the individual lines of the chorale in order to enable the members of the congregation to catch their breath and reflect. In Bach's organ chorale "Allein Gott in der Höh' sei Ehr'" ("Glory Alone to God in the Highest") this becomes especially clear. To be sure, we cannot claim that Bach is interpreting the text in this instance; rather, he made an organ toccata out of it that evoked not the verse "God takes pleasure in us" but rather the Last Judgment.

The harmonization is so daring and unprecedented for the times that we need not hesitate to term it revolutionary; in fact we must. But it is completely understandable that the congregation, in the midst of this and similar compositions, simply forgot to sing. And this occasioned a summons for Bach to appear before the consistory once again: "They rebuke him for having hitherto made many strange variations in the chorale, mixing many outlandish tones in it so that the congregation has become confused thereby." 53

That was true, but unfortunately the gentlemen now used the opportunity not for justified theological instruction or even admonition but to give Bach lessons in composition: "In the future, if he wishes to introduce a *tonus peregrinus,* he must prolong it and not shift too swiftly to something else, or, as he has hitherto been accustomed, even play a *tonus contrarius.*" This was of course combined once again with the reproach that he did not want to perform music with the students and with the demand that he explain himself within eight days.

When one reads the records more attentively, it becomes clear from what follows that the students had behaved in an uncouth manner toward the organist yet again during the worship service. The student Rambach, who was the appointed choir leader, did not even apologize but used the opportunity instead to blacken Bach's name by attacking his organ playing. It is true that he was condemned to the detention room for his bad behavior, but no answer was given to Bach's request that he be provided with a "competent director."

It is also remarkable that given his behavior the student Rambach had his turn with the authorities only after the organist had had to swallow a long-winded reprimand. And it is strangely affecting that despite the loutish conduct of the choir members, we read nothing in this or the other records about Bach's notorious bad temper. Apparently, the discovery of that character trait was entirely denied to his contemporaries. We do not read anything about it in Forkel either. It shows up for the first time as an invention of Spitta's, and his successors have copied it from him ever after, diligently and unthinkingly.

Bach had no intention of "explaining himself." The climate between him and his ecclesiastical superiors had entered an ice age in any event. His contract included no provision about this task, and after all, no answer is also an answer. He would have to experience that same kind of nonanswer himself ten years later in Weimar. But here the decision was up to him, and he was not willing to sacrifice his artistic standards to the interests of the church administration.

54   In all this Bach, who was supposedly so lacking in self-control, showed a notable degree of imperturbability. He fulfilled his con-

tractual obligations to the letter, on Sundays, Mondays, and Thursdays. Until his departure his superiors reproached him with nothing as to the performance of his duties, with one single exception. When on November 11 of the same year he was once again summoned before the members of the consistory because of the choir, the record states: "They further inquire by what right he recently had an unfamiliar maiden invited into the choir loft and let her make music there." Bach's answer is classic in its concision: "I spoke about it to Master Uthe"—not as though he had asked his permission; he had simply informed him about it.

With the exception of Rueger, who considers that the lady could also have been Maria Barbara's sister, all are agreed that the "unfamiliar maiden" must have been Bach's future beloved spouse. And it is rather implausible that the organist would have left his fiancée at home and taken her sister along "to the choir loft" instead. All are unanimous as well in assuming that in this case it was a question of completely private music making. "Were we to conclude that the singer made herself heard during the worship service itself, we would . . . be mistaken," Spitta comments, with reference to *tacet mulier in ecclesia*.

The apostle Paul's injunction in I Corinthians that "woman should be silent in church" has been of no benefit to Christendom into our own time. But in the Saxon-Thuringian area in Bach's day, it was still taken very literally. In Hamburg already less so: Mattheson reports that there some female singers were hidden behind columns, but then people not only wanted to hear them but also to see them. At Buxtehude's concerts in Lübeck, the customs were freer, no doubt, but that was not the case for worship services. In Leipzig during Bach's tenure of his post, the libretti for certain cantatas may well have been written by women, but we do not know that a woman was ever allowed to lift her voice in a performance.

And yet the text of the records gives pause to reflect. Bach did not simply "make music" in the choir "with an unfamiliar maiden";

55

he expressly invited her up so that she could make herself heard—
he "had her invited into the choir loft and let her make music
there." One does not "have someone come up and make music" if
nobody is listening. Nothing more than "I spoke about it to Master
Uthe" was to be extracted from the taciturn organist, however. He
saw no reason for an apology and even less of one "to explain himself," either in November or December or January. He stuck to his
duties and took care not to get mixed up in anything else.

And despite this professional frustration, Arnstadt proved to be
an extraordinary piece of luck for him. A relation from the widely
extended family of the Bachs, the sister of the widow of his deceased Arnstadt uncle (and thus his aunt) lived there as well. And
with this aunt, Miss Wedemann, lived his cousin Maria Barbara,
daughter of the late town clerk Bach from Gehren, an orphan like
himself. When the two met in Arnstadt, he was eighteen and she
was nineteen, a wonderful age to fall in love, and so they did, all
the more so because Maria Barbara had also been brought up on
music.

Good luck eventually came to his aid in his professional life too.
In Mühlhausen, less than 40 miles away, the organist of the St. Blasius Church, Johann Georg Ahle, died on December 2, 1706. Ahle
was a famous name, not just in Mühlhausen. His father, Johann
Rudolf, had already been organist there as well, and splendid
melodies devised by him are still found in the Protestant hymnbook, for instance, "Liebster Jesu, wir sind hier" ("Dearest Jesus,
We Are Here") and "Morgenglanz der Ewigkeit" ("Morning
Splendor of Eternity").

The son had continued the compositional work of his father,
though not on the organ. More important than anything else, however, was that Deacon Fischer made his home in Mühlhausen too.
He had already recommended the organ builder Wender and the
organ examiner Bach as well to the citizens of Arnstadt. He not
only knew who Bach was, but he also doubtless knew that he might
be available for the vacant position.

We might assume that Bach would have gone all out to seize the opportunity to leave Arnstadt for Mühlhausen. "The situation was intolerable," Schweitzer writes. But that too is only his assertion. For Bach, it was not that way at all; with the greatest serenity he let other applicants present their credentials, while December, January, February, and March came and went. We have to give him credit for extreme composure here and surmise that he himself considered his situation by no means "intolerable." On the contrary, he had held his own.

When they heard him in Mühlhausen, people were no less enthusiastic about his artistry than they had been three years earlier in Arnstadt. A month later, when the *conventus parocchiarum,* or parish council, convened, it was settled: Bach and no other. A city councilman was sent to Arnstadt to negotiate with the young man. His fee here also was much higher than that of his predecessor: It was as good as in Arnstadt. On June 14 Bach was in Mühlhausen, on June 15 he signed his contract, and on June 29 he returned the organ keys in the Arnstadt town hall and submitted his resignation.

The count's consistory of Arnstadt let him go in peace; his successor had already been found in the person of that same Johann Ernst Bach who had stood in for him during his journey to Lübeck. Furthermore, he performed music with the students and came considerably cheaper.

The virtuoso fee that Sebastian Bach had been awarded after his audition in Arnstadt had been an exception that was immediately repeated in Mühlhausen. This young man of twenty-two years was truly an extraordinary and deeply impressive expert at his art. To be sure, Rueger considers that this chiefly furnishes proof of Bach's unusual business sense and insinuates that he subsequently saw to it that his successors' salaries were reduced. To imply such uncooperative conduct on Bach's part is not exactly kind. That Bach, unlike his great contemporary Handel and his much lesser contemporary Mattheson, was unfortunately rather lacking in business sense can be clearly perceived from his Leipzig period. (Even if he did understand how to count.)

But for the time being, on September 14, his resignation took effect in Arnstadt, and Mühlhausen had even provided him with a furniture cart for the move. The only thing he still left behind for a short time was his bride. Otherwise he had finished with Arnstadt for good.

5

Bach's first phase in church positions can hardly be described as gratifying. He was neither the irresponsible person that Spitta portrays nor the incapable organizer and hothead that Schweitzer, Otterbach, and others depict. But in light of the incidents in Arnstadt it is also impossible to regard him as the gifted musician who felt driven from earliest childhood to serve his church, as Terry claims. His ecclesiastical superiors certainly did not see him that way, and in general the relationship between them and Bach was exceedingly distant, as the records make clear. At any rate, after three years in Arnstadt Bach could find no clergyman there whom he would have wanted to officiate at his wedding.

Although at this time he was already a citizen of the free imperial city of Mühlhausen, for the marriage ceremony, on account of his bride, he needed a license issued in Count Schwarzburg's domain. He obtained it without difficulty, but the wedding was performed on October 17, 1707, by the Reverend Lorenz Stauber in Dornheim. Bach had friendly relations with him. It so happened that the pastor had recently been stricken by a heavy loss, his wife having died. Yet the wedding of Johann Sebastian and Maria Barbara also had a happy sequel for Reverend Stauber, for Maria Barbara's aunt, Miss Wedemann, thereafter helped him to get over his great sorrow, and when the year of mourning was over, she moved into the vicarage in Dornheim as Stauber's second wife.

For his part, Bach discovered a wholly different service relationship in Mühlhausen from the one he had known in Arnstadt. This was a free imperial city and subject to no prince, even though its importance had strongly diminished as a consequence of the Thirty Years' War. Two weeks before Bach's arrival on May 30, 1707, the city had experienced a catastrophic fire in which 400 residences along with their stables were destroyed, a disaster that had reduced over half the city to rubble.

Bach was appointed as organist of the St. Blasius Church. Like the Church of St. Mary, this one had fortunately been spared by the fire. But taken as a whole the catastrophe was so great the councilmen reportedly had a hard time finding pen and ink in order to sign Bach's certificate of appointment.

Here he was dealing with councilmen, and the distinction is important. Bach was not subordinate to the ecclesiastical authorities of an imperial count's domain, as he had been in Arnstadt; instead, he was a city council employee, and the council valued him. It consisted in fact of three councils, which alternated in the administration of the city. (In Leipzig Bach would later encounter the same form of government.)

The changing of the council in Mühlhausen was a festive ceremony. We have a cantata Bach wrote for the occasion that was even engraved on copper and printed at the council's expense. That never happened to him again either in Weimar or in Leipzig; this is the only cantata of his that Johann Sebastian Bach ever saw printed in the sixty-five years of his life. In addition there are four others from the Mühlhausen period, and these first cantatas by Bach are just as remarkable as his first organ compositions in Arnstadt.

Already between nineteen and twenty-two years of age he steps into our ken as an accomplished master, and an incomparable one at that; we would look in vain among his famous contemporaries for works of such conceptual profundity and compositional virtuosity. The Halle musicologist Siegmund-Schultze writes of these early organ compositions: "The improvisational and virtuoso side predominates; the strictly worked out music is still absent. . . . The inspired spark is already perceptible in the early preserved works, but it does not come through." It seems he has never taken a look at what he is assessing here. Likewise when he immediately goes on to claim: "The further compositions of the Mühlhausen period continue the series of clavier and organ works of Arnstadt." It is a great loss that he did not share with us which works these might be; besides the Organ Prelude in G Major, no clavier and organ compositions from the Mühlhausen period have been found. And that is no coincidence.

The St. Blasius organ was in a deplorable state (Bach drew up a detailed proposal for its repair). Moreover, here he could finally devote himself to the work that in Arnstadt the obstreperous brats from fine families and the consistory had made impossible for him: ensemble music.

For here in Mühlhausen there was a strong musical tradition that extended to the villages in the surrounding area, and above all there was a "musical society" that united the singing and playing forces of Mühlhausen and its environs. Bach's predecessors had already performed music with it. In fact the organists of St. Blasius had contributed decisively to the local cultivation of music as long as anyone could remember.

Five generations of organists had laid the groundwork, even though Bach's immediate predecessor, Johann Georg Ahle, had not been equal to his father, Johann Rudolf Ahle, in talent and capability. He was not only organist of St. Blasius, but he had also been one of the mayors of the city: This tells us something about the importance of the post at St. Blasius in that period.

So it is understandable why the city fathers took their time, after the younger Ahle's death, in selecting his successor. The organist of St. Blasius was de facto a kind of municipal music director. With the musical society of Mühlhausen, the young Bach—twenty-two

61

when he took up his post—had a thoroughly competent musical apparatus at his disposal. That is evident from the demands posed by his Mühlhausen cantatas. Especially praised is the cantata "Gott ist mein König" ("God Is My King") (BWV 71), which he performed on February 4, 1708, in the Church of St. Mary for the aforementioned changing of the council, with three trumpets, two recorders, two oboes, bassoon, strings, timpani, and organ, along with a chorus and soloists—altogether an ensemble that was never available to him in Arnstadt and only rarely in Leipzig. And it went without saying that he conducted it himself.

To be sure, there are people who claim that since there were two organists there must have been a choirmaster too, but they will have a hard time finding him: Choirmaster *(Cantor)* was in fact not a church post but a school position, and neither the Ahles nor the Bach from Eisenach who became Johann Sebastian's successor are ever known to have used a choirmaster for the performance of vocal compositions. On the contrary, Bach developed a richly active role of direction and guidance in Mühlhausen; he virtually threw himself into that realm of musical endeavor which had been soured for him in Arnstadt. As his notice of resignation reveals, he bought music and instruments for his work with the society at his own expense and also looked after the church music in the surrounding villages—all things to which his employment contract did not oblige him but which opened up possibilities for his music. And that his cantata for the changing of the council was printed—which had never happened in Mühlhausen before and never did since—shows that the performance under his direction must have been seen as the high point of Mühlhausen's musical life at the time. Even after his departure he was entrusted with an important supervisory task and a further cantata for the changing of the council, and a quarter of a century later he could still refer to the lasting influence he had bequeathed after only one year of activity.

From all this Schweitzer draws an inconceivable conclusion: "The citizens believed that they had done their part when they had hired an artist on extraordinarily favorable financial terms, but he was not capable of reorganization."

As for the "extraordinarily favorable financial terms," Bach states expressly in his notice of resignation that "however simple my way of life may be, what with the payment of the house rent and other necessary expenditures, I can hardly make do." The same goes for the alleged incapacity for "reorganization": We have no knowledge of disputes between Bach and his musicians, and vocal music never attained such heights in the township either before or since. Moreover, Bach delivered a very significant work of reorganization to the city before he departed: The thoroughly thought-out plan for the renovation of the organ in the Church of St. Blasius.

It was a very economical plan, since it provided for the expansion of the organ at a good price by incorporating a smaller, unnecessary organ into it. It was a very well considered plan that revealed him to be not only a master of organ disposition but also a precise expert in mechanics. And it was a bold plan, since Bach proposed to enrich the organ with chimes, which was quite unusual (and Bach's own invention). The organ builder was the same Wender whose organ Bach had inspected and inaugurated in Arnstadt, and the members of the parish council, which was composed of city councilmen, were so enthusiastic about Bach's proposals that they not only agreed spontaneously on all points but were even prepared to pay for the chimes out of their own pockets. The council also went so far as to assign the supervision of the construction to him even after his departure.

So it is obvious that Bach's superiors in Mühlhausen appreciated him without reservation. Nonetheless he remained in Mühlhausen for barely a year, when his stay was spoiled once again. And again it was his superintendent who made the fulfillment of his goals impossible. Bach defined these goals in his notice of resignation to the city council in a phrase that has become famous: "a well-regulated church music to the glory of God and in conformity with your wishes."

What hindered him was the devoutness of the superintendent and chief pastor of St. Blasius, Johann Adolph Frohne. He was a supporter of the trend in Lutheran theology known as Pietism. For his part, Bach had been raised in the Lutheran Orthodox tradition; his schools had imparted the theological teachings of orthodoxy to him, and the theology in Arnstadt had also been Lutheran Orthodox.

"Orthodox" means "right-believing" and *pietas* means "devotion." The endeavor to infuse the firm doctrines of orthodoxy with a piety that sprang from within was not new. About 100 years earlier the writings of Johann Arndt, Philipp Nicolai, and others already tended in that direction. The movement became virulent in 1675 with a book by the Frankfort preacher and later high court chaplain in Dresden, Philipp Jakob Spener. The title of this work, *Pia desideria (Devout Wishes)*, gave the trend its name.

The desire for inner renewal of the inherited beliefs was not limited to the Lutherans. In France and the Netherlands, the Jansenists and, in England, the Puritans increased in number. Common to all these movements were the clashes to which they gave rise. The pope excommunicated the Jansenists in the bull *Unigenitus* and brought about their persecution. In England and Scotland, the Puritans shattered the absolute power of the monarchy and won victory in the English Revolution.

Taken as a whole, the religious conflicts of the seventeenth and eighteenth centuries were of a fierceness that we can hardly grasp today and that even the nineteenth century had already left far behind. Religious disputes not only triggered the Thirty Years' War but propagated themselves throughout the century. All these religious trends were alike in that they wanted to take the "true faith" far more seriously than the established church, whether Catholic, Anglican, or Lutheran Orthodox. And none of their followers became merrier people as a result.

64   With his Reformation Martin Luther had brought the Savior out of the churches and monasteries to be present among the people again. At last they could discover what the Holy Scriptures con-

tained and read them in their own tongue. And they enthusiastically sang their spiritual songs, their hymns, to secular melodies. "It is a joy to be alive," Ulrich von Hutten professed at the time.

Things subsequently changed again, and original sin once more triumphed over Christian freedom. The most pious among them espoused a renunciation of the world. The Orthodox also espoused such a renunciation, yet not so resolutely, and they bristled when others questioned their devotion. Of course a conservative attitude is necessary to the preservation of a pure dogma. But some claimed to be more conservative than others, that is, to maintain an even purer faith.

Many studies have been written about the nature of Pietism; it has become a regular field of research. And from Johann Sebastian Bach's short stay in Mühlhausen, it has been inferred that he too had Pietistic views. This is not a difficult case to make: Pietistic thought could also be shown to underlie the hymns of Paul Gerhardt, who was quite distant from the movement. And since the tune "Wie schön leuchtet der Morgenstern" ("How Beautifully Shines the Morning Star") constitutes the setting to music of a poem by Philipp Nicolai, who can be counted among the forefathers of Pietism, it is not hard to make a Pietist out of Johann Georg Ahle as well.

But the spiritual content of Pietism and its differences with Orthodoxy may simply not have mattered much to Bach. The wonderful and deeply religious interpretation Bach gave to his texts in his sacred compositions transcends all dogmatism. At no time did he adopt his opinions and professions of faith from the theological superiors for whom he worked; similarly, he did not derive his harmony from either Böhm or Buxtehude. He was as little a follower of this or that religious movement as he was the disciple of this or that composer.

The Leipzig theologian Martin Petzoldt has tried to demonstrate that Bach's spiritual and intellectual life had its roots in his (rather meager) association with his father confessors, and he has

65

investigated this relationship as a source of Enlightenment ideas. He does not seem to know that the Enlightenment strongly opposed the imposition of theology on others and so was in the worst hands among father confessors. According to Kant, enlightenment is "the ability to use the mind without the help of others," and precisely this ability Bach possessed from childhood on to an outstanding degree. His faith had nothing to do with the theological quarrels of his time, and these disputes could not possibly have influenced his beliefs any more than his music.

But they could interfere with it appreciably, and in Mühlhausen they did. His superintendent and head pastor at the St. Blasius Church, Johann Adolph Frohne, was a devout Pietist. As such he was opposed not only to any kind of activity on Sundays but also to all earthly pleasures and diversions in general, which the Pietists abhorred as sinful. And music was one of these, especially the more elaborate developments of church music.

For example, in 1697 Gottfried Vockerodt, a Pietist professor in Jena, published *The Abuse of the Free Arts, Especially Music,* in which he spoke out in detail against "sonatas, toccatas, and ricercari" as well as operas and comedies. Vockerodt was a relative of the Mühlhausen mayor of the same name. Frohne had been in his post since 1691, and there is no indication that he did not more or less share Vockerodt's views.

"Nothing tells you more about a person than a joke he is offended by," Lichtenberg observed. The Pietists were offended by every joke. For a serious Pietist, even a liberating laugh was sinful. "Guard yourself against idle laughter," Spener had written; "especially when others laugh about jests and foolishness, take care that you do not laugh with them. For it is not pleasing to God, so why is it pleasing to you?"

More valuable than Sunday worship services, than Word and Sacrament, were devotional exercises in the domestic circle, when the faithful sang their pious hymns not loudly and powerfully but quietly and introspectively. In this regard, Herder wrote in 1780 in

66

his letters on the study of theology that the Pietists "toned down the church chorales to chamber singing with sweet tunes, melodies full of tenderness and dilly-dallying, so that they lost all their heart-commanding majesty."

We can only shake our heads when under such circumstances Siegmund-Schultze flatly claims that Bach "felt very drawn . . . to the powerful sentimental values of Pietistic teaching." And others claim similar things. But what good was a religious movement such as this for a young musician of the creative energy of Johann Sebastian Bach? It pulled the rug out from under his feet; upon it he could not found that music for which he came into the world. Frohne, to whom Spitta dedicates a detailed and well-disposed character description, complete with a sample from his sermons, may have been a gentle and godly man. But he did not countenance the wider development of church music, since that ran counter to his deepest convictions.

Now in that respect the head pastor of St. Mary's Church, Georg Christian Eilmar, was quite different. Already when he had come to Mühlhausen in 1699, as a devout Orthodox Lutheran he had railed against Frohne's messages. But since Pietism had just as many fervently convinced followers there as the old Lutheran tendency, the situation reached the point of genuine turmoil. The city council had had to intervene with a formal ban. Such things did not happen only in Mühlhausen. In Eisenach in 1712 the duke had had a decree against sectarian Pietism read out from the pulpits, and in Arnstadt before Bach's arrival the superintendent, Johann Gottfried Olearius, had successfully fought against the Pietistic home devotions of the Weimar court music director, Samuel Drese. In Weimar Bach would encounter the dispute between Pietists and Orthodox once again, and nowhere was it conducted with the biblical saying in mind: "Behold, how good and how pleasant it is for brethren to dwell together in unity!"

Unquestionably, the Pietism disseminated in Mühlhausen was disadvantageous to Bach's work. And with regard to proof of

"Pietistic elements," caution is always called for: "Pietistic elements" could also be detected without difficulty in the case of certain esoterics today, as well as in the Catholic hymnbook—or even as early as in St. Francis of Assisi. What is decisive is not really the body of thought connected with Pietism but rather the narrow-mindedness and formation of parties that it implied. For in Bach's time, Pietism, as we can see from the facts cited above, was by no means just a devout spiritual current; it was a militantly secular one that triggered massive political conflicts and interventions by the authority of the state.

In Mühlhausen the city council's ban did not bring an end to the disputes at all. Precisely in Bach's time they flared up again. We know that Bach's cantata for the changing of the council was not performed in the Pietistic Church of St. Blasius, though St. Blasius and not St. Mary's was the principal church of the town. Thus it is likely that it was also mainly for theological reasons that, as Spitta reports, in his compositions Bach's predecessor "restricted himself to religious arias and small pieces for several instruments." It must have still been possible to reconcile that much with Frohne's Pietism. But that Bach's conception of the spiritual mission of his music was not compatible with Frohne's is only too easy to comprehend, as is the fact that under the prevailing conditions he became friends with Eilmar. What cannot be comprehended is how someone could hit upon the idea that "the Pietistic movement strongly appealed" to Bach. How could it, when it had no room for his music?

Eilmar at St. Mary's did have room, and what is more, he represented the doctrinal teaching Bach had grown up with. The only problem was that Bach could not be Frohne's organist and Eilmar's friend. That he preferred Frohne's declared enemy was understandably resented by Frohne's congregation of followers, especially since Eilmar continued his attacks on Frohne so vigorously that the city council had to intervene once again on May 8, 1708.

"Though I would gladly have fulfilled the duties of my appointment in every way, it has not been possible to accomplish this without adversity, and at present there is little indication that any change will take place . . . in the future," as Bach himself, in his letter of resignation to the city council, describes his dilemma and the failure of his endeavors. He adds that in his new post he sees himself in a happier position with regard to "the attainment of my goal of a well-regulated church music . . . without any further vexation." Since the city council was very well disposed toward him, Bach could not have been implying that they caused this "vexation." Bach had provoked that through his friendship with Eilmar and through his music. He had, yet again, made a superintendent angry with him. He apologizes formally to the city councilmen when he asks that "they content themselves for now with the meager services I have rendered" and promises that "if I can contribute anything to the service of Your Honors' Church in the future, I will do so more in acts than in words."

As we can see, he would have got along well with the city council. Here again it was his church that did not allow him to create his "well-regulated church music."

6

I<small>N</small> W<small>EIMAR THE COURT</small> organist Johann Effler had given up his post because of old age. The court at Weimar knew Bach, and Bach knew the court, or at least he believed he did. He applied for the position and obtained it. As in Arnstadt and Mühlhausen, his audition before Duke Wilhelm Ernst brought him an immediate increase in salary over that of his predecessor. In economic terms he had bettered himself decidedly through the change: In Mühlhausen he received along with payment in kind 85 florins; in Weimar he received 150, 20 more than his predecessor, Effler.

Everywhere Bach received more than his predecessors, which again tells us how much his outstanding talent impressed people. His successors were immediately reduced again to the salary level of those who had gone before him. Leipzig formed the only exception: There he was paid less well than his predecessor, and later his income was even lowered—by way of punishment. But that did not happen until the period of his highest development, namely, after the performance of the *St. Matthew Passion*.

The move to Weimar did as much to improve Bach's finances as it did to improve his art. Here music could be made on the organ, in the worship service, and as chamber and orchestral music, and here it was not hindered by any Pietistic animosity toward worldly matters. But socially, this was no advancement for Bach: The citizen of a free imperial city had now become a prince's most humble lackey once again. He would come to know very precisely the difference between the two. And as for his position among the musicians of the court, he was next to last in rank; after him came only the city musician as temporary staff. As court musician he also figured only in the middle third of the servants, above a coachman or groom to be sure, but beneath a body servant or ducal gardener. His social position in Weimar was thus quite low.

In Weimar in 1708 Maria Barbara gave birth to her first child, Catharina Dorothea, and Reverend Eilmar made a special trip from Mühlhausen to be the godfather at the christening. The friendship between Bach and Eilmar thus continued even after Mühlhausen. Twenty children were granted to Bach, but only once more was a clergyman named a godparent. That gives pause, as does the fact that of the fifteen godparents the Bachs appointed during their ten Weimar years, only two were from Weimar and only one of those from court.

The conditions of government in the duchy of Weimar were somewhat difficult to comprehend. In order to prevent his domain from being divided up, Duke Wilhelm had determined that his two eldest sons, Wilhelm Ernst and Johann Ernst, should share the government with equal rights. So there were two courts—two personal courts maintained out of a common budget. Officially, Johann Ernst was considered the equal of his brother Wilhelm Ernst, his senior by two years, and in 1703–1704 Bach had been "personal music lackey" to him. All that had changed: Johann Ernst had died in 1707. His elder son and successor, the nineteen-year-old Duke Ernst August, maintained no musicians of his own. Thus Bach was now a member of the "joint court ensemble."

Without exception, Bach's biographers paint the character and government of Duke Wilhelm Ernst in the most glowing colors. 72 "This man was among the most distinguished and best-educated princes of his time, and he was wholeheartedly devoted to art," writes Schweitzer. "Among the small-scale rulers of central Germany at the time—who mostly denied their Germanness as much as possible, were concerned only about their own welfare, and had no idea of the duties of a sovereign—Duke Wilhelm Ernst of Saxe-Weimar stands out as a distinctive, conscientious, and deeper-rooted personality," writes Spitta. In 1708 "Bach came to Weimar to serve a prince of unusual seriousness and high purpose. Wilhelm Ernst, Duke of Saxe-Weimar, was conspicuous among the sovereigns of his period," writes Terry.

The same tone has continued into the present: "This [duke] was intent on not having the feud between the Pietists and the Orthodox fought out at his court; and in general under his reign an enlightened, 'progressive' spirit prevailed. . . . In a way, the foundations were laid for the cultural flowering of Weimar that proved so attractive to Goethe and Schiller," writes Otterbach. And we know where he gets it from, since in Siegmund-Schultze we read: "The reigning Duke Wilhelm Ernst, an exceptional figure among the princes of his time, made serious efforts toward cultural improvement. In many respects he laid the foundations for the flowering of Weimar at the end of the century." And shortly before he speaks of an "early-Classical atmosphere."

This effusive praise from so many quarters seemed a little too general to me. I wanted to enrich the image of such a splendid sovereign with a few details in order to make it still more vivid. But although the portrayals of the musicologists agreed with admirable unanimity, unfortunately a somewhat different image emerged from my study of Thuringian regional history.

The duke, born in 1662, had reigned since 1683 and was forty-six years old when Bach took up his post. When the government passed into the hands of the duke and his brother, the duke immediately negotiated a contract with his brother that safeguarded his own authority. Then only two years later, by legal means, he imposed alterations that reduced the rights of his brother and expanded his own. After two more years he laid claim to the highest judicial office of the land for himself alone; by so doing he had practically demoted

73

his brother. The latter finally had to turn to the emperor in order to recover his sovereignty, if by no other means then by a division of the duchy. But after four years of waiting, he was denied his request in 1702, whereupon Johann Ernst completely withdrew from government affairs. In nine years of feuding, Wilhelm Ernst had achieved what he had wanted from the very beginning.

He is depicted as a pious man, but he thought nothing of brotherly love. When in the winter of 1706–1707 his brother lay mortally ill in his palace, Wilhelm Ernst never even paid him a visit; for him, Johann Ernst had ceased to matter. Yet his brother's sons, Ernst August and Johann Ernst, were still of interest to him, and against their mother's will he succeeded in getting guardianship over them. It so happened that Ernst August, the elder, felt the same kind of compulsion to get his way as his uncle, and he was determined to regain the powers of cosovereignty of which his father had been despoiled.

This led to the shabbiest of squabbles between the two sovereigns of this miniature state, which were naturally taken out on the skins of their subjects. Duke Wilhelm Ernst once billeted his state police, the "rangers," in the villages from which Ernst August drew his income. Duke Ernst August in turn had twelve of the thirty soldiers to whom he was entitled collect tolls from the inhabitants on the roads that led to Wilhelm Ernst's villages. Whereupon Wilhelm Ernst took the soldiers' horses away from them.

Wilhelm Ernst was somewhat rigorous in his decisions. When his wife, Charlotte, from the house of Hessen-Homburg, did not agree with him, he immediately divorced her and locked her up in one of his chateaux for the rest of her life. No less forceful was his "foreign policy" toward his neighbors. Before he had completely stymied his brother, he quarreled with Saxe-Eisenach over his claim to Jena, and he even took the matter before the imperial court council. A little later he started up a precedence fight with Saxe-Gotha and another one shortly thereafter with the imperial count Anton Günther II of Schwarzburg over the districts of Arnstadt and Käferburg. This struggle lasted almost thirty years and ended up once again before the imperial court council, where Wilhelm Ernst finally lost the trial.

Because of this affair, at the beginning of the century he had even had to send his chancellor to Vienna, but the imperial count held better cards in his relations with the emperor. The duke stationed 100 men from his militia in billeting in Arnstadt when the opportunity arose. In 1706, 1707, 1708, and 1713, his squabbles led to extensive disputes at the meetings of the Ernestiner-Saxon rulers, without bearing any fruit. The princely participants could rightly have said of him what the Leipzig city council later claimed about Bach, that he was "incorrigible."

His most important foreign policy achievement was that he kept his duchy out of the Northern War by refusing to send auxiliary troops to Saxony. They would not have earned him anything, and his domain was poor, dreadfully poor. Already in 1681 there was an edict against begging, and between 1704 and 1715 the duke repeatedly issued new decrees against it. Since he did not know how to eliminate the causes, he corrected the conditions without further ado by having his rangers chase beyond the borders anyone who had been reduced to beggary through some sort of misfortune. Gypsies who tried to travel through the region were kept off the roads by being locked up in prison. This was how he maintained order and rectitude in the duchy, for he did have a prison. Bach's biographers praise it as an "orphanage," but the title is incomplete: It was called the "prison and orphanage" and was an improvement insofar as the duke provided shelter to orphans at the prison. (In Hanoverian states they were raised in lunatic asylums.)

It is further considered to his great credit that he introduced compulsory school attendance for all children. In this respect he was in fact not at all ahead of his contemporaries: The same measure had applied in Gotha and Eisenach for some time, as well as since 1685 in the electorate of Saxony. But the curriculum he imposed is interesting. Voltaire instructed his peasants in Ferney in farming, horticulture, and livestock breeding and rightly believed that this was much more useful to them than the alphabet. Wilhelm Ernst also thought along economic lines and found that out of reading, writing, arithmetic, and religion, the catechism and reading were quite enough. The poor could not make much use of those perhaps, but they could also look forward to receiving a free burial from their benefactor.

There were eighteen different taxes in Weimar; even socks and shoes were taxed. But if Wilhelm Ernst could hardly help his subjects to prosperity and his country to wealth by this means, then he attached all the more importance to religion. This was his greatest passion. Already as an eight-year-old he had delivered a sermon, which his proud father had immediately had printed. He loved to gather the Weimar clergymen around him in the full regalia of their vestments. The post of high court chaplain in Weimar was a very important office, not as a guide to the duke's conscience (he did not recognize anyone besides himself as such), but as the head of his Weimar state church.

For such was the church in his domain. Attendance of the worship service was a duty for all his subjects, and whoever took the Bible or even his hymnbook along to church was already suspected of laxity in matters of faith. It was entirely possible for the duke himself to stop a citizen after the worship service and question him about the content of that day's sermon. The churchgoers also had to allow themselves to be catechized before the assembled congregation. The duke listened to his servants recite Bible quotations and determined accordingly in what order they could go to Holy Communion. In his prison and orphanage, praying was ordered as a punishment.

And he was a stickler for strict morality. Emperor Joseph II, who so mercilessly intervened in the organization of the monasteries and convents, set up a maternity clinic for unwed mothers in Vienna. His mother, Maria Theresa, had been less lenient; during her rule fallen women's heads were shaved. Wilhelm Ernst thought little of such softhearted actions. In his duchy unwed mothers were locked

76

up for two weeks on nothing but bread and water as soon as they gave birth.

Order also prevailed under him in other ways. In summer at nine and in winter at eight, the lights went out in his castle, and all Weimar had to retire for the night. As we see, no "enlightened, progressive spirit" predominated at all, even if the duke did accumulate a library (which his subjects never laid eyes on, of course) and enjoyed spending time with his coin and curiosity collections. To oversee these he paid a special employee, the consistorial secretary Salomo Franck, who thus found time to write religious poetry.

Under no circumstances did the duke have any understanding for the "liberation of man from his self-imposed dependence on others," as Kant defined the Enlightenment. Citizens who think for themselves cause difficulties for a determined ruler. The duke set great store by keeping his subjects on the leash of strict exercise of the Orthodox Lutheran religion. Enlightenment would have been a nuisance to him; his school lessons—catechism and reading—had nothing at all to do with that. Anyone who claims otherwise has not paid any attention either to the duke or the Enlightenment.

It seems more than a little bold when Werner Neumann affirms: "His measures to foster culture and the education of his people helped prepare the way for the golden age of Goethe and Schiller." Those two would hardly have felt at ease with the duke.

True, he did found a secondary school. Yet on closer examination that was clearly nothing but the need to catch up: Eisenach had already established its Latin School in the previous century, Arnstadt and Jena as well; those of Gotha and Ohrdruf were already quite famous—and Weimar still had none at all.

The school was finally created in 1712, the twenty-ninth year of Wilhelm Ernst's reign. The duke had not been in much of a hurry to educate his subjects. Naturally, an institution such as this had to keep up appearances: He enlisted the headmaster from Ohrdruf for his school, and when the young private tutor employed by a Jena theologian attracted attention through a pedagogical publication, he brought him over as assistant headmaster. His name was Johann Matthias Gesner, and we will meet him again later.

There was music all the same. But it was certainly not chamber music that the duke loved and cultivated. Nothing about that is to be found in Georg Mentz's history of the state and sovereigns of Weimar or anywhere else, nor is there any indication that he played an instrument. What he appreciated was pomp: impressive church music or splendid hunting music, as hunting was one of his few pleasures. For sacred music, besides the organist and ensemble, he had twelve and sometimes even eighteen trained singers at his disposal, and for hunting music he could add six trumpeters. On such occasions the sixteen musicians of the joint court ensemble had to play in Hungarian uniforms so they would look more magnificent.

The post of court music director had belonged since the previous century, with only a short interruption, to the Drese family. Adam Drese, to whom we owe the beautiful melody "Jesu geh voran auf der Lebensbahn" ("Jesus, Lead the Way on the Path of Life"), had been court music director in Weimar; a little later his son took over the position, and Wilhelm, the grandson, already held the rank of assistant music director.

We might think that under these circumstances Bach would not have had very much to organize for the court ensemble, but court music director Drese was sixty-four by that time and had become idle and sickly, and his son possessed little ambition. So both Dreses were quite content when the new organist (since he also played in the orchestra, after all) at first took on one thing or another and then more and more of the work.

But there was chamber music in the nephews' residence, the Red Palace, with Ernst August and Johann Ernst, who had already received music lessons from Bach when he was still in service to their father. And they were both musical, particularly Johann Ernst, who wrote some remarkable compositions. Two of them Bach arranged as organ concerti, and his cousin Johann Gottfried Walther did the same with another. They are equal in invention and substance to the concerti of Vivaldi.

Ernst August was a good violinist, but he had the same fierce will to succeed as his uncle, and he urgently wanted to recover the cosovereignty rights his uncle had wrested from his father. Of course, Wilhelm Ernst was vigorously opposed to that, and so began the great feud between uncle and nephew, just two years after Bach took up his post. When the nephew raised his claims against his uncle, the latter locked up his nephew's officials without further ado. A public trial ensued, the provincial diets were drawn into it, and only the mediation of the Ernestine duke of Gotha brought about an armistice—though by no means a reconciliation.

The pious duke had made his own personal selection from the Bible. "God is love," St. John had written, but the stern old bachelor in the Wilhelm Castle was absolutely uninterested in love. He attached no importance at all to such sayings as "He who says, 'I love God,' and hates his brother, is a liar," or "I give you a new law, that you love one another." As applied to himself, he rejected them. The enmity between Wilhelm Castle and the Red Palace remained an established situation, and the fact that his nephew did not wish to resign himself like his father only made matters worse.

That did not concern Bach much. He served as organist and as a member of the joint court ensemble; he kept his contract, which bound him to both courts. Moreover, in the Red Palace he knew two passionate musicians who were his friends. By contrast, with the lord of Wilhelm Castle there was no chamber music to be performed.

The duke was also unconcerned about Bach's music in the Red Palace. He knew that he was the stronger, and when his nephews were playing their music they did not get in the way of his governing. On top of that, he had made quite a wise choice by hiring the young Monsieur Bach, who was twenty-three when he took up his post; there was no such organist for many miles around. Nor did he 79 limit himself to his contractual obligations: When something needed doing, he tackled the job. The performance standards of the court orchestra notably improved after his arrival. (The absolute untenability of Schweitzer's judgment about Bach's organizational talent is also made manifest in that he never had any quarrels with his musicians—not in Mühlhausen nor Weimar nor Cöthen nor Leipzig.) In addition, in Bach the duke possessed a superb composer, a better one than he had ever had before.

The duke acknowledged this without any reservations. In the succeeding years he further increased the salary of his organist, in 1711 by 50 florins and in 1713 by 15 more. "The pleasure His Grace took in his playing spurred him on to attempt everything possible in the art of the organ," we read in Bach's obituary. This makes clear that the duke knew very well how much this man Bach was worth. After all, in the meantime Bach had become the guiding spirit of all the ducal music.

The duke gave him more money; however, he did not consider raising his rank. For this, Bach first had to appeal to him with a formal petition. Then the duke finally granted him the position of concertmaster, which he had long since taken over in practice; so it became official as well. In so doing he even raised his salary yet again by 35 florins.

In this regard it should be noted that the influence of the concertmaster, which still remains crucial for an orchestra today, was at that time far more important. As late as the premieres of Haydn's London symphonies, the concertmaster Wilhelm Cramer figured on the program sheet in full equality with the conductor, Haydn. The concertmaster normally led from the harpsichord. That Bach as concertmaster in Weimar was a far stronger artistic personality than Drese, the incumbent assistant music director, made him in effect the conductor of the orchestra as a whole.

The pay increases came just at the right time for Bach. Instead of the 85 florins he had received in Mühlhausen, here he now earned 250. Biographers readily recount how much and what kind of music he made in Weimar. Most of them say nothing about his household. Yet it was very extensive and needed to be taken care of.

The children came: Catharina Dorothea in 1708, Wilhelm Friede-mann in 1710, and Carl Philipp Emanuel in 1714. And sorrow also visited the house: In 1713 Maria Barbara bore twins who died shortly after birth. So the young Bachs stood for the first time before the graves of their children, and it would not be the last.

At Wilhelm Friedemann's christening Reverend Eilmar's daughter was named one of the godparents; the relations with the Eilmars continued. In the case of Carl Philipp Emanuel, Telemann became godfather, traveling from Eisenach, where he had been employed since the end of 1708 as concertmaster at the court. He was four years older than Bach and just as much of a musician through and through.

But not only children filled the house; there were also pupils. Johann Martin Schubert, twenty-seven by this time, had apprenticed himself to Bach in Mühlhausen. In Bach's parents' home in Eisenach, there had constantly been apprentices, and instruction, the transmission of his own experience and knowledge, was a passion that remained with Bach until the end of his life. A large number of his compositions consist of didactic works, from the *Inventions* to the *Little Organ Book (Orgelbüchlein)* and the *Art of Fugue*. Such titles as *Keyboard Practice (Clavier-Übung) I, II, III,* and *IV* suggest things that are to be taught and learned; they are not the notation of purely musical ideas like *écossaises*, impromptus, album leaves, romances, or songs without words. But it is wonderful that works Bach wrote mainly for instructional purposes outshine so many others in musical power.

At the beginning of his years of service in Weimar, Bach gave precedence to continuing his great works for the organ; almost half of all his organ compositions were produced in Arnstadt or Weimar. This is not music that is tied to the church: These are free organ works that never cease to amaze us as we study them. Not only are they unique as a whole, but each one is unique in itself. And Besseler is wrong when he claims that Bach's master years did not begin until his appointment as concertmaster. Bach had been filling this position for some time even before his appointment (which only took place at his request), and apart from this, the works of his great organ period are anything but journeyman's pieces: "The pleasure His Grace took in his playing spurred him on to attempt everything possible in the art of the organ." And in the end he was allowed to rebuild the organ according to his own conceptions in 1714, even though it had just been renovated when he took up his post. Again he inserted a glockenspiel or carillon. We find it only in the disposition of the two organs in Weimar and Mühlhausen that Bach designed, which goes to show that this organ expert had an exceptionally personal idea of disposition.

7

It is striking that in spite of all the recognition and all the possibilities for development and activity in Weimar, Bach cannot have regarded his post in the joint court ensemble as a lifelong position. (A couple of years later in Cöthen, although he was without an organ there and far removed from church music, the matter looked quite different.)

The duke permitted him to travel. Bach must have been in contact with his cousin in Meiningen at the time and visited him there. At any rate, we know of a splendid organ concert he gave in Kassel; the mother of the two young lords in the Red Palace hailed from there. In the fall of 1713, we find him in Halle, where in the Church of Our Lady the construction of a mighty new organ, with sixty-two resounding registers, was nearing completion. In the previous year Friedrich Wilhelm Zachau, Handel's teacher and himself a remarkable composer, had died there.

Bach took a look at the organ, the parish council offered him the post that had become vacant, and Bach was immediately inclined to accept it. He even composed a cantata as an audition piece. That would hardly have happened if he had felt totally happy in his position at Weimar.

A good many people claim that he traveled to Halle only in order to assure himself a salary increase in Weimar. But it seems somewhat out of proportion for him to have composed an entire cantata and performed it in Halle merely with a view to obtaining more money in Weimar. A person goes to that much trouble only when he has serious intentions.

The matter came to nothing in spite of a favorable inclination on both sides, because the Halle officials would not or could not pay the Weimar salary. In any case Bach's request for the position of concertmaster in Weimar was answered affirmatively, and he procured a new raise. It is noteworthy that despite his refusal of the post in Halle, after the completion of the organ there the officials invited him to test it in 1716. This became a memorable organ examination. The choirmaster of St. Thomas in Leipzig, Johann Kuhnau, and Heinrich Rolle from Quedlinburg were also on hand. The organ was found to be good in all its parts, and an opulent banquet at the city council's expense crowned the inspection.

All this goes to show that Bach had great freedom of movement in Weimar. He was not, like the duke's rejected consort, locked up in the castle. And in general it is absolutely untrue that his life was spent in a highly narrow sphere, as his biographers have traditionally maintained. Instead, he was amazingly well informed about many things, knew many different musicians and their compositions, looked at a great many organs, and learned as many details as he could about other instruments that he could not examine himself. Not only did he know many people, but he also was well known and widely esteemed. Though his compositions were not printed, they circulated in handwritten copies. An example is given by Johann Mattheson of Hamburg, a man of many-sided talents, who earned his reputation and fortune as a singer, harpsichordist, organist, composer, diplomat, and writer about music.

In 1717 he wrote in his *Beschützes Orchester (Defense of the Orchestra)*: "I have seen things by the famous organist in Weimar, Mr. Joh. Seb. Bach, for voice as well as for the keyboard, that are certainly so constituted that one must highly esteem the man." Mattheson perceived this even though there was nothing of Bach's that was printed. Indeed, when we compare Bach's compositions with those of his contemporaries, it is little wonder that musicians went to the trouble time and again to copy them out. Yet this did not prevent a Leipzig musicologist from asserting that "as a composer, [Bach] possessed no great name."

In fact Bach maintained relations with the courts in Kassel, Meiningen, and Weissenfels. That he and Telemann were befriended with each other went without saying, and a special closeness existed between him and his cousin Johann Gottfried Walther. Walther was only a half year older than he, both lived in Weimar, and both were organists, one at the castle, the other at the city church. In competition with each other, they created something that can be found only in their works: the arrangement of contemporary instrumental concerti into concerti for organ alone. Bach wrote two concerti after Vivaldi and two after compositions of the young Duke Johann Ernst; Walther also wrote such works after Albinoni, Torelli, Meck, Telemann, and others, and one is wholly his own invention.

In his *Italian Concerto* Bach then applied to the harpsichord the principle of an instrument playing in the concertante style, as a foil to itself. And if we want to get an impression of his absolute virtuosity, we must compare the musical structure of the notes in Bach's arrangements with what we find in Walther's. Bach's are disposed in an incomparably more difficult fashion; yet as the accounts of contemporaries confirm, he knew no difficulties when playing the keyboard.

But all that was of course not sacred music; none of it was for use in the church service, just as the great organ preludes and fugues were not so intended. Schweitzer, it is true, thought that they should be played in the worship service and the liturgy shortened accordingly, but this suggestion would hardly meet with the approval of theologians. Music is indeed as indisputably a part of the worship service as the liturgy, but a church service is not a recital. 85

Bach's organ works are absolutely immense in both their dimensions and their demands. Even Felix Mendelssohn-Bartholdy, who was a splendid organist and who performed not only the *St. Matthew Passion* in Berlin but also the organ works of Bach in Leipzig, admitted that he had had to practice some of them a long time. "As clavier-player and organist he can certainly be considered the greatest of his time; his organ and clavier compositions provide the best proof of this, as they are held to be difficult by everyone who knows them. But for him they were not so in the slightest; rather, he executed them with ease and skill as though they were only musettes," wrote Johann Adam Hiller thirty-four years after Bach's death.

Bach derived pleasure from the complexities of counterpoint; for him making music for several voices was not complicated, and the difficulties did not hamper his inventiveness but spurred it on. When we look at the contrapuntal works of Simon Sechter, the superb counterpoint teacher of Bruckner, we appreciate above all their astonishing precision. But in Bach counterpoint is not only musical; it is downright musician-like: His organ fugues overflow with the joy of making music, as do his toccatas for the harpsichord.

And like the great organ preludes, the virtuoso pieces always lead to the fugue as the main feature, as the real culmination of the free play of music. Bach's fun with fugues, his amusement with them, knows no end. Such grandly planned, clearly worked-out fugues as his were not achieved by any of his contemporaries nor by any of those who immediately followed him, and each is unique in itself. Martin Geck, the Dortmund musicologist I have already quoted several times, describes the fugue as a "*static* structure that makes its own law for itself." He could not have uttered greater foolishness if he had claimed that rivers are standing waters limited to their beds. But in another passage he claims that a fugue has no form at all—he is a very open-minded professor. The greatest merit the Jena musicologist Besseler ascribes to Bach's fugal compositions is the invention of something he calls "character theme," which he parses with academic thoroughness in his essay *Bach als Wegbereiter (Bach As Pathfinder)* in order to prove Bach's genius on this point. This is a case of love's labor lost. He could have found the carefully dissected "character theme of Bach" just as well in Buxtehude, Handel, Legrenzi, Porpora, Zachau, Walther, or Johann Caspar Ferdinand Fischer. What is more, fugal themes appear in Bach that cannot be cobbled into Besseler's "character theme" even with the greatest industry. If he had looked around somewhat, he could have saved himself a great deal of erudition; unfortunately, none of his professional colleagues pointed out his mistake to him either.

In fact it is not the thematic material that makes for the greatness (one would like to say the immensity) of Bach's fugal compositions; it is the process by which, from these beginnings, he develops something almost unbelievable. The first eight notes of Beethoven's Fifth Symphony are in themselves a long way from being a stroke of genius. The true inspiration is the way he builds up a foundational symphonic phrase out of these eight notes, which, in its totality, wholly eludes such analytical methods as those Besseler has applied. It is the immutable tragedy of musicology that it must rely on inappropriate means as soon as it abandons its firm footing as an auxiliary discipline. Inevitably, talking about music is not musical.

Bach's *Little Organ Book,* which he probably began about 1716, has also given rise to overinterpretation. Bach is supposed to have written it for his son Wilhelm Friedemann when the boy was only six years old and his feet did not reach from the organ bench to the pedals. That there were other pupils in Bach's house does not make for as lovely a legend. Schweitzer has said of the *Little Organ Book* that it is "the dictionary of Bach's tone language" and "one of the greatest events ever in music in general." That has also been repeated in more or less modified form by other authorities. Bach would hardly have been enthusiastic about so much praise: He himself considered his *Little Organ Book* a work for beginners.

Schweitzer further states: "The characteristic motifs of the various chorales correspond to just as many expressions for feelings and images as Bach dares to reproduce in tones." One can of course boldly claim something like that, but one cannot prove it. When we look closer, many different pieces in this collection are far more likely to prove the opposite. "The meaning of music is a peculiar thing," said someone who must have known, as a composer, pianist, conductor, and teacher: Leonard Bernstein. And he demonstrated that Rossini's overture to *William Tell* can just as well be defined as film music for an American Western. After excursions into many different tendencies in music interpretation and their mistaken meanderings, he comes to the fundamental conclusion: "The meaning of music is in the music, and nowhere else." With that he unfortunately removes the basic groundwork from under the feet of hordes of music exegetes. They will not miss it, however; they have done without it wonderfully up to now.

Besseler voices his surprise that Bach does not later repeat the stereotypical method of chorale treatment that he applied in the *Little Organ Book*—although it was intended, as the composer stresses, for purposes of instruction, for "beginning organists." And he goes on to claim that no similar work ever occurred to others. That is not correct: In Telemann, Zachau, and Walther there certainly are parallels. This does not belittle the beauties of the *Little Organ Book* in any way; Mozart loses nothing in uniqueness either merely because he did not invent the symphony. And Bach did later employ stereotypes similar to those in the *Little Organ Book*. Besseler need only have recalled the well-known chorale prelude "Wachet auf, ruft uns die Stimme" ("Awake, the Voice Calls Us!") or taken a look at the Neumeister collection. The system is extended, but the principle is retained.

Bound with his appointment as concertmaster was the obligation for Bach to "perform new cantatas every month"—the duke did not grant his favor without requiring something in return. He had not made such a demand of other concertmasters, and one can gather from this factor as well that he was practically appointing Bach to the post of music director, since the music director normally determines the repertoire. This new obligation opened up further possibilities for Bach: In addition to the court orchestra, there was a choir—not very large, but capable—and kettledrums and trumpets to boot. And so we come to Bach's Weimar cantatas.

The very first of the series, "Ich hatte viel Bekümmernis" ("I Had Much Distress"), is one of Bach's genuine masterpieces. The performance fell on the third Sunday after Trinity Sunday. It was not only a cantata of new beginnings but also one of farewell, for Prince Johann Ernst, who because of his bad health was about to make a journey to the baths. He would never return: He died at barely nineteen, a young musician who would still have had much to say to his time.

The cantata itself is remarkable in many respects. Its libretto, like that of the others, derives from Salomo Franck, the consistorial secretary and administrator of the duke's collections. His religious works are recognized as having a literary value beyond their sacred use. All the same the objection has been raised that the structure of this text is illogical, since the opening verse ("I had much distress, but your comfortings refresh my soul") already holds forth consolation and so deprives the composer of first working his way through to it. But with his music Bach proved the opposite, and his way of handling the preexisting words is utterly "Bachian": He re-composes their meaning and uses the text for his own purposes, only to leave it far behind in comparison with his music.

Eleven years later, in his *Critica musica*, Mattheson printed Bach's text treatment with all its repetitions but without Bach's score. It reads terribly, and certain people believe he wanted to mock Bach by doing this. But Mattheson placed in front of this quotation, in regard to Bach, the notable words: "Thus he does not repeat to bore us!"

For this cantata, Bach had a whole orchestra with kettledrums and trumpets, solos and choir at his disposal. So nothing would have been more understandable than that he should have fully exhausted this great array of instruments right at the beginning, in a fortissimo of distress.

But not so Bach: He begins the great work with pure chamber music, and whenever he has the solo singers perform he returns again and again to chamber-music transparency. He does not avail himself of everything he has at all but rather selects from it whatever he needs. He changes the effects in a wonderful way: solos, duets, interchanges of voice and solo instruments, all the way up to the vocal quartet with the choir as a background. Not until the end, when the comforting becomes a certainty and the distressed soul is happily consoled, does he bring in the kettledrums and trumpets, kept silent through all the previous passages, and so what began with sighing he brings to an end with rejoicing. In this way he not only forms a chain of artistic compositions based on contrast but also draws from the biblical saying of the initial chorus the plan for a grandly structured musical architecture. And when a critic considered that the duet between Jesus and the soul needy of consolation represented a "wandering off into the dramatic," he underestimated that wandering. The way in which Bach handled his libretto gives the cantata a dramatic development in its entirety.

By no means did Bach compose only sacred music, although his music as a whole was for him a holy thing to which he was absolutely committed. The most devout person can also very well be the most open-minded, because he has an unshakable standpoint in this world and so does not have to close himself off from it. Similarly, Bach's music making was not bound only to the church; because of his steadfastness in the faith, it was a music that remained open to the world. A beautiful example of this is the *Hunt Cantata* of 1716, which he wrote for the court of Weissenfels. Duke Wilhelm Ernst had close connections there; it was a place where theater, music, and hunting were fondly appreciated. There was even an opera in Weissenfels that enjoyed no small reputation. The people of this court were experts at celebrating, to such an extent that in 1712 Augustus the Strong, as head of the Wettiner lands, personally had to intervene to prevent bankruptcy there. Wilhelm Ernst was also occasionally invited into this cheerful circle from his gloomy Wilhelm Castle, and he came, especially pleased to join the hunt. Of reciprocal invitations of the Weissenfels connections to Wilhelm Castle there is no report, just as the Prussian king

Friedrich Wilhelm enjoyed visiting the king of Poland in Dresden but the latter traveled to Berlin only as a great exception.

It was in Weissenfels in February 1716 that Bach performed the *Hunt Cantata*—"Was mir behagt ist nur die muntre Jagd" ("What Pleases Me Is Only the Merry Hunt") (Franck also wrote this highly secular text)—and that Bach later performed it from time to time shows how fond of it he had grown. When we try to survey the fullness and range of his Weimar creations, we can only be astonished over and over again by the skill and absolute certainty of design they display. And we have to shake our heads over Besseler, who (in his work on Bach's "master years in Weimar") pronounces the judgment: "Only late did he reach maturity."

BACH'S DEPARTURE FROM WEIMAR has been described by most biographers quite inaccurately or even, as by Terry, with complete lack of judgment. Terry does not comprehend at all how Bach could give up such a good position. The only one who gives precise details about his departure is Weimar church council member Reinhold Jauernig, who prepared the materials with exemplary thoroughness. True, he too gives only half the story, but he provides considerably more of it than all the other authors put together.

For Bach, 1716 proved to be an extraordinarily successful but also disastrous year, though he would realize this only later. He was thirty-one at the time, and it was the year in which Mattheson confirmed from Hamburg the spread of Bach's fame.

Internal political events were at the root of the trouble, events to which he apparently attached too little importance for his own good. According to his father's will, the pious Duke Wilhelm Ernst was obliged to share sovereignty in a fraternal fashion, but he was not the least bit willing to concede his nephew more rights than he had conceded to his brother; that is, he would give up next to none at all. And the feud between uncle and nephew intensified. In 1716, when the nephew claimed 16,000 florins from the state treasury for a building project, the "broad-minded and responsible" ruler (as Spitta calls him) immediately demanded 50,000 from his side for his collections. The nephew's money remained within the country, whereas the uncle's was spent beyond its borders. But he had become annoyed, and for that reason he reduced his nephew's candle allowance for the evening lighting in the Red Palace. The candles came from the "joint treasury."

By 1716 the nephew had had enough of the high-handedness and self-satisfaction of his uncle, and in pursuit of his rights he directed himself to the imperial court council. There his uncle already had proceedings in progress because of his quarrel with the imperial count of Schwarzburg that did not look promising for him. Let us recall that only the year before the family council of the Wettiner had had to occupy itself for the fourth time with the duke's bellicosity. He stood out plainly from the princes of the surrounding area in that he did not associate with them. The opinion his Altenburg and Gotha relatives held of his deeds had not interested him ten years earlier.

But under these circumstances the complaint of his nephew before the imperial court council was highly inconvenient to him. After he had already cut back his candle allowance, he thought up further ways to sour his life.

Religion offered a good opportunity. The uncle had nothing against the Pietistic body of thought, insofar as it served to persuade the natives of his duchy to renounce the world and so embrace patience and simple needs. But he absolutely did not countenance the Pietistic way of individual practice of the faith; indeed, he combated it because its followers felt encouraged to split off from his state church. His nephew understandably had little inclination to pray together with his uncle, and so he organized his own devotionals at home. Now the uncle forbade these as Pietistic.

The old high court chaplain, general superintendent, and consistorial councilor, Johann Georg Lairitz, died in April 1716, and Wilhelm Ernst obtained as his successor the highly respected theologian D. Teuner. Above all he expected him to intervene actively on a religious plane in his feud with his nephew. But unfortunately, with the best will in world, Teuner started off on the wrong foot: He considered it necessary to have a serious talk with the uncle as well. The pious uncle stuck to the biblical saying, "Whoever is not for me, he is against me," and did not receive him again until he had mended his ways.

Now the uncle acted against his nephew on yet another front. Since the younger man loved and cultivated music, nothing could be more obvious than to withdraw from him his right to use the joint court ensemble. Since the nephew had hardly paid any attention to a decree in this regard—after all, his uncle's blood flowed in him too—the uncle took measures against the members of the orchestra, forbidding them to make themselves available to the nephew musically in any way whatsoever or else they would pay a fine of 10 thalers, a great deal of money.

Here was the point where Bach got mixed up in the affair. As concertmaster he looked upon himself as the leader of the ensemble and not simply a member of it. The nephew was seriously interested in music; for the uncle, it was only a question of pomp. Bach had direct and friendly affinities with the nephew; with the uncle, none at all. Besides, Bach had his contract, and the contract expressly obliged him to make music at both courts. Bach saw no reason to violate his contract, and so he continued to perform music at the nephew's palace, and with the nephew himself.

We can hardly describe the conditions in Weimar in 1716 as very pleasant, even if out of decency Teuner later said of the duke: "Among fifty princes in the surrounding area, we will not find one who leads such a pious, thrifty life and who has so put in order the finances of the state; raised the level of public order and morality; created primary schools, a secondary school, a prison and an orphanage; and lent so much support to the advancement of learning." (This was all true enough, as long as one did not go into the details.)

All in all, the old bachelor in the Wilhelm Castle did not come across as a friendly or sociable person. The nephew in the Red

Palace was not exactly a model prince either, but he was livelier and on more intimate terms with Bach. In January 1716 he finally got married, to the widowed Duchess Eleonore Wilhelmine of Saxe-Merseburg, sister of the reigning Prince Leopold of Anhalt-Cöthen. The wedding was, predictably, not held in Weimar but at Nienburg Palace in Anhalt-Cöthen. It is not known whether the uncle attended this wedding, but it is highly unlikely that music was not performed on the occasion. The prince of Cöthen was an enthusiastic music lover, and through his new brother-in-law he had made the acquaintance of his life in the person of Bach.

But for the time being everything ran its usual course. In February Wilhelm Ernst was invited to the birthday festivities of Duke Christian of Saxe-Weissenfels; there would be opera and the pleasure of the hunt. The duke took his concertmaster along, and the latter performed his cantata "What Pleases Me Is Only the Merry Hunt" as a musical entertainment. The relations with Weissenfels, which opened up for Bach in this way, continued to exist for a long time to come. During his period of office in Leipzig, he was even granted the title of Weissenfels court music director, from which he did not profit much in Leipzig, except that Weissenfels became for him a place of musical retreat and relaxation.

Duke Ernst August and his consort in the Red Palace were also eager to become acquainted with the *Hunt Cantata,* and so Bach performed it there in April of this same year, 1716. Since the Weimar musicians were not at his disposal owing to the prohibition of the duke, he had to make use of the musicians from Weissenfels. The latter offered a double advantage: First, they had studied the piece; and second, Wilhelm Ernst could not oppose their appearance because of his friendship with the Weissenfelsers. And indeed, he said nothing. In August came the memorable organ inspection in Halle, and Bach kept on making music in the Red Palace. Since Wilhelm Ernst remained silent about it, he apparently had no objection.

In the meantime an acquaintance or even friendship had begun rto grow with the assistant headmaster of the secondary school,

Johann Matthias Gesner, hired the previous year. He was a lover of the arts and an enthusiastic admirer of Bach's music. Also in the previous year, the third boy after Wilhelm Friedemann and Carl Philipp Emanuel had been born to the Bachs, and he was christened Johann Bernhard.

During his years in Weimar, Bach delivered to the duke a series of beautiful cantatas of the modern type, with arias and recitatives. At the time this trend was made out to be an intrusion of opera into the church and was occasionally combated with vigor. Spitta speaks of opera as the "troubled waters of an unthinking artistic creation"; in Spitta's eyes, then, the operas of Handel must have seemed like veritable swamp flowers.

Bach was obviously not of his opinion: He had immediately seized the opportunities to enliven church music that arose from contact with theatrical poetry, and he used what his librettist Salomo Franck offered him in this regard after the model of Erdmann Neumeister. He wrote more than twenty cantatas in Weimar, which means that he also performed them. The duke had good reason to be content with his concertmaster. When on December 1, 1716, the old music director Samuel Drese departed this life, Bach must therefore have taken it for granted that the position as music director, which he had long since held in practice, would now be officially conferred on him.

He was utterly mistaken. He had made music in the Red Palace, and the duke had made note of his concertmaster's violations of his orders. For him, a person who did not respect his orders was not acceptable as music director. He was vindictive and determined to extract the price for Bach's insubordinate behavior. But he did not inform him of his intentions at first. He even added four more thalers to the concertmaster's salary, almost as though to demonstrate what a benevolent ruler he was. Yet secretly he had decided to spoil Bach's enjoyment of his position as thoroughly as possible. Telemann's abilities had already caught the duke's eye in Eisenach. Since 1712 the composer had been municipal music director in

97

Frankfurt on the Main, and there he was not only engaged in lively concert activity but also proving his aptitude for various administrative tasks.

The duke had brought in as headmaster of his secondary school the headmaster of the well-reputed Ohrdruf school; when the young scholar Gesner attracted his attention through his writings, he had engaged him as assistant headmaster. In his consistorial secretary, Franck, the administrator of this collections, he possessed a widely acknowledged religious poet and in his high court chaplain a recognized luminary of theology. Telemann seemed to him a felicitous addition to his collection of eminent people.

But Telemann was doing very well in Frankfurt, he knew Weimar through Bach, and he knew Bach himself. And when the duke made him a commensurate offer, he wrote back to him that in Bach he already had the best musician he could want as court music director. On his part Bach, undoubtedly privy to Telemann's answer, addressed a formal request to the duke for the post of music director. He had earlier had to apply for the post as concertmaster with a formal request too.

But this time he obtained no answer. He wrote a most humble reminder. It too remained unanswered. He requested an audience. He received none. The duke, after the refusal of his preferred candidate, was determined to prevent his concertmaster from becoming music director at all costs.

It got about that he would appoint the younger Drese as the successor to his father. This speculation made the rounds almost until the end of the year, and in end the rumor proved to be correct. With that the duke had demonstrated the true level of his musical standards: When he could not get a first-class musician, he was fully satisfied with a third-class one. The musical level did not particularly matter to him.

98 But the Bach case was still not closed for him; he took yet a further step. Every year up to this time, Bach had received a ream of double-sided music paper for his compositions at state expense.

The duke did not want to hear any music by him anymore, so he canceled the paper allotment forthwith.

When the prince of Cöthen learned that Bach would be passed over for the title of Weimar music director, he enthusiastically offered him the post of court music director in Cöthen. The position at his court was vacant, and he knew from his own experience what Bach was worth, particularly what he was worth to him. After all, he himself was a passionate musician. And he made him a marvelous offer: 456 florins instead of the previous standard of 316, a subsidy for rent and firewood, sole supervision and determination of all princely music (whether court, chamber, or entertainment music), musical accompaniment of the prince, and instruction in performance and composition.

How splendid the financial side of this offer was is revealed by the fact that forty years later, when the richest magnate of Hungary, Prince Esterházy, engaged a certain Joseph Haydn as his court music director, he did not offer him more even then. And he was the wealthiest prince in the Habsburg lands.

But it was not a matter of the money alone. For Bach, the promotion also meant an enormous social advancement, which is usually not mentioned in the biographies at all. In Weimar Johann Sebastian Bach was and remained a lackey. In Cöthen, with the status of court music director, he moved up among the officers of the court; he would outrank the mayor of Cöthen, and only the chamberlain would stand above him at court. And let no one underestimate the importance of social advancement in those times.

Besides, Bach had practically been demoted through the duke's decision. The discontinuation of the music paper shows that Bach the composer was finished in Weimar. There were no more cantatas to be written, and if any were to be performed, Bach would have to subordinate his exacting standards to a musician of unquestionable mediocrity.

In view of these facts, the great Bach biographer Terry wrote: "Bach's migration to Cöthen offers a problem to his biographer."

99

For Bach, it was no problem. When one is no longer proposing to foster someone, one does not propose to keep him anymore. So he thought. At the end of May, he submitted his letter of resignation.

It too remained unanswered, just like his previous petitions and his request for an audience. The duke was no longer available to him; a reigning lord is not accountable to a lackey. And for the duke this fellow Bach was no more than a lackey.

Bach had no experience in dealing with ungracious potentates. In Arnstadt the discharge from service to the imperial count had gone forward smoothly, and he had also approved the marriage of his subject Maria Barbara Bach with the citizen of the free imperial city of Mühlhausen without any resistance. In Weimar as well his contract had earlier been canceled by Duke Johann Ernst without any problem. After the direction of the ensemble had been taken away from him and not even his compositions were in demand anymore, he certainly neither could nor wanted to remain. Indeed, the treatment he had received readily suggested that he was not at all expected to remain.

Given the circumstances, it is fully understandable that Bach signed the contract with the prince of Cöthen, which engaged him as court music director from August 1, 1717. The resignation from his post in Weimar must have seemed like a sheer formality. Yet it was not that by any means for the duke. He stuck to the biblical saying from the Old Testament: "But I want to come among you and flog you, and you must love me." When August 1 arrived, Bach still had no answer. And consequently he was stuck.

We might ask—though admittedly, not a single one of Bach's biographers has ever raised the question—why he did not simply withdraw from ducal service, since after all he had entered the duke's employ voluntarily. Why not just travel the 30 miles to Cöthen without waiting for a discharge? He had taken it upon himself to exceed his leave on the trip to Lübeck with perfect sangfroid. Why not undertake such a short trip as this one to Cöthen as well?

Now here we really get into the legal and juridical circumstances of this case and this period, which it would be absolutely dishonest to neglect at this point. Let us recall: serfdom was not abolished in Prussia until 1807, and even later elsewhere. According to the rules of the Weimar police and the state itself, no one was allowed to accept a new job without a dismissal letter from the previous one. Without the express permission of the duke, no servant whatsoever could leave his domain, and Bach ranked as no more than a lackey.

The professor of jurisprudence Georg Wilhelm Böhmer had explained this as follows: "As soon as you are born under the jurisdiction of your prince or as soon you have placed yourself under his protection, your duty toward him as a subject commences as well." The Leipzig legal scholar Christian Thomasius had stated in his *Institutiones jurisprudentiae divinae:* "Princes are in regard to their subjects what parents are to their children, and have the right to decide for them and to punish them." And Baron Samuel von Pufendorf, the founder of natural rights and the law of nations at this time, had emphasized that "the obedience of subjects to their superiors, since this must necessarily be complied with, can not even be reckoned to their free will."

So Bach found himself in a truly dire situation: If he wanted to, the duke could actually bury him in his pious Weimar.

Prince Leopold of Anhalt-Cöthen tried to intervene. Direct negotiations with Duke Wilhelm Ernst would certainly have seemed pointless to him, since he was linked by marriage to the opposing camp, as brother-in-law of the nephew Ernst August. But he did what he could to facilitate Bach's removal. On September 10 he sent a groom to Weimar who took accommodations at the Elephant Hotel; hardly two weeks later he even sent two of his servants, whom his brother-in-law hid in his village Tannroda and who stayed there a whole week. Consequently, the prince must also have promised Bach his full personal protection. But Bach could not rely on that.

For without the formal dismissal of the duke, he could not risk the move at all. According to the Lex Carolinga enacted by Emperor Charles V, by defying his sovereign he would not only have forfeited every right as a subject but also his entire property. Indeed, even if he had obtained an imperial letter of safe-conduct, for that very reason he could have been convicted as a rebel. According to the Saxon-Thuringian state regulations, the duke could even demand his extradition from any prince in the entire Holy Roman Empire of the German Nation. That this law was still fully obeyed Countess Cosel had found out the previous year. She had fled to Halle, in Prussian territory, after she had been successfully slandered by the ruling Saxon minister, Count Jakob Heinrich von Flemming. Friedrich Wilhelm I of Prussia had extradited her to Augustus the Strong of Saxony without further ado.

Thus Bach had gotten into an extremely bad situation by playing music with the hated nephew and by overestimating the duke's interest in his art. It was not at all the petty situation it is usually portrayed as being, and Bach must have been well advised of exactly where he stood. Friedemann Meckbach, a doctor of jurisprudence, was one of his closest acquaintances and belonged to the circle of his children's godparents.

A further anecdote will clarify the seriousness of his dilemma. In the 1630s, when Bach's patron, the artistic Duke Ernst August, had succeeded to power, his first trumpeter requested to be dismissed. Ernst August had the man thrashed, and when he then incomprehensibly still wanted to leave, he locked him up in the tower. On assuming office he had threatened with six months in jail "any subject who should dare to grumble."

So much for Weimar's "early-Classical atmosphere."

9

I N THE MIDST OF THESE DIFFICULT AND in fact dangerous circumstances, an invitation to Dresden reached Bach in the fall of
1717. He possessed a very extensive circle of acquaintances;
there could have been no question at any time of the "quiet and
monotony of his artistic creation," as Spitta claims. From everything we know, he had never been to Dresden before, but he had
acquaintances there, quite distinguished ones. For example, the
concertmaster of the famous Dresden court orchestra, Jean Baptiste Woulmyer (who was more correctly named Volumier, since
he originally came from France). The music director there was
the very capable Johann Gottfried Schmitt, and in 1717 the superb and to this day widely underestimated Johann David
Heinichen also arrived in Dresden. The electoral prince Friedrich
August had engaged him in the previous year in Venice for the
court of Dresden. An Eisenach acquaintance was there too, Pantaleon Hebenstreit, a violinist who was also famous for his virtuosity on the dulcimer, from which he knew how to conjure wondrous tones.

Bach accepted the invitation to Dresden. He could travel to
Dresden, because in doing so he still remained in Wettiner lands. It
is not known whether he obtained a leave of absence for this from
his stubborn duke, but permission to go to Dresden was in any

case hard to refuse. Augustus the Strong was the patron of all the Wettiner lands.

And then there was something remarkable about Dresden in general. The biographers treat Bach's journey there as a mere interlude, as though he might just as well have traveled to Plauen or Magdeburg. They are mistaken. In this period Dresden was the most brilliant, wealthy, and splendid court after Versailles. London, Madrid, and St. Petersburg paled by comparison. Even Vienna, as the seat of the emperor, with its newly built Schönbrunn Palace, could not keep up with it, and not only because the Dresden court opera was the best in all of Europe. (When Handel needed stars for his opera enterprise in London, he brought some over from Dresden. He could pay them even better than the king, for at that time, thanks to his London patrons, he was far and away the richest opera entrepreneur in Europe.)

Dresden music ranked with Venetian music in its prestige. But neither the opera not the orchestra made the magnificence of Dresden; both were only embellishments of the court. Dresden was above all the seat of the king of Poland. From the point of view of national law, it is simply incorrect to speak of the Wettiners of that time only as the "house of the elector," as the Bach Society deems it necessary to do. A Leipzig professor still remains a professor outside of Leipzig, and since 1697 Augustus the Strong was, as Augustus II, the legitimately elected king of the elective kingdom of Poland, just as his son after his death was the legitimately elected Polish king Augustus III. In contrast, Friedrich I, Friedrich Wilhelm I, and Friedrich II were by national law electoral princes of Brandenburg and only kings *in* (East) Prussia. That did not change until the division of Poland in 1772, even if the Brandenburg electorate by then had been calling itself Prussia for quite some time.

Being the "king of Poland" was not a mere formality, and no matter how much the Polish aristocracy strove again and again to restrict the power of their king, his was not an empty title. The splendor of the electoral Saxon capital was based not least of all on the royal dignity conferred on the two Wettiners by the Polish crown. Under the reign of both these Saxon kings, the Polish-Lithuanian empire experienced a cultural and economic apogee, as well as the longest period of peace in its history. Even present-day Polish historiography, including the episode of Marxist historiography, still describes the period of the Wettiner kings as a very fortunate one, and in fact the connection between Saxony and Poland was beneficial for both. Saxony was regarded as the most prosperous of all the German lands, a state of affairs that did not come to an end until the Seven Years' War. At that point, after invading Saxon territory Frederick the Great financed his campaign to a large extent with the money he mercilessly wrung out of Saxony.

Augustus the Strong had an important position in the Holy Roman Empire not only as king of Poland but as elector of Saxony as well. As the first among the electoral princes, he came immediately after the emperor in rank; he was his deputy and on occasion acted on his behalf as his representative. That is why close connections existed between the court of Dresden and the imperial court in Vienna. And in contrast to the court of Berlin, where Friedrich Wilhelm ate with his family off of tin plates, Augustus loved to reign in magnificence. Not only the Saxon but also the Polish nobles were in attendance at court. The king's plenipotentiary minister, Count Jakob Heinrich von Flemming, was linked to the cream of the Polish aristocracy, and his Polish estates were larger than the entire electorate of Saxony. Traveling to Dresden meant something. Neither Vienna nor London nor Madrid nor St. Petersburg could offer a similar splendor, to say nothing of Berlin and the other German courts.

So in the fall of 1717 Bach traveled to Dresden. The invitation had not been extended without reason: The Dresden orchestra had run into difficulties. A certain Louis Marchand was staying of late at the court of Dresden; a celebrity, he had until recently been the court organist and harpsichordist of the king of France at Versailles. 105

The encounter of Bach with Marchand (or rather the encounter that did not take place) is usually dismissed quite summarily as well. This tendency is already manifest in Forkel, the first of all Bach biographers. Not without a hint of patriotism, he merely portrays the incident as the victory of a true German musician over French arrogance, and a number of subsequent writers have followed his approach. Eschewing the nationalistic tone, others have depicted the contest between the two masters as simply an anecdote of one of Bach's artistic journeys that had an especially fortunate outcome.

That is because no one has considered it necessary to devote any attention to Marchand himself. Yet he was by no means just a windbag who happened to be traveling through but a musician of high accomplishments. At fourteen he had already been engaged as organist at the Cathedral of Nevers; at twenty he became the organist of the Jesuits in Paris. At twenty-four he attained the title of "organist first class" and at thirty-one that of "organist to the king." He was one of the most important representatives of the French art of the organ in his time. His compositions earned him the epithet *le Grand*; he appears as "Marchand le Grand" in collective works. And he was possessed of an imperious spirit. The incident that made him lose his position at Versailles is typical of his character as well as the boldness of his manner. His wife was neglecting him, he left her, she sued for maintenance, and the king decided that half the salary must be paid to her. As a result of that, Marchand broke off his next concert before the king when it was halfway through and declared—before the assembled court—that if the king was paying half of his salary to his wife, then she should play the other half of the concert.

With that he had of course not only fallen out with the king but also with Spitta and Terry. Terry calls him "conceited, improvident, arrogant." Spitta writes: "The merits as well as the defects of his people marked him to a high degree. . . . Richly gifted for everything technical and elegant in his art . . . he combined with that art just as great a measure of vanity, arrogance, and capriciousness."

Here we can see how much Marchand has offended the true spirit of a German underling that Spitta represents. Certainly there were other "arrogant" people at the French court. When the young Voltaire returned from the Bastille, where the regent had locked him up for one and a half years for his impertinent behavior, he thanked him with the words: "Monsieur, I still find it very kind of Your Majesty to provide for my nourishment, but I beseech Your Majesty not to worry about my accommodations any longer."

Like Voltaire, Marchand le Grand knew his worth and drew from that a justifiable self-assurance. In his everyday appearance, to people who casually encountered him, Bach was undoubtedly a plain, conventional, upright citizen who never made much out of his person. But he also showed his self-assurance, in Arnstadt and Weimar as later in Leipzig; this was held against him too, and not only by Spitta and Terry.

When Marchand was expelled from Versailles, with good reason he turned toward Dresden: There was no more splendid court in all of Europe and none more appreciative of the arts. His appearance there inevitably triggered two opposite reactions. Court society was delighted that this gentleman from the French court behaved himself in Dresden as among equals, whereas the orchestra was indignant that he so audaciously ignored class differences. Court society was enthusiastic about experiencing French music from the source, so to speak, through such a witty fellow, whereas the orchestra was angry because the sensation caused by the French virtuoso detracted from the prestige of its own Italian style. And this state of affairs threatened to continue, since the king was thinking of binding Marchand to Dresden through an official court position.

In this regard one must understand that at the time the French and Italian styles were absolute rivals. In Paris there was a regular war between the French singers and the Italian comedians that the comedians won, perhaps because the Italian manner of making music was lighter and more impulsive than the French. The French style was based on the school of Jean-Baptiste Lully, who aimed at exactness and severity. The Dresden orchestra was perfectly familiar with this approach to music; several of its members had been active in Paris themselves. But this style was not theirs, and in the meantime they had developed a manner that was all their own. It is in the nature of things that artists cannot be tolerant when it comes to their art: They do not acquire it easily, but only through an untiring intensity, and consequently it becomes a part of themselves. The Dresden orchestra could not get along with Marchand at all—and not for nationalistic, but for artistic reasons. On top of that Marchand displayed that sovereign independence which, in Dresden just as at any other German court, was simply inconceivable.

Bach had long since enjoyed an almost legendary reputation as an organist, but he was just as adept at the harpsichord (his Weimar toccatas show how splendidly). Marchand was fully his equal in reputation. So for those who had something against him, nothing could have been more obvious than to bring the two together—or better, against each another. If Marchand was presumed to have challenged a local harpsichordist to a musical competition, that could only be useful to Dresden's prestige. If it was Volumier who invited Bach from Weimar to Dresden, that was in any case a clever move. There really was no better virtuoso, even if what underlay Bach's music was not virtuosity. That he would accept such an invitation if he could was almost a foregone conclusion, given his unquenchable curiosity about music. And the calculation worked: Bach was familiar with Marchand's compositions, so he also wanted to become acquainted with the man.

The outcome is well known: Bach arrived, and a competition was set up at the Flemming Palace. But Marchand left on the morning of that same day, and Bach ended up playing alone. Thus Marchand undid himself at this time through his cowardly flight, and the great German musician triumphed over the Latin spirit. At least that is how the story goes, as related early on by Forkel.

Why has no one yet noticed the utter bizarreness of this account? An inferiority complex could not possibly have been the cause of Marchand's departure. After all, he was allegedly "capricious, arrogant, and uncontrolled." Moreover, he could have count-

108

ed on the devotion of his audience at court: He had the advantage of being on his own turf. And no one disputes his enormous ability. Since the Bach biographers write exclusively about Bach, they immediately lose sight of Marchand after this. But Marchand converted his trip back home into a successful concert tour, returned to Paris without a single dent in his prestige, and went down in the history of French music as "Marchand le Grand." Why, then, at that juncture did he run away almost in the dead of night, intimidated by the organist of a petty princedom (Weimar had only about 500 houses)? It is not even known whether Bach had ever publicly performed on any another occasion in Dresden before this memorable concert.

Marchand was famous for the bravura of his harmonic modulations. Spitta noticed nothing of Bach's own boldness in this respect; for Schweitzer he is only "the culmination of Baroque music," from which nothing more proceeded. But Bach's superiors were fully aware of this penchant of his; the Arnstadters expressly reproached him for "mixing too many outlandish tones" into his chorales and demanded that "when he wishes to introduce a *tonus peregrinus,* he must hold it out and not shift too swiftly to something else . . . or even play a *tonus contrarius.*" Which means, to sum up, that they were thoroughly dissatisfied with his harmonic modulations; these were simply too novel for them. We can comprehend their reaction with the aid of the collection of chorales harmonized by Bach, as compiled by his son Carl Philipp Emanuel: A great many of them are so boldly harmonized that even today a congregation might "forget to sing to them." Bach was not only a daring but also a groundbreaking harmonist. Marchand was fundamentally an innovator too, but he did not possess something that Bach had been pursuing since his Arnstadt days: "well-tempered tuning."

The problem consists in that there is a difference between a purely tuned octave and twelve purely tuned fifths. Pythagoras had already discovered this in antiquity, which is why one speaks of the Pythagorean comma. The practical consequence of this inconsistency is that a keyboard "purely" tuned in C major sounds completely out of tune in B major: The impure fifths virtually howl, and that is why musicians in Bach's time referred to them as "wolf fifths." And this phenomenon starts with B major but becomes stronger as the sharps or flats in the key signatures increase. For that reason, one must correct "pure" tuning to "equal-tempered" tuning, in which all tones diverge by a small degree from "purity." In theory this problem had been solved for quite some time. Already in 1637 the French monk Marin Mersenne had published the results of his investigations relating to this matter, and the Halberstadt organist Andreas Werckmeister had done the same in German between 1686 and 1687. But in his own compositions he had taken great care not to explore the circle of fifths in its entirety. In other words, it was not so easy to convert the theoretical findings into praxis. This proved to be nearly impossible for the time being on the organ, where with the transition to "equal-tempered pitch" all overtone registers would have had to be changed accordingly; and here it was difficult enough to produce purity of tone. It also proved to be impossible with so-called fretted clavichords, which did not possess a separate string for each tone but rather, like the lute, produced intermediate tones through frets. Thus musicians more or less had come to terms with the rule that keys with four flats or sharps in their key signatures were only to be played with limitations and those with five or six not at all. We can verify this in the entire literature of the time, particularly in the compositions of Marchand. Even Bach's organ compositions reflect the trend: Pieces in F-sharp major or D-flat major are nowhere to be found, and four-sign key signatures are highly exceptional. But that Bach went to the limits of the feasible is shown by the appearance of occasional impurities when his works are interpreted on the organs of his great contemporary Gottfried Silbermann. Silbermann's organs were not yet "equal-tempered."

Bach had continued to work on a better tuning technique, since he absolutely required it for his composing. He was obliged to invent an entirely new method of "well-tempered" keyboard tuning, and he had no other assistants in the process than his own skill and his own two ears. But he was now on the verge of success. And two years later, in the *Chromatic Fantasy and Fugue,* he would bring the possibilities of "well-tempered tuning" to fulfillment and employ modulations that no one had ever dared to attempt before him.

In all probability, that was precisely the reason behind Marchand's premature departure. His compositions show how deeply he was preoccupied with the problems of harmony and what an expert he was on the matter. So he did not need to hear much of Bach's playing—a free improvisation or the tuning of the harpsichord would have sufficed—in order to recognize that Bach had come a great deal further than he had and already disposed of possibilities that had remained closed to him until then.

Of course, Marchand was not at all "capricious, arrogant, and uncontrolled." If he had been, he could not have held his own for even two weeks amid the tumultuous intrigues of Versailles. Nor did he let himself get "carried away" in his defiant sally to the king. The anecdote reveals thought-out staging: His wife had offended him, the king had offended him again through his decision, and so for him there was no point in remaining at court (at half salary to boot). But he did not leave without a word of farewell, and consequently he was certain that he would not be forgotten. That betrays keen calculation. With the same cool-headedness, with no word of farewell, he left Dresden on the morning of a battle that as an expert, he knew he could not win. He departed from Versailles in a sensational manner because he had lost, but he departed from Dresden in great secrecy because he did not want to lose. In this way the news of a defeat in Dresden would not precede his return to Paris; he would return with all his splendor still intact. He was not arrogant, since he knew his limits. And he was not uncontrolled at all; on the contrary, he behaved with cleverness and circumspection.

For his part, Bach appeared at the scheduled hour before the magnificent assembly of Marchand's supporters in the Flemming

Palace, and as a commoner from Weimar he cannot possibly have made much of an impression in his modest jacket, a mere clavier-player from the provinces.

But then he began to play, and the world was transformed. All too readily one resorts to the cliché of an "unforgettable" evening. But in fact it was such an extraordinary evening that people in Dresden never forgot this man Bach for the rest of their lives. It was a decisive evening for him as well (as I later show).

Bach recounted this story to his sons, it is found in his obituary, and Bach's first biographer, Forkel, still heard it from the mouth of Carl Philipp Emanuel. Yet for Schweitzer it hardly seems worth mentioning, and Geck claims flatly that the anecdote has not been verified and so did not take place. According to him, Marchand was not in Dresden at all at this time. Instead, Bach traveled to Dresden in order to study the Vivaldi concerti in the music library (which he long since knew from Lüneburg and of which he had just arranged three for the organ and half a dozen for the harpsichord).

When Bach returned home, the prince of Cöthen's riders had already been there and left again, and Bach's situation had not changed in any way whatever. Under these circumstances only one possibility remained to him: to defy the duke. He no longer felt obliged to furnish him with compositions; he did not even have any more music paper. As for his post as organist, he could have his most advanced student, Schubert, stand in for him. The Austrian Bach biographer Geiringer, working in the United States, reports that on October 30, when the 200th anniversary of the Reformation was celebrated with fitting extravagance, Bach did not even appear at the castle church but attended the worship service at the city church. Apparently he had decided, "If the duke refuses me dismissal, then I refuse him service." And what other alternative did he have? Since he had attained nothing by obeying the rules, to leave his post he would have to take some kind of risk. The duke's reaction followed without delay.

When on a previous occasion the nephew's counselors had advised him to do something that was not in accordance with his uncle's wishes, the duke had had them arrested. Since Bach was not behaving as he desired, he locked him up without further ado, in the ducal judge's chamber.

"Ducal judge's chamber" sounds cozy, almost like a mere house arrest in the refined home of a gentleman. Indeed, a good many people still assert that Bach wrote his *Little Organ Book* in the ducal judge's chamber, in the amiable leisure of his prison sentence. But that is quite implausible for two reasons. The first has to do with the purpose of the work: It was intended for "beginning organists," that is, for his organ pupils. But Bach was bent on going to Cöthen, where he would no longer have any students. (And Wilhelm Friedemann was just seven at this time.)

And in the second place, the ducal judge's chamber was the most unsuitable place imaginable for such a task. In fact there were three different jails in the Weimar of Duke Wilhelm Ernst: the prison and orphanage he had founded (where he locked up the Gypsies picked up on the road, among others); the city jail (the compulsory abode of unwed mothers after giving birth, for example); and the ducal judge's chamber, which was the prison for beggars, tramps, and what were generally described as "riffraff." It was the lowest and most humiliating place of detention that Weimar had to offer. The duke had his concertmaster locked up with the dregs of the society of that period in order to hammer home to Bach that in his eyes he was nothing more than a rebellious lackey.

What he had not reckoned with was that the incarceration of this rebellious lackey would cause something of a stir. The political reputation of the duke was not exactly the best, not by any means. The prince of Cöthen, the brother-in-law of his nephew, had excellent connections with the court of Berlin. And since his appearance before the court of Dresden at the palace of the governing minister, Count Flemming, Bach had acquired a very important trump card. The arrest quickly became public—of course Bach's 113 wife was still in Weimar, and she had no reason to keep silent. Only the previous year the duke had been reprimanded because of his conduct by the council of the Wettiners, and he had two proceedings in progress before the imperial court council, one concerning his own nephew and the other his unjustified claims against Imperial Count von Schwarzburg. He had not improved his situation by locking up with the riffraff such a superb musician merely because he wanted to be discharged. Perhaps it was inexpedient to pick a quarrel with Dresden's governing minister over a recalcitrant lackey. After all, he had already shown this Bach what he was capable of.

The denouement is found in the Weimar archives, in a notice written by the court secretary, Theodor Benedict Bormann: "On Nov. 6th (1717) the heretofore concertmaster and court organist Bach was detained at the ducal judge's chamber because of his stubborn testimony and his too forceful demand of dismissal. Finally on December 2nd the dismissal was accorded to him by the court secretary with express disfavor, and at the same time he was freed from detention." And a marginal note to this document reads, *"Vide acta"*—"See the records."

Even the sums paid for the horses' oats by the Weimar accounting office during this period have been preserved. Yet the records about the Bach case have completely disappeared, which can only mean that the duke made them disappear. He was so furious over his defeat that he insisted on erasing the case from his archives. He even saw to it that beyond his death the name "Bach" would remain anathema in Weimar.

When Johann Gottfried Walther published his musical lexicon in Leipzig in 1732, he did not dare to communicate more than the bare essentials about his cousin and friend because of Weimar censorship. He could not completely leave Bach out, since after all he was a resident of the city where the publishing house was located. But as late as Gottfried Albin Wette's *Historical News of the Famous Seat of Weimar—Brought to Light under High Censure and Approval of the High-princely Chief Consistory of Weimar,* published in 1737, the organists before and after Bach are duly cited and the existence of Johann Sebastian Bach is completely suppressed. The duke had decreed that no such musician had ever been active at his court. He wanted the name "Bach" blotted out forever.

In Spitta's words: "Among the small-scale rulers of Central Germany at the time, Duke Wilhelm Ernst stands out as a distinctive, conscientious, and deeper-rooted personality."

His motto was: "Everything with God."

10

WHEN BACH ARRIVED IN CÖTHEN at the beginning of December in 1717, he had been through four weeks in the worst Weimar prison and come to know firsthand the powers of a wrathful potentate. Yet the Halle musicologist Siegmund-Schultze arrives at the conclusion: "Bach surely did not find it easy to bid farewell to Weimar." And in considering the piousness of the duke, who even punished people with fines for missing their instruction in the catechism, obligatory for all subjects, he mentions once again "the lively intellectual and spiritual climate." In view of these circumstances, Terry voices the modest conjecture: "Probably he was beginning to find the martinet rule of his Duke irksome." But then he immediately goes on to wag his finger at the composer again: "There was, too, in his nature a disposition to irritability which swelled easily to pugnacity under provocation"—as though the demoted musician had any alternative but departure at all costs. Rueger, who does not seem to know that the duke had even canceled Bach's supply of music paper and thus clearly released him from all further composing, comments as follows: "Bach is offended. From then on he does not write another note." That is not correct, of course: Bach was almost always writing music. In any case, from 1717 we have the Prelude and Fugue in A Minor by him, though for the harpsichord.

"Bach's migration to Cöthen offers a problem to his biographer," writes Terry, and a little later he remarks that there the whole "atmosphere . . . stifled the fullest expression of Bach's art and challenged his most rooted convictions." Of course Bach's convictions were not being challenged there, but merely Terry's. That Bach cannot have felt too at ease in Weimar already for quite some time is revealed by his application for the post in Halle in 1713. That much cannot be disputed. Anyone who went to as much trouble as Bach did in this case has to have been serious about seeking a new position.

Terry (and with him a great many others) is thoroughly mistaken when he assumes that for Bach it was the essence of his existence to make music only in and for the church. The crux of his aspirations, his purpose in life, was not the church; it was music. In reality he had distant relations with all his ecclesiastical superiors. Reverend Eilmar in Mühlhausen and Licentiate Weisse in Leipzig remained the only exceptions. His sons tell about the numerous musicians who called on him and with whom he stayed in touch. About theologians they report nothing. That he is supposed to have absorbed the concepts of the Enlightenment from his father confessors, as Petzoldt would have us believe, is an absurd idea. As a musician he had decidedly more to profess to his church than his church did to him, but one cannot claim that his church took note of that. And it is also possible for someone to be a true and genuine Christian without depending on clergymen; look at the example of Schweitzer in the African jungle.

Thus Bach betrayed neither his faith nor his vocation when he went to Cöthen. He was no musical preacher, even though he did know very well how to sermonize through his music. What nobody has noticed up to now is that more than half of his life's work is *not* sacred music at all. This does not belittle in any way the greatness of the faith in his Passions and cantatas but only suggests that Bach had many more things to give besides those. He could say good-bye to the Weimar organist position without regret; in Weimar he had not written any organ pieces for use in the worship service. Even the *Little Organ Book* was primarily a teaching work, although the individual pieces—Bach was a practical man, after all—were eminently usable in church. And he did not have to bid farewell to the organ either. If the need arose, he had an organ with thirteen registers at his disposal in Cöthen. Those who think that such an instrument was too small for Bach to study and experiment on only demonstrate that they have no idea of all that one can perform on an organ that size, provided it is in fairly good shape. To this day no one has proved that it was not in working condition.

But it cannot be proven either that in his Cöthen period Bach sought to join the Protestant congregation there at all. The court and with it the majority of the subjects of Cöthen were not Lutheran but Reformed according to the creed of the Swiss theologians Zwingli and Calvin. They had abolished not only all images but also the Holy Mass and its core component of church music. Thus in the Reformed Church one did without a "regulated church music to the glory of God." Yet unlike his fellow sovereigns in Weimar, Prince Leopold was tolerant and allowed his subjects religious freedom. There was a Lutheran congregation alongside the Reformed one, and it is remarkable that on the occasion of his second marriage Bach held the wedding not at the Lutheran church but in his own personal residence. This caused complaints from the congregation. Bach defended himself by saying that the wedding had taken place at his home by order of the prince. That was merely a pretext of course, for the prince had nothing against the Lutherans otherwise, and Bach was on such friendly terms with him that he could easily have obtained permission for a church wedding, if only he had been interested in one. But apparently he was not interested in that in the slightest.

The dramatist Paul Barz, who otherwise proved himself to be a good authority on the subject with his play *Possible Encounter* (performed in many venues in the 1980s), reproaches Bach with sheer betrayal in his book on the composer. "The creator of great, serious church music seems forgotten—and one wonders: for Bach, did the thought of his career come before everything else? Is his faith not really so sincere after all? Once again Bach places an enigma before us. And again the struggle for existence of his early years provides a conclusive explanation: it had taught this man self-denial as well." With that he makes Johann Sebastian Bach out to be a person who denied his faith and even himself in order to pursue his career. He does not seem to understand that for Bach the point was not to make his music serve his faith but to serve his music and mankind from the depths of his faith, just as Schweitzer by no means gave up his faith when he became a doctor in the jungle.

All Bach's biographical admirers merely note in passing, as a regrettable feature, that the prince of Cöthen was of the Reformed creed. Not one of all those who refer to the "deep piety" of Duke Wilhelm Ernst finds the extraordinary tolerance of this prince (which he had absorbed from the example of his parents) at all remarkable. Indeed, one unavoidably (and not only here) gets the impression that for a certain genre of musicologists theological problems signify just as little as historical facts. For Leopold's tolerance was truly noteworthy in that period and unparalleled in the entire region.

Pietism had split off from Lutheran orthodoxy and was assailed by it, even though it had never abandoned its grounding in Lutheran doctrine. In Bach's time the Orthodox Lutherans and the Pietists were fighting to the finish. Renowned Pietists were literally driven away from their pulpits in Dresden, Erfurt, and Leipzig, and the duke of Weimar (but not only he) took action against Pietistic prayer meetings with rigorous bans.

The struggle against the Reformed Church was based on far deeper conflicts, however. For Pietists professed the doctrine of the Swiss theologian Calvin, and a half century later Voltaire could still only dare to settle on the outermost fringe of Switzerland because he was not a Calvinist.

The disagreements had age-old causes. Luther and Calvin were contemporaries, both of them Reformers. But Luther only protest-

120

ed against conditions in the Catholic Church at that time (hence the term "Protestants") and wanted to reform the Catholic Church as it then existed. For Calvin, in contrast, the point was to create a completely non-Catholic church. The opposition between the two men was so great that Luther refused even to discuss matters with Calvin; for him Calvinism was utterly out of the question.

In Brandenburg the great electoral prince professed Calvin's Reformed faith and pushed through its adoption with a tolerance act that was in reality more of an intolerance act. Thus the great Protestant lyrical poet Paul Gerhardt had to give up his post as preacher at the St. Nicholas Church in Berlin because he did not want to forsake his Lutheranism. In Leipzig, a stronghold of Orthodox Lutherans, the hatred of Calvinists was so great that up to 1812 even the university teachers had to declare in writing before their appointment that all Calvinists were heretics and had earned the fires of hell. Bach too had to sign such a document when he was appointed to his post in Leipzig in 1723.

If he had been serious about his ecclesiastical ties, with that he would have consigned his patron and friend the prince of Cöthen to eternal damnation. This he certainly could not have done lightheartedly. But he signed the testimonial without hesitation and then dedicated a moving funeral music to this alleged heretic. From his actions we can see that a matter such as this meant nothing more to him than so much theological red tape, which was wholly separate from his Christian faith.

One has to know about the deep disagreements between Lutherans and the Reformed in order to be capable of assessing what an enlightened spirit it took to keep both going simultaneously in such a small land as Anhalt-Cöthen. Their coexistence necessarily led to considerable quarrels between the two denominations, which the prince accepted with composure. He was really and truly (though neither Spitta nor Terry nor Schweitzer nor anyone else has noticed it) an enlightened prince and would have been far more deserving of the eulogies that Bach biographers dedicate without exception to the duke of Weimar. Decades before Frederick the Great declared that in his country "each may be blessed after his fashion," the exact same principle had long since been put into practice in the principality of Cöthen. And so Terry's claim that there the whole "atmosphere . . . stifled the fullest expression of Bach's art and challenged his most rooted convictions" is on further inspection even more incomprehensible. After the highly unedifying clashes with his ecclesiastical superiors in Arnstadt and Mühlhausen and the compulsory religious practices in Weimar, the freer religious climate in Cöthen can only have been welcomed by Bach and his family.

The Bachs moved to Cöthen in December. There are people who assert that Maria Barbara must have traveled ahead with the children, when the Cöthen riders were there and her husband was in Dresden or even when he was serving his sentence at the Weimar jail. But she cannot have been so unwise: According to the laws in effect, the duke could have demanded her extradition, put her in jail as well, and locked up her children in his prison and orphanage. The course Bach was steering was much too risky for her to get involved in such an undertaking.

On the arrival of the family, Prince Leopold immediately proved himself to be extraordinarily generous. On the spot he paid out to his new court music director the entire salary for the four months Bach had been prevented from taking up his post by the stubbornness of the duke. A house stood ready for the Bachs, with a rehearsal room for the orchestra downstairs. The court music director could thus hold rehearsals right in his own home. The princely treasury also took care of the rent and heating. It was a warm nest that the Bachs found in Cöthen, warm as far as the heart was concerned as well. The prince of Cöthen was no inaccessible and unsociable ruler like the duke of Weimar. He had engaged Bach not only for his orchestra but also for his personal companionship. Music was his life. He played the violin, viola da gamba, and harpsichord; enjoyed singing in his beautiful bass voice; and took lessons from his court music director in composition. So here was something quite

122

different from the position in Weimar; it could not be described as "the risk of a new service relationship with absolutism," as Siegmund-Schultze would have it.

And then above all there was the orchestra. It was not bigger than the one in Weimar, but it was very good. When Friedrich Wilhelm I succeeded to the throne of Prussia after the death of his father and began the great economies of his twenty-five-year reign, he immediately disbanded the court orchestra. It had never interested him. Prince Leopold, who had enjoyed his education at the Cavaliers Academy in Berlin and accordingly had close connections with the court there, fetched five of the musicians to Cöthen. And he attached great importance to fine instruments. He even sent his court music director to Berlin for a new harpsichord so that he could receive it there, test it, and bring it home. There were court orchestras elsewhere, but nowhere else did the prince himself play along as well. He joined in out of sheer enthusiasm: Music was his element, and this wonderful man Bach was his music director! He did not part from him even on his travels. When he journeyed to Carlsbad, he took him along, and a half dozen of his musicians as well; otherwise the whole trip to the spa was spoiled.

He had had very sensible parents. The country was administered in an orderly manner, without making much fuss about it. His father, of the Reformed faith, was above the religious quarrels of his time and had wedded a Lutheran. He was also unconcerned that she was not "befitting his rank." Gisela Agnes von Rath, whom the father married when he was twenty-three years old, was merely a modest noblewoman who was not elevated to countess until after the death of her husband. He died after barely eleven years of wedlock, in 1704. Leopold, as his successor, was then just ten years old, and so the mother took charge of the regency for him until his majority.

She proved to be a capable woman who clung all her life to her Lutheran faith. She had persuaded her spouse to erect a Lutheran church in Cöthen as well, alongside the Reformed one. She gave her son an excellent upbringing and sent him at sixteen on a proper educational journey, during which he became acquainted with England, Holland, and Italy. In Venice the opera filled him with enthusiasm; he took advantage of the sojourn in Rome to take lessons with the German opera composer Johann David Heinichen, later court music director to Augustus the Strong. He was no less interested in the visual arts. When he came home three years later, he had not only seen something of the world but also made full use of his time. When he assumed sovereignty at twenty-one, his mother was wise enough not to interfere in her son's governmental affairs and retired to her residence at Nienburg Palace.

Prince Leopold was twenty-three when he brought Bach to Cöthen. So Bach was nine years older than he, and to his musical authority was joined his greater maturity. In any case the high court chamberlain was there for Leopold's duties and Bach for the prince's delight. Under such circumstances—Bach was highly respected, free of care, not limited by any prohibitions but constantly spurred on anew by praise—it was a pleasure to make music for his prince and with him. And Bach extensively availed himself of his opportunities. It seemed to him that here he had finally found the position of his life.

He had not yet finished settling in when an organ examination summoned him to Leipzig. The organ builder Johann Scheibe had completed the new organ in St. Paul's Church, which served as the university church. Johann Kuhnau, the St. Thomas choirmaster, with whom Bach had inspected the organ in Halle the previous year, had arranged for the assignment. Apart from his post at St. Thomas, he was also the university music director. It is unlikely that Bach would have asked him about the position of choirmaster at the St. Thomas School at the time; after all, he had just found his place in the world. The abundance of his creations in that period is tremendous. He wrote only a few cantatas, but he dedicated himself all the more wholeheartedly to music for solo instruments, chamber music, and such unique orchestral works as the four suites and the six *Brandenburg Concerti.*

When he met the margrave of Brandenburg is uncertain. Most likely he encountered him in Carlsbad; it is quite implausible that Bach would have called on the margrave when he picked up the harpsichord for his prince in Berlin. It is true that the margrave, brother of the king, lived in the palace too; but his orchestra—it was the only one in all of Prussia—consisted of just six musicians, and if Bach really had called on him, he would have been informed about the paucity of this ensemble. Instead he clearly assumed that such a great lord would have at his command an orchestra such as those at the courts of Cöthen, Weimar, or Eisenach, and for that reason his concerti were doubtless played in Cöthen but never in Berlin. They were found there later, bound in green leather and provided with a French dedication, still unused. There are also no signs that the margrave ever expressed his thanks for them or showed his appreciation to Bach in any way. For him, these pieces were obviously worthless, and under Friedrich Wilhelm I the Muses led a starved existence in any event. His nobles hardly had any opportunity to cultivate the arts; he shunted them into the military, into his officer corps. He attached enormous importance to the army, and with that he founded a tradition that lasted until Prussia's downfall.

The reason the *Brandenburg Concerti* are particularly remarkable is that they are unparalleled in their period (if we disregard the concerti of the Dresden court music director Heinichen, which have remained unknown to every single Bach scholar). These works of Bach leave far behind them the solo concerti of the time, concerti such as Vivaldi, for example, produced in heaps, just as they surpass concerti grossi of the kind that Vivaldi, Corelli, Torelli, Albinoni, Geminiani, or Handel composed. For not only is the contrast between the tutti and the soloist group, the concertino, broken down again and again, but the group of soloists that plays opposite the tutti is individualized to a degree that did not exist before then. Bach really splits up the concertino into separate solo performances, and we can see how much he thought of his Cöthen musicians from the way he changed the soloist group from concerto to concerto. He had such splendid musicians that each time he could let new ones shine.

It was clear that these concerti were unusable for the margrave of Brandenburg. We can search a long time in music literature until we encounter anything similar. It is true that in Dresden Heinichen wrote comparable concerti, but Bach could not have known them because they were played only before court society and their scores were immediately locked away. To cite later parallels, Haydn sometimes devoted himself to the sinfonia concertante, though Beethoven's Triple Concerto and the Double Concerto of Brahms come most readily to mind. Bach's extreme refinement in the treatment of the chamber orchestra, in which he has no equal in his period, has universally gone unnoticed. Since his fifteenth year of life, that is, since Lüneburg, Bach had been closely acquainted through practical experience with the subtleties as well as the vagaries of handling the orchestra. Yet Terry arrives at the conclusion that in Cöthen he first had to explore the orchestral style in general. That is as original as Rueger's claim that Bach really started out as a violinist. (Were the scores he copied down at night in Ohrdruf violin scores, then?) Incidentally, there are also counterclaims: for example, that Bach wrote the three sonatas and three partitas for solo violin only under the influence of the violin virtuoso Paul Westhoff when he appeared in Weimar; or Schweitzer's opinion that with these violin works Bach "exceeded the limits of the artistically possible."

These sonatas and partitas are also a happy fruit of the Cöthen years, but we can grasp them only if we understand that Bach was the genius of music for several parts. Something that almost never occurs in Bach is a single melody accompanied by harmony, as it was later cultivated by the Viennese classical composers and representatives of the Vienna school. In fact we can often discover even in his one-part compositions a hidden music for several voices. Someone in whom composition for several voices was so deeply inborn also had to strive to extract it, as a necessity of his nature, from instru-

126

ments that were made for single lines of melody, such as the violin, the cello, and the lute. Bach was able to write the solo sonatas and partitas in this way precisely because, through long years of practical experience, he was familiar with the violin down to the last detail. Here the comparison with the great violinist Niccolò Paganini is interesting: Whenever he wrote polyphonic music in his solo compositions, he did it so that he could show off his virtuosity. Bach required virtuosity for the sake of polyphony.

Yet it is self-evident that he by no means began his professional career as a violinist. Indeed, it would really be more correct to say that he earned his first money as a choir member. That would also explain why the tendency toward polyphony was so extremely deep-rooted in him. Still, that too would be a superficial explanation: In music as in life, one can become only what one is. With Bach, however, we must take into account the universality of his gift. After all, he was not only the composer who had at his command the most superb contrapuntal feats as well as the most profound reserves of moving musical expression. He was not only the first to establish full "well-tempered tuning" in praxis and immediately apply it in his compositions with the highest mastery. He also possessed outstanding gifts as a virtuoso on the organ, the harpsichord, and (judging by his compositions) on the violin, the viola, and the lute as well.

As if that were not enough, besides playing all these instruments, he invented new ones, like the viola pomposa. And in addition to devising organ dispositions in a masterly fashion, he knew how to assess the craftsmanship of an organ's construction. If need be, he could give precise advice on its improvement, just as he also knew how to redesign the functioning of clavier mechanics. He was, according to Gesner's report, an outstanding ensemble director. And according to the reports of his students, he was an excellent teacher. He possessed as well an innate and reliable knowledge about the acoustics of a space: He did not need any complicated experiments but simply looked around and knew what to expect, as a practitioner through and through. Thus he combined a wealth of unique musical gifts, and anyone who sees him solely as an outstanding church musician knows very little about him.

The theologian Friedrich Smend speaks of "those happy years, in which Bach worked as music director in Cöthen." This too is a comment at which one can only shake one's head. True enough: it began splendidly. Bach was the most important person in the life of his prince, and his prince was a highly educated, merry, open-minded man. (We can see this even from one of his portraits; in it he does not wear a wig, which was unheard of at the time, but leaves his hair loose, without a speck of powder.) He was young and full of *savoir-vivre*. And he honored his friend Bach. When the Bachs brought another child into the world after Bernhard, the godparents were all court personages; indeed, the prince's sister came over from Weimar especially for the christening. And in Cöthen Bach had a very happy household, with four children and a wife whom he loved more than everything.

But then fate struck a terrible blow. When he returned from Carlsbad in July 1720 with his prince, his beloved wife lay beneath the earth. Death came more quickly at that time, more often and more mercilessly. Even appendicitis took its course with inevitably lethal results; the saving operation, today almost a petty affair, did not become available until the end of the nineteenth century. Medicine was far less well developed than theology, and death was a frequent visitor to humankind.

The death of his Maria Barbara was a deep wound in Bach's life. The self-assured young man whom a portrait from the Weimar period depicts can hardly be recognized anymore in the portrait that Johann Jacob Ihle painted of him in Cöthen. Great sorrow and unmistakable grief are deeply carved on this face.

128   That same autumn Bach made a journey to Hamburg. Spitta views this as merely a concert trip that was somewhat postponed by

the death of his wife. Siegmund-Schultze writes that he undertook it in order to console himself right away for her demise. Naturally, both notions are equally false.

In September 1720 the organist and sexton of the Church of St. James, Heinrich Friese, had died, and Bach was one of the eight candidates deemed worthy of succeeding him. Bach was well known in Hamburg, as the statements of the Hamburger Mattheson make clear, and he was particularly familiar to the chief pastor of St. James, Erdmann Neumeister. For Bach had set Neumeister's cantata texts to music and in so doing actively endorsed his views about the cantata form, and Neumeister had come to Hamburg from Bach's immediate vicinity. He had been court deacon in Weissenfels and court chaplain to the count of Sorau (where he had spoken out most forcefully against Pietism).

For his part, Bach knew Hamburg. During his Lüneburg schooldays he had visited the great Johann Adam Reinken there, and he knew perfectly well what kind of music could be made in that city. Yet there was no question of his improving his lot financially or socially in Hamburg. A court music director, no matter where he lived, occupied a higher position than an organist and sexton. Hamburg could hardly offer him what he already possessed in Cöthen. Then why did he write a cantata in Cöthen as an audition piece for Hamburg before he embarked on the trip? Why did he take any notice of the invitation at all? Merely to have a change of pace? Or as Terry thinks, in order to "return to his true vocation"? To do that he was truly in no hurry whatsoever, as becomes evident at the end of the Cöthen period, and his Cöthen creations are not the only ones that prove how much music he had to give outside the bounds of the worship service.

There is only one plausible reason for his accepting the Hamburg invitation and for going so far as to prepare himself for it: Cöthen, so happy up to now, had become for him a place accursed by inconsolability. Everything there reminded him of her, and he was willing to give up his prince, his freedom from care, his musical opportunities, and his social position in order to begin a new life elsewhere, far from the grave of his wife.

And so he traveled to Hamburg. This journey was no more of a trifling interlude in his life than the concert in Dresden. Neumeister, who knew much about the courts of the small states in central Germany, could fill Bach in on what it meant to pursue one's career in a great free trading city. Mühlhausen had also been a free imperial city, but a totally insignificant one. Hamburg was the most flourishing commercial center in Germany; at best only Leipzig could compare with it, but not Frankfurt, for example. It was one of the major ports of transshipment in Europe. The citizens managed their city themselves; no prince could meddle in their affairs, though quite a few of its citizens lived like princes. The city was wealthy, and there one could become wealthy in turn. Mattheson, whose writings on music were widely heeded in Germany, had started out as an unimportant singer but had come to own his own house, his own carriage, and his own saddle horses. Handel had come there without any means and had stayed for just two years, but in that short time he had earned all the money for his great Italian journey.

Hamburg was a musical city: The great Collegium Musicum in the Reventer performed music from Rome and Venice as well as from Vienna and Dresden. Of course, Hamburg was a very cosmopolitan place. It had its schools, its shippers' guild, its wealthy merchants, its trading bureaus from many different countries, even its own branch offices overseas. The narrow-mindedness of central German towns was completely unknown there. And Bach was no longer the eighteen-year-old student from Lüneburg who came to Hamburg to sit at the feet of an important musician, but a mature artist with thirteen years of professional experience and in full possession of his powers. Neumeister knew exactly what kind of man Bach was, and so he also knew how to explain what Hamburg represented and why it was worthwhile to give Cöthen up to move there.

The upshot is well known here too. Bach played audition pieces comprehensively; he improvised for half an hour on the chorale *An Wasserflüssen Babylon* ("By the Waters of Babylon"). And at the end the ancient Reinken, who at the age of ninety-seven still held his old position, said to him: "I thought this art had been lost, but I see that it lives on in you."

But the problem was that it was customary in Hamburg for someone who obtained a post to show his gratitude for it. After all, it would earn quite a bit for him before long under the conditions that prevailed in that city. Bach's fellow applicant Johann Joachim Heitmann, a Hamburger, thought 4,000 marks in gold was a perfectly reasonable price to pay for the privilege. The parish councilors thought so too. As for Bach, although he lived without any cares in the prince's favor, he could not set aside any savings with his large family. In fact he had never seen so much money together on a table in his entire life; it would have represented five of his annual salaries in Cöthen. In Cöthen nobody could boast of having that much, apart from the prince, perhaps; and from him above all, he could scarcely dare to borrow the amount. He could not even stay in Hamburg until the official audition and qualifying deadline. The prince's birthday was before that, and on his birthday Bach could not possibly leave him alone and without music. So the other candidate was chosen and poured out the bounty of his gratitude.

Neumeister was indignant, and Mattheson later quoted words from his Christmas sermon that have become famous: "He was convinced that even if one of the angels of Bethlehem had come down from heaven, one who played divinely and wanted to become organist at St. James, he would just have had to fly away again if he had no money." He was undoubtedly right. But the parish councilors of St. James were not music lovers like Neumeister; they were businessmen and dignitaries. Like the duke of Weimar, they were concerned mainly with pomp—and then also that finances remained in good shape. 131

Generally speaking, among politicians it is not easy to find one who subordinates pertinent policies to an enthusiasm for art.

Schweitzer asks: "What encouragement could Bach have found with authorities who preferred money to his art?" Yet Bach's colleague Telemann and later his own son Carl Philipp Emanuel got on with "authorities" like these very well. And even Schweitzer concedes: "The position offered far fewer difficulties—and occasions for humiliation—than the one he later took up in Leipzig." Terry simply writes: "What considerations guided Bach's refusal are not known. . . . Probably he discovered on the spot disadvantages not apparent from a distance." And a half century later Werner Neumann still appears to have no idea of Bach's financial circumstances nor any clue about the situation of the music world in Hamburg at the time. He explains: "That he did not seriously pursue the matter any further may . . . have been due . . . to some sobering insights into the professional situation in Hamburg." Yet Bach did apply for the position again from Cöthen. His letter has not been preserved; however, if it had contained a refusal on his part, Neumeister would have had no basis for his comment in the Christmas sermon.

But as we can see, not one of Bach's biographers has thought of these simple facts.

11

WHEN ALL WAS SAID AND DONE, FOR THE GENTLEMEN of Hamburg the court music director from Cöthen was just a poor devil, in spite of all his talent. They saw no reason to hire a man like him when another candidate would benefit the coffers of their church. So Bach stayed on in Cöthen and could only seek cold comfort in his great musical work.

It must have been a very bitter time for him. He clearly had a wealth of talent for the Hamburg position, but that only made his lack of money all the more painful. Here he was with his children and a maid, in a house that without his wife seemed dreadfully empty. She had instructed the help and run the whole large household, and now he confronted all this alone. There were four children to care for: Catharina Dorothea, at twelve the eldest; Friedemann, ten years old; and Carl Philipp Emanuel and Bernhard, just six and five. The little boy born in Cöthen had already died before his mother—he was the third child whose casket Bach had escorted to the grave. Yet the household had to go on, even if the housewife lay beneath the earth. Three times a day there were six mouths to feed; the maid had to have her orders about the work to be done; the firewood had to be brought in; provisions for the winter had to be stocked up; and then Bach also had to look after clothing and shoes and everything else besides.

The management of a household in the eighteenth century was no small matter; most of the modern conveniences we take for granted did not yet exist. Water had to be fetched by the bucketful from the well; in winter you had to make sure it did not freeze over. In general—above all in the wintertime, of course—you had to maintain a well-planned store of supplies. For meat, you had a salt barrel and a smokehouse, and at harvest time you bought up food that would keep well. But you could not buy meal for the morning soup in bulk: It was ground wet and got rancid after four weeks at most. Nor could you simply set a kettle of water on the top plate to boil: Stoves did not come into use until a century later. Everything was cooked over an open fire, and pots were hung directly over the flames. Firewood was not delivered in bundles but as logs that had to be split. In the evening an oil lamp was lit, but it did not burn very brightly, for the lamp cylinder had not yet been invented. Candles were a luxury; middle-class homes used a pinewood spill that was stuck in a ring on the wall. Indeed, there were no steel quills yet either: Johann Sebastian Bach wrote his entire life's work using goose quills alone.

The laboriousness of housekeeping at the time becomes most clearly apparent when considering Bach's move to Leipzig: Four full wagons were needed to carry the household goods. And the education of the children was a major enterprise in itself. Since compulsory school attendance for all children had not been introduced, it was the parents' job to teach them reading, writing, and arithmetic. Bach's wife had looked after that, the domestic regime, and more. Now the burden fell on him alone.

Despite these circumstances, he performed music, held his orchestra rehearsals, taught his students, gave lessons to his prince, wrote the six *Brandenburg Concerti* and the Orchestral Suites, and worked on one of his principal compositions: *The Well-Tempered Clavier*. By that time he had fully adopted the well-tempered tuning that had sometimes been described by other musicians but that had never been applied by anyone else in all its fullness. The *Chromatic*

Fantasy and Fugue may be counted as his first brilliant foray in this direction. In the new work he would execute a prelude and a fugue in each and every one of the possible keys, some of which had existed up to then only in the realm of theory.

The art did not consist of simply marking down a key signature of six or seven signs and then beginning in C-sharp major instead of C major, in D-sharp minor instead of E minor. The art consisted in the transition from one key to another, in modulation. In pure as in moderately tempered pitch, the customary one until then, a C-sharp major chord or a D-sharp minor chord sounded impure and was to be avoided. If a composer wrote in A major, he needed E major as the dominant chord, and because of that he fell into the "wolf fifths." But the way Bach had learned to tune his harpsichord, such chords sounded pure at last. He had closed the circle of fifths, and so he had in effect found the hidden connection, the Northwest Passage between the oceans of music.

It was no theoretical aspiration that had induced him to this, but a compositional necessity of his music. Nobody else in his time swept through the realms of the keys like Johann Sebastian Bach. Nobody else knew how to handle the transitions from key to key, from chord to chord with such sovereign skill. Consequently, nobody else felt as hampered by the open circle of fifths as he did. The impure F-sharp major, the impure B-flat minor were barriers he could not accept; thus he had to demonstrate they could be overcome. And he proved it to himself by writing twenty-four preludes and fugues for the complete circle of fifths. It was a unique and revolutionary achievement in its era. In the twentieth century Dmitri Shostakovich undertook a similar project, but by then the procedure had become self-evident; nor was he bound any longer by the strict laws of classical harmony as Bach had been.

In this light, Schweitzer's view that the "little organ book for beginning organists" was "one of the greatest events in music in general" becomes even more incomprehensible. For his part, Terry claims that *The Well-Tempered Clavier* formed "Bach's conclusive

135

contribution to the controversy raging round the tuning of that instrument." And he is amazed that "a technical controversy should have been resolved by a volume of gems so alien in feeling from the academic debate which invited them." We can easily recognize from this observation that Terry not only did not understand anything about the matter but was very far removed from musical praxis in general. The problem was first and foremost a practical one.

The work by no means represented a "contribution to the controversy." In that case Bach would have had to publicize it, in other words, publish it. It is one of the greatest curiosities of music history that this composition—because of its groundbreaking content the most influential work of the century—was never printed in Bach's lifetime. Its overwhelming importance for the period can be discerned from the fact that it circulated in handwritten copies. Indeed, it has remained *the* standard work throughout all musical epochs. Mozart profited from it just as Schumann and Mendelssohn did, just as Beethoven and Wagner did, and so forth up to the present time. It has always been the bible of all serious musicians who occupy themselves with keyboard instruments and with composition. If there had been an association for copyright protection in his time, Bach would have become a wealthy man from Prelude No. I, the one in C major, alone.

But he was never rich at any juncture of his life, and financing the engraved edition of this fundamental work would simply have been too expensive for him. It has been calculated that in that period a printed copy could not have been put on the market for less than 35 thalers. That was a horrendous sum, if one considers that later in Leipzig Bach's fixed annual income amounted to no more than 50 thalers. Although better paid than his colleagues in the cities, in Cöthen Bach was not wealthy either. He knew a great deal about the music market as a buyer (and preferred to copy out the significant works for himself right away). Thus he recognized from the beginning that no sales opportunities would be forthcoming here. And nevertheless, he wrote this wondrous work "for the use and benefit of the musical youth desiring instruction, as well as for the pastime of those who are already skilled in this study." All the same, it was basically for his own and his students' household use or, as one might say of this today, for the desk drawer.

As far as the practical requirements go, the little clavier book he devised for his son Friedemann, which contains sketches for *The Well-Tempered Clavier* as well as the two- and three-part inventions, would have been completely sufficient. All the rest he wrote of his own free will, on his own initiative, and because he owed it to himself. We would search a long time for contemporaries who did something parallel and to a similar extent. For Bach, it is characteristic.

Much ink has flowed about *The Well-Tempered Clavier*—which Spitta, by the way, does list among Bach's Cöthen works but otherwise never mentions further. One of the most original notions yet is the indication in Riemann's music lexicon that the work was inspired by Johann Caspar Ferdinand Fischer's *Ariadne musica* of 1706. This idea could occur only to someone who has never compared the two works with each other and who possesses very little musical judgment. Fischer's *Ariadne musica* is a collection of beautiful and ingenious pieces. But not only is Fischer's structure completely different, his forms are also much simpler; nor do Bach's bold chord combinations and harmonic modulations occur in them at all. Precisely those keys are omitted whose usability Bach was able to demonstrate in his work for the very first time: C-sharp major, F-sharp major, E-flat minor, G-sharp minor, and B-flat minor. Fischer did not yet have well-tempered pitch at his disposal.

Anyone who investigates the historic performance practice of the period can ascertain what complicated conditions existed then in the field of musical tuning. And at the time a composer who had dealt practically with his clavier and had attained a completely tempered pitch would have had something quite different from imitation in his mind when he sat down to display what he had achieved. There can be no doubt: Bach had as little to borrow from Fischer in *The Well-Tempered Clavier* as he did from Kuhnau in the *Capriccio on the Departure of His Much Beloved Brother*.

A researcher who had looked at all deeply into Fischer's works would certainly have had to notice that there is a parallel to Bach's Prelude No. 1 in Fischer's prelude *Clio* from the *Musical Parnassus*. Anyone who would dare to assert that Bach's piece was created by following Fischer's example, however, would be demonstrably in error once again.

Hermann Keller has written a whole book on *The Well-Tempered Clavier* in which he meticulously presents what one could basically work out oneself—provided one does not confuse Bach's opus with Carl Czerny's *Art of Dexterity*, as did the Canadian pianist Glenn Gould. Striking interpretations may be found in Keller too. For example, one of his remarkable insights is that Bach composed a reclining cross with the theme of the Fugue in C-sharp Minor (C-sharp—B-sharp—E—D-sharp); this can be shown by drawing lines between the first and fourth notes as well as the second and third notes. Here we can discern Bach's shatteringly deep religiosity. Moreover, this is no isolated case: The same occurs in other composers of the time.

The matter of the cross in Bach is nothing more than a bald assertion. But Keller is completely right about his second observation. We encounter the deep piety of the German people still more profoundly in the old folk song "Kuckuck, Kuckuck, ruft's aus dem Wald" ("'Cuckoo, Cuckoo' Rings out from the Woods"), for if one connects the first with the fourth and the second with the third note there, the cross stands out with incomparable clarity. And when subjected to the same method, Mozart's *Eine kleine Nachtmusik* (*A Little Night Music*) turns into an entire graveyard of crosses (luckily, one cannot hear them). We might also refer to the deep religiosity of mathematics, which cannot get by without the cross as a symbol for plus. And the St. Andrew's cross or *x*, symbol for the first unknown, undoubtedly points to the unfathomable nature of the divine will.

All this can be compared to the skills of a secretary who types little pictures out on a typewriter, which is technically easy enough. Yet that sort of thing has virtually become the accepted approach in the Bach literature. Siegmund-Schulze, for example, has discovered that in Bach's *Kreuzstab Cantata* the word "cross" appears at a D-sharp, at a D with an accidental, thus precisely at a "cross," and he perceives in this a definite symbolic content. If that were true, the fact that in the B Minor Mass the alto begins the Crucifixus with a canceled F-sharp, thus with an F, could no doubt be interpreted as a reference to the imminent dissolution of the body of Christ. And it is deeply regrettable that to this day musicology still has not deciphered the theological meaning of the accidental musical flat symbol ♭.

Another scholar points out that in the cantata "Dies sind die heil'gen zehn Gebot'" ("These Are the Holy Ten Commandments") Bach's theme consists of exactly ten notes and so virtually turns him into the inventor of a theological ten-tone series. But then in the chorale prelude by the same name (BWV 635) we count only nine notes. Either Bach miscalculated or he was more of a musician than a mystic. Since there was no book about the Cabala in Bach's estate, Friedrich Smend has busied himself with that topic and proved that Bach smuggled the Cabala into his compositions, that in fact he may even have produced them with its help. This idea has since been eagerly pursued by others as well. Fortunately, Klaus Peter Richter has ascertained that the application of the Cabala is almost invariably doomed to success, as Smend could have discovered for himself if he had ever read the memoirs of Casanova.

The reason one may heartily make fun of all these goings-on is that they have less than nothing to do with music and merely indicate the (almost hopeless) distance of the observers from their subject. The ring motif in Richard Wagner's *Rheingold* would not have gained in substance in the least if Wagner had composed it in the form of a circle, nor would Siegfried's horn call be more meaning-ful in the shape of a curve. Bach knew more and was capable of more in music than any other composer before or after him. But even where he may have been intent on symbols, one does not come closer to his music either through counting or through the theolog-ical transfiguration of accidentals. There is something else, by the way, that completely escaped Keller's notice in his speculations on the cruciform. The theme of the C-sharp Minor Fugue is none other than B-A-C-H ("B" standing for B-flat and "H" for B-natur-al), note for note, transposed two whole tones higher. Thus at that time Bach consciously avoided the temptation to inscribe his own name within his fugal work. Quite obviously he did not wish to ob-scure his sequence of notes through extramusical references. That should give his interpreters pause.

And here is more food for thought: Bach was by that time thir-ty-five and had a good position, a fine orchestra, and a wonderful employer. But his wife was dead, and all she had left him was their four children. Dörte, the eldest, was now twelve, but she showed no exceptional bent for music—and anyway, as a girl she was more in-volved with the housekeeping. Carl Philipp Emanuel and Bernhard were eight and six, still playing games, still little boys. Wilhelm Friedemann, at ten or eleven, was already more mature and also very musical. Bach did not dedicate the *Little Music Book (Notenbüchlein)* to his sons—as might have been expected, since musical training in his home was taken for granted—but to his eldest son alone. It is usu-ally said of Friedemann that he was Bach's favorite son.

There is something else that strikes us as well, as soon as we exam-ine the portraits of the Bachs. Bach himself, as well as Carl Philipp Emanuel, had the same body type as their forefather Veit Bach: broad-shouldered, sturdy, sedate, not plump exactly, but powerful. The adult Friedemann's picture shows an entirely different type: more slender, more delicate, more nervous. When he later sits for his portrait, with his artist's hat at a rakish angle, he makes the image of his brother Carl Philipp Emanuel look almost petty-bourgeois by comparison.

140

Bach's portraits too stand in considerable contrast to the painting of his brilliant son; there is no similarity there. And since the other Bachs are all so unlike Friedemann, there is only one possible explanation: He resembled his mother. In Friedemann most of all, Bach recognized his deceased wife, and it is only too understandable that he developed a special bond with his eldest son. At the time he was the most mature of the children and the most musical, and for Bach his dead Maria Barbara lived on in him.

Bach's relationship with Friedemann changed when he took a second wife. A year and a half after the death of his wife, Bach did marry again. In the various Bach biographies, it all sounds rather dull. "The grief over the loss of his wife does not prevent Bach from seeing plainly that his children need a mother, the house a housekeeper and himself a companion," writes Rueger, for example. Siegmund-Schulze remarks dryly: "Already a year later Bach, who could not leave the under-age children without a mother, got married." Terry recognizes exclusively moral reasons for the marriage: "The man whose children were taught to invoke the name of Jesus before playing a five-finger exercise would not be less exacting in the deportment of their daily lives. For that reason, above others, he deplored the void in his motherless house." Love, in these versions, plays no part in the matter. The same holds for Spitta, who writes: "According to the philosophies of life that prevailed in the Bach clan, it was rather self-evident that Sebastian did not remain in the widower status to which he had been condemned by the death of his first spouse." And another source, already quoted often, does not even bother about the family traditions but only comments: "In accordance with the custom of the time, fairly soon he looked for a second wife for himself."

All these authors admit nothing more than common sense and convention as Bach's reasons for remarrying. And although Otterbach informs us about such details as that the oboist of the Cöthen orchestra gave fencing lessons on the side, he passes over the deeply 141 decisive turning points in Bach's existence. He almost seems to have an eagle eye for the irrelevant.

Where Bach's second wife is concerned, no one cares about her situation at all. Werner Neumann writes in his "little Bach book," "But the artist, sixteen years younger than he, no doubt felt it a great good fortune to be chosen by the famous court music director as partner in life and mother of his children." A young woman of today would hardly deem it a special stroke of luck to marry, right after her twentieth birthday, a widower almost sixteen years her senior, with four children—particularly a young lady who was already practicing her own profession and not at all badly paid.

Anna Magdalena Wülcken was both independent and successful in a period when young women of that description were quite a rarity, since most girls only waited for the day when they could get married and become housewives and mothers. Mademoiselle Wülcken was princely singer at the court of Anhalt-Zerbst, and her own income amounted to almost half that of Bach's. Thus she was very well-off by herself and did not need to rely at all on an early marriage.

For his part, Bach is depicted as though the eligible daughters of the land were merely his for the asking. If that were the case, considered purely from the point of view of common sense and convention, this Mademoiselle Wülcken was by no means a wise choice. Why would the widower Bach select such a slip of a thing, more than fifteen years younger than he, used to going her own way, and totally inexperienced in running a household, much less in bringing up children?

As one discerns on closer inspection, the union contradicted all common sense, to say nothing of convention, on the part of both the singer Wülcken and the music director Bach. For that reason, a conclusion suggests itself that not one of the scholars quoted has ever reached: The two must have felt a great deal of love for each other. And it lasted a lifetime. Not only do Anna Magdalena's thirteen children bear eloquent witness to this, but it is attested even more by the many music manuscripts that prove with what devotion she attended to the compositions of her husband. As he had earlier for Friedemann, Bach soon devised for his Anna her own little music book. It is *not* intended as an instructional work but may rather be considered a collection of musical declarations of love, not one that incessantly alludes to yearning, affection, and kissing but one dedicated to mutual feelings and experiences, one that is thus far richer and more comprehensive.

We cannot assume that Friedemann received the advent of a stepmother with indifference, much less enthusiasm. His father's love had been bestowed on him to an exceptional degree, but now an unfamiliar young woman, barely seven years older than his elder sister, stood between them. Even if Bach loved "his big son" no less than before, he could divide his affections again, and they must necessarily have been unequal shares. The lively young woman, who with her love had restored him to life, simply had more to offer him than his eleven-year-old son. And at that time a delicate but deep rift must have arisen in the Bach home. As far as we know, after Bach's death his two elder sons, Friedemann and Carl Philipp Emanuel, never supported Anna Magdalena in any way, though they were both on thoroughly good terms with each other at the time. She was and she remained their stepmother.

At any rate, and in defiance of all Bach biographers, I must acknowledge that his second marriage was based neither on convention nor common sense. It was instead love that joined Bach and Anna Magdalena for the rest of his days.

And as before, Prince Leopold was generous: As the ruler of Anhalt-Zerbst had done, he engaged Anna as princely singer for 200 florins. As a result the Bachs became a working couple—highly unusual for the beginning of the eighteenth century—and with 600 florins a year plus donations were quite well-off.

The prince had been especially open-handed, and not without reason: He was happy as a lark. For at the age of twenty-eight, he too had fallen in love, with a princess from the house of Anhalt-Bernburg, about 12 miles away from Cöthen. Friederike Henrietta, with her raven hair and coal-black eyes, was definitely someone who could make an infatuated young man fall deeply in love with her. But on one point she differed from Anna Magdalena decidedly: She was not at all willing to adapt herself. Adaptation, she thought, behooved her spouse.

Prince Leopold readily complied with her every wish. In his eyes he had won a pearl. For the wedding, he had the entire palace renovated, and the ensuing festivities lasted four full weeks. We might assume that Bach had a great deal of music to create on that occasion.

But we would be mistaken. Bach wrote none at all. True, there are those who would have us believe that the wedding music was merely lost, yet that is quite implausible. Bach took his music much too seriously to treat its preservation lightly. Once for his prince's birthday he had written a whole chorus of homage based on a movement from the *Brandenburg Concerti.* That was an occasional work of no great importance, but it has come down to us. The funeral music that he later wrote upon Leopold's death was subsumed entirely into the *St. Matthew Passion.* But it was preserved separately as well. And yet the entire wedding music has simply vanished? Bach would certainly have given his best for the occasion; he would also have had ample leisure for the task. During the great wedding preparations, there was no time and no room in the palace for making music of any other kind. But there was no wedding music. For Friederike Henrietta did not like music at all.

She admired things military, and so Leopold formed a corps of guards at her behest. After all, he had enjoyed his training as an officer at the Cavaliers Academy in Berlin; he knew something about this domain, and whatever wish his beloved bride might express, it was his pleasure to fulfill. Siegmund-Schultze is badly informed when he claims that the reason Prince Leopold suddenly concerned himself so intensively with military things was because "now the small absolutist states also found themselves obliged to prepare for war, particularly in the vicinity of belligerent Brandenburg-Prussia."

His "tall fellows" who were abducted into military service were much too precious to Friedrich Wilhelm for him to expose them to

144

a war. The Northern War had just come to an end with a fortunate outcome for Prussia. Between Berlin and Cöthen very friendly relations existed. Besides, unlike his great son, Friedrich Wilhelm I never invaded a peaceful country in his entire life. No, there were no political reasons for Leopold's military expenditures; making his bride happy was reason enough. Music could wait for a while. A wedding did not take place every day; after the wedding, music would surely come into its own again.

But it did not come into its own again. Bach's creations of the Cöthen years are amazingly abundant, and he particularly lavished attention on the violin and cello during those years, composing unique solo pieces and chamber music for them. Three violin concerti in addition to the *Brandenburg Concerti* and the Orchestral Suites date from this time, but they were all written before the end of 1721.

On December 3 Bach married Anna Magdalena in a wedding at home (to the annoyance of the Lutheran congregation), and a week after that, on December 11, the prince wedded Friederike Henrietta of Anhalt-Bernburg. From then on Bach wrote no more music for the palace. The man Spitta described as "irascible," the man Rueger said was of "choleric temperament," wrote to a friend seven years later that "the impression arose that the musical inclinations of the Prince had become somewhat lukewarm, especially since the new Princess seemed to be unmusical *(amusa)*." The list of Bach's works shows that after the marriage of his prince, Bach wrote nothing but clavier music for his own domestic use—only clavier music from then on . . .

To put it more clearly: Friederike Henrietta had thoroughly turned Leopold's head and rendered his court music director superfluous.

12

THIS WAS THE THIRD TIME THAT BACH HAD FOUND himself stymied: In Mühlhausen the Pietistic fanaticism of Reverend Johann Adolph Frohne had made his "well-regulated church music to the glory of God" impossible. In Weimar the duke had subordinated him to a talentless music director, dismissed him from composing, and in the end had treated him like nothing more than a rebellious lackey. And once again in Cöthen, his services were no longer needed. He was effectively being sent into retirement at the age of thirty-seven. And so for the third time he stood before the ruins of his career.

Bach was patient. Again and again Bach endured a great deal in his life with almost unbelievable patience. What course should he adopt now? His nest was very warmly feathered in Cöthen. One did not throw such comforts away thoughtlessly. But he had become redundant, useless. And it did not look as though this situation would ever change: The prince was indeed happy with his "unmusical" wife, who had so deeply transformed his inclinations.

So Bach bode his time. But for a steadily industrious person— and Bach was certainly that—idleness is hard to bear. Then on June 5, 1722, the St. Thomas School choirmaster, Johann Kuhnau, died. Geck, who calls him "not very capable," has apparently not taken a look at his works. He had not been an inferior man; he had been quite competent.

Here was a vacancy, then. And Leipzig was almost as important as Hamburg. Siegmund-Schultze speculates that "the opportunity to work in the trade-fair and university city of Leipzig as choirmaster of the leading church, and to combine the creation of sacred music on a higher level with the duties of *director musices*" must have "appealed to Bach." But here he is also mistaken, several times over. The trade fair and university were not under the control of the city but of the king, the post of choirmaster did not belong to a church but to a school, and nothing whatsoever about all this appealed to Bach. After all, he was court music director, and as such he stood considerably above a schoolmaster in rank. The position clearly did not appeal to others very much either: It remained vacant for quite a while. July went by, then August and September, and finally the whole year of 1722.

By now the Bachs had been idle for an entire year. Musicians had been dismissed from the court orchestra; it was obviously no longer needed. All that survived was hunting music. Bach and his wife were actually receiving a gracious allowance, not a salary. But Bach did not apply to St. Thomas. He heard that Telemann had made overtures for the position from Hamburg, but the Hamburgers had responded right away with a salary increase. He learned that his friend Johann Friedrich Fasch, the court music director at Anhalt-Zerbst, had already taken a look at the vacancy. The court music director from Darmstadt, Christoph Graupner, a man of fine reputation, was also supposed to have applied, and several others as well. So there really must have been something to the post. But Bach clearly checked his enthusiasm for "the attraction of a city characterized by powerful enlightened forces and civic progress" (Siegmund-Schultze): He had no intention at all of soliciting the job.

148   It was late autumn when the "honorable and most wise council of the city of Leipzig" sent the Licentiate Christian Weisse, curate at St. Thomas, to approach Bach formally. One might think that at

this point he offered him the position. But that was not the case; he merely requested Bach to apply as well. The gentlemen by no means wanted to commit themselves; they simply wanted to have a wider range of choices. And Bach was already known to them through Kuhnau, from his inspection of the organ at the university church.

Incidentally, the "honorable council" converted the selection procedure into a gigantic horse-trade (one can hardly give it a more favorable name). In the entire council minutes between 1720 and 1730, no topic was debated with such frequency and yet such slowness as the filling of the school choirmaster post, which Bach finally obtained. Kuhnau had died on June 5, 1722. Telemann had long since declined. But even six months later, in the council meeting of November 23, Bach's name was still not under consideration. Not until a whole month later, on December 21, do the names of Graupner and Bach turn up in the minutes as new applicants, and the council members' sympathies are immediately with Graupner. At the end of December, Graupner performed a cantata as his audition piece. Three weeks later (on January 15, 1723) doubts arose in the council meeting as to whether he would receive the necessary discharge from his sovereign.

After Weisse's visit Bach had already agreed in December to perform an audition piece, but Graupner had clearly been preferred over him. Even at this point, after Graupner had declined, it was not Bach but a native, the Leipzig organist Georg Balthasar Schotte, who was invited to present an audition piece first. He delivered it on February 2, and not until the following Sunday, February 7, was Bach allowed to perform his cantata "Jesus nahm zu sich die zwölfe" ("Jesus Took unto Him the Twelve"). But the council was still not ready to give Bach a confirmation. First it required the written consent of his sovereign that he could be released from Cöthen, and that request was also issued only after two months had elapsed, at the council meeting of April 9.

Bach personally delivered the prince's declaration with great promptness on April 19. But only after Graupner, who could not free himself from Darmstadt, expressly recommended Bach for the position on April 22, 1723, did the council finally accept Bach's services, after eleven months of procrastination, four months of which were taken up with consideration of his candidacy. It took two more weeks until the contract with Bach was signed. Neither the negotiations with Telemann nor the negotiations with Graupner took as long as those with Bach. And what awaited him in Leipzig?

The St. Thomas School was the *schola pauperum*, the city's school for the poor. Since the municipality bore the costs of the school, the students had to make themselves useful. And since the council also had to take care of the churches of the city (the council, oddly enough, not the consistory, filled the ecclesiastical posts), the students had to provide the music for the municipal churches. For that reason, a teacher was appointed at the school who apart from teaching the Latin classes was responsible for the church music. (Incidentally, in Bohemia in the nineteenth century the combined post of teacher and church choir leader, called the *ludi magister,* was still common.) The instruction in Latin had no repercussions in the larger community, but what the choirmaster achieved as a musician could be heard in four churches Sunday after Sunday. It was not without reason that this *Cantor,* the music teacher who was also obliged to teach Latin, was equal in rank to the assistant headmaster: In a certain sense he constituted an advertisement for the school. That is why he also received an "immense" salary, 100 thalers a year. (In the Dresden court orchestra the least of the musicians was already earning double that.)

Leipzig Bach researchers have claimed that the name "school for the poor" attached to St. Thomas was merely based on an old tradition, that in reality when Bach took up his post there it was quite a respected school. But that is not the case. Citizens of any status in Leipzig sent their sons to the Nicholas School or engaged a private tutor, as, for example, the mayor Dr. Gottfried Lange did (and as Bach did in later years). If the Thomas School bore the title *schola pauperum* out of tradition, it was fully entitled to that label in practice as well. Until headmaster Gesner took up his post, we search the council's records in vain for any indication that it ever provided support to the school in any way. As a result, for the last 100 years the Thomas School had gone steadily downhill. It had once had 120 pupils, yet when Bach assumed his post the student body had declined to fifty-two. Many of these fifty-two did not even sleep in a private bed, and quite a few had to share one bed among three. And almost all the students had scabies.

The pupils of St. Thomas were also obliged to sing twice a week in the streets as *Kurrende,* or "serenaders," literally begging for money in return for their songs. From these alms fixed charges were handed over to the teachers as payment for their lessons. And to give an impression of the school's physical plant: because of lack of space, in the "main schoolroom" three classes usually had to be taught at the same time. There had been no structural changes whatsoever in the building for 200 years, nor were any deemed necessary. The general condition of the Thomas School was of such small concern to the city that in the council records up to 1730, unlike the maintenance of the hospital or the prison and orphanage, it does not turn up at all.

It is hardly plausible that Bach did not inform himself about these circumstances, and the only question that arises is why he was willing to take up the post in spite of this state of affairs.

The motives for his decision are diverse. Bach was condemned to idleness in Cöthen, and that was something he could not bear. Anyway, he could easily foresee that it was only a matter of time before the young princess would get rid of him too. He needed a new circle of activity, if only in order to guarantee his own security.

If he applied to Leipzig despite the miserable conditions at the Thomas School, it must have been because he considered those conditions inconsequential. It could only be clear to him, of course, that the Latin classes would take up a great deal of time. But his predecessor, Kuhnau, had hired someone else to replace him at the task, and if the job became too irksome this possibility was presumably open to him as well. True, that would cost him half his salary, and with 50 thalers a year he could not maintain a family of six and pay a maid, especially since as compared with Cöthen the payments in kind were also reduced and only the free rent remained.

But apparently he regarded his salary as only a supplementary income. In Leipzig generally there was music to be made again, and he was perfectly at home with church music. And then Kuhnau had also held the post of university music director, and music could be performed with the students as well. As to earnings, a point Licentiate Weisse must have elaborated on persuasively, they could be derived mainly from the many incidental occasions in Leipzig—weddings, christenings, funerals, and the like. These were all paid extra, and in such a big city, with 30,000 inhabitants, a considerable number of them had to mount up. He ought to be able to amass 600 to 800 thalers in a good year; that was a third more than both salaries in Cöthen put together.

It was of course a rather uncertain income, but there was something else: Leipzig really was the only city that was able to match the wheeling and dealing of Hamburg. And what could be earned in addition to the actual salary in Hamburg had been thoroughly described to him there by Erdmann Neumeister. This had been brought home to him by his successful fellow applicant Johann Joachim Heitmann when he took Bach out of the running by paying 4,000 marks in cash for a job. What Hamburg offered had to be available to a similar degree in Leipzig as well. In addition, there was an educational opportunity for his three sons: They could study at the University of Leipzig, and a university graduate always commanded greater respect.

Thus on closer inspection, the conditions at the Thomas School per se hardly made any difference. It was true that the current stock of pupils was poor, but the employment contract did give Bach the chance to participate in new admissions decisions in the future, as far as vocal talents were concerned. So he could build up something in that department. On top of this, Telemann had been interested in the post, and he had always been a good businessman. And his fellow applicants Graupner and Fasch were court directors of music like himself, yet both of them would readily have become the school choirmaster in Leipzig; this too implied that there must truly be advantages to the position. With it he would acquire the title of *director musices,* and so would rank above a mere music teacher in any case.

True, the city ensemble consisted of only seven people—three wind players and four strings—but he could train further instrumental forces at the school, and among the university students in Leipzig there were capable musicians as well. Their Collegium Musicum had already been in existence for over twenty years. Moreover, since the council had been so thorough and ponderous in the process of filling the position, he could only infer that it was extremely fond of music. Under circumstances such as these, the details of the contract did not matter much anymore.

Admittedly this contract was somewhat odd. For example, Bach was not allowed to leave the city without the express permission of the council. He had to consider not only the "honorable council" but also all superintendents and school headmasters as his superiors. At all funerals he had to walk in front of the coffin with his choir. Further, he had to pledge explicitly not to take on any university post. That surely could not be meant quite literally, since his predecessor had indeed held the post of university music director, to the benefit of the city, as it turned out. He had to commit himself expressly to teaching, even if the contract did allow him a replacement, provided that no extra costs to the council accrued from this. In regard to Telemann, the council had not been so petty: It even wanted to excuse him completely from giving Latin classes.

But after all, with Telemann the gentlemen of the council knew what they would be getting; indeed, they were familiar with him from earlier times. As a student in Leipzig he had already been very active. The music in St. Paul's Church had been entrusted to him, and he had founded the Collegium Musicum at the university. Since the Leipzig of his day had an opera ensemble, he had also

153

composed operas for it. He had to be forgiven for that peccadillo; Kuhnau had run into real difficulties because the young people had been more interested in performing music at the opera than at church. The opera had in fact as good as faded away in the meantime, but it was written into Bach's contract all the same that his music "must not sound too operatic, but rather encourage the listeners to worship."

The council also covered itself in other ways. It required that outside his service obligations Bach must musically instruct the pupils *privatim* (free of charge, of course), and that his music must always be at the disposal of the gentlemen of the council (gratis as well). There could be no question of conceding special terms to him, like those he had obtained up to now from all his previous employers. In Bach they were taking on a musician whom they did not know because those whom they did know from out of town were not to be had. And a local such as the organist Schott (or Schotte) from the New Church was naturally not a serious candidate at all. No man is a prophet in his own land.

Schweitzer was quite right when he wrote, "Recently it has become fashionable to make a cheap reproach to the Leipzig council for accepting Bach only after it had sought in vain to win over the 'shallow' Telemann and the insignificant Graupner. Very unjust. These two were well known in Leipzig and had a name among their contemporaries that Bach did not yet possess. One cannot expect from such officials that they should anticipate or predict the judgments of posterity."

The comment often quoted in this connection is that of councilman Abraham Christoph Plaz: "Since the best cannot be obtained, we will have to settle for the mediocre." It is cited for the first time by Spitta, and all the rest have faithfully copied it from him since. As it unfortunately does not fit in with the image of Leipzig as a "city characterized by powerful enlightened forces and civic progress," the New Bach Society later took great pains to soften the bad impression. The most original effort in this regard is an elaborate work by the Tübingen professor Ulrich Siegele, which extends over several issues of the *Bach-Jahrbuch*. In it he develops broad aspects of a "Leipzig cultural policy" and claims that the Leipzig council was something like a "coalition government under changing chairmanship of the parties." He asserts that there was a "choirmaster party" and a "music director party," with one in favor of Bach and the other against him, and he elucidates his views in great detail.

On what basis Siegele arrived at his theories is not discernible. I can only affirm with certainty that he does not owe them to a study of sources, for the Leipzig council records of those years plainly reveal that there can have been no question of a "coalition government" and "changing parties." Of course the three councils in Leipzig did alternate every year at the end of August, but that by no means led to a zigzag course in municipal administration. And Siegele completely departs from reality when he claims to perceive a "cultural policy" oriented to the music world. With the lone exception of its selection of the Thomas School choirmaster, culture plays no part whatsoever in the council minutes of that period, and Siegele's work remains pure invention throughout. In spite of that, it headed up three successive issues of the *Bach-Jahrbuch*, and none of his colleagues has ever contradicted him.

Much too much importance has been attached to Councilman Plaz's remark, which was torn out of the middle of a debate. It so happens that after the council clerk entered this opinion into the minutes, he suddenly had to leave the meeting because he was needed elsewhere, so he handed the further recording of minutes over to that same Councilman Plaz. But the latter neglected to continue them, and thus no one knows to this day how the meeting ended up. It cannot be ruled out that Plaz was then contradicted and that he had to defend himself; perhaps for that reason he did not get around to completing the minutes. It is even conceivable that his negative opinion of Bach, as preserved seven years later, in the minutes of 1730, has its roots in his not having got his way during the selection process.

In any case he did not have a clear notion of the music world of his time, as his judgment of Graupner makes clear. In the council meeting of January 15, 1723, he stated that "it was true he did not especially know H. Graupner. However, he presented a fine figure and seemed to be a worthy man. He also believed that he was a good musician, but it remained to be seen whether he would provide proper instruction at the school." One cannot possibly deduce great musical expertise from this contribution to the discussion; at any rate he was much less concerned about music than about the Latin classes.

But on the musical question the other gentlemen were equally in the dark. Thus Councilman Adrian Steger: "He was no musician and deferred to the judgment of the governing Mayor." Or Canon Jacob Born, who approved of Graupner "because Mr. Graupner was so highly thought of." Likewise, Building Commissioner Gottfried Wagner "voted for Graupner for the reasons others have cited." Councilman Johann Job: "He did not know Graupner personally, but many good things were said of him." Not a single one of these gentlemen expressed anywhere at any time a musical judgment of his own; all refer to general impressions or the opinions of third parties. Hence we come much closer to the truth if we understand that among the members of the council not one really understood anything about music and that the long to-and-fro in dealing with the selection of the choirmaster had its cause above all in that. The gentlemen had to make a decision on a matter about which they basically had no clue.

In contemporary local politics the same sort of thing still goes on. To its credit, the Leipzig council of 1723 conscientiously tried to avoid a mistake. Yet what means did it have at its disposal for making the right choice? None of the councilmen was an expert on music. They wanted to have the most remarkable musician possible for their money, but all they had to go on was their acquaintanceship with some of the candidates.

From his earlier activities in Leipzig, Telemann was still very favorably remembered, so he was desirable candidate number one. Graupner was a graduate of the Thomas School and the University of Leipzig to boot, so he was number two. Fasch had the same Leipzig training and could conceivably represent a third option. But the councilmen had to pay attention not only to music but also to the school. What they were willing to concede to the well-known Telemann as a special privilege, the exemption from Latin classes, they could not accord to everyone else or it might become a customary practice. After Fasch had declined the post as well, there was no particular celebrity among the other applicants. So finally they sent Licentiate Weisse to Cöthen—but only for exploratory discussions. True, Bach had not been to university, but he was willing to teach. And furthermore he had a recommendation from Graupner, an expert whom the councilmen knew.

Unquestionably, after so much searching out of town they could not disgrace themselves by taking a local man such as Schott in the end. Bach had performed his music with aplomb—he only had to beware of slipping into the theatrical—and he was not averse to teaching Latin. So for the Leipzig council he was the last resort. And for Bach, who could not remain in Cöthen any longer, the vacancy in the Thomas School was also the last resort. It was not a love match for either side. But if they could not get what they loved, they had to love what they could get. On closer inspection it was for both sides not an ideal but at least an acceptable solution.

Thus Bach came to the decisive mistake of his career, which his biographers would later consider the fulfillment of his life.

13

Bach was in Cöthen for five years and five months. He was happy there for just two and a half years; then his dearly beloved wife passed away. As a widower with four small children he wrote the *Brandenburg Concerti*, the *Inventions*, and most of *The Well-Tempered Clavier*. He had not even been in the town for three years when he tried to leave what had become the tomb of his joy. The attempt fell through because of lack of funds. Then he found a wonderful second wife, Anna Magdalena, but was forced to recognize that the woman whom his prince married at the same time would no longer countenance any music. If he had been tempted to leave as early as autumn 1720, it was certain by January 1722 at the latest that he would soon have to leave. And so his fourteen last months in Cöthen were marked by the realization that there was no room for him there anymore.

Despite all this, Terry concludes that the five Cöthen years were among the most "placid and happy" of Bach's life. Walter Vetter writes in his book *Bach the Music Director*: "However light-hearted the Cöthen years may have been, the music they produced was certainly not always light," and he speaks of the "merry hustle and bustle at court." Smend as well mentions "those happy years when Bach worked as music director in Cöthen." He also claims that Bach already performed a cantata in Leipzig in December 1722, though

Bach's name is not mentioned for the first time in the council records till three days before Christmas—without reference to a performance, of course. That would have been a minor miracle in any event, for in the pre-Christmas season church music came to a halt (which, as a theologian, Smend should have known).

The notion that Bach may have performed his *St. John Passion* already at Easter 1723 in the Thomas Church is also premised on a disregard of the facts. When the council finally decided to appoint Bach on April 22, it is true that Graupner's recommendation played a part. But surely during their meeting at least one of the gentlemen would have referred to the great Passion performance just experienced, had it really taken place. Similarly, Bach's audition piece on February 7 would have been superfluous if he had already performed a cantata eight weeks before. As such scrutiny reveals, experts can make assertions like these only when they are uncertain of the truth themselves and can be sure that their colleagues do not know any better either. In studying the Bach literature, I have encountered many passages that are merely composed of untested ideas.

In the main, ideas have also determined the desire to prove that Bach was first and foremost a music-making man of God. Accordingly, everything that cannot be described as music related to the church turns out to be more or less peripheral. As grounds for this view, Bach's definition of the thoroughbass is usually pressed into service: "It is played in such a fashion that the left hand plays the written-out notes, while the right adds the consonances and dissonances, so that the whole affords a well-sounding harmony to the glory of God and the permissible delight of the spirit. Where that is not observed, there will be no real music, but only a devilish din."

In order to misunderstand that as emphasizing religion, one must stand at a considerable remove from music. Bach refers nowhere to "impermissible" music but describes the "delight of the spirit" quite apart from music "to the glory of God" as expressly "permissible." Here he is explicitly comparing music for worship to music for "delight"—in other words, for entertainment. For him,

160

as for the music of his time in general, the thoroughbass was part of both. And he wrote both types of music too. In fact for him not only his *Coffee Cantata,* his *English* and *French Suites,* and his "little night music" (the *Goldberg Variations*) but also his Orchestral Suites were music for entertainment; the second of them ends with a piece revealingly called "Badinerie," musical "banter."

All these are certainly the works of a religious man, but not the endless devotional exercises of a pious man. A person who is at one with God does not have to pray all day long, and Bach was not among those who turn up their noses at such words as "pleasure" or "entertainment," or disdain the sheer enjoyment of music. He did not even scorn to use a popular tune at the end of his *Peasant Cantata.* So why would he have pronounced a moral judgment when he was addressing a question of performance practice? For the musician Bach, a "devilish din" ensued only if somebody struck the wrong chords to the bass. That was the point of his remark. One anecdote reports that because of such an error he even threw his wig at the head of the organist Johann Gottlieb Görner during a rehearsal. And when Wilhelm Friedemann was improvising one night on the harpsichord and broke off right in the middle, it is said that Bach got out of bed to bring the piece to an end. Anyone who merely smiles at this story cannot comprehend that for such a musician harmonies, and tones in general, can only have been solid and tangible substances, no different from boards for the carpenter or skins for the furrier.

Without a doubt, music is a mysterious thing: We cannot eat it, cannot wear it, cannot prove anything by it—considered purely as a phenomenon, it is utterly useless. Perhaps for songbirds it serves as an aid to mating (though no one really understands why larks soar from the meadows high into the air when they sing). But why the production of vibrations between 16,000 and 17,000 hertz is a need, a concern, a calling for human beings, can never be explained, just as little as why the most accomplished in this field meet with more admiration and even veneration than inventors, generals, or

161

statesmen. Nor why the inclination toward music is apparently innate to humanity: In a cave near Marseilles a flute has been found that is at least 20,000 years old. Humankind without music is obviously only a fragment. The preoccupation with it has even given rise to a whole branch of learning, musicology, though no music is produced by its efforts. One will hardly find an approach to the basic phenomenon there either. According to Felix Maria Gatz, musical aesthetics asserts that music "refers to an outside-the-tonal and therefore to a reality that is itself nonmusic" and that in any case "music never means itself."

But that really does sound too confused to be taken seriously; it leads us into a dimension where anything goes. In their incapacity to comprehend music as music, in their dismissal of music as only a prop for the sphere of nonmusic, lies the hopeless foolishness of such lucubrations. In this respect Wilhelm Furtwängler declared: "Clarity of expression in music is different from that of the word, but no less precise." And: "Art springs from spheres that are beyond the sphere of the will." One finds parallel remarks in Bernstein as well as in Beethoven. But if musicology ever took their comments to heart, whole branches would fall from its peculiar tree of knowledge.

The biographers generally agree that Bach's true work did not begin until Leipzig. ("Only late did he reach maturity," as Besseler expresses it.) What he became in the end, he became in and through Leipzig. Before approaching this opinion, we must realize that it was arrived at in two ways.

In their relatively early biographies, Spitta and Terry celebrate the Leipzig of Bach's time as a highly significant city, virtually the ideal backdrop for the religious genius of the composer. But in 1945, when Johann Sebastian Bach, along with Immanuel Kant, fell into the hands of the Soviet Union and its satraps, a completely new Bach image was called for. As a philosopher who labored under his misapprehension of idealism, Kant could virtually be dismissed. If anyone remembered the great citizen of Kaliningrad (Königsberg) in the Soviet Union, it was only when his works were exhibited in East Germany under glass. Bach and his music, however, lent themselves to a far greater sphere of activity; the authorities could not and did not want to abandon him by any means. But they could hardly continue to honor the music-making man of God, since the Marxist worldview staunchly embraces the creed of atheism. (Like any other dogma, the concept that the universe can make do without a divinity is a sheer leap of faith; and like any other creed, atheism lays claim to a monopoly on truth.)

In order to salvage Bach for contemporary Marxism, his image as a music-making man of God had to be revamped. The new objectives inevitably clashed with the old religious ideas, and so Johann Sebastian Bach was converted into "the musician of the Enlightenment." The president of the newly founded East Germany saw to this change quite personally at the commemoration, in Leipzig in 1950, of the 200th anniversary of Bach's death. It was the golden age of Stalinism. Through the president's words Bach became the composer who "freed music from the bonds of medieval scholasticism," the "pioneer of that great period of the Enlightenment," the innovator "who signified the newness that presses forward and points to the future." And he went on to claim that "until 1945 official Germany merely regarded Bach's work as a formalistic game," that the citizens "never fully recognized the great national importance of Bach," and that "the so-called cultivation of Bach" had turned into "a falsification and distortion of Bach that grew more and more pronounced."

I would not have had to quote in such detail if this program had not proceeded to influence Leipzig Bach research so pervasively. Henceforth the goal was less to gain new knowledge than to demonstrate a preconception, and Albert Einstein's hypothesis that "imagination is more important than knowledge" was proved in quite a novel way. On the occasion of the Leipzig Bach Festival of 1975 this same speech was published again in a collector's edition. Not only did it claim that up to then in Bach's work "the humanistic, progressive content had been deliberately suppressed," but at the end Bach was even declared to be a "harbinger of peace." And the text proclaims: "In his works we hear the cry of a tormented humanity that longs for peace and happiness."

The Leipzig New Bach Society had to adopt a similar tune from this time forward. After all, the new wisdom issued from a stronghold that also handed out the society's indispensable funding. And all its publications required the state imprimatur, so the members had to toe the official line of the German Socialist Unity Party. As the Bach Committee of the German Democratic Republic declared on the occasion of this new Bach celebration, twenty-five years after the president's speech: "At that time advanced musicology began to elaborate the outlines of a new Bach image that would overcome the biased views of earlier decades." It went on: "With that the whole attitude toward Bach entered a new historical phase."

But by then the reassessment had ceased to be an internal affair of East Germany alone. Leipzig was and is a center of Bach research. The political division between East and West was growing more and more acute. The sensible attempt to avoid severing relations opened doors in the West for the new East German trend, especially since its hypotheses seemed apolitical. Moreover, the most discordant notes of the president's speech recurred only as an exception—for example, in the writings of the "founder of Marxist musicology," Ernst Hermann Meyer. The portrayal of Bach's music as "the music of the Enlightenment" prevailed. In 1982 there was even a large scholarly symposium in Leipzig on "Bach and the Enlightenment." The participants by no means agreed on what was to be understood under "Enlightenment," but they were determined to champion the tag. The "new Bach image" was duly reinforced.

Thus Hans Pischner, director at that time of the Berlin State Opera, in a much-cited essay declared *The Well-Tempered Clavier* to be a "product of the Enlightenment" because it was "encyclopedic" and "the encyclopedic approach was in the air at the time." That notion was also made of air, since twenty years before and ten years after Bach concluded the work, only two lexicons appeared in Germany, and in Paris the Encyclopedists had not even met yet. But it sounded like a very pretty thought.

The "powerful Enlightenment forces" of Leipzig, whom Bach supposedly met on his arrival there, were naturally invoked. The most important of them was Johann Christoph Gottsched, though he moved to Leipzig after Bach did. The Marxist philosophers, however, failing to coordinate with the Marxist musicologists, did not even consider Gottsched worthy of mention in their *History of the Enlightenment in Germany*. And of course the musical scholars also cited Gottfried Wilhelm Leibniz and Christian Thomasius in relation to Bach. True, both were born in Leipzig, but they had already left the city thirty years before. Leibniz never really even tried to establish himself in his hometown. As for Thomasius, the great jurist and commendable opponent of the witch trials, the Orthodox Lutherans harassed him so tenaciously that he finally emigrated to Prussian territory, where he founded the University of Halle.

August Hermann Francke also found refuge in Halle, after the Leipzig Orthodox had made his existence a living hell because of his Pietism. In Halle the citizens were more open-minded and allowed him to found an orphanage. The Pietists themselves in Halle, however, were no more liberal than the Orthodox, and they denounced the rationalist philosopher Christian von Wolff to their king. He ordered Wolff's expulsion, and after that Augustus the Strong offered him a chair at the University of Leipzig. But Wolff had already been to Leipzig in 1701; he refused the post with thanks and preferred to go to Marburg, though he would receive less money there. He was familiar with Leipzig, and he knew what to expect from the Leipzig Enlightenment.

That happened in 1723, the same year Bach came to Leipzig. Augustus had already had trouble with the university there thirteen years before. At that time, when a chair at the university had come vacant, he had to wield his royal power to ensure that it would be dedicated to natural sciences. This became the first chair of chemistry ever founded. The establishment of a chair on fief law, natural law, and international jurisprudence similarly required the clout of his authority; the Orthodox had insisted to the bitter end on appointing an additional theologian. In this city of 30,000 souls, there were no less than thirty-seven theologians (not counting those at the university), a ratio of one for every 800 inhabitants.

The clergymen were appointed by the city council and came under the jurisdiction of the consistory only in ecclesiastical matters. The university, in contrast, came under the jurisdiction of the king, just as the Leipzig trade fair did. Even though the latter took place several times a year, it is never discussed in the Leipzig council records. The municipal government limited itself to exercising censorship at the book fair through a commission appointed especially for that purpose. Even ten years after Bach's death, that is how the city managed to prevent any book by that heretic of the Enlightenment, Voltaire, from ever being sold there. The council always harbored a smoldering enmity toward the university since its royal status exempted all professors, their relatives, and even their servants from paying municipal taxes. To make matters more galling, the academics were subject only to the jurisdiction of the king, so in certain ways they were virtually extraterritorial. The city took revenge by forbidding its employees to accept a university post, a proscription that also figures in Bach's contract. Like his predecessor, Bach did not pay any heed to that, but in another respect it would have some dire consequences for him.

In regard to Leipzig, the words of Johann Wolfgang von Goethe are often quoted: "I like my Leipzig. It is a small Paris and educates its people." But that was forty years later. The Leipzig that Bach moved to in 1723 was above all a bulwark of the Lutheran Orthodoxy, and accordingly archconservative. It was no minor obligation but a highly important clause of his contract that Bach expressly committed himself "to introduce no innovations whatsoever." He learned very soon how allergic the council and consistory were to newfangled ways. That wheeling and dealing thrived, that this city of Leipzig "flourished," had nothing to do with the intellectual and spiritual views of Bach's superiors. If "the great musician of the Enlightenment" had actually encountered in Leipzig those "powerful forces of civic Enlightenment" that are so readily invoked, he would have found the prerequisites for an ideal collaboration, not unlike the cooperation between Handel and his opera-loving lords in London. Lamentably, as we know, Bach's working and living conditions in Leipzig would by no means be so gratifying. And the claim that Bach encountered "powerful forces of civic Enlightenment" when he moved to Leipzig rests on a single, fundamental, almost unshakable basis: the intentional ignorance of its proponents.

14

On May 29, 1723, the *Holstein Correspondent*, Leipzig's weekly newspaper, reported the following: "Last Saturday at noon four wagons loaded with household goods arrived here from Cöthen; they belonged to the former Princely Music Director there, now called to Leipzig as *Cantor Figuralis*. He himself arrived with his family in two carriages at two o'clock and moved into his newly renovated residence at the Thomas School."

For a long time, it was the only item about Bach's work that appeared in the newspaper; he was not in the public eye at all. The city council had had the choirmaster's quarters refurbished for about 200 thalers; the rooms were part of the Thomas School but had their own entrance. But we cannot infer from this that the council had shown any great generosity: Eight years later the residence already had to be renovated again. No more than the bare necessities must have been attended to before Bach moved in. That the repairs cost a pretty penny—twice as much as the choirmaster's annual salary—only indicates the wretched physical condition of the building as a whole.

Prior to Bach's departure there had been another decisive turning point in court life at Cöthen: After little more than fifteen months of happy wedlock, Leopold's young wife had suddenly died.

People with feeble powers of imagination may think that Bach could therefore have stayed on, that the prince would immediately have reached for his violin bow once again. The more empathetic should comprehend that the prince was not at all in the mood for playing music after this stroke of fate. It is remarkable that none of those who claim the wedding music was lost has noted the absence of any funeral music in honor of the princess. It likewise was never written. In the short time of her stay there, the young princess had completely changed the atmosphere in Cöthen; not until after Leopold's remarriage did music gradually reassert itself, though not with its previous splendor. The *Holstein Correspondent* was, however, mistaken in alluding to the "former Princely Music Director there": Bach was allowed to bear that title until the prince's own death.

Before Bach could be installed in his new post in all solemnity, he had to pass a doctrinal test. The consistory also had a say in his appointment, and its members could not countenance a musician who was unfamiliar with the subtleties of Orthodox theology. Thus about original sin Bach had to state that the Flacian exaggeration of the doctrine was to be rejected as contravening all articles of Christian faith; about the concordance formula, that good works were neither necessary to salvation nor were they detrimental to it; about Christ's descent into hell, that the whole Christ in spirit and flesh descended into hell. He also had to know by heart the three basic errors of Pietism: He had to explain how the terms "Piety "and "Orthodoxy" were wrongly interpreted by its proponents, how they misunderstood the whole concept of Orthodoxy in particular, and how they mistaught the relationship between spirit and flesh as well as spirit and letter. As opposed to all this, Orthodoxy constituted the absolute agreement of theologians and laymen with the Church's profession of faith. (In the eyes of its representatives, the official version is always the only correct one.) But the most important point of all was the contrast between Orthodoxy and the Reformed Church, or Calvinism. It had been conclusively determined

170

that the teaching advocated by the latter deviated from the words of the Holy Scriptures; thus Calvinism was a heresy that led to nothing less than the loss of eternal salvation. Though Bach had previously been serving as court music director to a Calvinist heretic, he was able to recite that precept too without any hesitation. Once he had signed the entire list of inspection articles, for the time being the consistory placed no further obstacle in his path.

His official inauguration took place on May 5, 1723, in the main classroom of the Thomas School. On three chairs sat Mayor Gottfried Conrad Lehmann, Chief City Clerk Carl Friedrich Mense, and Licentiate Christian Weisse (as representative of the consistory); on ten chairs on the other side of the room, the headmaster and the rest of the gentlemen in attendance. Minutes were carefully taken of the entire ceremony, but they say nothing of a chair for Bach. The Thomas choir sang, the mayor made a respectful speech, and Bach answered with some fitting and well-chosen words.

But then came the row. Licentiate Weisse also dared to address a few words of welcome to the new choirmaster on behalf of the consistory. He had received instructions to do so in a decree issued by the consistory to Superintendent Salomo Deyling; Weisse even displayed the document in question beforehand. The greeting consisted of a single sentence.

But Mayor Lehmann was deeply offended and declared on the spot that such an installation by the consistory had never happened before and therefore constituted a novel departure from the norm. Chief City Clerk Mense agreed with him entirely and promised to render a complete written report about this "unlawful innovation" forthwith to the "most wise council." Weisse tried to apologize, but it was already too late. A welcome to the new choirmaster by the consistory had not been customary up to now, and the council was determined to take action against this "unlawful innovation" at once.

There was subsequently a sharply worded correspondence between council and consistory. Here we must bear in mind that both bodies held their meetings in the center of the city, barely

300 yards from each other. Instead of writing letters, they could have reached an agreement by shouting across the way—if they had really wanted an agreement. But the council insisted on its supremacy and the consistory on its independence. This correspondence at a stone's throw, entered into merely because the consistory had dared to welcome with a single sentence the man who would provide music for four churches, shows better than anything else what Bach had got himself into in this new job. According to protocol he had to go "behind the chairs"; in fact from the beginning he stood between the chairs of council and consistory, as a subject of both.

The official duties of the school choirmaster were many and varied. The classes began at seven in the morning and lasted until three in the afternoon. The lunch period was from ten to twelve. On the first three days of the week, he had to give singing lessons twice, at nine and at twelve; early on Friday he had to attend the worship service in the church with the students. In addition, daily from seven to eight he had to teach Latin grammar; he had Thursdays off, but in exchange he was busy on Sundays. Every fourth week he had to carry out the inspection of the school as well. This entailed living with the pupils and spending the night at the school, going to bed with them at eight in the evening and getting up with them at five in the morning (in winter at six). Over and above that, the school choirmaster had to furnish the music for the four main churches of the city, the Nicholas Church, the Thomas Church, the New Church, and the Peter Church. The fifth one, St. Paul's Church, was under the jurisdiction of the university, yet on high holy days he had to provide for the singing at the church of Saint John's Hospital too.

The choirmaster had to direct a cantata on Sundays, alternately at St. Nicholas and St. Thomas; he was allowed to rehearse on Saturday afternoon in the pertinent church. Because the choirmaster could not divide himself in four parts, for the other three churches he had to appoint choir directors from the ranks of the pupils and train them for service; these were the so-called prefects.

Since Bach could not be content with the musical materials he found at hand on his arrival, he began to write new cantatas himself. This meant that week after week he had to create about twenty minutes of music for soloists, choir, and orchestra. He had to obtain the texts, compose the music, write out the part books, and rehearse and direct the performance as a whole. If he wanted to improve his instrumentalists, he had to train them *privatim* outside the hours of school. At funerals he had to walk in front of the coffin with the students; he had to provide the music for weddings and christenings; and in accordance with his contract, he always had to be at the disposal of the council members for their musical needs.

"Now if one adds that the choirmaster, as music director at the two main city churches, also supervised their organists—as well as the city band members and violinists who helped perform the sacred music—his professional duties are all accounted for," Spitta writes. And he continues: "It cannot be claimed that these duties were very onerous." Schweitzer comments: "His activities at the school were not demanding." But both authors overlook the fact that the bulk of Bach's income in Leipzig consisted of earnings on the side and that those thalers could be had only through a separate schedule of work. Going with pupils to a stranger's funeral was certainly not "demanding," but it had to be paid for in the currency that is most expensive for hardworking people: time.

In fact I still have not listed all the tasks to which the school choirmaster was heir. On top of everything else, he had to devote his attention to the university. Johann Kuhnau rightly attached importance to his post as university music director: That was how he got his musicians. Nothing much could really be done with the seven members of the town band, even if among them the trumpeter Gottfried Reiche was superb. And four choirs had to be filled with the fifty-two students of the Thomas School. That did in theory give thirteen boys for each choir. But nowhere near all of the pupils were musical, not all of them had usable voices, and a good many were sometimes sick or hoarse. Even if he assigned smaller choirs to

New Church and Peter Church, Bach could afford to draw instrumentalists from among the choristers only on a very limited basis.

Kuhnau had already made petitions to the council about the deplorable state of the choirs. After never receiving an answer, he recognized there was no way he could improve matters, and so he resigned himself to the fact. The headmaster, Johann Heinrich Ernesti, was in his seventies and had held his position for more than thirty years. In his entire period of office, he had altered absolutely nothing. Six years prior to the time Bach took up his post, the deficiencies of the school had given rise to a general inspection. After that, in 1723, some very important changes did take place: in the titles of the teaching staff. From then on the four lower teachers were no longer called *baccalaureus funerum, baccalaureus nosocomici,* and *collaboratores primus* and *secundus,* but simply *quartus, quintus, sextus,* and *septimus.* That was the extent of the great reform.

The intellectual state of the school was on a par with the condition of the building in which it was housed. The school rules had been in effect since 1534—for 189 years—virtually unchanged. The sole difference was that Friday had once been the choirmaster's day off; that had changed to Thursday. The Latin catechism of Martin Luther, which served as one of the Latin textbooks, was just as old as the school rules; the other Latin textbook, the *Colloquii corderi,* had been in use only since 1595, a mere 130 years. And Latin played an important part in the curriculum. Yet Latin classics like Caesar, Cicero, Livy, and Ovid were completely absent. Church Latin was taught exclusively, and since the texts were of purely theological content throughout, the Latin lessons as well were little more than religion classes in a foreign language. The natural sciences were wholly left out. And although the class time—from seven to three—sounds considerable, classes were canceled whenever the students were needed more urgently elsewhere, at funerals or weddings, for example, or to sing as serenading beggars in the streets.

Spitta has accurately described the sharing out of the funds collected in that manner. "Out of the money that was gathered during the strolls at Michaelmas and New Year, after the deduction of a thaler for the headmaster, the choirmaster received an eleventh. And after the deduction of a further eleventh for the assistant headmaster and sixteen thirty-thirds for the singers, the choirmaster also received a quarter of the remaining amount." Here the term "penny-pinching" comes to mind, and we can only imagine the arguments that must have preceded such a detailed division. But salaries at the school were meager, and the other members of the teaching staff by no means disposed of earnings on the side like the choirmaster. To them he must have seemed like a veritable Croesus.

Spitta sifted through the Leipzig council records only in regard to Bach. If those who extol "enlightened Leipzig" had ever taken a look at them, they could easily have challenged Ulrich Siegele's theories about a municipal "cultural policy." The council had more important things to attend to. For instance, a city clerk was injured by a dog, and so a report had to be prepared "about the big dogs that do so much damage." Then the "brewing citizens" complained that they could not make a living what with the low price of beer. Consideration of that matter was postponed. Then the eight members of the inner council circle, the "restricted committee," requested advances of 400 thalers. Those were granted. A city clerk's residence was in need of repair; that was put off. The municipal syndic Job asked for more money and received 500 thalers. The council wanted to buy old coins. The roof of the hospital was due for repair. The council clerk was accorded 75 thalers; the head council clerk, 100. Then the "royal lieutenant-general and governor" (of Pleissen Castle, which lay within the municipal boundaries) demanded that the city gates be left open longer in the evening. That was vigorously rejected by a council resolution, "for it would increase lewdness and luxurious living." Similarly, the brewing of beer was allowed only on the condition "that it must be very weak beer and must be sold cheaply."

175

In these council records we gain an overview of small-town life, with its many petty concerns that are handled in petty ways. A bare minimum was spent on city operations, yet money was always there for council members. The citizens were kept on a short lease, if possible. The higher authorities were simultaneously criticized and courted. The council owed 200,000 thalers to the king, which both annoyed it terribly and compelled it to be obsequious. When a meat tax was decreed throughout the land, the councilmen opposed it, of course, as it was not a city tax, but then they swiftly submitted. When a daughter of Augustus the Strong visited Leipzig, the council bestowed a "present of 1,000 ducats" (equal to 3,000 thalers) on the "royal princess" without further ado. (Incidentally, although the Leipzig council referred to this lady as a "royal princess," as anyone can verify in the records, "a princess from the electoral house" is the highest honorific she would have been entitled to according to the Bach Society, and even that only questionably, since she was an illegitimate child of the king.)

What we do not learn from any Bach biography, but what we cannot fail to see by studying the Leipzig council records, is that there can be no question of a "coalition government of changing parties" at any time. Rather, the term used in this period, "city council society," is fully justified. The council members regarded themselves as a class apart. What may seem outrageous to us today the Leipzig council in its entirety took for granted: that its chief purpose was to provide its members with official posts. Whenever the expansion of the council was proposed, the motion foundered on the argument that it was already impossible to provide its members with suitable (that is, lucrative) posts as it was.

Accordingly, direct relations with the council were highly important. It was a standard procedure that in filling the post of choirmaster the councilmen first inquired who knew whom and who had said what about whom. April 26, 1721: "As Saturday preacher Mayor Plaz proposes Master Hebenstreit, who is a learned man and who was tutor to his children for ten years." That completely matches his comment during the selection of the choirmaster: "In Pirna there is said to be a good man too." As a private tutor at the home of a gentleman on the council, one had considerable prospects of promotion, as well as the liberties brought by patronage. The benefits could be impressively experienced long before ten years had elapsed; credit and protection could be equally enjoyed.

In 1845, in his essay "German Conditions" (Deutsche Zustände"), Friedrich Engels wrote the scathing sentence: "Nothing could compare with the infamous behavior of the petty-bourgeois aristocrats of our cities fifty years ago; and indeed, we could hardly believe Germany was like that then, if those times did not live on in the memory of many who still remember them." That is precisely the impression we get from examining the Leipzig council records. Bach was already able to gain some insight into this on the day of his inauguration, but his later experiences unfortunately also show us that Engels did not exaggerate.

15

RIVALRY AND JEALOUS VIGILANCE of their own authority also characterized the relationship between council and university. Perhaps it would be more appropriate to say "between university and council," since the university came under the sovereignty of the king; thus in order of rank, although it was not entitled to give the council orders, it did have precedence over it. Its members were not governed by the council's authority to issue directives, nor were they subject to the municipal jurisdiction—and they paid the city no taxes at all. The council came to terms with this but not without some gnashing of teeth. If the university sometimes seemed like a burden to the citizens, the city still existed hand in glove with it in another sense. The notables took conspicuous pride in their university; it was prestigious for a man to say that he had studied not out of town but at "our very own University of Leipzig." Mayor Lange, for example, had even earned his doctorate there.

All three of the applicants the council had initially considered for the post of choirmaster at the Thomas School—Telemann, Graupner, and Fasch—had studied in Leipzig and helped to develop the Leipzig music world in their university years. Telemann's Collegium Musicum was a student activity. The worship services at St. Paul's Church were organized by the university; in fact the whole church was under its jurisdiction. In the past, municipal employees had also held a university post. The aged Ernesti, headmaster of the Thomas School, was professor of poetry at the university (we would probably call it "literary studies" today, perhaps even "poetics" or "aesthetics"). Kuhnau and his predecessors, apart from the position of choirmaster, also held that of university music director.

This had changed: In his employment contract Bach had expressly committed himself not to accept any university post. For its part, the university did not wait for the appointment of a new school choirmaster either. It used the intervening time to appoint its own university music director, the organist Görner who played at the Nicholas Church. The council was not only powerless to prevent this but not at all interested in the question; it did not take note of it in its records. But for Bach, the new *director musices* of four Leipzig churches, the matter looked quite different. Given the extremely modest forces he had at his disposal for his music, he was totally dependent on reinforcement from the university. In addition, Bach certainly had not come to Leipzig in order to continue the musical carelessness that had become habitual there. Carelessness was not his cup of tea; what he did, he did properly and thoroughly, and this became the cause of much frustration in his life. Many of his biographers have later reproached him for being unreasonable, obstinate, and so forth. But to a large degree genius consists precisely in the ability to pursue a goal with far more intensity than mediocre talents do and the incapacity to do anything halfway. Lazy geniuses do not exist, by definition.

When Bach came to Leipzig, he believed that the council had pondered his selection for so many months because it wanted him to achieve something in this post. That was his far-reaching mistake. Above all, in fact, the gentlemen wanted him to leave them in peace. But he immediately set to work.

For years, he wrote a new cantata every week. He was bent on creating a stock for himself, they tell us. But why? Preexisting scores were surely at hand. After all, Kuhnau had had to perform a cantata every Sunday, the same as his predecessor, Johann Schelle. Are we to believe that all these works had suddenly disappeared? And would that explain why only Bach's cantatas are mostly still available? The performance of cantatas and motets was an established routine, introduced long before. If Bach was laying up a whole supply of cantatas of his own, there can be only one reason: The ones by earlier composers were not good enough for him.

At last here in Leipzig he saw the opportunity to realize a "regulated church music to the glory of God" such as he imagined it, a music that it had not been granted him to create in Arnstadt and Mühlhausen. He assumed that the councilmen who had selected him for his post would appreciate his achievement.

To attain his goal, however, he needed access to the students of the Collegium Musicum, an access he could most easily gain through the post of university music director. But that too was a complicated issue. The linkage of the Thomas School position to the university post was a mere convention, not an official mandate. The main responsibility of the music director was to provide for the worship service at the university church. But that actually meant two separate services, the "old" and the "new." Originally, worship services had been held at St. Paul's Church only on high holy days—that was the "old" service. On the introduction of regular worship—the "new" service—thirteen years before, the student Fasch had crossed Kuhnau's path. He had volunteered to perform at the new worship service with his Collegium Musicum. In the end Kuhnau had received permission to conduct it by dispensing with any additional payment. But when Kuhnau died and there was still no prospect of a school choirmaster, the organist of St. Nicholas seized the opportunity to run the new service, and the university was happy to rid itself of that half of the linkage with the Thomas School position once and for all.

Even before his inauguration, on the first high holy day of Pentecost, Bach asserted his rights to the old service and performed a cantata, determined to abide by the Leipzig rules. Görner continued to maintain his recently won control of the new service. But in

181

addition to these there were also the university celebrations. Since they had already been introduced at the time of the old service, Bach considered them as belonging to him. Again things were spoiled for him by a factor he had already paid insufficient attention to in Arnstadt. There he had to learn during the clash with the Arnstadt secondary school students that the interests of local citizens always take precedence over the claims of a newcomer. Here it was no different: Bach was quite new to Leipzig, and Görner was a Leipziger. He also received his fee out of what had formerly been paid to Kuhnau, whereas Bach received nothing. After the first six months of his official activities, Bach finally applied to the university for the payment due to him—and was promptly turned down. As the unanimous resolution read: "Bach would be turned down because he had applied too late and had no *ius prohibendi* at all." A fair amount of arrogance is obvious in this statement: The authorities were simply trying to get rid of him.

Bach, decried by his biographers for his violent temper, swallowed the rejection quietly, continuing to perform—with the greatest composure but without any fee—the duties to which he was entitled. On high holy days and eventually at university celebrations, he could count on a loyal circle of listeners among the professors and students. In this way he could demonstrate that his music was more than acceptable and in any case better than Görner's. Obviously, the authorities could not object to getting something for nothing. In December 1723, for the inauguration of Professor Kortte, he furnished a *dramma per musica;* and in May 1724, when the king came to Leipzig once again, he provided the musical part of the ceremony. But after Bach had shown patience for two years and was finally forced to realize that all his efforts had still borne no fruit, he turned to his king and elector with a petition.

There are people who think that he should not have gone so far "so soon." If he had petitioned against the university to the court tribunal that held sole jurisdiction over it, however, he would not have got very far. Its chief justice was professor of law at the univer-

182

sity, and he would hardly have decided against his own institution. So Bach really had no alternative but to pursue the matter in higher official channels. On September 14, 1725, he sent his letter, and on the 23rd, scarcely a week later, the university received orders from Dresden to grant his appeal forthwith and to "render the supplicant without any further complaint."

But the academic authorities had no intention of doing so. Rather, they merely informed Bach that they had replied to Dresden on the subject. What they had written they did not reveal. So now Bach had to send a message to Dresden requesting a copy of the university's letter. He received it just as promptly as he had the answer to his first missive, suggesting that he enjoyed considerable esteem there. And that is quite understandable, as he had just given two organ concerts there on September 19 and 20. It turned out that the university's reply was full of deliberate falsehoods: The authorities had not set out to elucidate the facts of the case but only to put Bach in the wrong.

Bach thus had to explain the true situation again in a more detailed letter. The officials in Dresden evidently lent more credence to him than to the university: They directed that from that point on the latter had to grant Bach Kuhnau's previous income and even to reimburse him for the salary it had denied him up to then. Moreover, they formally accorded him the "old post" of his predecessor. Görner was allowed to keep his position, to be sure, but now the university had to dig into its own pocket for him as well, unless he would perform his duties free of charge. As we can see, for the academic authorities this wise decision was by no means a happy ending to the story. The royal order, written, according to Spitta, "in by no means definite wording," did have very definite consequences.

Bach's music making at the university, gratis up to then, also had definite consequences for his artistic reputation. He had shown what he could do, and at the university there were people who could appreciate his work with exactitude: the students. The professors' *concilium* had suffered a defeat at the hands of a nonacademic, but the students had discovered a musical master. Needless to say, under those circumstances Bach's next run-in with the university authorities was already preordained, and it occurred less than two years later.

On September 6, 1727, Augustus the Strong's consort, Christiane Eberhardine, passed away. In acute contrast to her spouse, she had declined for her part to accept the Polish royal crown and had remained simply an electoral princess, for the prerequisite of coronation had been conversion to Catholicism. Even though Augustus was the patron of the Protestant faith in the entire Holy Roman Empire of the German Nation, he had said to himself, to paraphrase a famous remark of Henry IV of France: "Poland too is worth a Mass." For that, Christiane Eberhardine, Protestant to the core, never forgave him. She had no appreciation for the political ascendancy of her husband; she left him and lived henceforth in the vicinity of Wittenberg at her Palace Pretzsch on the Elbe, constantly accompanied by two clergymen for her personal edification until the end of her life.

At no time was she a worthy partner to Augustus; in her grim piety she was an adversary who exercised a considerable effect on internal politics. The clergymen of Saxony felt betrayed by their elector since he had turned Catholic: A gale of indignation blew from their pulpits. The king took it with composure, even forbearance, but in Dresden he had to order some of the reverends to hold their tongues when they went too far. To be sure, that hardly served to intimidate the others; if they had to control themselves during their sermons, this only strengthened their indignation.

Throughout all, the electoral princess stood as a Protestant rock in the sinful sea of heresy, and her influence was all the more powerful because she never appeared in public. To the devout Saxons she meant something similar to what King Ludwig II, who scarcely ever let himself be seen by the people, would later signify to the Bavarians. When she went to Dresden and her consort received her, he always treated her with the greatest chivalry—from which one could, of course, infer his guilty conscience. No one gave him credit for restricting Catholicism to his household and for not allowing any widespread Catholic propaganda at all. Electoral Princess

Christiane Eberhardine was and remained the example of all virtue, and because of her self-sacrificial firmness of faith she enjoyed the honorary name "Saxony's pillar of prayer." But even pillars cannot stand forever; on September 6, 1727, she died. National mourning was a matter of course.

But a good many contemplated doing even more. After all, Leipzig was virtually *the* stronghold of Lutheran Orthodoxy. Both the university and the city council considered holding a special funeral service but immediately dropped the idea. After all, on closer examination this was a very delicate political affair. On the one hand the council together with its clergy naturally stood behind Christiane Eberhardine; on the other hand it owed the king 200,000 thalers, and a funeral service might possibly be interpreted as a hostile act. The university found itself in the same dilemma: If it celebrated, would it be commemorating the king's consort or the king's opponent? Responsible authorities in such a case do what cannot be wrong under any circumstances and still leaves open the possibility of making some excuse: nothing.

But once again the professors had not reckoned with their students. Among the latter there was one who wanted to organize a funeral service no matter what, a young gentleman of the nobility who had brought his court chamberlain along and who was not without means, a certain Hans Carl von Kirchbach. He followed a path that had not occurred to either of the two official bodies: He submitted his request for approval of a funeral service directly to the king in Dresden. He duly received the royal consent, taking both university and city out of the danger zone; henceforth the whole funeral service had become a private affair.

But not completely. For *studiosus* Kirchbach was a member of the university, and after the professors sloughed off their political responsibility they remembered their right to give directives. This funeral service was not an actual university celebration and consequently did not belong to the domain of the old worship service. Accordingly Görner, the university music director appointed by the

185

academic authorities, was entitled to its arrangement. But young Herr von Kirchbach knew perfectly well how to distinguish between the musical qualities of Bach and Görner, and that is why he commissioned Bach for the job. Here was a worthy occasion for the university to demonstrate that when it came to know-it-all attitudes, it was definitely a match for the "honorable city council."

When Kirchbach commissioned the composition from Bach, Görner objected to the academic authorities. The young lord was summoned before the *concilium* and instructed to assign both composition and performance to Görner. Kirchbach, however, had no intention of doing so; sure of his man, he had even paid Bach in advance. Whereupon the professors threatened him that they would not allow Bach to perform; whereupon Kirchbach retorted that he would make the whole celebration fall through. Then the *concilium* convoked Messieurs von Kirchbach and Görner (and certainly not Bach), and Kirchbach declared himself willing to pay just as much of a fee to Görner for remaining idle as to Bach for composing. But in addition, Görner insisted on a written declaration from Bach that such an incident would never be repeated. This was immediately drafted, and a university servant was sent to the Thomas School posthaste to obtain the choirmaster's signature. The whole course of events leaves us with the impression that the emolument was less important for these gentlemen than the goal of humiliating Bach, even against the resistance of a young nobleman.

At this point in the saga, Bach did the only right thing: He simply left the university's envoy standing outside; after an hour of waiting in vain, the messenger went away. We even know the exact time of day: He came at eleven in the morning, and as of twelve Bach had to give his music class. After the servant had been ignored, the university lawyer was called upon to clarify the institution's legal position. He suggested that if Bach refused to sign, then the solemn piece of paper should be handed to Herr von Kirchbach. But there the immediately dispatched envoy got only as far as the lord's court chamberlain, and in the latter's care the document was inexplicably destroyed.

Bach faced the Leipzig professors with the same steadfastness he had shown toward the student louts in Arnstadt. He had won no friends this way, but in the *concilium* did he have any to lose? He collaborated only once more on a university ceremony: the funeral of the professor of poetry, Johann Heinrich Ernesti. The latter had been the headmaster of the Thomas School as well, so on this occasion the choirmaster's right could scarcely be disputed.

An important man who could very well have intervened for Bach kept out of the whole affair with marked circumspection: Professor Gottsched. Since Gottsched was a highly respected man of letters, Kirchbach had requested him to compose the text of the funeral song, and his decisive intervention could perfectly well have influenced the course of events. But Gottsched was on his guard. He was only in his third year at the university and still in the process of making a career for himself. Just then he was in a somewhat awkward situation: Unlike the professors of theology, law, and medicine, he had a hard time attracting any students.

He had come to Leipzig in January 1724, fleeing the Prussian recruiters. He was unusually tall, and Friedrich Wilhelm I had his men capture "tall fellows" on the street and in the fields, exactly like the slave hunters did in the African bush. The soldier-king locked them up in his barracks and drilled them for his personal pleasure, thus founding the fine tradition of the Prussian army. It was completely indifferent to him whether the "tall fellow" in question was a peasant serf or a university teacher—only the height was decisive. And for Prussia's glory, we must surely forgive him such pranks.

Gottsched had studied at the University of Königsberg. He had defended a treatise there on the monads of Leibniz at twenty-one, and the year before arriving in Leipzig he had been extolled, at twenty-three, as the "teacher of wisdom." In Leipzig he immediately succeeded in obtaining a position as private tutor in the home of university professor Johann Burckhard Mencke. Less than two months later, owing to his exact knowledge of poetic theory, he was admitted to membership in the Leipzig Society for the Cultivation of German, a literary association of some influence, and in a short time he had become its president through his tireless industry.

A year later the tax-comptroller, Henrici, under the nom de plume Picander, wrote a satirical poem about him. But a trifle like that could not disconcert him; he had studied universal wisdom, and as he wrote:

> We all know that the number of people of understanding has been very limited in every epoch. . . . But that is also why nothing is more uncertain than their approval. Who among us carefully considers what an invaluable member of the body the tongue is? Without it we could not talk, but without talking man would in a certain sense remain man no longer. Now speech is so necessary to the use of reason that we should respect our tongue all the more highly. We can all talk; only very few can talk cleverly and sensibly. We all have to talk too; but if only we all knew how to strike the right balance, so that we do not talk too much.

So much for a sample of Gottsched's universal wisdom. When the electoral princess died in 1727, he was ensconced as professor of logic, metaphysics, the art of poetry, and universal wisdom at the university. In Königsberg he had learned how to write according to the rules of reason under court counselor Pietsch, and he had also thoroughly studied the writings of Leibniz and Wolff. He wrongly believed (as Bernays reports in *German Biography*) that in this way he had, in his own words, "gathered ample powers in order to advance into many different intellectual and artistic fields with confidence, and establish himself in any one he liked." Bertrand Russell once identified the real tragedy of this world: that the stupid are always self-confident and only the clever full of doubts. Doubts cannot be found anywhere in Gottsched's writings, though the dubious is found in them in ample measure.

Kirchbach had commissioned Gottsched to write the funeral ode, and as a poet Gottsched could very well have had a say in the selection of the composer. No doubt he was not only too cautious for that but also convinced that given the academically demonstrable excellence of his work, the music was only a minor matter anyway.

The literary oeuvre of Gottsched does not exist in any current edition. At the beginning of the twentieth century, a Gottsched Society was founded in Leipzig with the aim of publishing Gottsched's collected works. But it had overestimated both the scope of the task and the public interest in the result, and gave up before it had completed a quarter of its labors. The verses of the funeral ode have more or less been preserved only because of Bach's composition. They are written strictly according to the rules and begin with the somewhat ambiguous lines:

> *Let, Princess, let one more ray*
> *From Salem's starry vault shoot forth . . .*

The Leipzig Bach specialist Werner Felix describes Gottsched's composition as "a work of high artistic quality"; presumably, he did not finish reading it. Yet his claim naturally has a motivation: Since East German intellectuals were determined to make a "philosopher of the Enlightenment" out of Bach "the man of God," Gottsched simply had to become one too, and a gifted poet to boot.

Bach was admittedly of a different opinion with regard to Gottsched's poetic qualities, for he rewrote the poem. He resolutely broke up Gottsched's nine strophes of measured evenness and transformed them into a cantata in ten movements. It goes without saying that in his composition he did not stick to lines of verse that click-clack along perpetually in step; here again he made music with numerous repetitions of the text, anticipating its meaning. He always proceeded that way. He repeated the first four lines of verse seven times in various segments, and so freed them completely from their harness.

189

But poets, when convinced of the academically justified evenness and impeccable erudition of their work, are wounded by few things in this world as deeply as by the revision of one of their immortal texts. Gottsched was offended, and as a craftsman he was cut to the quick. The professor just quoted, Felix, is amazed that from then on, with a sole exception, there was never another collaboration between Gottsched and Bach. But what use could a Gottsched have had for a composer who did not discern the reverence due to the incontestable academic correctness of his poems, and who through his music transformed a literary artwork into an amorphous hash?

Gottsched had his own high opinion of his poetic writings:

> That people in general almost never judge poetry as fairly as they should comes from the fact that they do not recognize its true value. Anyone who wants to esteem it according to its dignity must have a mind that is of no common type. It takes a more than ordinary skill, a peculiar temperament, a correct, penetrating, thorough, and all-embracing mind, a fertile, lively, and pure imagination. This lofty gift cannot be attained either through art or through study: it is absolutely a gift from heaven.

The reader will find this and much more in the works of the "spokesman of the Leipzig Enlightenment." A man of letters of the education and greatness of a Gottsched plainly could not collaborate with a man who had so unappreciative an attitude toward literary achievement as Bach, and who mutilated its creations in such an unseemly fashion. It is incomprehensible that no one in the Leipzig New Bach Society perceived that.

Bach had won three victories over the university authorities. Contrary to their intentions, he had won his fee and his rights to the old worship service. He had not let them take the commission for the funeral ode away from him. And he had shaped a superb musical work from Gottsched's learned doggerel and performed it before the cream of Leipzig society.

190   As a result of this, the academic officials wanted nothing more to do with him for the rest of his life.

The self-assured, thirty-year-old artist in Weimar
(Erfurt, Angermuseum. Photo: AKG London)

Georg Christian Eilmar was the only theologian besides Pastor Lorenz Stauber in Dornheim with whom Bach had friendly relations in the course of his career.

The quarrelsome Pietist Johann Adolph Frohne spoiled Bach's tenure as organist in Mühlhausen through his hostility toward music.

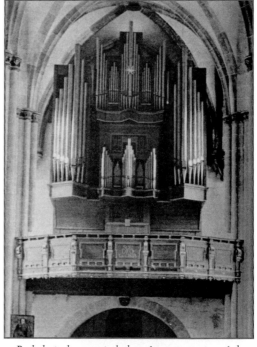

The organ of the Church of St. Boniface in Arnstadt still looks exactly as it did in Bach's time.

Bach devised economical plans for a renovation of the city church in Mühlhausen; they were adopted once again when the organ was rebuilt in 1959.

Johann Mattheson of Hamburg, four years older than Bach, enjoyed a high reputation in the musical world of the age because of his critical writings linking theory and practice.

Duke Wilhelm Ernst of Saxe-Weimar gave Bach his support at first, then later put him in jail and wished his name to be expunged from Weimar history.

After the memorable recital, Count Jakob Heinrich von Flemming, the all-powerful cabinet minister of Augustus the Strong, saw to it for the rest of his life that Bach's requests received preferential attention at court.

Duke Ernst August of Saxe-Weimar, Wilhelm Ernst's nephew and co-sovereign, was his uncle's successor; he threatened any discontented subject with half a year's imprisonment.

Erdmann Neumeister never forgave the citizens of Hamburg for rejecting "his Bach" because of money.

Louis Marchand, the most famous harpsichordist of his time, took flight from Dresden before Johann Sebastian Bach.

The interior of St. Thomas Church in Bach's day. Because of the various built-in fixtures, the acoustics at the time were totally different from those of today.

The Church of St. Thomas.

In 1721 Georg Philipp Telemann took up the
post in Hamburg that Bach had been unable to
pay for in 1717. He and Bach held each other
in the greatest esteem.

The highly celebrated and much-reviled
Johann Christoph Gottsched later publicly ac-
knowledged Bach's great importance for
Leipzig.

Headmaster Johann Heinrich Ernesti (the
elder) put up with the deplorable conditions at
the Thomas School without changing a thing,
nor did he lift a finger for Bach.

Johann Matthias Gesner completely reformed
the Thomas School and decisively improved
Bach's position. During his tenure, Bach experienced his only happy years of service.

The Dresden court music director, Johann Adolf Hasse, and his wife, Faustina Bordoni, a singer famous throughout Europe, were among Bach's special friends. He visited them a number of times in Dresden, and they both visited him often in Leipzig.

Imperial Count von Keyserlingk paid Bach the highest fee of his life, 100 louis d'or in a silver goblet, for the Goldberg Variations.

Johann August Ernesti (the younger, not related to the elder Ernesti) methodically ruined Bach's church music and excluded Bach's pupils from his classes.

The Bach monument by Karl Seffner was erected on the south side of the St. Thomas Church in 1908.

16

THE FIRST SUBSTANTIAL CLASH with the ecclesiastical authorities of the city, the consistory, occurred at Easter in 1724. In his short time in Leipzig, Bach had been extraordinarily active. People were already talking about his completely new cantatas. And we can readily ascertain how great the artistic difference was by comparing them to those of other composers of the age, even such acknowledged masters as Buxtehude or Telemann. For Reformation Day on October 31, 1723, Bach reworked and expanded the splendid cantata from his Weimar period, "Ein feste Burg ist unser Gott" ("A Mighty Fortress Is Our God"). It was far and away the best music Leipzigers had heard up to then in a Reformation worship service. The Christmas present he gave them was a Magnificat that is among his most superb musical creations. And he had intended his *Passion Music According to John* for Easter. In view of these and his many other achievements on the side, it naturally followed that the early morning Latin class at seven, and teaching Latin in general, became irksome to him. So he very soon made use of the right assured him in his contract to find a stand-in for those duties. Assistant Headmaster Siegmund Friedrich Dresig took over the job for 50 thalers a year, half of Bach's salary.

The *St. John Passion* is written on Cöthen music paper, and the handwriting has been described as hurried in parts. From this the conclusion is sometimes drawn that Bach composed the work in Cöthen and had already performed it before his inauguration in Leipzig. But that is implausible if only because of what the work requires: It calls for at least fifteen musicians, and almost a third of it is sung by the choir. Besides, the music paper tells us nothing about the date of origin; paper acquired in Cöthen would not have been thrown out because of the move to Leipzig. Nor does the handwriting prove anything; its hastiness could suggest a shortage of time or that Bach was composing the notes more quickly than he could jot them down. The latter possibility implies two others: either that the music came to his mind especially swiftly or that he saw the notation of some parts as sheer routine that demanded no particular care.

At any rate it should be obvious that after the Reformation cantata and the Christmas Magnificat, Bach wanted to make the Passion music a special event as well. The performance itself (which anyone who has looked into the matter will confirm) involved extensive preparations: He needed the Thomas pupils who were at all capable of singing; the town band was too small to make up the orchestra, so he had to find reinforcements there; besides the organ and harpsichord already in place, he required a good deal of room for everything else. That is why he set the performance for Holy Friday 1724 at the Thomas Church, which contained an organ gallery far more spacious than that of the Nicholas Church.

But this was nothing short of an unprecedented audacity. For it was a long-standing custom in Leipzig that the Passion music was performed in annual alternation at the Nicholas and Thomas Churches. In the previous year it had taken place at the Thomas Church, so this year it was St. Nicholas's turn.

Bach had very serious reasons for avoiding St. Nicholas. Not only was the gallery smaller there, but both the organ and the harpsichord (indispensable for the recitatives) were urgently in need of repair, and the platforms for the choir were so rotten that he feared the singers would fall through them. Bach had pointed out these conditions to the church authorities in good time, and they had never contested the truth of his remarks. But they did not feel responsible for the situation. Here was another complex legal tangle again: The consistory was in fact only charged with ecclesiastical concerns, not the churches' upkeep. And as an ecclesiastical matter, it insisted on the performance at St. Nicholas. It did so all the more resolutely because superintendent Deyling, the head of the consistory, preached at that church, so it could by no means be neglected in favor of St. Thomas.

Furthermore, a city council resolution of 1721 had established the alternation of performance in the two churches. And in his contract Bach had expressly committed himself not to introduce any innovations.

But all that did nothing to change the simple fact that the harpsichord at the Nicholas Church was already eighty years old and that the organ had not been repaired in thirty-two years, to say nothing of the choir platforms.

The consistory explained to Bach that improving these conditions was not its job, but that of the city council. When Bach lodged a petition with the council to this effect, he received the answer—neither new nor original even then—that there was no money available for such repairs. And when Bach explained that in that case he could not perform the Passion music at St. Nicholas, the council replied that this was a problem for the consistory to address.

The consistory now expressed amazement at Bach's complaint, since in Kuhnau's time, after all, the instruments and platforms had still been considered good. It conveniently forgot that Kuhnau too had been reluctant to perform at St. Nicholas anymore—otherwise the council resolution of 1721 about alternation would not have been necessary. The performance of 1722 had taken place shortly before his death, so it was understandable that he had resigned himself to the situation at the time. In fact we have just as little information about the Passion music that year as we do about that of the following year.

As the new *director musices,* Bach wanted to present a genuine Passion music, a great and beautiful performance. That was impossible with an organ that missed notes or kept on playing because valves got stuck, and with a harpsichord that after eighty years of use was surely worn out. If the council lacked money and the consistory lacked understanding, then Bach had no choice but to act on his own. In the end the blame for a poor performance would be laid at the doorstep of neither the council nor the consistory, but at his and his alone. So without further ado, he had fliers printed to announce that the Passion music would take place in St. Thomas again this year.

Now he had really fanned the flames. He was immediately summoned before the consistory to answer for his unauthorized behavior: He had contravened not only his contract but also an express directive from the consistory. Yet it was precisely to his contract that Bach could refer, in that it bound him to perform the music for the churches "to the best of his ability." The state of the Nicholas Church had made it impossible for him to comply with this very point.

On further reflection, the superintendent would not be well served by a bout of caterwauling at St. Nicholas either. Since Bach had done everything in his power, to no avail, the consistory would deign to see about improving conditions there itself; this had now become an urgent necessity. It rose to the occasion at long last, and organ, harpsichord, and platforms were duly repaired. But the council also renewed its resolution by specifying "that the Passion music must be performed this year at St. Nicholas." And it added a clear reprimand for Bach: "The Choirmaster should for his part act accordingly." By the way, we also read in the council minutes Bach's statement "that the harpsichord needed to be repaired somewhat, which however could be done at little cost." And he "requests some opportunity to accommodate the persons needed for the music."

194   The council demanded of Bach that he draw up a fresh announcement, clarifying that the Passion music would take place at St. Nicholas after all. But he was not willing to pay for the printing

costs again. Thus we read further on in the minutes: "At the expense of the Most Wise Council the Choirmaster should have a message printed that the music will be presented this time at the Nicholas Church." True, that was only a minor cost by now: The organ repairs alone ("only the bare essentials") consumed 600 thalers. From this we can see how right Bach was about the deterioration.

Bach supplied the wording of the announcement. It can be called civil, to be sure, but by no account can it be called very friendly: "Since after the printing of the Passion texts was completed the Noble and Wise Council decided that the performance next Friday should take place at the Church of St. Nicholas, this is hereby made known to the listeners."

Bach had done nothing more than insist on the minimal prerequisites for his music, and he had succeeded in the end. But no one thanked him for his victory. His stubbornness had brought the council and consistory into conflict yet again. The new choirmaster was causing problems for both of these august bodies; he had not been hired for that. He was unwilling to adapt, this Mr. Bach: a querulous troublemaker.

And then in 1728 the Gottlieb Gaudlitz affair occurred. To understand that, we must first know something about Bach's ecclesiastical superior, Superintendent Deyling. His life-sized portrait may be admired to this day in the chancel of Thomas Church. He was a very learned gentleman, strictly Lutheran Orthodox of course—Pietists were not tolerated in Leipzig. In one of his *Observationes sacrae (Holy Observations)*, 150 Latin theological treatises in three volumes, he devotes eight lines to music, very much in passing. He obviously did not know what to make of it other than as a conventional feature of the worship service. It could not be said to have moved him. In Deyling Bach had certainly not found a sponsor of his striving for "a regulated church music to the glory of God."

Bach's Bible is preserved; in it we find some instructive annotations in his hand to the first and second books of Chronicles. In I Chronicles 25, we read: "Moreover David and the captains of the host separated to the service of . . . men who should prophesy with harps, with psalteries, and with cymbals." And a few verses later: "So the number of them, with their brethren that were instructed in the songs of the Lord, even all that were cunning, was two hundred fourscore and eight." Next to this Bach's handwritten note appears: "N.B. This chapter is the true foundation of all church music pleasing to God." The end of chapter 28 reads: "And, behold, the course of the priests and Levites, even they shall be with thee for all the service of the house of God: and there shall be with thee for all manner of workmanship every willing skillful man, for any manner of service." In his marginalia Bach calls this "a marvelous proof that along with other institutions of the worship service music was also especially ordered by the spirit of God through David." Finally, a third note is found in 2 Chronicles 5:12–14, in which the music of the Levites and priests in transporting the Ark of the Covenant is described. Bach writes: "N.B. In a devotional music God's grace is always present."

The notes show how deeply Bach's music was grounded in his faith. But they are not just evidence of his profound religiosity; they also demonstrate how highly he valued music itself: From his standpoint it was no less an element of the worship service than the sermon. In the Psalms he could have found many more references to worship through music; it is significant that he commented upon only these two "political" passages. To his mind, judging by the passages he annotated, in church the musician faced the theologian with equal rights. This was the point of view from which he created his music for the worship service.

For a church musician, there is to this day no better stance, though it is not the stance of all theologians. According to everything we know of him, there is little cause to think that this was Deyling's point of view. And so the most important of these three 196 annotations in his Bible expresses not only Bach's deep faith but also his faithful willingness to fight: "A marvelous proof that along with other institutions of the worship service *music was also especially ordered by the spirit of God* through David." The practice of his music was a matter of deep belief to Bach, and he believed in its defense just as deeply. His entire conduct throughout the Leipzig years must always be understood in light of this supreme and highly honorable integrity.

Leipzig was a city where the rights of each and every official were precisely meted out, and he had to defend those rights with equal precision if he did not want to lose them. This Bach had seen for himself right from beginning. That he could expect neither fairness nor friendliness in the process he had learned in the struggle over the post of university music director and on the occasion of performing his funeral ode. In Leipzig you had to fight back fiercely to keep from going under, unless of course you had the right connections—then everything looked different.

The Bachs were by no means friendless in Leipzig. Councilman Bose, a businessman who lived opposite the St. Thomas churchyard, and the lawyer Dr. Falckner were not the only ones who held Bach in high esteem. There was also the tax collector, Henrici, and Mrs. von Ziegler, both of whom wrote texts for his cantatas. But he maintained no close relations with the clergy. Licentiate Weisse, who had called on him in Cöthen to make the case for moving to Leipzig, had stood as a godparent at the first Leipzig christening. But there were no clergymen among the godfathers after that. Here one must not forget an important difference in rank. The ecclesiastics had all been to university, and so had the council members of the "restricted committee" who set the tone in local society. Bach was merely a musician without a university degree. It appeared that even the Latin classes at the school were too difficult for the man, otherwise why would he have given them up so quickly? And then came the squabble with Master Gaudlitz before the consistory.

Nowadays the minister usually picks out the hymns for the worship service and notifies the choirmaster or organist; that allows him to select the hymns according to the topic of his sermon. In

197

Bach's time the selection of the hymns, for which there was a fixed rotation, fell to the *director chori musices,* so they were the choirmaster's prerogative. Master Gaudlitz was newly established as minister at the Thomas Church when he altered this practice and chalked up the hymns himself. For a while, the "irascible" Bach looked on as patiently as ever. But since Master Gaudlitz could not bring himself to change his ways, Bach felt obliged to turn to the consistory. For his part, he had been forced to commit himself by contract not to introduce any innovations, yet this was an innovation, one that impinged on his rights and curtailed them.

Between two reasonable men the whole matter could have been settled through a conversation, provided that a trusting collaboration prevailed between minister and choirmaster. But it is typical of the relationship between the Leipzig clergy and Bach that no trace of such cooperation can ever be found, which is why all the Bach biographers meticulously avoid broaching the topic. Master Gaudlitz was not willing to reach an understanding with Bach, so Bach's only alternative was to petition the ecclesiastical authorities. Unfortunately, the latter could not find any way to justify the behavior of Gaudlitz; they had to uphold the right of Bach the musician to determine the hymns and explain to their colleague the illegitimacy of his conduct. That was a bitter pill, for Gaudlitz was one of their own, and this man Bach had already shown with the Passion performance of 1724 that he always had to get his way.

The whole affair took place in 1728, only a year after Bach had had to struggle to defend his funeral ode. He had not yet been in Leipzig a year when in 1724 he had been forced to fight to have the instruments and platforms repaired at the Nicholas Church. In the following year he had to vindicate his privileges at the university with petitions to the king. And now he had had to resist an affront to his prerogatives before the consistory. Yet that was far from all. For at the 198 school as well, his right to participate in decisions about which pupils to admit, based on their vocal qualities, existed only in theory. Headmaster Ernesti was in his seventy-fifth year, and he had worked at the

Thomas School for forty-eight of those years. During his entire tenure there he had never effected the slightest change. The aged Kuhnau had simply come to terms with his sluggish regimen. At this point Ernesti not only lacked the will but also the energy to support Bach's efforts. After all, at the school there were far greater deficiencies than the dearth of good singers. The number of students had been declining for a long time, so the headmaster could not afford to pay any closer attention to the voices of the new recruits.

In his first four and a half years as choirmaster of the Thomas School, Bach's tiresome standards of quality and obsession with a "regulated church music to the glory of God" had made him thoroughly unpopular with the council, the consistory, and the university. In addition, he had nothing left but 50 percent of the promised regular income from the school, and the singers it yielded were inadequate. He was in the forty-second year of his life, at the peak of his creative powers, and up to this time his work had garnered no appreciation from the authorities—more the opposite.

So much for what the Leipzig New Bach Society called the "powerful forces of the Enlightenment" Bach supposedly encountered on moving to Leipzig. These forces would treat him to more harsh blows in the future.

17

BUT WHAT DOES THE TERM "ENLIGHTENMENT" actually mean? The entire eighteenth century has been described as "the century of Enlightenment." Yet that is misleading: It was not an enlightened century but simply one in which a few enlightened people were trying to convey their insights to those around them. At the end of that century, as I have mentioned, Kant defined "enlightenment" as "the ability to use the mind without the help of others." But far earlier, in 1670, Spinoza had called for the "liberation of man from his self-imposed dependence." No one can claim, then, that the Enlightenment did not arise until the 1700s. In fact would-be "enlighteners" have existed from earliest times, and all share a common characteristic: They have always been thoroughly unpopular with the ruling class.

With his dialectical method, Socrates proved to his followers that on closer inspection things are completely different from the way they are conventionally perceived; as a result he was put to death as a corrupter of youth. Dante was also menaced with execution in 1302 and had to flee his native Florence. Guido of Arezzo, who invented the lines of the stave, was driven from his monastery. Descartes was forbidden to give lectures. Galileo's writings were kept on the Index for centuries, and he himself was silenced by the threat of torture. Spinoza was expelled from the Jewish community. When Voltaire exposed the stupidity and shallowness of the president of the Royal Prussian Academy of Sciences, Maupertius, he fell out of favor with the "enlightened" monarch Frederick the Great. The philosopher was forbidden to leave the city, whereas Maupertius remained president as before. At the end of his life, Voltaire was even denied burial in Paris.

These are only a few examples; the list could go on indefinitely. All those who sought to enlighten others wanted nothing more than to replace a false tradition with new knowledge and to prove that commonly held notions were not correct. Returning to the case of Leipzig, an interest in the "Enlightenment" can hardly be imputed to city authorities who expressly prohibited innovations among their employees and showed themselves resistant to change in other domains (we have only to study the council minutes), nor to a university where five theologians and eleven "philosophers" always had the final word in everything.

In those times far more than today, theologians strove above all to maintain doctrinal purity—an "orthodox" faith; by definition, then, they were strictly conservative. In Leipzig as elsewhere, the philosophy professors were obliged to toe the dogmatic line. In Halle the rationalist professor Wolff had learned what would happen to any philosopher who displayed an independent attitude: He was immediately accused of blasphemy by the theologians and expelled from Prussia by the king as a result. But this was a comparatively lenient procedure; in Voltaire we can read about the innocent people in Switzerland and France who were barbarously executed for alleged blasphemy in the so-called century of Enlightenment. In fact witch burnings were carried out up to the end of the eighteenth century (though not in Leipzig). Not until Frederick the Great took power was torture abolished in Prussia—and even then only partially. In Bach's time Leipzig still kept a city executioner on the payroll.

202

As for the arts, Leipzig professors such as Felix and Schneiderheinze have claimed that Gottsched was the central figure of the literary Enlightenment there and a spokesman of the Leipzig Enlightenment in general. Their assertions depend on the premise that the reader has never taken a look at his *Detailed Rhetoric* or his *Essay on a Critical Art of Poetry for the Germans*. Gottsched did indeed set himself up as a kind of high priest of German literature from 1730 to 1740, but of the literature he described as exemplary, just as little has remained as of his own. Starting in 1737, the celebrated German actress Caroline Neuber tried to transpose Gottsched's proposals for theatrical reform to the stage in an attempt to improve the dramatic arts. But she finally had to leave Leipzig in 1741: The audience failed to appear for theater based on Gottsched's principles, and the great man would not tolerate any other kind.

No, Leipzig was not "enlightened." It had neither room nor understanding for someone who really sought to enlighten others, as subsequent events in Bach's life will continue to prove. Claims to the contrary do not stand up under closer inspection, any more than does the assertion that Bach was an "Enlightenment musician."

That whole concept is meaningless in any case. Both the *Meditations* of Descartes and Wolff's *Reasonable Thoughts About Human Action and Inaction* certainly did promote the enlightenment of humankind, but those works had nothing to do with music, nor did musicians expound them in their art. With his *Chromatic Fantasy and Fugue* and *The Well-Tempered Clavier*, Bach had realized an expansion of harmonic possibilities only dreamed of up to then, but his music did nothing to promote political or philosophical Enlightenment. "Enlightenment painting" or "Enlightenment architecture" would have been equally powerless to do so, if there had been either such thing.

Some would pretend the opposite, of course. Connections between an artwork and a phenomenon of the times or between an artwork and the period in general can always be established somehow or other, in a purely speculative manner. Some claim that in his music for *The Magic Flute*, Mozart divulged the Freemasons' se-

203

crets. In the Mass he performed in Eisenstadt in honor of the English Admiral Nelson, Haydn supposedly paid homage to the French Revolution. We are also told that in his symphonies Beethoven was combating the Metternichian system. Respected musicologists have proclaimed all the above, but assertions such as these derive less from learning than from thoughtlessness or even outright audacity. Essays in musicology of that type merely recall the legendary hanging gardens of Queen Semiramis: We raise our eyes to them in amazement because they lack all foundation.

Similarly, I can say with considerable certainty that people who use expressions like "Enlightenment ideas" or "under the influence of the Enlightenment" have never seriously studied the subject. They have even gone so far as to establish especially for Bach the concept of an "Early German Enlightenment," whatever that means. It is unlikely that he adopted "Enlightenment ideas" by perusing Spinoza and Wolff, much less by discussing them with his Lutheran Orthodox father confessors.

I prefer to stick to the facts about Bach. And an important fact of this period is that in 1728 he bought up an entire year's worth of cantatas from his cousin in Meiningen. This tells us something about his attitude toward cantata writing in general. Up to then he had composed and performed a new cantata of his own Sunday after Sunday for years on end. Schweitzer was convinced that Bach's cantatas formed the centerpiece of all his musical creations. The strength of faith that comes to expression in them and the artistic mastery that they display are beyond any doubt. But it may certainly be doubted whether they are his principal achievement. That Bach undertook to offer a new cantata every Sunday on his own initiative is admirable enough; the compositional solutions he found are even more astonishing. A different man from Bach would inevitably have slipped into mere routine. Yet it is unthinkable that 204 a musician of such a wide range of creative powers would have regarded this compliance with his duty as the centerpiece of his life, consigning the rest of his works to a secondary status.

Serious musicians nowadays, confronted with the task of writing, rehearsing, and performing twenty minutes of music for solos, choir, and orchestra every week for years on end, would indignantly reject such a proposition, especially if they still had to attend to many other obligations besides that. Nor would it be easy to find a church choir in our time that would care to perform a Bach cantata every week, with at best a two-hour orchestra rehearsal and a total of eight hours' rehearsal in all.

About 200 cantatas by Bach are preserved. The canon of biblical texts for sermons followed a four-year rotation; the number of cantatas that have come down to us corresponds to that figure fairly precisely. And we can well understand that Bach had finally had enough of presenting a new cantata each Sunday after reaping no appreciation whatsoever from the council, the consistory, and the university, but only clashes and recriminations. The school, which cost him so much of his time, brought him very little in the way of income after he relinquished his Latin classes; academically antiquated, it was a boarding school that had gone to seed and could place only inadequate singers at his disposal.

At the same time Bach continued to hold the title of court music director to the prince of Cöthen, and he was appointed court music director in Weissenfels as well. It is true that Cöthen and Weissenfels were no more than insignificant foreign lands in the eyes of the Leipzig council, but all the same Bach enjoyed a considerably higher standing at these courts than he did in the city. So it would have been far more sensible to expand his activity in those two places and cut back on it in Leipzig.

But clearly this was a point of view that Bach could not possibly adopt. When he replaced his own cantatas with those of his cousin, he did so above all in order to free himself for a much larger task. A lesser man would no doubt have avoided any further complications and used some composition or other by one of his predecessors for the next Passion music that was coming due—but not Bach. Despite the adverse circumstances he now decided

205

to prepare a completely new, even grander, and more beautiful Passion music for the Leipzigers in the following year, when he would again have at his disposal the Thomas Church, with its superior possibilities. Surely he could win the community's approval with that, at long last. And so he asked his friend Henrici to write the text for him.

Henrici initially worked for the postal service; later he became a tax collector. As such he came into contact with a number of people, and he managed to remain both cheerful and respected in spite of his occupation, which generally affords little pleasure to humankind. On the side he was a man of letters for all occasions. He by no means wrote only for religious edification; he also sang of love and wine and current events. He represented a kind of Leipzig Anacreon in the days before his successor to that title, Gellert (who did not become a professor in Leipzig until a year after Bach's death). Now and then he also liked to deride a local personality, as in 1725 the pushy Professor Gottsched.

Since he frankly admitted that his compositions cost him some trouble and that occasional verse might be inspired by payment if a kiss from the Muse were not forthcoming, he is reproached with not having been a true poet. Such remarks betray scant knowledge of poesy. Verses do not occur in an ecstasy even to the highly gifted; poetry too is bound up with work. But even under the pressure of a deadline it still becomes poetry in the hands of poets, and even in ecstasy it remains only dross in the hands of others.

Henrici's religious texts are sometimes described as bombastic, but in this he merely complied with the prevailing tastes and was certainly no worse an offender than Gottsched. Yet genuine lyric poetry full of deep thoughts is found not only in the *St. Matthew Passion* and the *Christmas Oratorio* but in other works from his pen. Henrici also supplied his friend Bach with the texts of his *Coffee Cantata* and *Peasant Cantata*, two masterpieces of occasional verse. His pen name was Picander, but all Leipzig knew that this was none other than Henrici the tax collector.

The *St. Matthew Passion* was what Bach was working on in 1728 under circumstances that would have daunted anyone else. And he needed time for it. He had not only his daily duties at the school and the many funerals and weddings that furnished the bulk of his income but also the monthly school inspections that kept him away from his composing room fully a quarter of the year. There were many different reasons to give up, but he trusted his mission in life and his music, and he still believed that he had but to show the authorities what splendors he was capable of creating in order to win them over to his side.

He did not take into account that they not only understood nothing whatsoever about music but did not care to understand it. All they wanted was an obedient employee, a teacher of Latin and music who furnished the essentials at worship services or funerals, weddings, and the like, and who did not make further demands of any kind. They wanted an employee who was content with what he accumulated in income on the side and with the musical resources at his disposal, just as they were, without any improvements.

But all this was precisely what Bach could never be for the authorities, even if he had tried to meet their requirements. To be sure, he did not try. Their standards were incomprehensible to him. He was a musician. Music was not simply the center but the entire meaning of his life. As I have said, the chief ability of a genius consists in pursuing his objectives with a far greater intensity than average people can even imagine. The most graphic example of this is the great Newton. For millennia, human beings had seen apples fall to the ground and had thought nothing about it. But that common occurrence suddenly struck him as something utterly out of the ordinary, and he became so focused on the question that he discovered the laws of gravity.

So it was with Bach and his music. Quite certainly he was what we would call a gifted musician. And yet such a gift is anything but a pleasure; it is something to which one is doomed. Thus Lessing had his character the painter Conti pronounce a startling insight:

207

that Raphael would undoubtedly have become the greatest genius of painting even if he had been born without hands, for he was simply condemned to paint. In exactly the same way, Bach had no choice but to explore the cosmos of his music. For that very reason, he did not understand how to do what Gottsched managed so skillfully and that people of his ilk still excel at today: placing their own ego center stage.

For Bach, the deeper objective was always more important than his person, and that objective—music and its divine mission among humankind—was sacred to him. Some observations Schopenhauer made in his essay "Of Genius" might readily be applied to Gottsched and Bach:

> Mere men of talent always come at the right moment: for just as the spirit of their time and its needs must give rise to them, so they only suffice for that and nothing more. . . . However, to the next generation their works are no longer congenial; they have to be replaced by others, and these in turn will not fail to appear. The genius, on the other hand, shoots across his time like a comet across the planetary orbits; to their well-ordered and easily grasped routine, his own eccentric course is utterly alien.

Here he has portrayed precisely the relationship between Bach and the Leipzig authorities. For Bach, to whom music was the entire purpose of his life, it was simply incomprehensible—indeed, it was not even conceivable—that the Leipzig authorities should have as little understanding of his music as of a sermon in Chinese. He thought that if he only preached loudly enough they would get the message all the same.

And so he sat down and wrote the most splendid, most powerful, and most shattering Passion music the world had ever known, a work of such grandeur and sublimity that it has still not found its equal to this day. Much ink has flowed about the *St. Matthew Passion*, and anyone who writes about Bach feels obliged to worship at its altar. But no one has ever recounted how wretched the circumstances were when Bach created this work or how miserable the conditions when he performed it. The premiere took place during the Easter week of 1729, and we know that only because Henrici had the date printed on his text. For the rest, the event was hushed up. Strictly speaking, this performance was a thorough flop, a flop that brought Bach an almost endless series of nasty consequences in its wake. From then on, his already damaged standing with the authorities went even more swiftly downhill.

18

For the *St. Matthew Passion*, Bach mustered everything he had and everything he could possibly get hold of. There were two organs at the St. Thomas Church, so he used two organs. If he assembled all his usable Thomas pupils, he could fill two choirs at best, so he used two choirs. And two choirs called for two orchestras, so he had to divide the one at his disposal in half. Luckily, for some time he had no longer been obliged to rely only on the town band and possibly on instrumentalists from the Thomas School but could count on students from the Collegium Musicum. Just then the latter was undergoing a radical change. The organist Schotte, who had been directing it up to now, had found a position with better opportunities in Gotha. The Leipzig council had already given him to understand five years earlier, when it turned down his application for the post of Thomas choirmaster, that he could expect no advancement there. That Bach took over the direction of the Collegium in his stead in April 1729, precisely at Easter time, proves that he already had connections with the institution. And it also demonstrates something else: that the students themselves esteemed the choirmaster of the Thomas School. Otherwise they could just as well have chosen Görner, who was, after all, the official university music director. By selecting Bach, they were deciding in favor of the more unpopular of the two, as far as the authorities were concerned.

As important as it was for Bach's objectives that he take over the post, it is far more significant that the students were giving him a signal vote of confidence. For this was not a position that could be filled as though it were merely an empty chair. The Collegium was an entirely voluntary organization; it also played in completely private surroundings, at Zimmermann's Café, and it chose its conductors itself. When it offered the post to Bach, some members of the group had already had experience with him from the cantata performances. So they were well aware that his music was difficult and that he himself was quite demanding. But they also knew that he was the finest musician in the city, and no hint of any quarrel between Bach and the students, in all the time that he made music with them, has come down to us. It is clear that he could require from them whatever he wished, and they would give him their loyalty. Later they even fought with the city council on Bach's behalf, and the council got back at him for that too in the end.

Two choirs, two organs, two orchestras—it was all Bach had, and he would never write for such a large ensemble again. This time he brought everything into play. He could depend on his musicians. Good people were at the organs, at the bigger one Görner, who had moved from the New Church to the Nicholas Church. The primary risk to the whole performance lay in the quality of the singers; Bach simply had no other choir at his disposal but the Thomas choir. A second threat was posed by Bach's commitments on the side: In February 1729 he was at the court in Weissenfels, and although he spent the first week of March in Leipzig, the following three weeks he was with Anna Magdalena and Wilhelm Friedemann in Cöthen.

212 It was a sad occasion that took him there: Prince Leopold had died, at less than thirty-four years of age, and the Bach family had been asked to provide the funeral music. Bach took a portion of his

just-finished *St. Matthew Passion* to Cöthen for the purpose, not only because he had no time to write something new but because this was the finest music he had to offer. Reinhold Raffalt has taken it amiss that for a "petty prince" Bach performed music that was consecrated to a holier purpose. But this was not just any "petty prince"; he was the best employer Bach ever had, his only benefactor and patron. He must have mourned his passing with all his heart; he would never find a second Prince Leopold in the rest of his life.

In all Bach had only three weeks for the rehearsal of the Passion, and in those three weeks three cantatas also had to be performed. It goes without saying that under circumstances like these, he could not rehearse the immense vocal sections without assistance. For this, he had the prefects at his command. There were three of them: his son Wilhelm Friedemann, Johann Ludwig Krebs (highly regarded as an organ composer to this day), and the less well known Johann Ludwig Dietel.

From the start the prefects had been the real mainstays of all Bach's labors with sacred music, as he could neither be in four churches at the same time on Sundays nor do all the necessary rehearsals—choruses and solos—all by himself. Otherwise he would have had to be not only a composer but a voice coach as well, and the singers would have been governed by his own schedule instead of the school's.

Since all this was impossible, the prefects formed the backbone of his music; for it to succeed, he had to be able to rely on them absolutely. They had to be capable of asserting themselves with their younger schoolmates as well as those their own age, but above all they had to be sound, dependable musicians themselves. Bach could not train all pupils in music equally; the prefects necessarily had to take over part of the others' instruction, so it was their musical education on which he concentrated the most.

213

The following has never been mentioned in any biography, yet it can be proved: To rehearse the entire *St. Matthew Passion*, a work of more than three hours' duration, Bach had all of twenty-four lesson periods, plus a few Saturday sessions at which the cantatas also had to be practiced. Thus the whole production was carried out under considerable pressure in terms of time, and of course this music was extremely demanding. A hundred years later the experienced conductor Carl Friedrich Zelter, who had the well-schooled singers of the Berlin Singing Academy at his disposal, still considered the work too difficult to perform (just as forty years after that, the artists of the Vienna Court Opera would judge Wagner's *Tristan* to be technically impossible). In any case, Bach was taking a big risk with such an ambitious performance, given the time restrictions and limited artistic resources involved. He had no choice but to rely on the experience of his young singers.

But besides the choruses there were also the great solo parts. For these as well, Bach had only students. Although his wife was a trained and talented singer, women were still not allowed to perform in the Leipzig churches at this time any more than they had been twenty-one years earlier in Arnstadt. With the move to Leipzig, Anna Magdalena had lost her profession into the bargain.

We can only conclude that the rehearsals must have taken place at a very hectic pace. Spitta reports that during one of them Bach threw his wig at Görner in a rage. To a polite German researcher in the era of Wilhelm I and Queen Victoria, that must have seemed like an incredible lack of self-control. Spitta's claim that Bach was irascible, repeated almost unanimously throughout the entire Bach literature, has its origin there.

Had Spitta ever been present at the orchestra rehearsals of the imperious autocrat of German conductors, Wilhelm Furtwängler, he would probably have imputed fits of temper to him too. As for Arturo Toscanini, one anecdote reports that at a rehearsal he threw his gold watch at a cellist in an outburst of fury. The orchestra members were better informed than Spitta about the nervous states to which a conductor is prey: They pooled their money and presented the maestro with a new, shockproof timepiece the following day.

Incidents of that kind are not the rule in the music world, but one must really be far removed from musical praxis to infer a violent temper from a single toss of a wig. Unlike industrious researchers, great musicians have always been equipped with notable temperaments; without them their notable music would never have been achieved. As a matter of fact, the "enmity" between Bach and Görner has also been exaggerated. After Bach's death Görner acted as his executor and looked after his family; he surely would not have done so if Bach had been hostile to him throughout his life.

The first performance of the *St. Matthew Passion* took place on Good Friday of 1729, and the sole review that has come down to us is the comment by an unidentified noblewoman: "God save us! It's just like being at an opera comedy." Scholars have subsequently tried to play down this remark in the interests of Leipzig's reputation. They have argued that no one knows who the lady was or whether she was to be taken seriously at all; they have virtually apologized for her remark. All this was completely unnecessary: In fact she was right.

There is no reason to disapprove of the word "comedy" in this context; it has nothing in common with our modern idea of a comedy. The Neuber troupe often put on very serious plays, yet they remained "comedians"—"comedy" was simply synonymous with "play." And that the lady was reminded of opera by Bach's Passion music is understandable. One need only listen to Handel's *Brockes Passion* or Graun's *Der Tod Jesu (The Death of Jesus)* in order to appreciate the giant stride that Bach had made in the direction of musical dramaticism.

It was not the musical dramaticism of Handel's late oratorios, which even today are still performed scenically on occasion. Bach's music is not scenic but dramatic in and of itself. This is true not only in the passages that are obviously full of excitement,

215

such as the "Crucify Him!" chorus or the concise depiction of the rending of the temple-curtain. Throughout the work, Bach does not offer any transfiguration; in all its beauty, it is not just beautiful music. Instead it compels us to empathize, and that is why the unnamed lady had to ward off its effects with the term "opera." Without any visual support at all, the *St. Matthew Passion* makes the great events come alive, not on a stage but in the soul of the listener. In that regard Bach's Passions differed markedly from any Passion music that had been heard up to then in Leipzig. The lady had grasped that fact; she had become ill at ease because this music had moved her.

In invoking the musical dramaticism of opera as a key to Bach's work, I certainly cannot subscribe to Spitta's views about the "troubled waters of an unthinking artistic creation." Instead I refer to Erdmann Neumeister's definition of the cantata: "A cantata should seem like a portion of an opera." Bach agreed with him right from the beginning; at no time was he averse to the dramatic, even if (unlike his colleagues Telemann and Reinken) he did not compose any operas per se. He called the cantata he created for the inauguration of Professor Kortte a *"dramma per musica."* And the deeply moving, dramatic element in the *St. Matthew Passion* was fully intentional: He had suited the strength of his expressive means to the greatness of his theme.

But by doing so he had, of course, contravened his contract. In it he was expressly bound to see to it "that the music should not last too long and not sound operatic." The unnamed lady had experienced something totally different, and her remark would not have been preserved if it had been regarded as a mere absurdity. Bach had by no means won over the members of the council, his superiors, with his music; once again he had gone too far.

Shortly after that he went even further. The performance must have turned out in a manner highly unsatisfactory to himself as well. Paul Hindemith once voiced the opinion that if Bach was able to perform his cantatas and Passions with such a small ensemble, then in the Thomas choir he must have had quite a fine resource at his disposal. Yet after the performance it was precisely this choir that Bach felt so extremely dissatisfied about, because it was not even remotely capable of achieving what he needed it to do. If he wanted to avoid a repetition of the debacle, then the right to have a decisive say in selecting new pupils, as guaranteed in his contract, finally had to be granted to him in reality.

The opposite occurred. Among the newly admitted students, only five had been deemed suitable by Bach, whereas four of those accepted he had rejected as unworthy. He could not expect any support from his headmaster in this matter: Ernesti was in his seventy-eighth year, and it was destined to be his last. He had been born in Leipzig, had grown up in Leipzig, and had gone to university in Leipzig. He had served as assistant headmaster at the Thomas School before becoming headmaster in 1693, and he had always resisted any kind of change with the greatest success. Although a general school inspection and revision of the school regulations had already been announced for 1717, nothing took place until 1723, and then the upshot was that everything went on virtually the same as before. Ernesti knew how to deal with a bureaucracy: He constantly pretended to be undertaking reforms, but he actually altered nothing, thus sparing difficulties for the authorities and for himself. In his effort to advance his musical concerns, Bach knew that with Ernesti he was fighting a losing battle. So finally he addressed a petition to the council.

As we can gather from this, he still had a completely false idea of the council's attitudes; he could not have done anything to annoy its members more thoroughly. His predecessor, Kuhnau, had submitted two petitions about the same matter and had never received a reply to either of them. And when he had declared his reluctance to perform the Passion music at St. Nicholas anymore because of the deficiencies there, the council had simply resolved that everything should stay as it had always been, and that was that.

Bach believed that if he explained sensibly and carefully what was needed to improve the choir, then the gentlemen would see reason, especially since they had been able to hear the debacle with their own ears. After all, he had created a work without precedent in the annals of music, and he hoped that this would finally be acknowledged. But Bach's contributions were not supposed to be noticed; on the contrary, he had to make his music so that it would not last too long or sound "too operatic." He had contravened both requirements. (The first demand has its parallels in music history. The prince bishop of Salzburg similarly stipulated in Mozart's employment contract that his music would not be permitted to last too long. But that was more than a half century later, and Mozart was a worldly-wise young man; when he got wind of the clause from the archbishop, he reacted by leaving Salzburg right away.)

Bach did not yet want to leave Leipzig at all; he only wanted to be able to make proper sacred music at last. For a musician of his refinement of feeling, it must have been an unending and almost unbearable agony to hear his music performed Sunday after Sunday, for years on end, in nothing but a defective manner. And it is admirable, nearly incredible, what infinite patience this great man showed under the circumstances. But patience, a long, persistent patience was characteristic of him. He had already shown it again and again in earlier years—in Arnstadt, in Mühlhausen, in Weimar, and even in Cöthen, where he had sat around idly for almost a year before considering the post in Leipzig. Why has no one ever perceived this before? Bach's enormous patience is far easier to prove than his alleged bad temper.

We know exactly how many singers Bach disposed of for his choirs in the *St. Matthew Passion;* in his petition we read: "*summa* of usable pupils 17, not yet usable 20, completely incapable 17." Seventeen "usable" students: This was the total available for two and on occasion even three choruses, not to mention the solos. Hindemith claimed in his Bach commemorative speech of 1950 that only this "chamber music" ensemble would let all the subtleties of the composition come to the fore. An extensive offering of recordings of old music on the market features historic instruments and historically scaled-down ensembles. An attempt to cope with all the choruses and solos of the *St. Matthew Passion* with a total of only seventeen singers is not among them.

The American Joshua Rifkin has arrived at the opinion that Bach invariably set his choruses for only one voice per part because only one part book for each vocal part has come down to us. Bach's petitions of 1729 and 1730 clearly reveal the opposite, yet Rifkin's completely groundless notion has actually been taken seriously by some experts as an "interesting hypothesis." That Bach in his petition had expressly ruled out such a possibility was of no interest to them—who ever reads petitions? In all this discussion no one stopped to think that in an orchestra two violinists are regularly accustomed to playing from one part book, that thus two or even three boys, if not hindered by instruments, could very well sing from a single part. But for that to occur to them the scholars involved would have had to possess at least as much knowledge of their subject as a stagehand at a concert hall. In fact Bach did not require more than three singers for each vocal part in his "Brief, Though Most Necessary Draft for a Well-Appointed Church Music." For two choirs, that would have made a total of twenty-four singers instead of seventeen. The council found this modest request an indescribable impertinence.

After all, here a mere employee was actually daring to instruct the gentlemen of the "honorable and most wise city council." To make things worse, right at this juncture the council truly had more serious worries on its plate. For example, the chief officers of the militia were demanding that along with the lieutenant commander to which they were already entitled they also be given a vice-lieutenant. The administrator of the city hospital had just died, and no 219 fewer than sixteen candidates had applied to succeed him. Besides that, the St. Peter's Gate was in urgent need of repair. Furthermore, the onerous debt with the state treasury in Dresden—which now amounted to 270,000 thalers—continued to hang over the heads of the councilmen like a sword of Damocles, and it would have to be redeemed at some point. Amid this mountain of problems and concerns—they are all recorded in the council minutes—the choirmaster of the Thomas School was bothering them with a request for better singers.

The school was already causing them enough difficulties as it was. The headmaster had died in the autumn of that year, and the assistant headmaster was seventy years old. School discipline had reached new lows, and the teachers were scrapping over their rights to the meager supplemental income. Now the choirmaster was making trouble again, and what a choirmaster he was. Leafing through the council records, we will search in vain for a man who was grumbled about so often and so unanimously by its members. There is certainly no talk of the "cultural policy" Siegele attributes to the council, but we do find that Bach's standing rapidly declined after the performance of his *St. Matthew Passion*. It had been much too long for the councilmen's taste—and worse, it had been much too dramatic. They had already upbraided Bach for the same fault five years earlier, on the occasion of his *St. John Passion*. But had he taken their reprimand to heart? On the contrary: he had exaggerated the tendency still further.

Even before Bach submitted his petition, the council had lashed him with a storm of recriminations. No municipal employee had ever arranged for leaves of absence as often as he. He had his prefects give singing lessons to the other boys while he stood by and watched. Moreover, he had the effrontery to shirk his Latin classes altogether. They failed to realize that at the singing lessons his first concern must always be the training of the prefects, since on Sundays they had to stand in for him at the other three churches. Not a single one of them recalled that Bach's contract expressly granted him the right to find a substitute teacher for the Latin classes. The central point in their minds was that this choirmaster had done nothing but cause them trouble over and over again. All he did was fritter away his time with the Collegium Musicum at the university and travel thither and yon just as he pleased. To top it all off, he had paid no heed to the council's admonitions up to now.

The members' joint conclusion was expressed by Court Counselor Adrian Steger: "The choirmaster is incorrigible!" And they passed a resolution "to reduce his pay." This meant that apart from the meager 50 thalers left to him after he gave up the Latin classes, he was now excluded from the supplemental income distributed among the teachers. The decision of the council was unanimous. In all the minutes of the sessions when Bach was discussed, not *one* good word for him is recorded. Nor is there a single indication that any of the clergy ever lent Bach his support at any juncture, in any way, including Superintendent Deyling— whom Schweitzer describes as Bach's "patron." The council had disagreements with the choirmaster? Then the consistory stayed out of that. After all, his mulishness in the quarrel with Master Gaudlitz had not been forgotten. Bach's enormous creative achievement in the past six years—the *St. John Passion,* the *St. Matthew Passion,* the Magnificat, the roughly 200 church cantatas, enough for a life's work in themselves—simply did not signify anything for the authorities. Not a single member of the council contradicted the summary assessment of councilman Christian Ludwig Stieglitz: "The choirmaster does *nothing."* That is what was recorded in the minutes, and Bach was informed of the resolution without delay.

At this point a practical-minded person would rightly have said to himself, "If they do not want me, then they can do without me," and would have sought income elsewhere to replace the money lost. But Bach's patience persisted; they had not brought him to that extremity yet. He did not waste a word on the reduction of his earnings. He did not wish to argue about the disparagement of his person, the misrepresentations of his conduct, the disdain for his

221

accomplishments, the violation of his contract. He swallowed all of that. But at least they had to let him make music; after all, it was in their own best interests. Or so he thought. And instead of defending himself against the council's accusations, he suppressed his justifiable bitterness. He sat down and wrote a precise and purely objective account: his "Brief, Though Most Necessary Draft for a Well-Appointed Church Music, with Some Modest Reflections on the Decline of the Same." It was an exact description and explanation of the minimum means he needed to perform an adequate sacred music in the churches.

He did not even receive a reply. In all these years on the job, the only response he ever obtained from the honorable and most wise council of the city of Leipzig was a reduction of his pay. But now they had finally brought him to the point where he wanted to leave.

Yes, he wanted to leave. On October 28, 1730, he wrote a detailed letter to his old schoolmate Georg Erdmann, who had earlier paid him a visit in Weimar and who had since become Russian consul in Danzig. This document has gone down in the Bach literature as an "autobiographical sketch." Bach's ponderous style always bristles with formalities, but anyone who has scrutinized this missive more closely cannot help but read it as a cry of desperation: Here a man is pouring out his heart and pleading for help. Bach surveys his whole life up to that time; he describes his family circumstances and makes a point of mentioning that his children are also adept at making music. Yet again and again, Bach's caustic assessment of his seven years of service in Leipzig has been downplayed: "The authorities are odd and have little interest in music . . . so I must live amid almost constant vexation, envy, and persecution."

Such was the true Leipzig of the "Early German Enlightenment" as Bach got to know it. In none of his previous positions had he ever found so little appreciation as in that city. He wanted to leave, but where could he go? He had a big family, with seven children to provide for. So a post as organist, as his brother had had in Ohrdruf, would never have sufficed unless he too started farming and raising livestock.

He was forty-five years old and had become a Protestant church musician once and for all. For a man in that walk of life, lucrative positions in the Holy Roman Empire of the German Nation were few and far between. The Reformed Churches, as in Prussia or Cöthen, had no need of church musicians. And in Catholic lands a Protestant would be unthinkable; there they would not even let him audition. He lacked connections with the southern German Protestants in Augsburg, Nuremberg, Württemberg, and Franconia. His room to maneuver was very limited.

As for Erdmann, we do not know whether he ever answered Bach's letter. But we do know that the Leipzig council did not stop with cutting back its disobedient choirmaster's emoluments. A good city council looks to economize wherever it can. And its investigation of the Bach case had revealed that the university musicians who reinforced the orchestra for the cantata performances were being paid by the council in the customary way. But was not this Bach, instead of giving his classes at the school as he should, also directing the students' Collegium Musicum? Did not that mean that by hiring its members for the cantatas he was providing them with additional income out of city coffers? Clearly that dubious practice could not be continued; all funds for extra musicians were canceled forthwith.

Not all the students came from wealthy homes by any means; consequently they had to look for income elsewhere and failed to appear when Bach needed them. So Bach had to make do not only with inferior singers but a less capable orchestra as well; the quality of the music he produced could only suffer. Yet that in turn would be regarded as simply one more sign that despite all the council's reproofs, he did not propose to mend his ways. It was a screw without end. The council had no intention of providing him with better singers and had cut back his pay and his orchestra alike. Never before had Bach been forced to perform his music with such inadequate, such wretched resources.

And a solution was nowhere in sight. Nowhere did Protestant Germany offer an acceptable vacancy to its "master of all masters," its "fifth evangelist." By comparison, the disputes with the church authorities in Arnstadt had been little more than a trifle. Then in Mühlhausen Pietistic fanaticism had made his "well-regulated church music" impossible. In Weimar the duke's vindictiveness had stymied his further development. In Cöthen an unmusical princess had rendered him useless. And now in Leipzig a resentful and obtuse city council had gutted his musical resources. With what was left to him, great sacred music could never be produced; that was now definitive.

The despair of Bach's situation did not dawn on Spitta, who collected all the facts so carefully, nor did Terry grasp the truth. Following Spitta's lead, Schweitzer dismisses all these mishaps as "external annoyances" and claims that the years before and after the *St. Matthew Passion* were the happiest of Bach's entire life.

On the contrary: after seven years in Leipzig, at the age of forty-five and at the height of his creative powers, Bach had sunk to the lowest ebb in his existence up to then. His prospects were hopeless.

Schweitzer comments: "We cannot say that Bach suffered because of these tensions. They superbly served his own need for independence, for he could play the consistory off against the council and the council off against the consistory. Meanwhile, he did as he pleased."

None of that is true. Yet apart from the English writer Esther Meynell, no one has ever contradicted Schweitzer's words.

19

JOHANN SEBASTIAN BACH WAS A RELIGIOUS MAN; that is what all his biographers say, and leave it at that. They see the religiousness in Bach without realizing that it is also inherent in their own approach to him. Religious biography does have its place, since biography is never only a compilation of names, dates, and events. Humans are composite beings; they consist of soul and body, of a spiritual as well as an animal component. Only in their polarities can they be fully grasped. By exercising our wills, we assume half the responsibility for our fates, and so it is up to us what we make of our lives. But that is only half the story. What comes of it is an act of divine providence.

Bach always exercised his will by moving straight ahead, as he did on his epic walks: from Ohrdruf to Lüneburg, from Lüneburg to Hamburg, from Arnstadt to Lübeck. In his art he never swerved and knew no compromise. In Arnstadt he was not cowed by the students, nor did he "resume instruction again in a more moderate form." In Mühlhausen he refused to let Frohne, the Pietist, put a damper on his music. He succeeded in obtaining his discharge from Weimar when the duke curtailed his opportunities for development. And he left the warm nest in Cöthen when his music could no longer flourish there.

But this too is only half his life story. The other half, no less wondrous and impressive, is that whenever a door slammed shut another one opened up for him, over and over again. The offer from Mühlhausen arrived when he could not achieve anything further in Arnstadt. When his "regulated church music to the glory of God" was rejected in Mühlhausen, the post as organist in Weimar came free for him. And when the duke effectively demoted him, a friendly prince offered him social and artistic advancement in Cöthen.

Relentless and unfathomable, fate robbed him of his dearly beloved wife, but after that, just as inscrutably, it brought him fresh happiness with the young Anna Magdalena Wülcken. All those are coincidences that in retrospect may well seem like miracles or even acts of providence. But Leipzig took on a different aspect. All his years of sincere effort had brought nothing more than an artistic checkmate, and no new door opened onto another path. Bach had gone to Leipzig with high hopes, and they were utterly dashed. The old adage "Man proposes; God disposes" had proved itself in the nastiest way.

Or so it seemed. As far as anyone could judge, there was no prospect of improvement on the horizon. True, old Headmaster Ernesti, who had always let Bach down so reliably, had died in the previous autumn. His successor, Johann Matthias Gesner, had occupied the post since July. By definition the new headmaster had to be a friend of the council; in its interests he would no doubt pursue his duties with greater vigor. There was no reason to believe that that would entail any improvements where Bach was concerned, even though Gesner was a long-standing acquaintance of his. It would be extremely unwise of him to quarrel with the council over Bach right off the bat.

Gesner was indeed a friend of the council, or at any rate a friend of the council had recommended him for the position. Ministerial president Bühnau in Dresden had strongly vouched for him. During Bach's Weimar years, Gesner had been assistant headmaster at the secondary school there. Replacing the consistorial secretary Salomo Franck, he had then become administrator of the ducal library and coin collection; he had been sponsored for the post by the duke's chancellor, Greiff. That is why when old Duke Wilhelm Ernst passed away, his nephew Ernst August dismissed Gesner on the spot—the only thanks he received for thirteen years of faithful service.

But a kind hand ruled over Gesner as well. After his departure he became headmaster of the secondary school in Ansbach, and there he carried out the extensive reform program he had already proposed in print before assuming the position in Weimar. He knew the conditions in Ansbach particularly well, as he had grown up as a pupil at the school there. That was also the reason he could assess the conditions at the Thomas School with exactitude. In his schoolboy days in Ansbach, he too, like the Thomas pupils in Leipzig, had had to wander the streets as a "serenading beggar."

Of course, that was not what had clinched the decision to hire him as the new headmaster. A renowned scholar, both a pedagogue and a classicist, Gesner had made a name for himself that reached as far as Holland. Moreover, he was regarded as an energetic re-former, and it was high time for some changes to take place at the Thomas School. At thirty-nine, Gesner was just the right age for the task. Not only did he have a fine reputation, but as the former headmaster of Ansbach he also had the necessary experience.

In Weimar Gesner had been a sincere admirer of Bach's art, and he later voiced his appreciation in splendid Latin prose in one of his books. We can only assume that when they were reunited in Leipzig, he must have greeted Bach in the friendliest manner. But after seven years in Leipzig, Bach knew a lot more about it than Gesner. And despite his friend's arrival, he was eager to leave the city, a further sign of how deep his disappointment and bitterness must have been. He could hardly think that Gesner's friendship would change the fundamental situation.

Indeed, in the first three months things did proceed exactly as before. But Gesner was what Bach never was and what his deepest nature would never allow him to be: a diplomat. At first Gesner did not appear to have any effect on Bach's life. But then came the mir-acle. He altered everything.

227

From the beginning he set to work with extreme caution, with calculating shrewdness. He knew that this was the only way to make possible what had seemed impossible up to then. The transformation bordered on magic. In short order he entirely and decisively changed what had gone untouched for 196 years, virtually hallowed by age—he altered the curriculum. He managed this in agreement with the council, which looked upon nothing so suspiciously as innovation, and despite the vigilance of the theologians, who jealously kept watch that the teaching of dogma would not be shortchanged in any way.

He made the curriculum of the Thomas School unbelievably modern, a model for all other schools of its time, yet the council could find no grounds to raise an objection. He got rid of the outdated Latin textbook, the *Colloquii corderi* of 1595. Abandoning the exclusive use of church Latin, he introduced the study of classical Latin and the writers of antiquity, things we take for granted today but that were completely unheard of at the Thomas School. He had recognized the importance of reading ancient sources in order to overcome the narrow-mindedness of focusing only on religion. Accordingly, to the Latin courses he added instruction in Greek.

He also realized that a proper secondary education combines the natural sciences with the humanities. In his curriculum higher mathematics, geography, and natural history were joined for the first time with the more traditional subjects. It was Gesner who introduced such practices as course readings and extemporaneous Latin tests, and his teaching program even included such innovations as art courses and physical education.

This new curriculum was revolutionary indeed, yet Gesner contrived to keep the gentlemen of the council from finding it novel at all. And he managed something even more extraordinary. He persuaded the council, which pinched every penny, to renovate the entire Thomas School from top to bottom. Heretofore, for 200 years, the city had done nothing more than make the most urgent repairs. Gesner had been at the school for just nine months when major work began on its physical plant, an extensive restoration that lasted over a year.

And the miracles began for Bach as well. "The righteous man must suffer much, but the Lord succors him in all his travails." He would now experience the truth of this biblical saying in all its vigor. The choirmaster's residence was revamped from cellar to roof; the Bachs found another place to live during the reconstruction, and the council even paid their rent. Incidentally, five of the Bachs' children had died in the Thomas School residence prior to its refurbishment; after the renovation, there would be no more deaths among their children there.

But Gesner did even more for Bach: He saw to it that with the introduction of the new curriculum the choirmaster was released from any obligation to give Latin classes. That meant not only an official exemption from language instruction but a doubling of his salary as well. From then on Bach did not have to hand over half his emoluments to the assistant headmaster for replacing him.

Gesner succeeded at yet another adroit and beneficent move. The rebellious choirmaster had been a thorn in the council's side to date; to its relief Gesner arranged to have him placed under the control of the headmaster in all matters in future. The council was glad to shift the unpleasant clashes with Bach to a lower level of jurisdiction, and Gesner could use his post to defend the composer against the council's incomprehension.

This automatically put a stop to the councilmen's complaints about the choirmaster, which allowed Gesner to see to it that Bach's full income was reinstated. Since Bach answered to the headmaster from then on, his leaves of absence were also subject only to the latter's approval. And so the renovation of the school had hardly begun before Bach made trips to Dresden—where he gave a splendidly successful concert at the Sophia Church—and to Kassel, to which the crown prince invited him. The crown prince treated him 229 in truly princely fashion. He placed servants and sedan chairs at the disposal of Bach and his wife for the duration of their stay, asked him to dine, and presented him with a valuable ring at his departure.

Through Gesner's intervention Bach was finally able to assume his social position as a truly great musician and to assert his influence at the school as well. After eight years of waiting, he could at last exercise his right to have a say in the admission of the students. The headmaster not only defended Bach's prerogatives, but he was interested in his music. This was not merely a question of personal taste; as a pedagogue he recognized—unlike whole generations of schoolmasters since—the fundamental importance of the arts to education in general. Under his guidance, music attained a status in the curriculum equal to that of the humanities and sciences.

Gesner stands out as the only superior in Bach's twenty-seven years of service in Leipzig who recognized, admired, and fostered his greatness as a musician. Years later, long after he had left Leipzig, the classicist still retained his enthusiasm for Bach, and when he edited Quintilian's work on rhetoric, *De institutione oratoria*, his memories inspired a fulsome footnote that actually had no relevance to a new edition of a Latin author:

> You would think but little of all those ancient musicians, Fabius, if conjured back from the underworld, you could see Bach (to cite him in particular, for he was my colleague [note that Gesner does not write "my subordinate" or the like] not too long ago at the Thomas School in Leipzig) playing our clavier, for example, which contains many citharas in one, with all the fingers of both hands, or hastening over the keys of that instrument of instruments, whose innumerable pipes are enlivened by bellows, with both hands and nimble feet, producing all alone whole armies of quite various yet matching notes; if you could see him, I say, in an achievement that many of your citharists and countless flautists playing together could not attain, not only, like a citharist, singing with one voice and keeping up with his own part, but governing everything at once, and holding thirty or even forty musicians to the rhythm and beat, one with a nod of the head, another by tapping his foot, a third with a

warning finger, giving the proper note to one from the top of his voice, to another from the bottom, and to a third from the middle—and all alone, in the midst of the loudest playing by the musicians, even though he himself is performing the most difficult part, noticing right away if something goes awry somewhere, correcting the players wherever needed and drawing them all together, restoring steadiness whenever there is wavering, feeling the rhythm from head to toe, sensing all the harmonies with his unerring ear, and with his voice alone producing all the tones of all the voices. Ardent admirer of Antiquity though I am, I do believe that our friend Bach, and whoever may resemble him, single-handedly surpasses Orpheus by several times and Arion twenty times over.

For a classicist, that was a truly unusual note to a text from Roman times, but Gesner was an unusual person. He had taken up his post in July 1730, and already in March 1731 the renovation of the entire school had begun. By the spring of 1733 it was no longer recognizable, from within or from without: It had become a modern pedagogical institute in a modern building. Ideally, he would have remained the headmaster of Thomas School.

But great minds of Gesner's caliber do not know how to strike a balance. He was not satisfied with being headmaster of the Thomas School; he was a classicist of fine repute, and once he completed the inner and outer renovation of the school, he aspired to pursue his vocation as a professor at the university. The gentlemen of the council had not opposed him up to this point; they had gone along with a number of things, but this simply went against their grain. His predecessor at St. Thomas had indeed held a chair at the university simultaneously, but that was the very origin of the school's neglect. Hence the council's resolution (which can be read in the minutes): "But now he should stay the course and not be switching to something else all the time." Accordingly, Gesner's request for permission to apply for a university post was denied, unanimously.

Gesner had done enough for the school; from then on it could get by without him, if it came to that. He agreed to relinquish the headmastership if he obtained a chair at the university. But he was not exactly welcomed there with open arms. The worthy professors still remembered their Virgil: *"Quidquid id est, timeo Danaos etsi dona ferentes"* ("Be that as it may, I fear the Greeks even when they bear gifts"). That the councilmen would release this man Gesner so he could take a professorship seemed suspect; the university did not see eye to eye with the council. It seemed clear the councilmen were trying to sneak a spy into the groves of academe. But the professors would not let themselves be taken in so easily. Mr. Gesner's application was rejected—again unanimously—on the grounds "that he is too close a friend of the council."

As we can see, the "powerful Enlightenment forces" of Leipzig kept their own deep deliberations, and here they had struck once again.

Gesner was not the type of man who could renounce research and teaching for the rest of his life and content himself with an administrative post, even a more exalted one than his position at St. Thomas. For example, the king of Prussia offered him the supervision of all the Prussian schools, encouraging him to reform them according to his own ideas. But Gesner had good reason to distrust his sincerity. After all, here was a monarch whose reputation was such that his subjects usually ran away if they merely set eyes on him. It is recounted that on one occasion he pursued one of them right into his home. To the royal question "Why do you run away from me?" the cowering citizen replied: "Majesty, we are so deathly afraid of you." Whereupon His Majesty lit into him with his cane, admonishing him with the words: "You're supposed to love me!" A common saying among the people was: "Nobody becomes a Prussian unless he has to."

232 So Gesner decided instead to accept an offer from the electoral prince of Hanover and settle in Göttingen, as a professor with diplomatic rank. It is a mistake to aver, as Leupold does, that he was

appointed to the university there: The University of Göttingen was not founded until 1737, and in fact by Gesner himself, which proves once again his high standing in the academic world of the era.

Most Bach researchers seem ignorant of all that. Martin Geck tells us nothing about the reforms Gesner carried out at the Thomas School starting in 1731; he merely claims that Bach "apparently came to terms with the conditions" there, citing as evidence "that he did not write any more petitions." Professor Geck never even mentions Gesner's name, and the only event from this period he deems worth noting at all is that during the renovation of the Bachs' residence the city executioner of Leipzig cleaned out their privy.

The New Bach Society in East Germany did no better by Gesner. Following up on the presidential speech of 1950 (the most significant political achievement of Wilhelm Pieck's entire career), in 1976 a great symposium was organized on the topic "Bach and the Enlightenment." After all, what had been claimed so boldly twenty-six years earlier finally needed to be proved by research results. But Gesner's name was never once brought up in the entire conference. The previous year, on the occasion of the Third International Bach Celebration, the Leipzig Bach researcher Armin Schneiderheinze had already demonstrated in his essay "Bach and the Enlightenment" that he had no idea whatsoever of the true nature of Gesner's work in Leipzig. He wrote: "Under the Thomas School headmaster Professor Johann Heinrich Ernesti ... and under Johann Matthias Gesner ... Bach remained largely undisturbed in his endeavors." In fact, old Ernesti had left him at the mercy of the council's vindictive dissatisfaction, whereas Gesner had changed Bach's employment conditions, his ability to work on his music, his influence, his housing opportunities, his entire life. If anyone represented the Enlightenment, then it was Gesner.

Why did the scholars of the Leipzig New Bach Society unanimously give their blessing to Schneiderheinze's superficial and totally misleading depiction? Why did the Leipzig Bach researchers at

233

their great symposium similarly fail to mention Gesner's unquestionable contributions at any point? Why have the Bach specialists of Leipzig generally considered it unnecessary even to notice them?

There are good reasons for this. To the University of Leipzig, Gesner appeared untrustworthy, and the city council soon became displeased with him because he "always wanted something else." Because of their attitudes, he had not remained in the city very long. So there was no motivation to remember him—he had not been a Leipziger at all.

Without further ado, the Leipzigers chalked up all Gesner's contributions to his successor, Johann August Ernesti, a young man of astonishing circumspection and drive. (As far as we know, he was no relation to the elder Ernesti.) After two years of university studies in Wittenberg, he had come to Leipzig in 1728, and he immediately found the right access to the city's inner circle, as private tutor in the home of Mayor Stieglitz. At the university, with equal cleverness, he attended the courses of the reigning intellects, Professor Gottsched and Superintendent Deyling. Gottsched in particular must have welcomed him heartily, for the previous year he had complained that the students stayed away from his lectures. Stieglitz took a great fancy to the assiduous young man, and when in 1730 new employees had to be found for the positions of both headmaster and assistant headmaster at the Thomas School, he personally saw to it that Ernesti, who had just turned twenty-three, received the latter post. His motives were not unselfish; they were the result of shrewd calculation: The ambitious young man would now be obliged to show him gratitude, and this way he had someone who kept him very well informed about all the goings-on at the school. Gesner, the new headmaster, enjoyed an excellent reputation, of course, but surveillance was called for with regard to such a restless spirit.

234   A comparison between the careers of Gesner and Ernesti is instructive. Gesner was the son of a poor country parson. After his father's death he had entered the boarding school at Ansbach, and

during his schooldays and his university years in Jena he had had to undergo the harshest deprivations. Nor did his term of office in Weimar or the headmastership in Ansbach bring him prosperity; throughout his career he remained very respected but never wealthy. In Göttingen as well his annual salary amounted to only 700 thalers; although he could live on that with his family, he could not amass any riches. All the same, he remained faithful to the electoral prince of Hanover both as a university professor and as a diplomat, turning down more splendid offers. To his particular credit, in Göttingen he stayed in touch with his former assistant headmaster and continued to foster Ernesti's academic works from afar.

Ernesti was the fifth son of the electoral Saxon superintendent of Tennstedt in Thuringia, and he received his initial education from a private tutor there. When his father died, he entered the famous Latin School of Schulpforta, displaying an industry that impressed his teachers right away. Endowed with a brilliant academic record, he took up his philosophical and theological studies at the University of Wittenberg, then immediately found the right connection in Leipzig. With that he proved that he was not only a hardworking but also a very worldly-wise young man. After he had proved himself in the eyes of his patron, Mayor Stieglitz, it virtually went without saying that on Gesner's departure he would become the new headmaster.

Even though he was a closer friend of the council than Gesner, access to the university was not denied to him. Gottsched (who was rector of the institution five times) and Deyling spoke on his behalf. The council did not object when he became a full professor there in 1742, nor when he completely gave up his position at the Thomas School in 1747. He was a man of signal gifts, and he knew how to use them. Not only had he managed quickly to become an assistant professor while still remaining headmaster of the school, but as a full professor of theology he also preached at the university church. He became virtually indispensable to the Leipzig upper crust thanks to his eulogies and speeches, in Latin as well as

German; and as a man of high standing, he required handsome fees for his services. (The usual price was 50 thalers, half the annual salary of a school choirmaster.) His wife, Rahel, died in her first childbirth; he remained a widower and taught his daughter, Sophie Friederike, Latin and Greek. He was a well-known and important man, distinguished by numerous academic publications, as respected as he was rich. After his death, the sale of his library alone brought 7,500 thalers, and in addition to his townhouse in Leipzig he owned two country estates. He had made a career for himself.

20

JOHANN MATTHIAS GESNER LIVED IN LEIPZIG for less than four years, and that period, between 1731 and 1735, was the only happy one in all Bach's twenty-seven years of service in Leipzig. At the same time, it was a time of great change in Bach's family life. Through his father's good offices, Wilhelm Friedemann, by then twenty-three years old, was invited to apply for the post as organist at the Sophia Church in Dresden, and he effortlessly won the job over all the other candidates with his virtuoso organ playing. Carl Philipp Emanuel went to Frankfurt an der Oder to study law; Friedemann had also studied law for three years in Leipzig. Of course Carl Philipp Emanuel too was supposed to become a musician, but a university-educated man always commanded greater respect, as Bach himself had had to recognize so often over the years.

The Bach household was still large enough to cause some worries to the head of the house. There was no prospect of a bridegroom anywhere for Dörte, the eldest; the Bachs had to assume that she would remain unmarried. Gottfried Heinrich, still a child, was mentally deficient and would have to depend on the help of others all his life. But Bernhard, twenty at this point, was already proving to be a capable musician; it was about time to find a position for him as well. On behalf of his son, Bach reminded the authorities in Mühlhausen of his own earlier activities in their city; he was still remembered with such esteem that his Bernhard immediately secured a job there, not as organist at St. Blasius, like his father, but at St. Mary's, where the Lutheran Orthodox harbored no Pietistic resentment of sacred music.

The performance resources at Bach's disposal were also undergoing changes. One of his most reliable singers, the younger Schemelli, left the school in 1734; the prefect Johann Ludwig Dietel, who had always been so dependable, also departed the following year; and the wonderful Johann Ludwig Krebs, one of Bach's all-time favorite pupils ("the only crawfish [Krebs] in my brook [Bach]," he liked to joke), moved on as well in 1735. Bach had already given lessons to the boy's father in Weimar, and then the elder Krebs had sent his son to Leipzig in turn because he knew that more could be learned from Bach than from anyone else. How much the younger Krebs learned from Bach can be gauged to this day from his organ compositions.

In the position of first prefect, he had a choirmaster's son by the name of Gottfried Theodor Krause, twenty-two and regrettably already on his way to the university as well. In April 1736 Ernesti wrote a recommendation for him and five other pupils as "six youths who give grounds for good hopes and whom he authorizes to dedicate themselves to the comforts of philosophical studies" ("*sex bonae spei adolescentes de commodis ex historia philosophica capiendis dicere jussi*").

The working conditions at the school, after the transformation of the building, the curriculum, and the regulations, were splendid. Bach had a decisive say in the admission of pupils on the basis of their musical abilities, the choral singing notably improved, and Bach's music blossomed. How beautifully it must have flourished at this time we can gather from the remark of the old noblewoman about the *St. Matthew Passion*. The complete story reads:

Many high ministers and aristocratic ladies, gathered in the pew of a noble family at the church, sang the first Passion chorale from their books with great devotion. Then when this theatrical music began all of them fell into the greatest bewilderment; they looked at each other and said: "What will come of this?" An old widow of the nobility said, "God save us, children! It's just like being at an opera comedy."

In the year this account was published, 1732, it could hardly be referring to the lost *St. Mark Passion* of 1731. The old reminiscence about the *St. Matthew Passion* was relevant at this time because Bach's music was increasingly winning the reverence of the congregation precisely around 1732, thanks to his improved performance possibilities. But not all the Leipzigers were music lovers. The clergyman Christian Gerber, in his book *Unrecognized Sins,* had expounded on the abuse of church music. Armed with the anecdote about the noblewoman's remark, other people would also find themselves in a position to denounce this music that was steadily gaining in influence and popularity.

Another feature of these years is worthy of observation: In 1733 Bach applied to Dresden for the title of court composer. To that end he composed two sections of a Latin Mass (the later B Minor Mass), proof of just how important the whole matter was to him. We should recall that in this year Bach was still securely under Gesner's wing. He had been released from his duties as Latin teacher, his old income had been reinstated, and his music had been elevated to its due place in the school curriculum. Gesner had in fact removed all obstacles from his path. The position that Bach had imagined he would hold when he took up his post in 1723 had become a reality, thanks to Gesner. Bach could be content with his situation at last.

Nevertheless, in Bach's letter of application for the court title we find the notable wording, "and thus deign to take me under Your Most Mighty Protection." Bach is seeking the title not so much as an honor but as a measure of protection, and his reasons 239 immediately follow: "For some years and up to the present time, I have directed the music at the two principal churches of Leipzig, but through no fault of my own I have had to suffer one injury or another, and on occasion a reduction of the emoluments accruing to me in this post; but these injuries would vanish altogether if Your Royal Highness would grant me the favor of conferring upon me a title of Your Highness's Court Ensemble."

As we can see, the application letter is in reality a call for help. A genuine friendship undoubtedly existed between Bach and Gesner (otherwise we could not explain why Gesner later speaks of him not as a "subordinate" but as a "colleague"—*collega*). Accordingly, it is very likely that Bach conferred about such an important letter with his friend. Indeed, is even more likely that Gesner, who was such a judicious and diplomatic person, actually suggested that Bach apply for royal protection along with the title.

By this point Gesner must have recognized fairly accurately the true character of the Leipzig authorities. In the coming spring he would abandon the city altogether because the council and the university had blocked his further opportunities for development. In the summer of 1733, he must have been fully aware of the insecurity of Bach's position. That Bach applied for royal protection during a period when he should normally have felt more at ease than ever before can only be explained by Gesner's insights and influence over him.

In his reform Gesner had delineated the areas of authority of the assistant headmaster and choirmaster with precision: One was responsible for the academic subjects and the other for the musical instruction at the school. It was thus only logical that on Gesner's departure Ernesti, who had served as assistant headmaster up to that time, was promoted to the post of headmaster. A very capable young man, he also had a committed patron in Mayor Stieglitz. There was no reason to seek a headmaster elsewhere. The promotion did not affect Bach except in one minor detail: Ernesti went from being his colleague to being his superior. As the older man, however, Bach showed that he sincerely esteemed him. He invited the headmaster to stand as godfather to the next

240

two children that Anna Magdalena gave him, plainly indicating that for him their relationship was more than just a professional one. Bach was virtually including the unmarried young man in his family (Ernesti would remain a bachelor up to his thirty-seventh year).

To this period we owe one of the gayest and most beautiful of all Bach's works: the *Christmas Oratorio*. It rang forth for the first time during the holiday season of 1734–1735, not as a unified work but in the form of six separate cantatas, performed between December 25 and January 6. That has inspired various authors to claim that the cantatas are entirely without connection to one another, and so no "oratorio" can be said to exist at all. The awkward thing about this conclusion is that not a soul would notice the inconsistency during a full performance, since the "disjointed" cantatas join together seamlessly. On the contrary, it is separate performances that spoil the great arc of the whole.

As the oratorio makes clear, Bach, the great contrapuntist and harmonist, was an incomparable musical architect as well. (Schleuning has examined the astounding architecture of which he was capable in the *Art of Fugue,* and along the way he reaches some conclusions that are equally astonishing.)

Discussions of the *Christmas Oratorio* always stress that Bach subsumed other compositions into it, ones he had not written for church purposes at all but for highly secular occasions—above all the homage cantatas to the new king and elector Augustus III. Schweitzer believed that Bach created the *Christmas Oratorio* only "so that the most beautiful pieces from the 'Wahl des Herkules' ['Choice of Hercules'] and the homage cantata 'Tönet, ihr Pauken' ['Sound, Ye Drums'] would not go to waste." A woman who for many years exercised considerable power at the Ministry of Culture in the defunct government of East Germany denied any religiosity whatsoever to the work. She characterized it as a "high statement of human self-awareness" and averred that with it Bach had proved yet again that he was "a great figure of the German 241

Enlightenment." It was probably the tragedy of her life that she could not make him into an out-and-out atheist. That she was by no means alone in sounding this note shows what momentous achievements East German musicology was capable of, at least in the margins of the discipline.

More important, this feature of the oratorio draws our attention to the frequently mentioned "parody procedure" in Bach. It is nothing unusual for a composition of his to reappear in a different context, for him to employ it more than once. In this he differs from other composers of the period, who preferred to write something new each time, though their efforts were nowhere near as long-lasting, partly because they did not have as much to invest in their work as Bach in terms of both musical substance and skill. Bach always invested a great deal of himself in his compositions. Whatever he fashioned, he fashioned with the greatest solidity. He simply could not do sloppy work or go easy on himself; when he composed, he composed with the utmost intensity. Thus what he achieved justifiably seemed too good to him to throw away. For the most part, architects are outlived by their buildings; painters' creations remain visible to the eye. The sound of a composition dies away, and yet there was more than a little art and accomplishment in its creation—so why not let it sound forth again?

Schweitzer was of the view that we would do better to perform the secular cantatas that underlie it instead of the *Christmas Oratorio,* since he believed that the music had a far closer connection to the original texts. But in all the great Bach arias the music is never there for the text. Rather, the text is always there for the music, and the music has indisputably been elevated into a much higher framework in the *Christmas Oratorio* than it had occupied in the *Choice of Hercules.* By employing the same passages again in the *Christmas Oratorio,* Bach 242 rededicated them to a loftier purpose, and they proved themselves to be fully worthy of that purpose. There are numerous examples in his work where he reutilized secular music for sacred ends, but there are no examples of the reverse phenomenon: What he had conse-crated to the worship service, he did not carry back out into the world again. (Similarly, flowers are drawn from the light of the out-side world into the church, but it would be a terrible profanation to take one from the altar and stick it in one's buttonhole.)

Above and beyond all the practical expediency of reusing music, there was as well a more fundamental reason for doing so: the safe-keeping of creative achievement. Bach is one of those composers who maintain a special attachment to their work because they have "succeeded" at something while writing it—they have solved a self-imposed problem with which they became deeply involved as soon as they jotted down the initial idea.

Is it not astounding and almost incredible that Haydn, who cre-ated so much music in his life, could still draw up a list of his works from memory at seventy, and in the process remember almost every single one of his themes? He had wrestled with those ideas, had tried out each of their possibilities, had come to a stop at dead ends and barreled down open roads with them, had brought them to the summit of their potential and then to their blissful end. And as they evolved, they had become a part of him.

The glimmer of an idea, though it first has to dawn on one, is already a great deal, to be sure, and yet by itself it is still nothing at all. It cannot live out of itself, but at the same time it already makes its own claims, bows to them, and struggles against any further de-velopment. And in the case of Bach's music, it does not merely pre-sent one melody with its accompanying harmony, for all the melodic voices make their demands at the same time. And all this skill was supposed to manifest itself for a mere twenty minutes, only once and never again?

Bach had no reason not to reuse his music. He did not do so ar-bitrarily but according to the good sense that was inherent to his nature. In the "Choice of Hercules," the lullaby of sensuality was quickly exhausted as an allegory. Only as a lullaby for the just-born Son of God did it attain permanence. And Picander's new words 243 went far beyond the original text in depth and beauty. After "Sleep, my dearest, enjoy thy rest" came originally "Taste the joy of the lusty breast, and know no bounds." In the oratorio it read: "Refresh the breast, experience the joy where we gladden our hearts." Schweitzer's claim that parts of the new libretto are "totally colorless and could never have given rise to such music of themselves" is incorrect. Surely in order to compose a lullaby to such jarring phrases as "Follow the lure of inflamed thoughts" one must be utterly uninterested in the text.

Henrici had to create new words for music that already existed. Not just anyone could have carried out that task, and he introduced many a beautiful thought into the Baroque formulations. Schweitzer does him a grievous wrong when he judges, "One is surprised that the master felt attracted to such an unrefined and unpleasant person." To Henrici's credit we may point out that this supposedly "unpleasant person" remained bound by friendship to Bach in all those years when the council, the school, the university, and the church authorities had long since distanced themselves from him.

Unfortunately, it cannot be said that the biographers who so admire Bach's greatness have treated him with equal friendliness: Even the word "civility" would be unsuitable where they are concerned. Rueger claims in all seriousness: "If he had evinced only an iota of deference or at least respect towards the council members, he would certainly have been spared a great deal of trouble." But he does not cite any examples of where this might have changed anything.

For the biographers, all Bach's negative traits would come to light in the "prefect quarrel" with Ernesti, of which Schweitzer contends that Bach "made a mountain out of a molehill through his precipitate blindness." But when we delve a little more deeply into the course of events at that time, the affair takes on quite a different coloring, as we will see in the following chapter.

244   But first we should take a closer look at Bach's endeavors to cultivate his Dresden connections. With assiduous energy, he strove to maintain his standing at the Dresden court. A great deal had

changed there. The old ruling minister, Count Flemming, whose favor Bach had won in 1717 through his brilliant recital after Marchand's departure, had died in 1729, and Augustus the Strong had passed away in February 1733. Flemming's successor was Imperial Count Heinrich von Brühl, who had started as Augustus's personal page and then became chamberlain. In 1731 he was named ruling minister, and after the death of his king it was he who exercised the real power behind the throne in Saxony and Poland.

It is regrettable that Augustus the Strong's successor, his son of the same name, did not possess the sovereign personality of his father. But his father was still able to wed him to a daughter of Emperor Franz I, a cousin of Maria Theresa. After all, the Saxon elector was the premier electoral prince of the empire and the emperor's deputy, so close connections with the Habsburg dynasty were only natural. Frederick the Great would consider it his right in the Silesian Wars to invade Saxony without declaring war and to wring the costs of his campaign from that prosperous country. But that story will have bearing only on a later stage of Bach's biography.

Like his father, Augustus III enjoyed going to Leipzig. The music of homage on such occasions lay in Bach's hands, and he strove to do his best. The opening chorus of the *Christmas Oratorio* was originally composed for a homage cantata to the king that began, "Sound, you drums; sing out, trumpets!" Bach did not limit himself to homage cantatas in Leipzig; he also took care that he was remembered in Dresden. He was well acquainted with several of the soloists of the Dresden court orchestra, and he was a close friend of the famous Hasse, who held sway over the court opera, and his no less famous wife, the singer Faustina Bordoni. Both visited him in Leipzig, just as he was fond of visiting the Dresden court opera with his son Friedemann in order "to hear the pretty little songs." 245 This proves once again that the great church musician was by no means averse to music "for the recreation of the mind," in other words light music. We also know of a two-hour recital by Bach in 1731 on the Silbermann organ at the Dresden Sophia Church. Friedemann became organist there in 1733 through his own great skill, no doubt, but his father's influence certainly did not hurt.

Bach submitted his petition for the title of court composer shortly after Augustus III took power, so there is some connection between the two events. Despite the favor he must have won with his great cantatas of homage, Bach's request remained in the balance for the moment, perhaps because of the king's concerns about his own status. Through Brühl's adroitness, in January 1734 Augustus III had duly been elected king of Poland, like his father before him, but an opposing French faction in the Sejm countered his claim by putting forward the Pole Stanislas Leszczyński as king. It was not a question of national pride but a purely political decision; the French influence on Polish history in that period is not to be underestimated. In this case, however, it did not prevail, and Stanislas Leszczyński was driven from the country. From 1736 onward it was settled once and for all that the only rightful king of Poland was the Saxon Augustus III.

In this year Bach certainly needed the protection afforded by a court title more urgently than ever. The "prefects war" had broken out.

21

Wars do not erupt like volcanoes. One of the reasons Emperor Franz Joseph started World War I—with Emperor Wilhelm backing him up—was because it offered a welcome chance to absorb the kingdom of Serbia into Austrian territory. The matter began with an ultimatum that had been meticulously reworded so as to ensure it would be rejected. The death of the heir to the throne and his consort was deeply regrettable, but it was a convenient motive for launching an attack.

The prefects quarrel did not erupt like a volcano either; it can be shown to have been carefully prepared months in advance. The misconduct of the prefect Krause offered nothing more than the desired pretext. The quarrel has been referred to many times and described in exhaustive detail. Spitta gives an almost day-by-day account of the successive incidents. The clergyman Johann Friedrich Köhler conveys it in the most concise form in his *History of the Leipzig Schools* of 1776:

> He [Bach] fell out with Ernesti completely. The occasion was the following. Ernesti dismissed Krause, the general prefect, for having punished one of the younger pupils too vigorously, expelled him from school when he fled the premises, and selected another student as general prefect in his place—a prerogative that really belongs to the choir-

master, whom the general prefect has to represent. Because the student chosen was of no use in performing church music, Bach made a different selection. Recriminations arose between him and Ernesti, and the two became enemies from that time forward.

That is all the text has to say. But after "the Enlightenment" came to the fore in Bach studies, the prefect quarrel was reinterpreted accordingly and portrayed as a tragic clash between two of its greatest proponents. In fact the claim that Bach was advancing the Enlightenment with his *Christmas Oratorio* is no more sensible than the assertion that Ford built his car in honor of the U.S. president. But ever since Wilhelm Pieck's presidential speech the Enlightenment had seemed like the most obvious means of wresting Bach away from the church. And since Gesner was undesirable as a witness for the Leipzig Enlightenment (see the minutes of the 1976 Leipzig symposium "Bach and the Enlightenment") because council and university had virtually driven him out of the city, from then on the anointed representative of the Enlightenment was inevitably the younger Ernesti. With that we now had two great pioneers of the Enlightenment side by side, and their tragedy was that they were at war with one another, even though they were both fighting on the same side of the barricade. To be sure, there was no barricade at all in the Leipzig of that time (unless it was one against the Enlightenment), but it all made for a very pretty picture. It placed both Bach and Ernesti in a positive light and seemed convincing on top of that.

The only drawback is that the tale is a pure fabrication; it has absolutely nothing to do with the truth. Bach was just as much a man of the Enlightenment as the goldsmith Dinglinger or the architects Pöppelmann and Bähr in Dresden, and to compare him with these three contemporaries of his does not belittle him. It only points to the fact that just possibly artists have something different to achieve from philologists and philosophers.

Another explanation of the prefect quarrel has been offered as well: that in this period the increasing division of the academic cur-

248

riculum from the musical program corresponded to the "spirit of the times." That is what Spitta and Schweitzer asserted—and after that "Enlightenment" and the "spirit of the times" went admirably hand in hand. The "spirit of the times" is a very compliant creature that can always be summoned to stand in when we do not have the facts at our fingertips: "Johann Sebastian Bach met a demand of the times with his 'Well-Tempered Clavier'" (Besseler); "the encyclopedic was in the air at the time, you might say" (Pischner); "a new age was dawning" (Schweitzer). That kind of statement makes it sound as though an author knows whole epochs of history in such detail that he can survey them summarily, whereas in reality he can speak only summarily because he has not researched the factual details at all. (Which led Goethe to remark, "What you gentlemen call the spirit of the times is usually only your own spirit, in which the times are reflected.")

In the case of the Thomas School, despite the rapid progress of the sciences and the expansion of the curriculum, the cultivation of music persists there to this day, and in fact "the times" at no time required a downplaying of the musical component. If we think of other schools for choirboys today, whether in Dresden or Vienna or anywhere else, the same holds true, although the academic demands since Bach's time have if anything increased.

As headmaster, Ernesti in any case made a somewhat peculiar contribution to the academic activities of the Thomas School: He reduced the curriculum. He cut back on the teaching of Greek because he had an aversion to it and considered it unimportant. Then he pared down the classes in mathematics, getting rid of algebra and limiting the instruction to geometry and arithmetic. His strong point and primary interest (apart from theology) was Latin. But in that domain he opened his own classes only to upper-level students who already possessed a large stock of knowledge; he did not wish to teach beginners in the language. "He was not well disposed to- 249 wards what one habitually calls 'fine literature' after the example of the French," writes his biographer Friedrich August Eckstein in the

General German Biography. That is why he also diminished the Latin curriculum and threw out the Roman poets like Ovid and Virgil.

On what grounds the Bach biographers can describe him as an advocate of the "academic school" thus remains somewhat mysterious; it seems obvious that they need to look into the matter a little more closely. Incidentally, they all report that Ernesti punished the prefect Krause too harshly for his misconduct. The only thing we miss in all these accounts is the question: *Why* did he do so? After all, Ernesti is not known to have been such a severe brute otherwise; on the contrary, it is reported that under his headmastership school discipline became much too lenient.

But again, all these biographers focus their attention only on Bach. Why has no one scrutinized headmaster Ernesti? Eckstein wrote a vivid biography of the man; why has no one bothered to read it? Among other things we find the remarkable observation there: "He was not well disposed towards the singing institution that flourished among the students under Bach because as an enemy of church music, he found that it detracted from academic studies." So he was what one has to call an "unmusical" man, paralleling the "unmusical" princess of Cöthen. He was fundamentally opposed to musical education.

To Ernesti the curriculum as it stood was certainly not congenial. Gesner had established its academic and musical components as having equal rights. For that reason, his assistant headmaster and his choirmaster also had equal rights. That is how Bach's music was able to develop; he could draw to the school a choir of gifted singers whom he could train as befitted their talents. This was the foundation of his success. Nor had the Collegium Musicum of the university by any means become worse under his direction. Thus at Easter 1736 he could even risk a new performance of the *St. Matthew Passion,* and no spiteful remarks about it are recorded from that year. Whenever the king came to visit, Bach was also able to present something splendid before a still broader public. All the conditions were fulfilled for his reputation and renown to increase considerably at this time.

Ernesti had been extremely ambitious since his earliest youth, as is conspicuously revealed by his career. He could not possibly have derived much pleasure from the fact that Gesner treated the choirmaster as his equal. And once he was headmaster and Bach had become his subordinate, he still had to stand by and see his inferior accumulating kudos. To make matters even more galling, Ernesti held music in the lowest esteem, yet it was precisely through his music that Bach was eclipsing him. It was nothing unusual for pupils to apply to the Thomas School for no other reason than to study music with Bach. Through it all the composer, in his jovial and upright way, remained extremely friendly and accommodating toward his superior, who was twenty years his junior. In fact he was friendly and accommodating to everyone; that is widely attested. Bach must have felt a genuine trust in the headmaster, otherwise he would not have invited him to stand as godfather twice in a row.

In that, however, he was subject to a fatal error: Ernesti had grown jealous of Bach's popularity. We know from his association with the Collegium Musicum that Bach was really well liked by young people. Ernesti did not enjoy this good fortune. Of his university lectures, his biographer notes: "Conciseness and clarity commended them; they were not characterized by liveliness." And about his sermons at the university church: "The composition of the sermons in German caused him a great deal of trouble, but he did not please the congregation because he lacked geniality and warmth." Bach possessed both; later too, pupils would continue to flock to him. Taken all in all, this was a highly unequal situation: The choirmaster was far more generally appreciated than his headmaster. It was only to be expected that Ernesti's envy would be aroused. If he did not take action, all his hopes for preeminence were dashed: The choirmaster had stolen the show from him.

But it would not be easy to redress the balance. Since Gesner's reorganization, the council had no more complaints about Bach, and he gave no cause for criticism at the school either. Indeed, he even set great store by a friendly relationship with his young superior.

It would be necessary for Ernesti to proceed with caution. In order to suppress the unwanted musical activities at the school, music had to be spoiled for Bach in general. If he could no longer perform his music well, its influence would recede and Bach's own prestige would dwindle accordingly. An elegant character assassination was called for; the attitudes of Bach's biographers have subsequently proved that Ernesti pulled it off to perfection.

The prefects were the key; they were the mainstays of Bach's sacred music. Without them he could not cope with the task of providing for the performance of cantatas at four different churches Sunday after Sunday. Bach himself was not open to personal attack; he was too loyal to the headmaster for that. But Ernesti could strike him a devastating blow by getting at his prefects. As the events would show, Ernesti was already determined to do that in November 1735. In order to carry out the plan, the only thing missing was an appropriate pretext for war, something on the order of the assassination of the heir to the Austrian throne. Of course it could be a far slighter event; what mattered was to make something out of it. When some misconduct on the part of the student Gottlieb Theodor Krause came to his attention, Ernesti saw that his time had come.

The duties performed by Bach's prefects were not only musical but also disciplinary. Without discipline no choir can produce adequate singing, and the pupils in Bach's choirs were not always enthusiastic musicians, much less paragons of good behavior. Young people between twelve and sixteen are notoriously difficult for educators to deal with from time to time. Krause was Bach's first prefect, the "general prefect." In the choir he directed, there was one genuine brat who was causing him a lot of trouble and about whose conduct the congregation had already complained. Then at a wedding service in the spring of 1736, his malicious disruptions became so terrible that Krause felt he had no other recourse but to take him out and thrash him.

252

But he had picked the wrong person, for Kastner (such was his name) was the son of the tax collection director at the silver mines of Freiberg. Backed by a father of that importance, he was not about to swallow a beating from an older student, no matter who was in the right. Kastner complained to the headmaster; he said he had been struck so hard that his back had bled.

Neither the school barber-surgeon nor his assistant could detect any wound, but that did not matter. The main point was that Headmaster Ernesti had found his opportunity at last. He was not deterred when Krause apologized, expressing regret for his harsh and precipitate action. The headmaster ruthlessly condemned him to a public caning before the assembled school. That was the most terrible punishment that a headmaster could mete out. The last time it had been applied was eighteen years earlier, and after that the delinquent had never been able to show his face in the city again.

What nobody has emphasized up to now is that this severe punishment did not correspond at all to the gravity of Krause's offense. After all, beatings at school were completely customary in those times; they were virtually part of the instruction. The cane was a perfectly ordinary instrument of power in the hands of the teacher. In the lower levels of secondary schools in the first third of the twentieth century, the cane was still wielded every now and then; there was at least a sharp thump on the head when attention waned. Krause had perhaps hit too hard, but he had done nothing abnormal by the standards of the day. At most a reprimand would have been appropriate, along with disciplinary measures not only toward Kastner but his accomplices in provoking Krause's reaction in the first place. Yet Kastner and all the other boys got off scot-free; clearly, Ernesti was aiming only at the removal of Bach's general prefect.

The misconduct had occurred not at the school but at the church, in Bach's area of competence. All the same, Ernesti imposed the devastating sentence without even consulting the choirmaster. And he also saw to it right away that Bach had no opportunity to confer with him. As soon as he pronounced his judgment, he went out of town until the morning when the punishment was due to be carried out. In addition, he cautiously withdrew any authority from his deputy, the assistant headmaster Dresig, to intervene in the matter.

Krause had been a reliable and capable young man up to then. When Bach learned about the furor—from Krause, not from his headmaster—he cannot have been anything but stunned. And by his absence the headmaster had taken away from him any possibility of resolving the situation.

Krause wrote a petition to the council in which he expressly apologized for the incident. But that did not help him at all, and in the end it all boiled down to this: He could submit to the public caning or evade it by fleeing the school. His reputation was ruined either way, so he chose to abscond. When the headmaster reappeared on the appointed day (and not a day earlier), Krause was no longer there. Ernesti had successfully put to flight the invaluable mainstay of Bach's sacred music.

After his coup, the headmaster was finally available to voice his deep regrets to Bach: what an unfortunate conspiracy of circumstances and what a lamentable mistake on the part of Assistant Headmaster Dresig. Since Krause had not let himself be thrashed, Ernesti confiscated all the student's possessions, including his savings. They amounted to 30 thalers, a lot of money for a young man, and Ernesti had no right to them whatsoever. The council must have brought that home to him, for Krause turned to it with a second petition, and Ernesti was obliged to comply by returning the student's property. He immediately made use of the occasion to show Bach that he was fundamentally a warmhearted man, willing to forgive.

254   He had long known how to preserve this mask of friendship superbly; anyone who wants to take somebody in must pick a propitious time to get at him. What mattered was to foist off on Bach as

unfit a prefect as possible in place of a competent one. Ernesti had him pegged already. His name was also Krause, and he was now the third prefect, the one at St. Peter's; only the weaker singers were assigned to that church anyway, so there was not much damage that he could do.

Six months earlier Ernesti had found the ideal moment for a decisive negotiation with Bach regarding this point—which shows just how long he had been preparing his attack. He and Bach were riding home in November 1735 in a good mood after a wedding feast, in perfect harmony together. In that context, when the discussion must have made a purely theoretical impression, he proposed Krause II to Bach as a successor to Krause I in the post of first prefect.

Bach had misgivings, but Ernesti could argue that Krause II had a right to the position as the senior member of the prefect staff. Bach saw no reason to protest vigorously at that late hour, since it was a mere private chat and anyway the matter was not yet ripe for making any decision, so he did not voice anything more than some cooperative reservations. But Ernesti had already attained what he was after.

Johann Gottlob Krause—Krause II—had anything but a good reputation at the school. In one widely known incident, for example, he had had a tailor make him an expensive jacket and then had shown no intention of paying him. The tailor had naturally seen to it that this story got about, and in general Krause was considered a dirty dog. As far as we know, he never developed a close interest in music, then or later. During that coach ride, however, Bach was willing to entertain the idea of granting him the important position of general prefect. And soon he would experience the debacle that Ernesti had been aiming at by bringing up the question to begin with.

After he had driven Krause I away, the headmaster appointed 255 Krause II as his successor, referring to Bach's November agreement. He could dispel Bach's misgivings by saying that, after all, he had just shown Krause I what vigorous measures he was prepared to take, and he would apply them in Krause II's case too if disciplinary problems arose. He virtually vouched for Krause II, at the same time leaving Bach no chance to contradict him.

It went as was to be expected. Krause II soon proved to be careless. He made no effort to keep order among his singers, and the accuracy of their singing was equally unimportant to him. The headmaster, who was supposedly so concerned about school discipline, put the entire responsibility for the worship service on Bach's shoulders and refused to intervene in any way. On top of everything, he could point out that when he had stepped in to censure Krause I, Bach had only reproached him for it. Meanwhile, Bach had to watch and listen to the way Krause II, with his talentless insouciance, ruined not only Bach's reputation but above all the sacred music that he had built up with such care.

Authors who merely describe music from a distance can of course dispassionately observe something like that, calmly contemplating the destruction of many years' work. Bach's inexcusable crime is that he was not capable of doing so. His admiring biographers have all judged that he behaved with complete wrongheadedness in the events that followed, yet they neglect to explain to us how he should have proceeded instead.

Headmaster Ernesti refused to take any action whatever in Bach's favor; he merely referred him back to the school regulations. A petition to the council would not have helped him either, for according to those same regulations he was no longer subordinate to the council but directly to his headmaster. Moreover, Ernesti had excellent connections among the councilmen. And in any case they had never answered a single one of Bach's many petitions up to then.

He could not hope for any help from the consistory either. True, the ecclesiastics had once—reluctantly—admitted he was right in the Gaudlitz case. But here they could easily stay out of the affair altogether, commenting that they had no authority over the school and so were not responsible for what went on there. The writers who have criticized Bach can turn and twist the matter any way they want: Ernesti had successfully maneuvered his choirmaster into a hopeless position, exactly as he had earlier done with Krause I. Whatever step Bach now took, it could always be interpreted as a grave mistake.

But Bach's most serious error of all was simply this: He was not a schemer; he was a musician. He was defenseless against Ernesti's crafty malice and at the same time incapable of enduring bad performances. His headmaster had let him down, and he could expect neither the consistory nor the council to come to his aid. Meanwhile, he was being held responsible for the music that was now in shambles.

Bach's admonitions did not worry Krause; he knew that the headmaster was behind him. One Sunday morning, when he could not bear the situation any longer, Bach summarily dismissed Krause as general prefect and replaced him with the second prefect, Kittler. He then announced his decision to the headmaster, in accordance with school regulations.

Krause promptly complained to the headmaster. Ernesti, who up to then had been painstakingly careful to leave things to run their calculated course, referred him back to Bach. Bach explained to Krause that as choirmaster he alone had the right to determine the appointment and dismissal of prefects. Krause immediately reported Bach's words to the headmaster, and with that Ernesti had exactly the chance he wanted. With all appearances of solid justification, he could accuse Bach of having refused to comply with his headmaster's orders in word and in deed.

Bach still did not realize what was going on in this morass. He formally apologized to Ernesti and even promised to appoint Krause again on a trial basis. But in the next singing class, Krause conducted the choristers so abominably that Bach gave up. (That cannot have happened without prior consultation with the headmaster, for nowhere is it recorded that Krause even attempted to

257

improve.) Ernesti conclusively had the upper hand, and when Bach did not reappoint Krause after a written demand to that effect, Ernesti did so himself on his own initiative. According to school regulations, he was of course not at all entitled to appoint a prefect. But the "irascible" Bach had still by no means lost his composure, even after this open snub.

The superintendent was responsible for overseeing the worship services. With the high-handed reappointment of the incompetent Krause, Ernesti had decidedly spoiled an essential element in their proper presentation. Therefore Bach turned to the superintendent and explained the facts to him in detail. His explanation was clear. Deyling was certainly not one of Bach's friends, but he had to admit that the choirmaster was right, and he promised to settle the matter. Consequently, sure of the superintendent's support, Bach dismissed the slipshod Krause from the worship service and reinstated Kittler in his place.

Bach had presumed too much on the correctness of his point of view (in which Deyling had reinforced him) and on the steadfastness of Deyling himself. After Bach left, Ernesti came to see him in turn. Ernesti had been Deyling's star student at the university. What master would ever betray his model disciple? Deyling switched to Ernesti's side in the dispute. Ernesti, sure of his ground from this time onward, appeared in the choir loft just before the vespers service, expelling Kittler and reinstating Krause II. In addition he forbade the pupils, under penalty of the severest punishments, to obey any prefect appointed by Bach.

The question whether Bach exceeded his authority in what followed, as certain biographers claim, becomes completely idle at this point: The headmaster had so far exceeded his own that he had put himself completely in the wrong as Bach's superior. After he had been unable to force the choirmaster to his knees through his intrigues, he resorted to sheer brute force. He was not entitled to appoint a prefect; Bach was always responsible for the proper implementation of the church music. Since Krause could not achieve this aim (and obviously had no intention of trying to, either), Bach had no other choice but to prevent him from continuing in his post.

But after the threats issued by the headmaster in the choir loft, no other student dared to direct in his stead (he had already proved in the case of Krause I what he was capable of should the situation arise). Bach's wonderful ex-pupil Krebs, who had since gone on to the university, happened to be on hand, and so he took over the direction. As Spitta depicts the further developments:

> On the following Sunday [August 19] the same annoying quarrels were repeated. Bach did not want to let the prefect appointed by the headmaster conduct and lead the singing; among the remaining pupils no one dared to do so. Bach had to resolve against convention to direct the motet himself; as choir leader, a university student came in again. The very same day Bach directed a third written complaint to the council. . . . But the urgently necessary intervention of the council did not come about.

The incident with Krause I had occurred at the beginning of July. Since then there had been a constant war. July passed, and in August there were open scandals; the council merely looked on while the choirmaster was demoted to performing the duties of a prefect. It kept silent through all of August and all of September and on into November. One recalls Siegele's claim that there was a cultural policy in the council and a party that defended the interests of the choirmaster. But in this case as at other times, it never manifested itself. The regulation of church music was among the obligations of the council, just as the appointment of the clergymen was. But the members of the "noble and wise council" did not feel at all responsible. We cannot ward off the impression that they must have found the circumstances positively amusing.

259

Finally there was an event that gave Bach some hope. On September 29 the king came to Leipzig on a visit, and Bach again drafted a petition soliciting the title of court composer. But the king departed without fulfilling Bach's request. In November Bach finally drew up a petition to the consistory; after all, it was the body with jurisdiction over the ecclesiastical hierarchy, and as such it even had precedence over the superintendent as well. Then, when Bach no longer expected it, he was overwhelmed by tremendous surprise and joy. On November 21 he received from Pleissenburg Castle, where the governor of the king resided, the longed-for certificate of appointment as composer to the court ensemble.

That seemed like a deliverance. For this was actually more than an empty title: As composer to the court ensemble, Bach was a court personage from then on, under the personal protection of His Majesty the king and elector. The council would have to respect that and take note of his newly won distinction. Or so Bach thought. He shelved the complaint to the consistory and rushed to Dresden, where in the deep exuberance of his gratitude he gave a magnificent recital on the great Silbermann organ at Our Lady's Church in the presence of numerous court luminaries. The all-powerful Count Brühl had signed the certifying document, and no less than Count Keyserlingk, the ambassador of the Russian czaress, had seen to its rapid transmission to Leipzig. Here was ample proof that Bach had important friends and patrons at the court in Dresden.

But in his present case, with respect to the Leipzig council, they were unfortunately of no help at all. The council considered itself under no special obligation toward a royal electoral court composer, not in November, not in December, and not in January. In its view Bach would just have to muddle through with his music as best he could. Finally, after four months, he handed over his petition to the consistory after all, on February 12 of the following year. Spitta writes:

Six days before, at city hall, they had indeed roused themselves to the enactment of an order. But it was not carried out for two months: on April 6th it was served to Ernesti, on the 10th to Bach, and on the 20th to Deyling. The council had gone to no great trouble to get to the bottom of the dispute; it chose the easiest means of resolution and put both parties in the wrong. Incidentally, Johann Krause, "whose stay at the school comes to an end at Easter," remained first prefect. Easter fell on April 21st.

At that time the council could be certain that its decision would be of no more use to Bach in any way. With its precisely calculated delaying tactic, it had given its favorite, Ernesti, as much encouragement as possible; it had conclusively demonstrated that it was not interested in Bach's sacred music at all. Spitta carefully weighs up the legal situation of the parties. Nor does he forget to mention that Ernesti resorted to underhanded means in the end, not shying away even from calumnies and the charge that Bach was bribable—in a word, Ernesti proved the utter baseness of his character. But in that he was a superb match for the council and the consistory, which for its part remained completely unperturbed by the whole affair and resolutely let it peter out.

A legal examination of this prefect war is simply useless and overlooks the heart of the matter. We have no need of any knowledge of the law but only some common sense to see that the person who is responsible for the music must also have the authority to make it. The choirmaster alone was capable of deciding who should represent him, and the very fact that the gentlemen in charge never reached such an obvious conclusion as this shows how far removed all of them were from any artistic understanding. We might assume that the *Christmas Oratorio* of 1734 or the Passion music of 1736 must have made some small impression at least on the ears of these worthies. A couple of these citizens, we might think, must have realized that Leipzig possessed in Bach a man of exceptional talent and qualities. But we would be mistaken. The ruling circles of Leipzig merely saw him as a bothersome quarreler. And they had taught him a lesson once again.

"Nothing could compare with the infamous behavior of the petty-bourgeois aristocrats of our cities," Friedrich Engels writes in surveying this period—as though he were considering Bach's fate.

22

Ernesti emerged from his war with an unlimited victory. He had proved his ability to prevail, and he had consolidated his position. Henceforth it was settled once and for all that Bach would not find any backing from his superiors: The choirmaster was stymied. With his status enhanced, Ernesti could also finally rid himself of an irksome duty. As for himself, he discontinued the inspections that obliged him to spend the night every fourth week next to the pupils' dormitory, assigning the duty to the *quartus*. As a result, Bach did the same. He left it up to the headmaster to find a substitute for him, since at church he had appointed someone to stand in for him with such insistence. "This neglect had the most unfavorable influence on the moral education of the pupils," writes Reverend Köhler in his *Notes on School History,* but he does not write that Ernesti did anything about it. He was an academic after all, and he wanted to be teaching at the university; the fate of the Thomas School concerned him only insofar as it promoted his interests.

Schweitzer asserts:

What happened here at St. Thomas was typical of what was going on in the schools of that time in general. It was an epoch when the school system was being reorganized. Studies began to be pursued for their own sake. That is why it did not do to grant so much attention to music in the scholastic program. Music was ousted. The choir boarding schools had had their day, like the old student choirs in the churches in general. A new age was dawning.

But this too is all pure fabrication and does not apply to Ernesti's behavior in any way. Apart from reducing the curriculum, he did not change anything whatsoever. He never dreamed of removing music from the scholastic program. For he would have had to fight not with Bach but with the council over that, and a good careerist naturally takes great pains to avoid any clash with his superiors. And what would Superintendent Deyling have said if he had tried to prevent the Thomas pupils from singing anymore? He certainly would never encroach upon church music at his school; he simply wanted to make Bach incapable of performing it properly. He did not care to eliminate music from the curriculum; it was only Bach himself that he intended to drive into isolation. At that he succeeded beyond all measure. In the end Bach wanted nothing more to do with this ungrateful slanderer. For ten long months, Ernesti had systematically ruined his sacred music for him.

Surely no one will pretend that Headmaster Ernesti asked the school choirmaster for his opinion about the admission of new students in 1737. Nor was there any teacher left in the entire school who would have stood by him. The teachers were obviously on their guard. Since Gesner's time, music had been separated from the rest of the curriculum anyway, but in addition the headmaster had plainly shown how dangerous it would be for anyone to oppose him. He had connections and knew how to use them. Bach had so completely underestimated Ernesti's cunning during the quarrel that he even agreed to accept Assistant Headmaster Dresig as the mediator in an arbitration meeting. Of course if he had refused to go along with the idea he would only have handed Ernesti a proof of his irreconcilable attitude. Dresig was probably no more prejudiced than anyone else; in all Leipzig there was no one Bach could have proposed as a mediator. It goes without saying that in the end the assistant headmaster agreed with his headmaster on every point under discussion. That he even went along with the mediation at all shows how much naïve trust Bach still possessed in his colleagues or perhaps how abandoned and without any recourse he already felt.

What is known in Germany today by the English word "mobbing"—making life so unpleasant for a coworker that he leaves of his own volition—Ernesti had achieved to perfection: He had taken care of Bach. At the end of the prefects war, there was not a single person, neither at the school nor in the consistory nor in the council, who would have been willing to speak up in the choirmaster's defense. His performance resources were successfully gutted, and he himself was excluded, converted into a nonperson without any rights.

Yet the Bach specialist Christoph Wolff describes all that Ernesti achieved for his own gratification as "Bach's self-ordained quasi-retirement." In the process all his superiors had proved emphatically enough that for them he was nothing or less than nothing, and the slights did not stop. The title of court composer, which made him into a court personage, was for them above all a reason to show him their disdain.

What shabby form this social exclusion could take is demonstrated by an episode of April 10, 1737, when a Thomas pupil sang off-key during communion. Normally the incident could have been dealt with through a short talk with the choirmaster after the worship service; it was his responsibility, after all. But the ecclesiastical authorities simply did not speak with that man any longer, and so instead of complaining to Bach directly, the superintendent immediately went over his head to the city council. And the council, which had always refused any reply to all Bach's petitions, summoned him posthaste to deal with this important matter and issued him a reprimand: "The choirmaster should reproach the choir leader and in the future place capable persons in these duties." That

265

it was the gentlemen of the council themselves who consistently hindered him from obtaining competent people for his work did not even occur to them.

On the whole the year 1737 became another of the lowest points in Bach's life, a life so rife with disappointments. No second Gesner appeared. From then on all Bach's superiors were against him, and that situation would not change up to his death.

Not only was he isolated, not only was his "regulated church music to the glory of God" in shambles, but other, more intimate sorrows also took their toll. He had secured a job for his son Bernhard at St. Mary's in Mühlhausen by risking his own personal reputation. The citizens there still remembered the senior Bach with pleasure and deep respect, but the young one went too far: He played so fiercely that they had to call in an expert to test whether the organ had suffered any damage. So the young man had to leave, and Bach again made use of his connections to find Bernhard a new position in Sangerhausen. But there he only caused his father still further grief. He abandoned the post, leaving behind a mountain of debts to his landlord, and simply disappeared. In vain, Bach had interceded for him twice; Bernhard had brought him nothing but shame, and on top of that Bach had to pay his debts. (Two years later he would learn that Bernhard was dead.)

In this same awful year, the Scheibe commentary added to his troubles. Johann Adolph Scheibe was the son of an organ builder in Leipzig; already in his Cöthen days Bach had inspected his work at the university church and awarded the organ a certificate of approval. Who was the younger Scheibe? His life is included in the *General German Biography* of 1858:

He was born in 1708 in Leipzig, son of the university organ builder Johann S. In 1725 he left the Nicholas School there in order to study law but was soon forced by the difficult circumstances of his family to give up his plan and turn to music instead. He learned to play the organ and the clavier, began to compose, and tried to earn his living as a teacher and concert musician. Around 1735 we find him in Prague, then in Gotha; in 1736 in Sondershausen, and after that in Hamburg, seeking permanent employment wherever he went. His ambitions for a post at the Hamburg Theater were dashed when an opera he submitted could not be performed because of the sudden bankruptcy of the management. He then pinned his hopes on writing about music, and in 1737 he founded the newspaper *Critical Musician*, which appeared in irregular installments until 1740.

In one of the first installments, in May 1737, after he had praised Bach's virtuosity to the skies, he wrote the devastating lines:

This man would be the admiration of whole nations if he had more amenity, if he did not undermine the naturalness of his pieces through turgidity and confusion, and did not obscure their beauties through an excess of art. Since he judges by his own fingers, his pieces are extremely hard to perform; for he requires that singers and instrumentalists should do with their voices and instruments whatever he can play on the clavier. But this is impossible. All the ornaments, graces, and everything else included in the performance method, he expresses completely with notes; and this not only deprives his pieces of the beauty of harmony, it also makes the melody inaudible throughout. All the voices are supposed to work with each other and be of equal difficulty, and one does not recognize among them any principal part. In a word: he is in music what Mr. von Lohenstein used to be in poetry. Turgidity has led them both from the natural to the artificial, and from the lofty to the obscure; and one admires in both the laborious work and uncommon effort—which nonetheless are applied in vain, since they conflict with nature.

He supplemented this opinion in the following year in a circular letter to his colleague Mattheson: "Bach's church pieces are increasingly artificial and arduous; and by no means of such vigor, convic- 267 tion, and reasonable reflection as the works of Telemann and Graun."

Here we are reminded of the Berlin music critic who, after a performance of one of Beethoven's string quartets, wrote the following judgment: "Mr. van Beethoven will never attain the supple grace of Kozeluch's string quartets." (He was right, but who still plays Kozeluch?)

If we take a closer look at Scheibe, we will discover both that he was no match for Bach and that he was anything but a real musician. "All the voices are supposed to work with each other and be of equal difficulty, and one does not recognize among them any principal part." But "one" is solely Scheibe, who blames Bach because a fugue is beyond his ken. He is certainly not alone in his limitations: In the next century a certain Hanslick could not cope with the harmony of Bruckner and Wagner. And more than two centuries later some musicologists would still find Scheibe's criticism completely justified.

Scheibe furnished practical samples of his lack of judgment in his own compositions. His biography says of them: "Already in his lifetime he met with less approval for his music than for his literary works; his choruses were reproached for a conspicuous chromaticism and as a consequence, for excessive difficulty; his arias, for a lack of coloratura; his recitatives, for an excess of emotion; the greatest and most general flaw of his music is in any case a poverty of invention." And if this assessment of his compositions is accurate (as a matter of fact, none of them has come down to us), it demonstrates yet again that Bach's style simply went beyond Scheibe's comprehension. In another passage he asserts that if for no other reason, Bach cannot be a great composer because he has not studied universal wisdom under Professor Gottsched (as Scheibe himself had done), along with rhetoric and the art of poetry. Here he becomes utterly ridiculous, and we cannot excuse him by noting that other theoreticians besides Scheibe (Mizler, for example) held similar pseudorationalistic views. "By their fruits ye 268 shall know them," the Bible says, and it is characteristic of all these people that not a one of them produced anything of importance, even though certain other theoreticians praise them highly as theoreticians. "In art, practice always comes before theory," said Pablo Picasso. Theory simply does not create any music.

To sum up, there is no reason whatever to take Scheibe seriously; if he had not attacked Bach, he would rightly have been forgotten long ago. His reproach that Bach was not a composer but a man with no education betrays remarkable stupidity. Worse, it is simply underhanded, hurting Bach when he was already wounded to the quick by the outcome of the prefects war. Everything came together to drag Bach down: the headmaster, the authorities, his son Bernhard, and then the mud Scheibe slung at him.

He had been in Leipzig for fourteen years by this point, and after his second seven-year stint he was even worse off than after the first. Nor at fifty-two could he see any more prospects for a change of location; he was no Goldoni, who in the fifty-fourth year of his life moved to Paris and kept on writing in French. Carlo Goldoni had to take care of just himself and his wife, and he was not only a playwright but also a sophisticated lawyer. Bach was a musician through and through. He was doomed to music, not a man like Scheibe who could take it or leave it.

Given the situation in which he found himself in 1737, he certainly would have had every reason to give up. But we can only wonder what is going on in the mind of a prominent musicologist when he speaks of a "self-ordained quasi-retirement." Another one claims in all seriousness that Bach actually strove for this state of affairs, yet God knows he did not choose it for himself. The headmaster had proved to be his mortal enemy; the teaching staff ostracized him: It was only sensible for him not to set foot in the school any longer. Nor did he leave his children there; instead he engaged a private tutor for them, his cousin Elias. As Bach's children, they could not hope to benefit from the Thomas School; only an idiot would have expected objectivity from a headmaster who had shown himself to be as grossly biased as Ernesti.

269

No, Bach certainly did not leave the school at that time on his own initiative. The adjective "self-ordained" is a complete distortion of the facts. And the word "retirement" is equally false. Under circumstances that might perfectly well have impelled a man to lethargy, Bach continued to work. He persisted with the calm steadiness of an albatross circling the Antarctic seas. Many biographers leave us with the impression that Bach's only occupation in life was that of school choirmaster. They are pleased when they can pin some flaw or other on his character in that context, in order to prove their own "objectivity." But where is the writer who shows an appreciation of his unwavering character at this juncture, his firmness in will and faith? We can only bow down before his steadfastness and strength, with the deepest admiration.

If at this point he had scrapped the whole business and withdrawn from public life, who could hold it against him? Yet he continued to work, not only undeterred but thoroughly industrious, though he was so sick and tired of Leipzig he could no longer take pleasure even in his Collegium Musicum.

There was no retirement there or elsewhere; in fact the bulk of his duties took place outside the school, and these remained to him. Even under the circumstances, the entire responsibility for the Sunday church music continued to be his. The cantatas for the changing of the council also had to be written and performed. And there were the constant christenings and weddings and funerals at which he, "the great Thomas choirmaster," a lowly city employee, had to walk in front of the coffin with the "serenading beggars." But each funeral brought him his thaler. Since he had all of 100 thalers in fixed income, he had to keep busy with the special events in order to support his family.

But Bach was industrious all his life; annoyance and grief could not keep him from his work. Moreover, he was not completely deserted; he still had friends. At the university there was Master Johann Abraham Birnbaum, who undertook his defense against Scheibe with great vigor and an astounding knowledge of the subject. And Johann Gottfried Walther, Bach's cousin in Weimar, agreed with Birnbaum publicly.

There are still musicologists who attach importance to Scheibe's views as a "sign of the times." But his criteria remain objectively false, and his further career shows all the characteristics of bustling mediocrity. He did manage to become music director of the Copenhagen court orchestra, but he was already retired after five years, at the age of forty-one—and surely not because of his outstanding achievements. Then he concentrated on composing again; besides numerous sacred works, he wrote 150 flute concerti alone, thirty violin concerti, and seventy symphonies in one movement. Again: "The greatest and most general flaw of his music is in any case a poverty of invention," notes the *General German Biography*, which otherwise speaks very positively of the people included in its pages.

Birnbaum's retort was excellent, and its fullness of detail demonstrates how close to his heart this matter lay. He was not Bach's only friend; we have already alluded to those in Dresden. Even as far away as Bohemia, to which he probably never traveled, he had his admirers. There lived Count Johannes Adam von Questenberg, a man obsessed with music, who introduced musical instruction into the schools of his domain in Jesomerice. He was personally acquainted with the leading lights of the Vienna music scene—the world-famous court music director Johann Joseph Fux and his equally celebrated assistant music director, Antonio Caldara. (Fux created the standard work of the century on counterpoint, the *Gradus ad Parnassum*; it was highly esteemed by Bach, who recommended it as a textbook.) The orchestra of Count Questenberg was important in both Bohemia and Moravia; that he was among Bach's admirers and stayed in contact with him is historically verified. The same goes for Count Sporck, who had his manor house in Lissa near Prague and who was befriended with Questenberg. Henrici had already dedicated his *Collection of Edifying Thoughts* to Sporck in the holiday season of 1724–1725, suggesting that he was well acquainted with Leipzig. Both Questenberg and Sporck were Catholics, but this did not diminish their enthusiasm for the Protestant church composer by any means. After all, Bach did not

271

write sacred music exclusively; the bulk of his creations were not even intended for church use.

In this period of his total isolation, Bach wrote four short Masses (*Missae breves*)—that is, Masses without the Credo, Sanctus, and Agnus Dei. Much ink has flowed about how *Missae breves* were also employed in the worship service of the Orthodox Lutheran church, and without further ado these Masses have also been declared "Protestant." The only problem is that we do not have the slightest proof these Masses were ever performed in Bach's time, at Bach's churches, or by Bach. And that they could have been intended for Leipzig is absolutely implausible to begin with. If such short Masses in Latin were needed in Leipzig, why did Bach never write one before 1730, at the time of his cantatas, the Magnificat, and the Passions? Why of all times would he compose them at a point when he had reached an absolute low in relation to his ecclesiastical superiors, and when he had neither an occasion for performance nor the means to carry it out? These are demanding works of quite some scope—in fact some of Beethoven's symphonies are shorter. They are totally unsuitable for performance in a normal Protestant worship service, especially in a city where one expressly attached importance to music's "not lasting too long." And at this of all times, amid his worst humiliations by the school, the council, and the consistory, not to mention the breakdown of his performance resources, Bach is supposed to have had nothing more urgent on his mind than presenting his superiors with no less than four such splendid and extensive compositions? That really seems quite unbelievable.

It seems much more credible that these Masses in their original form, without any alteration, had a place in the Catholic worship service. The only necessary requirement was that the Catholic parish involved be headed up by a secular ruler. In that period Catholics and Protestants alike were still far away from the ecumenical movement; their relationship to each other was of a more hostile nature. Whether Bach said a Hail Mary after the Lord's Prayer must have been a matter of complete indifference to Sporck as well as Questenberg. But performing a Mass by Bach in their own places of worship with their own choirs and orchestras must have afforded them an incomparable joy.

Consequently, those who think that Count Questenberg or Sporck commissioned Bach to write these Masses must come considerably closer to the truth (though Sporck would already die in 1738). The Protestant theory does not seriously hold water. In any case it is wonderful that Bach found a client somewhere, in this period of his greatest setbacks, who eagerly sought his musical treasures and assured him that outside Leipzig they were still deeply esteemed.

In 1737 Bach was so fed up with Leipzig that he even relinquished the direction of the Collegium Musicum. Yet Christoph Wolff, for many years the editor of the *Bach-Jahrbuch,* reached the surprising conclusion that practically all the concerti, overtures, and chamber music, including many sonatas, date not from Cöthen but from the mid- and late 1730s in Leipzig. That would mean that during the five years when Bach was in charge of the orchestral and chamber music in Cöthen, he did not write anything at all; but when his work had been spoiled for him to such a degree that he was thinking of renouncing his orchestra, he suddenly created orchestral and chamber music in lavish abundance.

Unfortunately, Wolff lacks a musicological explanation for this unusual phenomenon. But there is no shortage of foolhardy theories from other sources. For example, Schleuning, for whom even the reasons for Bach's departure from Cöthen are "unclear," sees in the prefects war nothing more than a "jurisdiction struggle among different social groups." He considers the whole affair a trivial question of detail, does not concern himself with the repercussions for Bach's sacred music, and makes use of the subject mainly to tax Bach with "his own inconsistency and false steps." If that sort of thing is regarded as musicology, why not allow that Bach composed most assiduously for orchestra right at a time when he no longer wanted an orchestra?

273

Yet Bach slipped away from his orchestra for only a short time. The prefects war was not over for him even then. Since the consistory did not want to take a position on the matter, as royal court composer Bach finally turned to his lord and king in October 1737. On December 17 a demand came from Dresden that the consistory concern itself with Bach's grievance at long last. This exigency was set adrift in the slow meanders of official channels. Finally, four months later, on February 5, 1738, the consistory required of the council and the superintendent . . . a guarantee of Bach's right to control the performance of his sacred music? No, not so fast. The ecclesiastics did not need to study Parkinson's books on bureaucratic procedures; they had long since acquired sufficient experience in that domain, and they required a report. On the double now, within fourteen days. . . .

Spitta does not tell us whether he found the two reports, one by the council and the other by the superintendent. But another force had to be reckoned with in this affair, the king himself. He decided to visit Leipzig again for the Easter fair in 1738, so it went without saying that a music of homage would be needed, and this time the council was determined that Bach would not present it. A person with whom one had had so much trouble was hardly a suitable representative of the city of Leipzig any longer. And if he was "court composer"—well, so what? After all, besides the council's own town musicians, the performers would be the students, and Görner was still the university music director. That meant he, and not the "court composer," was entitled to the music. Or so the council thought.

But the students thought otherwise. Even though Bach had handed over the direction of the Collegium Musicum to Carl Gotthelf Gerlach, they wanted to play the music of homage under Bach. And since they alone had the say as to who would direct them, the council felt it could not risk a quarrel and eventually acquiesced. A royal letter was still lying around unanswered in their city; on further reflection, perhaps it would be too terrible an affront in any case to prohibit the king from hearing his own royal court composer in Leipzig.

The students had won, but so had Bach. On this occasion he managed to finish his business with the council through help from Dresden. We can only assume that some influential gentleman of the court must have complained to the council about the treatment of Bach. From Easter 1738 the quarrels stopped—for the time being, that is. The council waited patiently for the opportunity to pay Bach back for his victory and duly found the occasion the following year, during the Easter season of 1739.

We have no record of any Passion music for Easter 1738, nor of any Passion music with the prefect Krause II for Easter 1737. But for Easter 1739 Bach wanted to perform his *St. John Passion* again at last.

It would not come to pass. The council forbade him to perform the work on the more than flimsy grounds that "the choirmaster omitted to have the text approved by the council in accordance with the regulations." That was certainly an extraordinary omission, since this Passion had already been performed in Leipzig several times. But wherever a humiliation could be invented, it was exercised on Bach. And the council still felt obliged to teach him one more lesson. It had the decision delivered to Bach by a well-chosen man; we know his name and his profession: He was subcoroner Bienengräber.

The "noble and most wise" councilmen of Leipzig could not have proclaimed more clearly what social rank this choirmaster occupied in their eyes.

23

MUCH TOO LITTLE ATTENTION HAS BEEN ACCORDED to that momentous event of Easter 1738. For it was definitely momentous that the young people of the university disregarded the council and insisted that Bach, a man who had run so completely afoul of his superiors, should conduct them. Görner was not bad, and Gerlach was not bad either—after all, he officially directed the Collegium Musicum. But for this occasion they absolutely had to have Bach.

We can only conclude that Bach was very popular among the musical youth of Leipzig and enjoyed an extraordinary reputation. And that was not the case only among the university students. After Ernesti had finally driven Bach out of his school, something remarkable happened. He got rid of Bach but not the musicians. Anyone with an inclination toward music who enrolled at the Thomas School could be certain of Ernesti's wrath, yet young people kept on becoming Thomas pupils for no other reason than that this way they could receive instruction in music from Bach.

Anyone who studied with Bach was excluded from Ernesti's classes; such pupils were not even allowed to listen to his words of wisdom from the adjoining room. We know that he called those who were keen on music "beer fiddlers," from which it follows that those who took lessons with Bach would not have an easy time of it and would have to reckon with severe discrimination. But despite all this, Ernesti did not manage to fend them off. Pupils who wanted a thorough musical training came to the Thomas School and received instruction from the great Bach. Schleuning ventures the bold hypothesis that for Bach the point was to found his own school. But he really had no need of that. He taught anyone who possessed talent and wanted to learn from him, and for that he did not have to place any advertisements in the newspapers.

Something more should be added in this regard. There are Bach biographers who pretend that after his expulsion from the school Bach was finished and everything that followed was no more than a postlude. The nonsense about a "self-ordained quasi-retirement" is not unique. Spitta entitles his chapter on the years 1737–1750 "The Last Period of His Life"; Terry dubs them "The Last Years." After reading headings like those, we instinctively envision an aging man who walks through Leipzig with his cane, forgotten by the world and absorbed in esoteric musical conundrums. Geiringer stressed this notion to the maximum by presenting his portrayal of that time under the sad words "Heading for the End."

In speaking of a "quasi-retirement," Wolff obviously starts from the premise that Bach came to Leipzig in order to become the Thomas choirmaster (Cantor) with his music. But he did not go to Leipzig only in order to perform his job as choirmaster. And when the post was spoiled for him in every respect, he still kept making his music without interruption. True, from then on he discharged his choirmaster duties as a secondary activity, with few exceptions. But once Ernesti had driven him out of the school, the headmaster never again interfered in the appointment of Bach's prefects. In this respect Bach had a free hand; the territories were clearly marked. After the council formally forbade him to present his Passion music in 1739, he persisted in performing it in 1740: He directed his *St. John Passion* again and even revised it for the occasion.

278

Here we meet with a further hallmark of Bach's creations, one that is no less important than the "parody procedure" discussed in

Chapter 20. Bach wrote an almost incredible quantity of music, but for him his works were never finished; he continued to work on them. He saw them not as works for specific occasions but creative ways of looking at problems to which he returned again and again. (That is also the path that led him to *The Well-Tempered Clavier*, part 2.) And in addition he occupied himself with things that were not needed at all, like the *Organ Mass*, the B Minor Mass, and the *Art of Fugue*. So if the handwriting in manuscripts of his orchestral and chamber music points to the second half of the 1730s, that does not amount to proof that he first composed them at that time. He may very well have revised them in this period, in remembrance of better days and precisely because by this later time, sadly, he no longer needed them.

But one theory is utterly absurd: that he withdrew from public life and wrote his works while sulking in a corner, so to speak. The founding of the "Great Concert" in 1741 by the merchant Gottlieb Benedict Zehmisch, in which Bach did not participate, is always invoked in this connection. But biographers overlook a question: Why should he have taken part? He was not dependent on Zehmisch; he had already taken charge of his Collegium Musicum again. Neither Zehmisch nor Bach had a monopoly. Apart from Bach's Collegium Musicum there was Görner's as well; at no time was Bach the only musician in Leipzig. Nor did he bury himself in esoteric, antiquated musical problems, in the *stile antico*, as Schleuning, Wolff, and others would have us believe. Above all, he could never be out of fashion because at no time was he a fashionable composer to begin with. Yet up to his final days students came to him, young people who wanted to learn something. According to the testimony of his son Carl Philipp Emanuel, his house resembled "a dovecote in its liveliness." That does not point to his being forgotten, and it certainly does not indicate that Johann Sebastian Bach had "gone out of fashion" in his lifetime. Was the duke in Schwerin really being old-fashioned when in the last year of Bach's life he provided his court organist Johann Gottfried Müthel with a scholarship so he could study with none other than old Bach? And was the young Müthel already so senile that he did not have anyone more modern to propose?

In this context scholars always allude to the advent of the "gallant style." Exactly what is to be understood by that phrase the musicologists harbor as a deep secret in their hearts—"that's the way it is, and that's all," as Leo Stein has his Merry Widow say. The phrase "gallant style" had already been used by Kuhnau, Bach's predecessor in his post, so around the middle of the century it was hardly something that was just coming into fashion. Schweitzer's classification of Bach as the "culmination and end of Baroque music" implies that up to Bach's time all composers subscribed to polyphony and spun out countless fugues. But that was absolutely not the case. And when Bach died and the "gallant style" had supposedly left him in obscure retirement long before, there was no composer anywhere around who could eclipse his name, as Mozart's would overshadow Haydn's despite his brilliance.

When Bach began rehearsals of the revised version of his *St. John Passion,* he had overcome the malice of headmaster, council, and consistory. In spite of all his intrigues, the headmaster had not been able to oust music from the school. The council had had to learn that it would get in trouble with the king if it wanted to mistreat the royal court composer, so it preferred to let things alone. And the consistory had shown all too obviously that it did not propose to concern itself with Bach and his musical interests. He was consequently a free man. He organized the ongoing sacred music from his home; his prefects were all dedicated young men who by taking on their posts had clearly decided for him and against the headmaster. He could rely on them. As for the university students, they had proved to Bach repeatedly that they knew how invaluable he was. The Passion music of 1740 must have been excellent.

280   But Leipzig did not consist merely of the school, the council, and the consistory. Bach could not play splendid music for years every week in Zimmermann's Café and Garden without having his

keen supporters. Nor were such people as foolish as Johann Adolph Scheibe: They would very quickly have stopped frequenting Bach's student concerts if they had not derived any pleasure from his music, if it had seemed old-fashioned or "confused" and "turgid" to them. We have only to listen attentively to the pieces by Bach that people got to hear at that time, his harpsichord and violin concerti, for instance. They display not only the finest artistic mastery but lively musicality as well, far removed from all dryness. People who worship Bach's music as the epitome of loftiness and profundity overlook the fact that he left us a great quantity of catchy tunes, themes we cannot get out of our minds for days on end after hearing them the first time, that are so infectious we beat time to them with our hands and feet.

We can be sure that if Bach did not have his superiors on his side, he did have his public. (Of course, nothing annoys the authorities more than when people they dislike are showered with acclaim, especially when despite their "most wise" work they garner none themselves.)

That Bach was now court composer reaped him no advantages with his superiors, but with his Leipzig following it did bring him something after all. In September 1737 a gentleman from the Dresden court, Mr. von Hennicke, moved to the vicinity of Leipzig. He was an influential man who had risen from the status of lackey to that of a powerful person of rank and had even received a title of nobility. The estate of Wiederau in the district of Pegau had been bestowed on him, and on September 27, 1737, he took up residence there as "Johann Christian von Hennicke, hereditary liege lord of the manor at Wiederau, true most trusted privy counselor to his royal majesty of Poland and serene elector of Saxony, state minister and vice chamber president, as well as director of the foundation at Naumburg and Zeitz, etc."

Such a lofty gentleman had to be greeted appropriately, and in the estimation of those who had a particular interest in the matter a homage cantata would befit the occasion. Under the circum- 281 stances the only possible candidate for writing the cantata was the court composer, and Bach duly produced a magnificent piece. His friend Henrici wrote the text for him; this was only to be expected, since the tax collector was among the gentlemen who wished to present their homage to Hennicke in this fashion.

The incident shows that Henrici was anything but insignificant; on the contrary, he must have been a highly respected figure in Leipzig society. The other persons of rank who took part in the event were magistrate Beiche and Chief Magistrate Schilling. Chief Magistrate Schilling was well acquainted with Bach as well; five years earlier he had stood as godfather to one of Bach's children. Picander's text observed all the proprieties of court homage, no less than the one Gottsched composed at Easter 1738 for the homage cantata to the king.

Incidentally, that was the second and last time Gottsched delivered a poem to Bach to be set to music. It must be said to his credit, however, that he long since figured among the Leipzig personalities who appreciated Bach. Not only did he point out that Leipzig could be proud of this great artist, but he also gave the Bach suites to his betrothed as a present. And the later Mrs. Gottsched, who is said to have been superior to her husband, complained to him that the pieces were devilishly difficult. She was right about that, but unlike the know-it-all Scheibe, she did not reproach the composer for this as a failing.

When Bach conducted the homage cantata for Hennicke, Gerlach was already directing the Collegium Musicum. But the students placed themselves at his disposal for the performance all the same, just as a half year later they insisted that Bach present the homage cantata to the king with them. They could not do without him: In 1741 he had to take over the Collegium once again, and he continued to direct it until 1744, possibly even 1746. Since young people are enthusiastic mainly about novelty, this demonstrates that Bach seemed anything but old-fashioned to them. That should give pause to musicologists who claim that at the time Bach had totally turned away from "modern" music to a *stile antico*. (I return to this point later.)

Spitta made a significant but not exactly glorious comment about this period in Bach's life as a composer: "He had developed early and swiftly; he also came earlier to a standstill." This thesis is perfect unto itself: false both front and back. Bach did not develop early or swiftly by any means. He did grow up with music from his earliest childhood, yet he did not compose much of anything before he was twenty. So the "early and swiftly" part must be discarded. And the second half of Spitta's judgment is just as much of a pure invention, for how can it be pretended that Bach ever came "to a standstill"?

To be sure, the abundance of occasional compositions abated; that was only natural. The church did not require any more pieces of that kind, and he no longer needed to write a new cantata every week; he had done with that Sisyphean task. The necessary teaching works were also completed. But then came the four great *Missae breves*. And in 1739 his *Keyboard Practice III* appeared, also known as the *Organ Mass (Orgelmesse)*. That summer his son Friedemann came over from Dresden with two other musicians, and there was family music for four weeks in a row. In September he gave a concert in Altenburg, in October he took up his work with the Collegium Musicum again, and in November he traveled to Weissenfels. Standstill? He had pupils; for his own pleasure he compiled for a second time twenty-four preludes and fugues, ranging through all the key signatures; he published works of other composers—his colleague Hurlebusch; his favorite pupil, Krebs; his son Friedemann. And as Carl Philipp Emanuel reports: "No musician was likely to travel through the area without making my father's acquaintance and playing for him." That Bach needed his cousin Elias for five years not only as a private tutor for his children but also as a secretary for himself, shows best of all how much his general activity increased after his withdrawal from schoolteaching. (After having intimidated the choirmaster, Ernesti in the end had to appoint a music teacher to replace him. The council authorized him to do so without any difficulty.)

None of the compositions Bach wrote from his withdrawal in 1737 until his death can be qualified as works of old age; they do not betray any "standstill" whatsoever. In the twenty-four preludes and fugues generally known as *The Well-Tempered Clavier II,* a sense of fun, of untrammeled pleasure, bubbles from every phrase. Great contrapuntal music has never been written more amusingly, more variously, or more entertainingly. And the same holds true for *Keyboard Practice IV* from 1742—that is, the *Goldberg Variations.* The name is actually wrong; more correctly they should be called the "Count von Keyserlingk Variations." Bach wrote them for him, and Keyserlingk paid him in a princely manner, with a silver goblet filled to the brim with 100 louis d'or.

Imperial Count von Keyserlingk was an interesting man. Of ancient Baltic nobility, he was an important diplomat, equally at home at the courts of St. Petersburg, Dresden, Vienna, Warsaw, and Berlin. His cousin Dietrich von Keyserlingk was an intimate friend from youth of Frederick the Great, whom he jokingly called "the swan of Mitau" or "Caesarion." The imperial count was Russian ambassador in the service of Czarina Anna; her successor, Peter III; and finally Catherine the Great until the end of his life. He was a man of high culture "who combined the rarest honesty with excellent statesmanship" (as it says in his obituary). He was also an enthusiastic music lover. When the count came to Dresden, Friedemann was still organist at the Sophia Church, the court church at that time. He invited Friedemann to his home, just as he did many other famous musicians from the court of Dresden. From 1740 his son attended the university in Leipzig, a reason for repeated visits there. That he visited Bach as well cannot be doubted; after all, we know that he invited Bach to his home in Dresden 284 along with his cousin and secretary, Elias. Elias later reported that he "had enjoyed much undeserved favor in the house of this great ambassador."

On one of his journeys, probably in Königsberg, Keyserlingk had come upon an unusually gifted boy named Johann Gottlieb Goldberg. He took him in and saw to his education, first with Friedemann Bach and then with his father. Goldberg, who later entered the service of Count Brühl, became Keyserlingk's house musician and must have developed virtually fantastic abilities as a keyboard player. It is said that he played the most difficult pieces from sight, even when the music was placed upside down.

Because he suffered from insomnia, Imperial Count von Keyserlingk ordered a little night music from Bach for Goldberg to play. For such a purpose, any conventional composer would have produced a composition that encouraged sleep—not music that was boring, of course, but something soothing nonetheless. It is remarkable that this most obvious approach did not cross Bach's mind at all. On the contrary, though he did begin with a very soothing aria in the vein of a folk song—a lullaby, really—he then produced thirty variations on it that are anything but soothing, that are extremely exciting piece for piece. A cultivated connoisseur like Keyserlingk could only fall over himself with enthusiasm (and he did, as Bach's honorarium shows).

For Bach, it would have been normal to end with a fugue, but here he finishes with a quodlibet, one that conspicuously demonstrates the intimate terms on which he must have stood with the count. His opening with the melody of the song "It's So Long Since I've Been with You" is an unmistakable allusion to his visit to Keyserlingk's home with his cousin and secretary, Elias, and "Cabbage and Turnips Drove Me Away" can only be a joking reference to the delicacies they enjoyed. But Bach takes things even further; at the end he virtually escorts the imperial count to his bedroom when he strikes up the song "With You, with You, to the Featherbed, with You, with You, to the Straw." What choice was left to the count then but to go to bed? As we can see, the *Goldberg Variations* 285 are not only a masterpiece of Bach's counterpoint but also a proof of his hearty humor.

Serious people usually consider it beneath their dignity to accord fun the importance it definitely possesses in a lively existence; they regard as important only what no one can laugh about. Spitta remarks about the *Peasant Cantata,* which dates from the same period as the *Goldberg Variations:* "It should not put us off that Bach was ready to undertake the composition. No doubt he paid no attention at all to the ethical side of the matter." Werner Neumann avers that "most likely the social-critical aspect of the piece" has "been overestimated considerably" and speaks of an "esoteric occasional composition in an idiosyncratic style."

I find it rather difficult to accept such an assessment, which would have to be applied to the *Coffee Cantata* as well. But quite apart from that consideration, Bach reused a whole long aria from the cantata *Der Streit zwischen Phöbus und Pan (The Quarrel Between Phoebus and Pan)* in the *Peasant Cantata* by means of the parody procedure, and Neumann did not tax the original for being an "esoteric occasional composition in an idiosyncratic style." And if we look closer, there are also other compositions by Bach on which we could pin this designation if only it were accurate.

The *Peasant Cantata* is a homage cantata to Chamberlain von Dieskau. That a wholly different tone is adopted here than in the cantata to von Hennicke—and all other homage cantatas in general—should make us reflect. Like von Hennicke, the chamberlain was a gentleman of high rank, someone normally approached with a deep bow. First, then, we have to be amazed that the homage bearers were allowed to take the liberty of such a disrespectful tone. There is no other homage cantata in which such a familiar tone is adopted. And second, we should wonder why the homage bearers took this tone. It testifies not only to a pronounced familiarity but to a genuinely friendly relationship. This seems all the more peculiar in a society of strictly separated ranks, with its rift between the bourgeoisie and the upper nobility.

There is yet another peculiarity. In the case of the homage cantata for von Hennicke, we know precisely which persons of rank

286

initiated it. In the case of the *Peasant Cantata*, the donors are completely missing, with the exception of Henrici, who composed the text, a man well versed in social manners. Neumann reproaches him for not having risen to "aggressive social criticism" in this instance, as though what we know today as a political roast were already in vogue at that time and a homage might considered an appropriate vehicle for one. On this occasion a member of the landed gentry was being shown due respect combined with a heartfelt affection, and that must have been a tremendous exception in those days. And there is another aspect we should note: Chamberlain von Dieskau was not a parvenu like von Hennicke but a scion of ancient and venerable nobility.

Von Dieskau was an unusual squire, however. In 1742 there was a war going on. Prussian soldiers were stationed near Leipzig—still as allies for the time being, though allies too eat bread. The biggest concern was that they were levying recruits everywhere. In Wiederau alone, within von Hennicke's jurisdiction, sixty young men had been obliged to enlist, and the peasants were left to see how they could finish their fieldwork without them. In Klein-Zschocher von Dieskau saw to rounding up the needed recruits in person. Oddly enough, he found only two suitable ones. And at the next review of troops not a single one had to report for duty anymore; instead, von Dieskau donated a barrel of beer to his men.

Here is another instance of his largesse: From time immemorial a tax was levied on fallow land ("lands that remain untilled"). Henrici was von Dieskau's state tax collector, and the tax procurator was the law court director Müller, who was very exacting about revenues. He threatened that whoever could not or would not pay his tax on fallow land would have his crop confiscated. When Dieskau found out about this, he ordered his state tax collector to abolish the tax on fallow land entirely.

We could list more such incidents. All in all the villagers of Klein-Zschocher had received more good turns from von Dieskau in five months than in all the fifty years before. We do not need to

287

study local history in order to learn about them. They all figure along with other local lore in Henrici's cantata text—the deeds of Dieskau's administrator Ludwig, the thrift of Dieskau's wife, and that the Dieskaus had five daughters but still no son and heir. We also hear about how the peasant lads were allowed to stay on the farm and how the master gave them free beer. According to the text, Klein-Zschocher seemed too immoral to the local clergyman; this was an especially amusing matter since the minister was suspended from his duties for three months owing to his own mores.

Neumann regrets that Henrici cast only the first lines of this memorable homage cantata in the Saxon dialect. Yet he may be sure the performers had a sufficiently good command of Saxon (at that time still regarded as the standard language of the town of Meissen in Saxony) so that Henrici could save himself any further trouble in spelling it out.

On the whole this *Peasant Cantata*, with its many-faceted, instructive text and its absolutely unique form of homage, can hardly be overestimated as a document of the time. No other chamberlain from this period is remembered through such a monument to his character and activity. That Bach did not take this "occasional work" lightly is revealed in that it contains no less than twenty-four musical numbers, of which only a few are borrowed from earlier works and none used again for other purposes. At the end, with "Now We're Going Where the Bagpipes Drone in Our Tavern," he wrote a regular pop tune.

Doubtless Spitta found the whole thing questionable because of the opening passage, where the male singer, a peasant lad, confesses to the female singer, his betrothed, "how good a bit of spooning tastes" (for "spooning" young people today would probably say "necking"). But the betrothed was not born yesterday, and she contradicts him: "I know you all right, you filthy thing. After that you'll only want to go further and further." And where he wants to go we learn from Bach right away, for his music intones the song

"With You, with You to the Featherbed, with You, with You to the Straw."

Before bristling with moral indignation, Spitta should have recalled that Bach had also ended the *Goldberg Variations* with this song. He could have found it again in Robert Schumann—it rings forth at the end of his *Faschingsschwank aus Wien (Carnival Farce from Vienna)*.

But when Spitta maintains that Bach "no doubt paid no attention at all to the ethical side of the matter" he becomes unjust. For the ones who commissioned the work can only have been the peasants of Klein-Zschocher; city customers would have appeared as urban dwellers on such an occasion and not as peasants, nor would they have had any relationship to the references in the text. Under the circumstances depicted, the Klein-Zschocher peasants not only had an obligation to respect their master but a reason to pay him special homage, out of gratitude. That is surely one of the most beautiful reasons in the world. Bach lovingly fulfilled their commission and, in contrast to Spitta and many others, fully recognized "the ethical side of the matter."

24

THE *PEASANT CANTATA* DATES FROM THE SAME YEAR in which Bach wrote a little night music for a sleepless elderly gentleman. That music, the *Goldberg Variations*, appeared in print as *Keyboard Practice IV*. The work that preceded it, *Keyboard Practice III*, is generally called the *Organ Mass:* a collection of splendid chorale arrangements and four duets, framed by a prelude and a fugue. The fugue, in E-flat major, has become known as the *St. Anne* or *Trinity Fugue*, in allusion to its triple character—three themes are separately introduced and then interwoven with each other. Since there are three themes, Schweitzer posited the reference to the divine Trinity, not without carefully distancing himself from the idea: He states that an organist (unnamed) drew his attention to the correlation. Rueger then expands on the insinuation in his Bach biography, pointing out that not only the fugue but also the prelude is tripartite.

The structural observations are correct, but identifying the work as a detailed portrayal of the central Christian belief undoubtedly goes too far. With complete impartiality, we might conceivably recognize the first fugal theme as the ascent of God's spirit from the depths. But if the second theme depicts Jesus Christ, we have him speeding by on roller-skates, and the third evokes a Holy Ghost who clanks along like a knight in armor. We can always ascribe all possible and impossible meanings to music without its gaining any meaning in the process. That is true even when the composer has expressly introduced a programmatic meaning into his work. To appreciate *Till Eulenspiegel's Merry Pranks* by Richard Strauss, we do not need any inkling at all of the individual episodes; even for someone who does not know who Till Eulenspiegel was, the piece remains a splendid concert rondo. Beethoven's bombastic music on Wellington's victory at Waterloo, with its nerve-racking clarity, has rightly been forgotten despite its obvious program. If not the first two, then the third theme of the triple fugue lingers unavoidably in the listener's memory, yet Bach can hardly have intended to make a catchy tune of the Holy Ghost. Many have read their Goethe a bit flightily and consider that "man believes, when he hears tones, that something needs to be thought about them too." But music is a higher revelation than all wisdom and all philosophy, precisely because it eludes the grammatical thinking of speech. The *Trinity Fugue* is no contribution to the doctrine of the Trinity.

Nor can we simply classify Bach's great chorale preludes, or more properly organ chorales, as church music. They go beyond the scope of the worship service. Schweitzer even maintains that some of them surpass the limits of music, though he does not let us know where these might lie for him. In any case we must not understand the *Organ Mass* as though Bach were interested solely in the textual background; his spiritual approach was at the same time a deeply musical one. The *Little Organ Book* was oriented to both "beginning organists" and church praxis. That is clear from the generous conception of the whole, even if he composed only a portion of the chorale preludes he originally planned. Those of *Keyboard Practice III* by far transcend the scope of these praxis-related works in several ways; organ music itself, not the liturgy, is their ultimate aim.

292   In this respect Bach's great organ chorales are free organ music as well. That does not mean any renunciation of their spiritual content, but the roots of inspiration lie in their melodies, not in their texts.

We can never overestimate the musical power of the old chorale melodies. They have maintained their vital force undiminished for centuries, and it is remarkable how many of them have induced composers to write chorale preludes, organ chorales, and chorale fantasies, over and over again. There is a vigor in them that leaps over religious barriers. No one who is receptive to music can resist the power of the choral hymns in the *St. Matthew Passion* or the *Christmas Oratorio*. But the same holds true for the organ chorales of Reger or the *Reformation* Symphony of Mendelssohn. "Silent Night" is not the only Christmas carol; Luther's "Vom Himmel hoch" ("From Heaven on High") is almost 500 years old, and older still is the tune of "Innsbruck, ich muß dich lassen" ("Innsbruck, I Have to Leave You") in the hymn "Herzlich tut mich verlangen" ("My Heart Is Full of Yearning"). It was not only obvious but virtually inevitable that in Bach's hands organ compositions would arise from a body of song like this that far transcended the needs of the worship service. In regard to those "needs," Bach had his own standards in any case: Whatever he began, his music demanded room for development. No one could have danced to his suites, and his organ chorales would have stuck in the throats of the congregation if they had tried to sing them. And so he composed his *Organ Mass* not for churchgoers as such but "to delight the spirit of music lovers, and especially connoisseurs of this kind of work" (as he says in the dedication). He had a highly personal way of serving his church.

Why did he write so many cantatas? After all, a sufficient quantity of them by his predecessors was available. But they were not sufficient for him. What has become of the cantatas of Schelle or Kuhnau? Even the ones by Buxtehude are not sung very often. The Bach cantata stands alone, not as representative of the genre: It *is* the genre.

Incidentally, in the final part of his life Bach wrote a number of church cantatas besides the *Schübler Chorales*, the Eighteen Chorales, and the three epoch-making major works that no reasonable person would accuse of representing a "standstill": the *Musical Offering*,

293

the B Minor Mass, and the *Art of Fugue*. After his expulsion from the school, his life flowed along on a more regular course than in the preceding five decades, but that flow had lost nothing of its power.

There are those who impute a change in style to Bach after his withdrawal from the school. They are very sensitive people, for otherwise it would not easily occur to them that the Bach of the *French Suites* was different from the one of the *Goldberg Variations,* or that the Bach of the B Minor Mass was a different composer from the one of the *St. Matthew Passion* or the Weimar cantata "Ich hatte viel Bekümmernis" ("I Had Much Distress"). We truly cannot detect these distinctions by listening, all the less so since Bach continued to incorporate into his new works pieces he had written earlier. He would hardly have done that if he had "broken" with his previous style.

Schleuning even claims to know the reason for Bach's "stylistic change." His name was Mizler. Lorenz Christoph Mizler was from 1732 a pupil of Bach's for a while; he founded a Society of Musical Sciences (Societät der musicalischen Wissenschaften) that Bach steered clear of for a long time. But through Mizler, our author says, Bach arrived at new, quite lofty ideas. Who was Mizler?

His life story is bewilderingly multifaceted. He came from Ansbach, where he attended the secondary school under headmaster Gesner. A year after Gesner's move to Leipzig, we find Mizler there as well; he studied theology, returned to Ansbach as a preacher, came back to Leipzig as a student, and took his master's in divinity. Then he switched to jurisprudence, and from that he changed to medicine, while at the same time giving lectures on mathematics, philosophy, and music. In 1738, together with two other gentlemen, he established the Corresponding Society of Musical Sciences (Correspondierende Societät der musicalischen Wissenschaften), and in 1740 he even started composing, without much success. He went on to become court mathematician to a Polish count, but four years later he graduated in Erfurt as a doctor of medicine. Then he

294

returned to Poland again, where he received a title of nobility and became court counselor, court doctor, and court historian. He died as the owner of a print shop and a bookstore. As we can see, his was an eventful life, and music did not play a central role in it by any means.

Be that as it may, his society boasted some celebrated members. Telemann joined it as early as 1739, Handel in 1745, and the two Grauns in 1746. There can be no doubt that Bach was among the first to be asked; after all, Mizler was his pupil. But Bach must have said no pretty stubbornly, for nine whole years. Mizler was interested in the philosophical, historical, mathematical-acoustic, and rhetorical-poetic foundations of music—not so much in music itself as in everything that could somehow be brought into connection with it. Carl Philipp Emanuel Bach furnished us with a good explanation of why his father steered clear of this society for so long. "My late father," he writes in the obituary, "was no friend of dry theoretical stuff." And in another place he adds: "It is true that our late Bach did not occupy himself with deep theoretical reflections on music, but he was all the more outstanding in the practice of the art."

So we can well imagine that he would not have been enthusiastic about a piece of writing like Mizler's *Anfangsgründe des Generalbasses, nach mathematischer Lehrart abgehandelt (Fundamentals of Thoroughbass, Treated According to Mathematical Teaching)*, and that everything within him must have struggled against Mizler's declared aim for the society: "to bring music completely into the form of a science." Bach must have known better than that, in contrast to his apologists. (Wolff claims imperturbably that *Keyboard Practice III* manifests "a considerable theoretical-historical component," and Schleuning attributes the credit for this precisely to Mizler.)

It cannot be pretended that Mizler was a music connoisseur, much less an important musician, and his endeavor "to bring music completely into the form of a science" makes his relation to music seem dubious in any case. Music does require enormous knowledge 295 and ability, but an enduring work has never come into being with the help of musicology. Unlike knowledge that we can appropriate, the essential element in art cannot be learned; musicality can be cultivated, to be sure, but not acquired through study alone. So Bach must have smiled at the efforts of his former pupil, and when he did finally join the society after all, the reason must have been not Mizler's aims but the members the society had assembled. At any rate he kept his enthusiasm for Mizler's endeavors firmly under control for almost a decade.

Certain academic efforts come to fruition when a scholar has read his colleagues for so long that he arrives at a couple of additional ideas himself. Accordingly, there are theoreticians who claim that Bach composed his entire *Keyboard Practice III* merely by following old models, in order to demonstrate his erudition—that basically it is nothing more than the product of assimilating other people's works. It is striking that these individuals say such things about Bach, but take care not to assert the same about Brahms or Beethoven. And yet they could easily reproach Beethoven for having written his *Diabelli Variations* simply to prove that he too could compose like the great Diabelli, or Brahms for having shown in his *Academic Festival Overture* that he was incapable of having ideas of his own.

All this would be no sillier than insinuating that in his great organ work Bach wanted to copy other composers. Schweitzer goes one better when he avers that the Four Duets must have entered the opus inadvertently, because he does not know what to make of them. Indeed, Keller similarly says that he does not understand them. Of course, we might already ask whether anyone understands the triple fugue correctly when he sees it as the portrayal of God the Father, Son, and Holy Ghost. At any rate, we can approach the Four Duets much more closely if we try to analyze their harmony. In them Bach achieves in many different passages the de facto abolition of any tonal reference. In the Four Duets he introduces for the very first time a nontonally determined music; it is, so to speak, atonal music. Similarly, in the F Minor Fugue of *The Well-Tempered*

Clavier he presents a fugal theme that comes very close to a twelve-tone row (as Bernstein points out).

All those who talk of "stylistic change," of a "considerable theoretical-historical component," of a conversion to the *stile antico,* of number symbolism, of "macrostructures," "sound grids," and the like, claim of themselves that they possess an uncommon understanding of art. Few dare to question this. The nimbus of a specialized superiority surrounds scholars, no matter what their field of activity may be. But what escapes all these experts on art is an understanding of the working method of artists. For art (in this case music) is not their world at all but only the object of their studies. It is not something that takes place in them but something that once came into being outside them; not something they experience but something they merely observe, distancing themselves so they can examine it. But that is something completely different from art itself. The method associated with study is not creative; it is deductive and analytical: What comes from where? What consists of what?

The structure of Schweitzer's splendid (because enthusiastically written) book makes that quite clear (and if I take issue with him in one place or another, it is not in order to disparage his book but because it merits more attention than many of those that have tacitly set it aside). He too works deductively. He begins with a survey of the history of church music up to Bach: What comes from where? His portrayal is analytical too: aesthetic discussions, reviews, and analyses of works make up more than half the book—three-quarters even, if we include the performance indications. The biographical element, in contrast, represents less than a quarter of the whole. His real domain, in which he has no predecessors, is the analysis of Bach's tone language. (He describes the *Little Organ Book* as its "dictionary.") And there he makes some very interesting discoveries.

The problem is that with regard to Bach's instrumental works 297 that have no textual base, his analysis proves to be unproductive. (Probably his lack of interest in *The Well-Tempered Clavier* stems from that.) But we must also ponder his system in relation to Bach's organ chorales and chorale preludes: If for Bach there really were such preestablished forms of expression, then why did he create as many as nine very divergent treatments for the chorale "Allein Gott in der Höh' sei Ehr'" ("Glory Be to God on High Alone"), to cite one example? And the revelation of a "Bachian tone language" becomes still more dubious if we check it for its practical value: In listening to music as in playing it, it is as useful as an index of all the words Goethe used would be for understanding and performing his literary works.

Following, paralleling, and departing from Schweitzer, others have devoted themselves to similar analytical pursuits. They have counted Bach's notes and discovered arithmetic wonders in them, the causes for which are mere necessities of musical logic. They have found out that he produced his compositions with the help of the Cabala or exclusively because of the Cabala. They have inferred Bach's position on various Bible interpretations from the chords he noted down; conversely, they have investigated the influence of specialized theological literature on his harmony. The questions "What comes from where?" and "What consists of what?" virtually form the foundation of academic Bach literature. To be sure, it can hardly be concerned with more; at most we can fault these studies for being carried out here and there with considerable superficiality and often with far-fetched references as well.

Occasionally this sort of thing is not without its comic side, as, for example, when a theologically minded musicologist, referring to a Bach chorale, wonders in all seriousness whether perhaps "behind Bach's personal musical style" there is not "also an expression of personal involvement with the text." We can only enjoy the sensitivity of such musing and chuckle at its having been taken seriously by other academics in the field. A little later in that same piece, there appears a fundamental appreciation: "Bach's own achievement consists in the convincing mediation between musical expressions and theological material."

Now theological material has nothing whatsoever to do with belief, and musical forms of expression have just as little to do with creativity, but there is no mention of that. The statement could hardly be phrased more unartistically, in a manner more remote from any artistic feeling, yet here are no less than four Bach scholars who profess this thesis unanimously (and without being contradicted). But luckily, insights like these and their ilk share one great characteristic: Since no one can make music with them, they are completely useless and suited at best to persuade their authors that they know all about a subject that is completely inaccessible to them.

For all this has less than nothing to do with comprehension, with empathy for the working method of the artist. I have collaborated for decades with composers, conductors, directors, singers, and actors; they have allowed me much more than "a few insights into their work." There is one thing I can assure all those who are proud to be able to prove that Bach drew this from one place and that from another, that he composed this piece following Palestrina's example and that one according to the aesthetic categories of Gottsched, or even that he adapted his musical forms of expression to the views of contemporary theologians: In my entire life I have never known a single composer whose ambition was to write like any other, a deceased one least of all. Nor have I ever met a conductor who wanted to copy someone else with his tempi, his conceptions of a work. And if one can induce a director to look at a colleague's production at all, he does not think for a moment about adopting this or that from him; rather, what he will do, and do quite differently, occurs to him almost on the spot. This is not because all these people are fools on some tangent of their own; there is no other reason for it than that they are artists and so they are creative and have their own ideas. In their art they are compelled to express and to fulfill *themselves.* "It's about me when I write, always about me!" said Thomas Mann. The same goes for every artist. 299

Naturally, like all other human beings, all artists absorb the influences of their surroundings, the tendencies of their time. Writing in German means writing in a language that has shaped its habits of thought over 1,000 years; thus even the most modern writers are rooted in the past through their language. It is no different with music. But to search for influence directly, so that we can say afterwards that someone took this from that and that from this, and here wanted to write like this person and there like that one—collecting such influences, as academics have said again and again about Bach (of all people), corresponds exclusively to the thought process of a later and lesser generation. Mozart admired Johann Christian Bach, but he did not write like Johann Christian Bach. Schubert admired Beethoven, Brahms admired Schumann, Bruckner admired Wagner—but none of them wrote "under the influence of" Beethoven, Schumann, or Wagner but as Schubert, Brahms, and Bruckner. It is also characteristic that in the literature about those just named, the question "Now where did he get that?" never comes up at all; "Bachology" alone endeavors to push the "master of all masters" (and so on) into the role of a permanent imitator.

Even assuming that Bach really did know Fischer's *Ariadne musica* (which cannot be proved by merely reading similarities into it), then the one and only interesting point is still that he developed from the same idea something much greater, something groundbreaking and more complete.

But there are those who are not interested that Bach actually is the very first who wrote great preludes and fugues in C-sharp major and F-sharp major and E-flat minor and B-flat minor, and that on top of that in these pieces he modulated from those keys into others any way he wanted—all of which was unprecedented in such perfection at the time. For them, it is a certainty that he wanted to imitate Fischer. When he finally invented the electric light bulb, Edison presumably had no other intention but to imitate the
kerosene lamp.

25

THE INSINUATION THAT WITH THE *KEYBOARD PRACTICE III*
Bach wanted to demonstrate his study of other composers is all
the more inappropriate in that everything Bach took up immediately turned into Bach. His work was marked by a harmony unparalleled in his time. Although he may have differentiated
between his *French* and *English Suites,* we do not really hear anything
"English" in those so named. But we instantly identify them as
Bach, even without knowing the titles. And in the *Keyboard Practice
III* we rightfully recognize a connection among the prelude, the
four duets, and the fugue because all six are utterly unusual works
of art. What is utterly unusual (and never copied in the same
form) is the combination of three markedly heterogeneous fugal
themes in a unity that bubbles over with musicality, as well as the
juxtaposition of three themes in the prelude. We must advance far
forward in music history before we find another composer who
treats three themes in a single movement, by that point symphoni-
cally: Bruckner.

And in the case of the chorale settings, another question
arises. Bach had decided on his own initiative, without receiving
any commission at all, to create settings of the chorale melodies
that corresponded to Luther's catechism. Under those conditions,
how could he do otherwise than compose in a very different way

from before, especially since the publication was intended for connoisseurs of this kind of work? No reason existed to go back to the beautifully circumscribed limits of the *Little Organ Book*. Certainly it would have been advantageous in business terms if Bach had produced musical consumer goods for the market (and we could be grateful to him for that). But this was no longer an organ book "in which a beginning organist is given instruction in developing a chorale in various ways, and also in perfecting himself in the study of the pedal etc." Nor was it an artistic demonstration of theory ("Look, I can write like . . . "), for then he would have explicitly stressed what he intended, as he did elsewhere ("in the Italian style," *"in stilo francese"*). This work—and that is what is so unprecedented about it—was created out of the same impetus that would later lead Beethoven to write his symphonies. Beethoven did not compose them in order to show the world what symphonic development can be derived from a major and a minor third, from a simple triad, or from a simple fifth. Rather, he was compelled from within to supply musical problems with perfect musical solutions.

Back to Bernstein again: "The meaning of music is in the music, and nowhere else." For people who have no living relationship with music but only a theoretical one, that must be nothing short of unacceptable. What is one supposed to imagine about a piece of music if one is not supposed to imagine anything about it at all? Even if we remove all the meaning from music, it still remains music. But what remains of their theories without music itself?

"Thus it is not surprising that probably for the first time in Bach's creative production a collection of works . . . displays a considerable theoretical-historical component . . . in the juxtaposition of retrospective and modernistic styles of composition" (Wolff). That may sound extremely meaningful to a nonmusician. But a musician cannot compose in such a manner unless he is marked by styl302 istic colorlessness and lack of character. He would have to resemble the unprincipled hack in Gustav Freytag's *Journalists*, who confesses: "I've written to the left and again to the right; I can write according to any line of thought." Bach was anything but unprincipled; from the beginning he possessed a pronounced personal style.

Certain scholars think themselves extremely important when they point out that here one composer and there another wrote something that reminds them of Bach. But when on that basis they attribute to Bach a permanent urge to imitate, they go astray. Musicologists are very proud when they can show in the bibliography of an article that they have assimilated the ideas of others in its pages. But when a musician adopts a style or melody from one of his peers, his colleagues immediately cry: "You copycat! You stole that altogether!" In art the only thing that counts is originality, and copying is held in contempt.

Yet that is exactly what all sorts of people would like to ascribe to Bach as a merit. They behave as though he became acquainted with the compositions of Grigny, Frescobaldi, or Scheidt only in Leipzig at the end of the 1730s, although they had actually been at his disposal since the Lüneburg days. It is even claimed that Bach first had to study the *Gradus ad Parnassum* of Fux in order to write in the old ecclesiastical modes. But the ecclesiastical modes were completely familiar to him; to this day many hymns are sung in them, so for an organist of the eighteenth century they were just as much taken for granted as the old C clef.

When Schleuning speaks of a "historicizing application of the old ecclesiastical modes" in the *Keyboard Practice III*, he is mistaken. Not only were they still in vogue in those days, but he would find them in the nineteenth and twentieth centuries as well: They occur in Liszt's Second Hungarian Rhapsody, in Sibelius's Fourth and Sixth Symphonies, in the Fourth Symphony of Brahms, in Debussy (for example, in *Fêtes* from the *Nocturnes*), and even in works by rock musicians like the Beatles. These ecclesiastical modes are in fact not antiquated at all; they facilitate extremely striking harmonic modulations.

The other part of Schleuning's assertion—that Bach wanted to show he could write "modernistically"—is completely wrong as

303

well. After all, no "modernistic" style was available to him, so he could not write in that manner. The word seems to imply that he was following some contemporary's example. But the musicologists do not tell us where else they have come across a style resembling Bach's. It would be lovely to find out that Bach availed himself of the same harmony as a Mr. X, in order to show that he could be a match for him as well as for the old composers.

There is another element for which there is certainly no room in such imaginative coordinates: individuality. Many scholars feel scholarly only if they can conclude that a great mind is composed of nothing more than a batch of influences. In every passage of an artist's work, they would like to demonstrate where he got what he created. It is their pride and joy to convert a unique oeuvre into a patchwork quilt.

No great artist is a fool, off on a tangent of his own. From his earliest youth until his final days, Bach looked around him in the musical world; his thirst for information was virtually unparalleled, beginning in his childhood when he took the scores from his brother's cabinet at night in order to copy them out. From the start, Bach educated himself, but already in Arnstadt he was writing in his own individual style. Nowhere in Böhm can we find an organ chorale comparable in power of expression even to Bach's "Glory Alone to God in the Highest" of 1706; nor in Buxtehude a single fugue of Bach's architectonic greatness. Naturally, Bach learned from both of them, just as he did from Telemann, Marchand, Vivaldi, Handel, and many, many others. He was not so silly as to despise the successful composers of his time; his mind contained a whole compendium of music. But when he composed, he composed as Johann Sebastian Bach, and even the early *Capriccio on the Departure of His Much Beloved Brother* does not display the slightest similarity to Kuhnau's *Biblical Sonatas*.

304   That is why Bach could not have convincingly carried out the theoretical intentions ascribed to him by certain parties, if ever he had harbored them in the first place. His personal style was too

pronounced. At fifty-four he had more than four decades of artistic self-fulfillment behind him; his was a mature and distinctive personality. Personality as the mark of a character always means self-definition and determination as well. Up to then Bach had at no time written like anybody else. That at fifty-four he supposedly started doing so—or even trying to—is nothing but a fantasy.

Of course, in academic circles such observations are never expressed so bluntly. Scholars do not contradict one another; at most they supplement one another. So to put it in musicological terms: "With regard to the *Keyboard Practice III*, perhaps the perspectives of Wolff and Schleuning may need to be supplemented to a certain degree in various aspects in the near future."

We should not do things by halves. The completely inappropriate attempt to give credit to the medical student Mizler for Bach's "change in style" is not an isolated instance. In all seriousness, Geck wishes to prove to us that Bach was fulfilling the aesthetic requirements of Gottsched and Scheibe with his compositions and thus complying with their demands. Going into the greatest detail, he expounds on which works Bach wrote in Gottsched's "low," "middle," and "lofty" style, as though Bach would first have had to study those aesthetic dictates before he started to compose—as though they would have had anything to tell him.

Carl Philipp Emanuel expressly acknowledged of his father: "The deceased was no friend of dry theoretical stuff." But Geck frankly admits in other places that he gives no credence to the statements of Bach's sons. In his eyes they must have been real fibbers, and on no account can they have known their father as well as he, Professor Geck.

The idea that Bach's works could have been written according to the aesthetic categories of Gottsched and Scheibe is grotesque, even if that sort of thing is not an isolated occurrence (compare the Mizler case). The belief of those who cannot create that they could instruct those who can is quite widespread among certain

305

theoreticians. They think they know more about the matter on the basis of their studies. But though a scholar of theater may master all the details concerning Shakespeare, his plays, his times, and the Globe Theatre, the actress who must play Ophelia cannot use anything of that for her art. It helps her neither with her breath control nor with her speech technique nor with her physical gestures. It does not in any way enrich the ability that made her into an actress in the first place—the capacity to turn the emotions of fictional figures into her own and transmit them to an audience. Yet without this, all her acting arts are naught, and she leaves people cold.

Academic dealings with art are always nonartistic. Aesthetics can analyze art, no doubt, but cannot produce it, not even indirectly. Anatomy is different from procreation. Though the harem guard may know much about physical love from his own experience, the most essential element remains closed to him: eroticism itself. However much the ethologist may discover and communicate to us about the development, behavior, and psychology of dolphins, he is incapable of grasping the life of these intelligent beings in the seas, an endless world without landscape and sky. The breadth and depth of the oceans remain inaccessible to his experience. "Art has no enemies except those who cannot make art"—this shattering observation was made by Albrecht Dürer, who certainly did not lack admirers in his lifetime. To see Gottsched's and Scheibe's influence in Bach's compositions, one must be far removed from Bach and his music. That is how one arrives at such an assertion: "With the three parts of the *Keyboard Practice*, he conquered the field of keyboard music according to plan"—as though Bach had not already created heaps of "keyboard music" before that. That is how one concludes that Bach's *Little Organ Book* can best be compared with Beethoven's bagatelles or that a fugue from the last years of Bach's life presumably belongs to his *Art of Fugue* precisely because its theme does not appear in that work at all.

No less clever is Schleuning's claim that the *Goldberg Variations* were a preliminary study for the *Art of Fugue* since "the building principle of monothematic variations" they display points to the latter. We could explain with similar zeal that the bicycle is a precursor of the automobile, since it already has two of its four wheels, fitted with rubber tires like the car's. The learned author of this thesis should at least have studied Bach enough to notice that the fugue he dedicated as an eighteen-year-old to his elder brother was already "monothematic" and that incidentally monothematic treatment is virtually the characteristic compositional method for Bach. All his concerti are monothematic as well, from the *Brandenburg* series to the Italian; we can almost (with a few exceptions) describe him as a monothematic composer. Erudition that is not aware of even that much inspires little confidence.

Machiavelli says in *The Prince:* "There are three kinds of minds: first those that attain insight and understanding of things by their own means, then those that recognize what is right when others explain it to them, and finally those that are capable of neither one nor the other." After this excursion into musicology, let us return to Bach. We may count him in Machiavelli's first category. That ranking makes a great deal of scholarly hypotheses superfluous, but it brings us closer to understanding his exceptional nature.

We need not stick to the question of what company he kept in his maturity. Much more decisive is the path he had taken to become Johann Sebastian Bach. We know he made his way in a unique manner—as an autodidact. But what an autodidact! From his older brother he had acquired the musical fundaments; by playing the clavier he had surely learned thoroughbass and thus harmony as well. That was the musical alphabet, so to speak. But from what teacher, from what textbook did he absorb the difficult domain of counterpoint?

307

We know the curriculum and syllabus of the Lüneburg school, but we hear nothing about a counterpoint manual there.

Though some people pretend that Bach's first compositions were written under the influence of Böhm, not a one of them has claimed that Bach was trained in counterpoint by Böhm. In any case the contrapuntal feats the young Bach was already able to perform do not occur in Böhm at all. In Böhm as in Buxtehude there are passages where both composers merely rely on the sound effects of the organ, but in Bach such lapses are nowhere to be found.

Bach owed his knowledge and skill to neither teachers nor textbooks; rather, he acquired them from reading the music of his predecessors. Recognizing from the notes themselves the laws that governed them was an astonishing achievement in itself. But it was not the only one. Even more astounding is that he immediately began to compose contrapuntally in his very own style, peculiar to him alone. This is what Scheibe describes: "All the voices are supposed to work with each other and be of equal difficulty, and one does not recognize among them any principal part." When Scheibe finally notices that technique, Bach has already been practicing it with success for more than thirty years. From the beginning it was the vital element of his music, and there is not a single other musician of whom one can say that in the same way. No other wrote so many and such great fugues for his pleasure as Bach did, and the fugues are by no means his only polyphonic music, nor even his most rigorous. That honor goes to the canon, a form that delighted him again and again; he had fun with his puzzle canons and let others crack the nuts.

Another characteristic of Bach's is his amusement in building up a series, as he reveals in the headings of the *Goldberg Variations*: "*Canone all'unisono*," "*alla seconda*," "*alla terza*," "*alla quarta*," and so forth to "*alla nona*." If something like that does not give someone pleasure, he lets it drop. It also proves that up to the end of his life Bach never stopped exploring the mystery of separate voices making music with each other. Musical exploration was in general his greatest passion. We need only think of his truly revolutionary discoveries in the domain of harmony.

With regard to "well-tempered" tuning, scholars point out time and again that the solution was found long before Bach by the Halberstadt organist Werckmeister. That is simply not correct: Werckmeister described it, but he did not put it into effect himself. Actually, Werckmeister's equal temperament is not yet identical with Bach's at all; it only comes closer to it than before. Bach's equal-tempered pitch was still not commonly understood even after his death. His pupil Kirnberger worked out a tuning method that did surpass Werckmeister's but could not match Bach's equal temperament. As Forkel reports: "He tuned both his harpsichord and his clavichord himself, and was so practiced in the procedure that it never took him more than a quarter of an hour. But then, when he improvised, all 24 keys were at his command; he did with them whatever he wished." Kirnberger did not later attain this tuning to the same degree, and we must know that in order to recognize how far Bach had leapt ahead in his praxis at a time when his contemporaries were still obliged to experiment. Bach was no "friend of dry theoretical stuff," but on a practical level he had become immersed in the problems of harmony as early as his Arnstadt days. As a result, twelve years later he could modulate with absolute purity of tone through all the major and minor scales, a feat not even his great contemporary Handel accomplished.

Yet what was marvelous and unique about this great music-explorer Bach was that despite his grandiose theoretical knowledge, as demonstrated in his praxis, he never became coolly theoretical but always wrote and performed lively music. For him, singability was the basic criterion of all his art, and a cantabile performance was his main objective. Not one to comment thoughtlessly, Wilhelm Furtwängler was speaking from the deepest expertise when he observed that in his view Verdi and Bach were the greatest melodists in musical history.

26

Carl Philipp Emanuel Bach, Bach's second son, began his study of law in Leipzig. Then for reasons still unknown he transferred to the university at Frankfurt on the Oder, even though the law faculty there and the musical world as well were more or less in shambles, according to descriptions of the time. In 1738 he moved on to Berlin—as a musician, of course; he was never a practicing jurist. He almost accompanied the son of Imperial Count von Keyserlingk on a great journey abroad, but nothing came of it because the count, as ambassador to Dresden, opted to send his son to Leipzig to continue his education at the university. As already reported, the count's cousin Dietrich was an intimate friend of Crown Prince Frederick in Berlin. When he succeeded to the throne in 1740 as Frederick II, he did two notable things right away, in the very first year of his reign: He invaded Silesia without any declaration of war, and he engaged Carl Philipp Emanuel Bach as his harpsichordist.

He delivered an explanation for his attack on Silesia after the fact. He did the same in his succeeding campaigns as well; that was his concept of a declaration of war. Carl Philipp Emanuel Bach remained in his post for twenty-eight years, until March 1768; thus he knew the Prussian court from the closest possible perspective. No high praise of Frederick the Great on his part has come down to us; rather, when he broached the subject at all, we note signs of a clear reserve. Right from the beginning, as court harpsichordist he had more of a steady income than his father, 300 thalers. But as Frederick's flute teacher, Johann Joachim Quantz received 2,000, plus extra payment for each flute he made for the king.

All this would not be important in a biography of Johann Sebastian Bach except that it explains why he traveled to Berlin once again in 1747. Twenty-eight years earlier he had picked up a clavier there for the prince of Cöthen. The conjecture voiced by many that Bach may have wanted to look around for a position in Berlin is rather implausible. If there had been one available, his son would certainly have let him know about it, especially since he was all too aware of the conditions his father endured in Leipzig. But from the depths of his being, Frederick was no great patron of sacred music, nor did he pay particularly well. In a country like Prussia, in which 80 percent of the state budget was spent on the military, life was not very lavish. Besides, the two Grauns, Carl Heinrich and Johann Gottlieb, were already in Berlin, and both had long standing as musicians to Frederick and were of exceptional ability.

Naturally, Frederick had informed himself about the important father of his harpsichordist. Schleuning has discovered some very interesting parallels between the flute sonatas of Bach and those of Frederick. The only problem is that from this he draws the curious conclusion not that Frederick composed in the style of Bach but that Bach composed in the style of Frederick. Now *that* is original.

If Frederick was interested in the father of his harpsichordist, since 1746 there was another person who could give him a detailed report: the Russian ambassador to his court, Imperial Count von Keyserlingk, cousin of Frederick's friend who had died two years before. So it is certainly understandable that Frederick wanted to meet this man Bach, whose sonatas he already knew and about whom so much was recounted in the highest terms. Miesner, who investigated the life of Keyserlingk, turns the facts of the case wonderfully upside down: He imagines not that the king wanted to meet Bach but rather Bach the king, and that Keyserlingk arranged the necessary formalities for him.

We do not know whether the king insisted on observing formalities at his famous encounter with Bach, though through Forkel we are well informed about the events of Bach's visit. According to Forkel, Bach was on a journey with his son Friedemann to see Carl Philipp Emanuel. At the Potsdam gate their coach was stopped and Bach was summoned posthaste to the recently completed Sanssouci Palace, where the king was in the midst of his evening concert. Since these concerts usually began at seven o'clock in the evening, it must already have been later than that. In Forkel's depiction, Frederick immediately interrupted the concert with the words, "Gentlemen, the elder Bach has arrived!" Another version tells us that Bach had to wait at first in the antechamber. Yet another would have us believe that Bach stayed in the antechamber the whole time, listening to the concert from outside. These variants are all the more astounding since Forkel owed his portrayal to Carl Philipp Emanuel himself, who as harpsichordist was present at the encounter.

When the crown prince of Kassel wanted to hear Bach play during Gesner's period in office, he sent the composer and his spouse a formal invitation, placed servants and a sedan chair at their disposal, had him to dinner, and even presented him with a valuable ring on his departure. When Frederick II wanted to hear Bach, he had him intercepted at the city gate and summoned to him at once.

Bach was sixty-two at this time, and people aged far more quickly in those days. He had just completed a ten-, if not fourteen-hour trip by stagecoach, and the king had not even given him time to change into suitable clothes. Nor did he allow him a moment's rest. Bach had to try the pianos in all the different chambers right away and improvise on each one. First and foremost, the king was interested in impressing Bach with his musical treasures, as we can see from the course of his visit; that he found this necessary shows he secretly had some respect for Bach after all. Then Bach requested a fugal theme from the king and duly developed it. The next day he had to take a look at the Potsdam organs and try them out, and in the evening he had to appear at the concert once again. On this occasion the king challenged him to improvise a six-part fugue on the same theme as before. With that he had finally driven Bach to the limits of his art; this was something Bach could not achieve with Frederick's theme. But on a theme of his own he improvised a six-part fugue on the spot, an incredible feat of skill.

The rest is well known. Back at home again, Bach elaborated Frederick's theme in the most artful manner, as ricercar, as fugue, and canonically in many different forms. He added a flute sonata and several puzzle canons as well because he believed that in Frederick he had found a connoisseur. These splendid displays of skill kept him utterly on tenterhooks for many weeks, but exactly two months after the visit to Sanssouci he rounded off the work, had it engraved on copper, and sent it to the king as a *Musical Offering* with a humble dedication. For this unique homage, the great Frederick showed just as much gratitude and just as much generosity as he had for Bach's two-day guest performance: He totally overlooked the priceless gift and never expressed the slightest thanks, not even by a couple of friendly words to Carl Philipp Emanuel—otherwise Forkel would have reported them. Frederick's conscience toward Johann Sebastian Bach remained completely clear, however; after all, he never made use of it.

Among Bach specialists, various legends have grown up around the "royal fugal theme." Despite the opinion of Bach, who considered Frederick such a perfect musician that he dedicated puzzle canons to him, scholars have raised serious doubts about Frederick's talent. They have done so especially (but not exclusively) in East Germany, where it seemed incompatible with a "progressive consciousness" to ascribe so much excellence to a militaristic absolutist.

In fact Frederick did compose quite properly and even remark-
314 ably for his time. Since he had pursued music with thoroughness for more than a decade and a half by then, it was almost inevitable that some experience and knowledge would express themselves in

his work. The Swiss flute virtuoso Aurèle Nicolet has pointed out that the beginning of the "royal theme" shows parallels with warm-up figures that are commonly employed on the flute. The prerequisites for inventing his fugal motif were thus perfectly available to Frederick. The invention of a theme of eight measures is no great matter, above all if one can leave the elaboration of the fugue to someone else. The king, however, did not need to place the slightest value on its brilliant execution. The old gentleman in the shabby jacket could allegedly do anything, after all, and Frederick would not have been Frederick if he had not been bent on pushing him to the limits of his art.

That is shown by his challenge to a six-part fugue. Playing six parts on the harpsichord requires an extraordinary, indeed a total dexterity. A person only has ten fingers. The *Musical Offering* does contain a six-part ricercar, but a six-part fugue is found neither in *The Well-Tempered Clavier* nor in the twenty-four preludes and fugues of 1744, *The Well-Tempered Clavier II*. Thus Frederick was purposefully demanding something that he could predict would be impossible. It must have been a disappointment to him that Bach nevertheless managed to pull off the feat with a theme of his own. The king could not wring any surrender from this opponent on the battlefield of music.

But Bach called the theme an "excellent" one in the dedication of his *Musical Offering,* even if it was unusable for a six-part fugue, and with that the matter was settled for the researchers. The reason it could not be by Frederick was that it could not be by Frederick. From a strict scholarly perspective, the king must have got it from *somebody.* Rueger has even figured out where Bach got the whole *Musical Offering.* Published in 1691, the *Kunstbuch (Art Book)* of Johann Theile, a pupil of Heinrich Schütz, contains thirteen pieces as well. The idea of dedicating the work to Frederick did not come from Bach either, but from Giovanni Battista Vitali, who had once dedi- cated a similar work to a duke in Italy sixty years earlier. So here again Bach was nothing but an imitator.

But not Bach alone. Naturally, Frederick's "excellent" fugal theme could not be by him either. Arnold Schoenberg has figured the matter out: The king had the theme slipped to him by his harpsichordist, Carl Philipp Emanuel. Yet Frederick took great pains never to let anybody see his cards. The notion that he would have turned to Bach's son, of all people, for a theme he could pass off as his to the father presupposes either an effervescent imagination or none at all.

Yet Schoenberg did ascertain something important that seems to have completely escaped the theoreticians to this day: that this theme Bach termed "excellent" was anything but that. Schoenberg describes the theme as essentially a trap, a "theme that resisted Johann Sebastian's versatility." And he continues: "In the *Art of Fugue* a minor triad would offer many contrapuntal openings; the Royal theme, also a minor triad, did not permit a single canonic imitation. All the marvels that the 'Musical Offering' displays are attained from without, through countersubjects, counter-melodies, and other additions." But after reaching these extremely sensible conclusions, he returns to his Carl Philipp Emanuel theory all the same and declares: "Whether his own malice led him astray, or whether the 'joke' was ordered by the King, can presumably only be proven psychologically."

Accusing Bach's son of outrageous behavior toward his father, without any firm reason, does not exactly reveal high-mindedness on Schoenberg's part. Not a single unfavorable remark by Carl Philipp Emanuel about his father has come down to us. But with regard to the king it is a different story: "The sovereign does not even want to look at my own beautiful works! And how he wounded my deceased father: he had . . . gone to so much trouble over the 'Musical Offering,' and Frederick did not care to glance at the score. In his last three years my father hoped for some acknowledgment, all in vain." This raises the question, on what were Schoenberg's insinuations based?

But the most eccentric theory of all about the origin of the "royal theme" is furnished by Schleuning in his work on the *Art of*

316

Fugue. In his opinion the king obtained the fugal motif (unsuitable, according to Schoenberg) from none other than . . . Bach himself. Bach supposedly reckoned on Frederick's summons far in advance. Before beginning his journey, he sent this very theme ahead to Carl Philipp Emanuel so that he would foist it off on the king. He did so because he divined that Frederick would turn exclusively to Carl Philipp Emanuel for a fugal theme and that he would then proffer it as his own. Which brings Lichtenberg's comment to mind: If this is philosophy, then at least it is a mad one.

The theories about the origin of the "royal theme" range from gross implausibility to absolute folly. Poor Frederick! Here eight truly remarkable measures occurred to him for once while he was playing his flute, and these are the very ones nobody gives him credit for.

Incidentally, we can infer that the king was no admirer of Bach's at all. If he had been, Carl Philipp Emanuel would not have withheld it from us. But Frederick was a skeptic, even a cynic; nothing was more natural to him than to bait a widely praised man. Bach did not allow him to triumph; indeed, he later even turned the occasion into a triumph of his own. The king had little reason to be grateful to him for that. He had challenged him, but Bach had proved himself to be the far greater musician. The Russian ambassador had been right to extol him, and to Bach Frederick the Great owed a defeat.

If we try to view this whole course of events from Bach's standpoint, however, none of these ideas is of any interest. Bach had been challenged to prove his skill to the most important German prince of the time. He could not expect that this would be made easy for him. It was not his first time in Berlin; he was familiar with the king from the accounts of his son, so he knew that Frederick was no contrapuntalist. And if he received a theme from him that did not fulfill the necessary prerequisites, he could not possibly have suspected a malicious intention behind it; insufficient knowledge of contrapuntal requirements was a more obvious explanation. Just as little could it have occurred to him that the king was only out to impress him; if that were so, it was unlikely that Frederick would have sacrificed a whole second day to the effort. Rather, Bach must have sensed in him a far-reaching interest in his art, an interest that must have affected him all the more deeply since the music of this king, like that of his sons, took other paths than his own.

When we contemplate the course of Bach's life, we get the impression not that he fell increasingly under the spell of the past (a *"stile antico"*) but that he arrived increasingly at a greater consciousness of the uniqueness of his own art. The theory of the *"stile antico"* is built on sand in any case. Generally it is understood to mean the style of composition molded above all by Palestrina. But that style is still characterized by very modest counterpoint and very limited modulations—two traits so completely foreign to Bach that we can only be amazed by suggestions that he ever tended toward the *"stile antico."*

At any rate, when we compare the theme of the *Musical Offering* with that of the *Art of Fugue,* we receive quite a different impression: It would seem that the former gave the impulse for the latter. First we have a demonstration of how to master a really unsuitable theme, then a demonstration of all that can be achieved with an ideal theme. Yet the inappropriate motif must have exercised an almost magical attraction on Bach as well. He must have considered it a unique challenge. The incredibly short gestation period of the work can be explained only through an extreme devotion to the subject, through a truly obsessive focus on it.

Another event stands in direct temporal connection with the *Musical Offering:* Bach's joining of Mizler's Society of Musical Sciences. Here again something has been ascertained with extraordinary perspicacity that points to Bach's mathematical talent as well as to his marked superstition—that is, his dependence on the Cabala, the secret Jewish numerology. "Bach's number" was fourteen (or, to transpose the digits, forty-one). Since he could not wait until forty members were assembled in the society, because the number was restricted by the statutes to twenty, he supposedly bode his time until thirteen had joined, and then at number fourteen it was "his turn." This will be clear as day to any mind that is clouded enough. Superstition rules the minds of the relevant scholars more conclusively than it ever did Bach's.

But in Mizler's statutes we do find one motivation for joining that seems more plausible: Each year every member of the society had to submit a piece that was circulated among the members. Moreover, all the pieces collected in this way were to be preserved along with the portraits of the members. That Bach's art could be disseminated and preserved in such a manner, in the very best of company—that was quite a different reason to join. The impression Bach had made on Frederick cannot be compared with the one Frederick had made on Bach. A great king—Frederick stood at the apogee of his grandeur at this time—had dedicated two whole days to him and shown enormous interest in his contrapuntal gifts. This must have made him more aware than ever before of the uniqueness of his knowledge and his skill. Not that it swelled his pride in the way of Schindler, who would later boast of his days as Beethoven's servant. It simply must have become clearer to him that he had something to impart, something that no other composer possessed to an equal extent: the art of fugue. If that talent had interested a king, how much more must it interest other musicians.

Bach's genius is in fact particularly characterized by his quite exceptional capacity for polyphony. His clavier and organ fugues were to him nothing different from the musical ideas that great composers of the following century would turn into "études," "album leaves," or "songs without words." They were not just excellent constructions, as for a later contrapuntalist like Sechter; for Bach, his fugues were character pieces as well. In the 1740s he must have become increasingly aware that he stood alone in the mastery of this art. 319

A lot of nonsense has been scribbled to the effect that in his late creations Bach intellectually lagged behind the musical development of the century—that he was "antiquated," that the "gallant style" had passed him by, and that his sons were the forerunners of a modern art. But that sort of thing is superficial and thoughtless; it does not stand up to a confrontation with reality. In fact what is described (very hazily) as the "gallant style" was already in existence at the beginning of the century; we need only take a look at the music of that time. For example, where are the great polyphonic works, where are the fugues of Vivaldi, Tartini, or Albinoni, of Lully, Rameau, Couperin, Hasse, or Purcell? Were the oratorios of Handel, which he performed in that same decade of the 1740s, "antiquated" too? It is a strange "old style" that seamlessly matches everything that follows it. Since that decade marked the great victory of Handel's oratorios, then these must logically have been written in the "gallant style." But perhaps that classification would be a little grotesque?

Music is a domain that cannot be forced into pigeonholes. "Baroque music" was superseded by a "gallant style" just as little as "Classicism" was superseded by "Romanticism." Weber's *Der Freischütz*, Schubert's *Unfinished Symphony,* and Beethoven's Ninth Symphony were composed almost at the same time. We can point out that the "Romantics" Schubert and Weber already belonged to a different generation from the "Classic" Beethoven, yet for their contemporaries all three of them were writing "contemporary music." Rossini, who came to Vienna in Beethoven's time, was neither one nor the other. No one really wants to include Wenzel Müller, Ignaz Pleyel, or Johann Nepomuk Hummel in the fold of Classicism; at most Salieri and Dittersdorf might be admitted, with some reservations, just to play it safe. It would probably be better to consign them all to the "Vienna School." The "Age of Sentimentalism" was created especially for the organ composer Christian Heinrich Rinck, also a contemporary, without considering that his works show no trace of that trait anywhere—though they do reveal an unmistakable enthusiasm for contrapuntal music. Because of that he does not fit into any of the hackneyed categories, and so he becomes an unacceptable composer. (*Riemann's Music Lexicon* of 1961 still lists him, but he is missing from the *Brockhaus-Riemann* of 1979. In the prelude collection of the new Protestant hymnbook of 1993, he is included again: Although dead for scholarship, he lives in praxis.)

Endeavors to force music into pigeonholes do not further our understanding of either music or musicians; rather, they distract us from both, just like theories about how music reflects the "spirit of the times." When we speak of the "spirit of the times," we enter a space without coordinates, in which anything and everything can be averred, no matter how implausible it may be. It is an ideal realm for speculators: Without any risk they can claim to possess a fortune, because in reality they have nothing to lose.

Johann Sebastian Bach, in his most fundamental works, was never bound by his time. *The Well-Tempered Clavier* presupposed the ability to produce an equally tempered scale, and at the time of its creation this was anything but common knowledge. *Keyboard Practice III* in no way submitted to the requirements of the worship service, and whoever thinks the *Goldberg Variations—Keyboard Practice IV*—are just casual music for home use should sit down at the piano and dash them off at once. Certainly, when these pieces appeared in print they were intended for sale, but we cannot suppose that Bach viewed them as "popular editions" in the conventional sense. All were composed "to delight the spirit of music lovers, and especially connoisseurs of this kind of work." It was no different with the *Musical Offering*, and the *Art of Fugue* is a logically consistent continuation of the entire series. We may still believe in business considerations on Bach's part in the case of *Keyboard Practice I* and *II*—though with some reservations, for a work like the *Italian Concerto* is not simply any concerto; it represents the essence of the genre. But in the case of *Keyboard Practice III* and *IV*, his principal aim is to demonstrate the range of all that is musically possible. The *Musical Offering* and the *Art of Fugue* advance those expositions still further: They are the natural sequels of the earlier demonstrations.

Bach retains the term "keyboard practice" four times with a strange insistence. Similarly, Frédéric Chopin called his enchanting piano fantasies "études," in other words, "exercises." We are also reminded of Bertolt Brecht, who dubbed his masterly plays "experiments," and Adalbert Stifter, who referred to his artful stories as "studies." There is something about these oddly similar terms that gives us pause, for we cannot simply ascribe a common tendency toward understatement to such disparate personalities. Nor did any of them generally display an excessive modesty, except toward their art—perhaps because they could grasp it far more deeply than the rest of us.

27

O<small>F COURSE, BACH DID NOT INVENT THE EXPRESSION</small> "keyboard practice" any more than Chopin invented the term "étude." But what matters is how they used them. Chopin applied the word "étude" to pieces quite different from the exercises Czerny composed for the perfection of his pupils. That Kuhnau had already employed the phrase "keyboard practice" contributes nothing to the elucidation of Bach.

Certain scholars would have us believe that Bach never invented anything but merely rifled through the stock techniques of music history and devised illustrative examples of them. He never thought of fugal composition at all (according to Schleuning) until he was in his "self-ordained retirement." He derived his inspiration from young Mizler, who was translating Fux's *Gradus ad Parnassum* from the Latin at the time. We are meant to conclude that without Mizler's translation Bach would never have known the work, though it had already been available in Latin for twelve years and Bach had such a good command of the language that he could teach it. As a matter of fact, he even recommended Fux to others. But allegedly it was only at this point that he gave Mizler the "research assignment" of translating Fux, contenting himself with "accompanying" the text "compositionally"; in other words, Mizler translated and Bach made musical notes in the margins. Though the idea derives from Schleuning, he is certainly not alone in its propagation; and this is hardly the only scholarly hypothesis we owe to his irrepressible imagination. If we would go along with him, then Bach gave a recital in Cracow as well, and he was contemplating a performance of his ("Catholic") Mass in B Minor at the (Reformed) court of Potsdam. Bach had completed whole sections of the *Goldberg Variations* before Keyserlingk ordered them, and he did not create the work for Keyserlingk's pleasure but in order to fulfill his obsequious duties as court music director in Dresden. That he did not hold that position at all but had been appointed only as court composer does not matter in this kind of scholarship. At any rate, Frederick the Great did commission Bach to write the *Musical Offering*. True, there is no basis for the notion either in the dedication or elsewhere, but a learned mind must not linger over trifles of that sort. As Professor Galetti, famous for his bloopers in the lecture hall, rightly remarked: "Scholarship is concerned with pure knowledge. In the process, reason is completely eliminated."

In reading the secondary literature on Bach, we encounter assertions of the same ilk by the bushel. For example, we are told that in his *Art of Fugue* Bach mainly wanted to prove that he had studied the compositional theories of his cousin Johann Gottfried Walther as well as those of Angelo Benardi and that he knew and understood Mattheson's book *Der vollkommene Capellmeister (The Complete Music Director)*. If we are to believe certain authors, up to the fiftieth year of his life Bach was an utterly uneducated musician. He did not become acquainted with Palestrina's compositions until he was fifty-one and wrote his *Keyboard Practice III* merely to show he had examined the gamut of musical styles. That he devoted his attention to the *Art of Fugue* we really owe only to Mattheson, who in a paragraph of his *Complete Music Director* of 1739 virtually commissioned the work and set it into motion. On the whole, in that case and elsewhere Bach's compositions are not really music but a "theoretical reflection on a virtually experimental plane" (Wolff).

In the meantime, it has also come to light that the sixth *Branden-burg Concerto* is in reality the first and, like the *Musical Offering*, chiefly represents a musical imitation of ancient Roman rhetoric. It is also as good as certain that this famous "old-age work" of Bach's had already entered his mind much earlier; in 1735 Mattheson's *Finger-Sprache (Finger Language)* had appeared, and it must have immediately stimulated Bach's inveterate urge to imitate. Indeed, according to musicological assessment his harpsichord concerti were composed only under the inspiration of Handel's organ concerti, and the *Goldberg Variations* derive their origin from a series of variations by Scarlatti. As for the *Art of Fugue*, Schleuning recommends that we investigate the influence of Winckelmann. If we do, we arrive at in-structive conclusions: Bach was not interested in architecture, nor Winckelmann in music, and the latter's first book, *On the Imitation of Greek Artworks*, did not appear until five years after the composer's death.

I could dwell at much greater length on claims of this kind. Whoever considers the theses listed above to be gross nonsense should avoid perusing the works of serious musicologists; without exception, all these assertions derive from the writings of well-known scholars. If we wanted to refashion our image of the com-poser based on their findings, a very new and by no means more admirable Bach would come to the fore.

From earlier authors we already knew that Bach was hot-tem-pered, in other words, bereft of self-control; we also knew that he lacked any talent for organization. But the Bach authorities of our own time have further succeeded in proving that his most impor-tant compositions merely constitute an imitation of the works of others. He did not become acquainted with the most significant composers of his era until quite late; for the greater part of his life he was an uneducated musician. Yet in shaping his principal works, he mostly mimicked the forms of other creators. (Logically, that would mean that he must have known their compositions after all; musicologically, this is no contradiction at all.) In many of his works, he was simply reacting to the suggestions, challenges, and aesthetic insights of others, a tendency that points to an inferiority complex. His religiousness expressed itself on suitable occasions through the arrangement of his notes in a cruciform configuration. In addition, he endeavored to insert his name into his compositions as often as possible by playing with numbers. But I have not even come close to assembling all the curious findings of modern Bach research. I can only comment that up to now these scholars have failed to notice that Bach's compositions sometimes display crescent-shaped patterns of notes, especially in the transitional passages; this might possibly indicate his connections with Islam.

All in all, as the reader can verify, this is the kind of image that emerges from the research of the most eminent modern authorities on Bach. Of course, there can be no doubt that it is completely wrong. Presumably, the scholars who would protest against such a vision most resolutely are the very ones who brought it into being. But to repeat: it is verifiable as the sum total of their research findings. We can only ask: How could this happen?

There are at least three reasons. For one, they have exhibited not only simple ignorance on occasion but an absolute dearth of musical expertise. Second, they have often haphazardly used mere suppositions to fill in existing gaps in knowledge, passing them off as scholarly findings. Finally, many of these specialists set out not to demonstrate Bach's learning but chiefly their own. They were not interpreting Bach but indirectly proclaiming their own importance via Bach. And moreover, as I earlier observed, scholarly approaches to art are nonartistic by definition.

The only approach to art is art itself. Unartistic approaches to art lead to nothing more than dilettantism. It is a sad state of affairs when a professor would have us believe that, regrettably, Bach's *Italian Concerto* displays "a rather mechanical development." It is obvious that he is not only unfamiliar with Italian concerti in general, but he has never studied the absolutely amazing periodic structure of this concerto in particular. He is judging out of ignorance. And when in another passage he dismisses the magical melodic lines of the *Canonic Variations* as mere "music for the eyes," he manifests a troubled relationship with music as a whole.

Full of pride, another scholar reproaches Bach for his parallel fifths—in other words, for mistakes in harmonization. By doing so he simply demonstrates that he has never learned what passing tones are in harmony. Had he ever devoted any attention to Haydn, he would have observed that over passages that seem to contravene the scholastic rules, the composer would write *"con licenzia"*—"I am allowed."

At the same time, the same author also asserts that there is no rational explanation for the ban on parallel fifths. Of course, for the existence of music as a whole there is no rational explanation. But here we have a music professor who neither has ears nor has read Bach's own words. In Bach's thoroughbass rules, we find the sentence: "Two fifths and two octaves must not follow one another, for this is not only a defect, but it sounds bad."

A third scholar reports with a sense of importance that Bach worked out the same fugal theme twice. What escaped him was that Bach worked out the theme once from the tonic and once from the dominant. Unavoidably, each solution entails completely different harmonic combinations and so leads to a totally different work.

Juggling with number symbolism also belongs here. Supposedly, the first fugue of the *Art of Fugue* has exactly seventy measures only because the number seventy is the "numeric symbol" for Jesus as well as Bach. The inventor of this concept implies that the "master of all masters" was compelled to sign his name everywhere, just like a little boy. The fugue is in D minor for the same reason; the key permits the introduction of the letters *B-A-C-H* in all sorts of sequences, and this was of course what most mattered to Bach. (Did he have nothing more important to do in his music? His interpreters could not think of anything greater to ascribe to him?) 327

Ten notes can only mean the Ten Commandments; three themes, the Holy Trinity. Accordingly, Bach's works are so full of symbols I feel entitled to ask whether he also used his notes to make music. One scholar knows for certain that the *Art of Fugue* was composed because Bach suddenly turned to the past, to the *"stile antico"*; another announces the exact opposite—that Bach was heralding the new "Enlightenment ideas" in this work. Such authors are utterly convinced that the Christian faith could be professed with four notes. But wisely, they neglect to explain how Bach could proclaim "Enlightenment ideas" with twelve notes while pondering the *"stile antico"* at the same time. Eminent scholars of this caliber cast the seriousness of their discipline in a dubious light. As Brecht has Galileo say, one of the main causes of the poverty of knowledge lies in its pretensions to wealth.

"At universities, young people learn to believe," Bako of Verulam asserted, as Schopenhauer relates. Unfortunately, he does not reveal what particular faculty that pronouncement referred to; we are left to rely on conjectures.

Yet we sincerely owe a profound debt of thanks to many musicologists, because with boundless, carefully detailed work they have made treasures of the musical past available to us—treasures that would have been lost forever without their efforts. They are comparable to divers in the South Pacific, fetching pearls from the depths into the light of day, so that later, in the hands of jewelers, the pearls can become precious ornaments. These divers are true heroes, but they do not consider themselves experts in the field of marine biology. They do not claim that just because they dive for pearls they also understand everything there is to know about sharks and herrings.

The grotesque statements made by academic divers into aridity, of which I have cited only a few above, arise chiefly from their belief that notes must primarily represent something other than the written recording of tones. They also spring from the equally grave misconception that we can explain something by identifying where it came from. Whether the sixth *Brandenburg Concerto* was composed first or last is insignificant for the value of the work and insignificant

328

for its interpretation. And by the same token, the eventual precursors of a composition are completely unimportant to its meaning. Its origins do not matter at all; it is the use to which they were put that counts, what became of them. What difference does it make whether the pastoral melody that sounds forth in the third act of Wagner's *Tristan* comes from France, Ireland, or India? It expresses an infinite loneliness: That is why it belongs there. What difference does it make whether Mattheson published his *Finger-Sprache* in 1735? It is just as irrelevant as pointing out, in reference to the Alps, that mountains are also found in a certain part of Saxony. It is uninteresting to prove that Beethoven was preoccupied with the Ionic mode in his first symphony. Suppose someone announced as a great discovery that the scales in Tchaikovsky's *Pathétique* have precursors in Czerny's finger exercises? He would only make himself ridiculous.

What do we learn about Bach's music when someone explains that here something reminds him of Frescobaldi and there something recalls a work by Scheidt? It is completely insignificant where the sculptor gets his clay; the crucial question is what he can sculpt with it.

They rack their brains over where he got the clay, but they have nothing to say about what he made of it. In addition to the publications of their colleagues, perhaps these scholars should have read Lessing. "It is granted to the genius not to know a thousand things that every schoolboy knows," he wrote. "It is not the acquired stock of his memory, but what he is able to bring forth from himself that makes up his wealth."

Paul Dessau has penned a splendid and informative study on the "music for the eyes" of the *Canonic Variations*. There are profound notes on parts of the *St. Matthew Passion* by Leonard Bernstein. We will search in vain for those two contributions in the volumes of the *Bach-Jahrbuch*, however: They were written by musicians. They discuss music not as an object to be scrutinized but as a sphere in which they are at home, and instead of investigative findings, they furnish us with insights from their world.

What the great biographers entitle "The Last Period of His Life," "The Final Years," or "Heading for the End" spans no less than the whole second half of Bach's tenure of his post in Leipzig (namely, the years from 1737 to 1750). According to that schema, the entire Leipzig period could be divided in a completely dreary manner as follows: the first seven years of service until the reduction of Bach's salary; the second seven until the destruction of his church music; and the remaining thirteen, in which his existence drew to a close in virtual retirement. We may well lodge a protest against such a summarily pejorative survey of his later years—more than a quarter of his creative life. Anyone who would claim that in those years Bach discovered above all the *"stile antico"* has in fact unearthed extremely little.

In reality, already in his earliest years Bach wrote a vast amount of great music without any external cause, simply on his own initiative and so that he could give it to the world—but also because in doing so he was simultaneously pursuing the secrets of his music. For he was constantly on their trail. What mattered to him was not just writing down his inspirations but plumbing the mysteries of his art. That can be proved continuously at every stage of his development, at the latest from Arnstadt onward. His gift—which we may well consider an extraordinary gift of God, for nothing about it is explicable through biology—had put him in the position of being able to penetrate deeper into music than even highly talented musicians.

For instance, there is the anecdote handed down by Forkel about Bach's visit to the Berlin opera house. He looked at the dining hall and immediately recognized that in one corner of the room one could hear everything that was said in the opposite corner. No one had ever discovered that before; his eyes had told him all about it, yet he never attended a lecture on acoustics. He knew all about this the same way he knew what tempi the acoustics of a given church would permit him on an organ. It is recounted that he took tempi rather quickly, but never that he took them too swiftly (in contrast to those virtuosos who think they are playing Bach right when they play him prestissimo).

And yet those are only ancillary factors of his unique relationship with music. The real "Bachian phenomenon" is his polyphony. This is not to say that other musicians always wrote only melody and accompaniment. (Compare Glenn Gould's comment on Mozart's piano concerti: "They were really only written for the right hand.") That does not hit the mark. But no one could configure the four voices of a chorale as he could, so that they were independently singable and expressive. And it was quite natural that the master of polyphony virtually gained a new lease on life in his fugues and took an unqualified pleasure in the canon. He was almost incapable of thinking nonpolyphonically: It was the natural way of thinking for him. But it was unusual, just as unusual as his capacity for wholly new harmonic combinations never heard until then and without parallels in the music of his time.

The primary-source researchers as well as the cabalistic interpreters have failed to notice that all compositions comprise above all musical (musical!) ways of looking at problems, along with their solutions. At the beginning of all these endeavors, there is little more than the empty music paper and the idea of a possibility. But every note put down onto the paper opens up a wealth of further opportunities, of which one may be feasible, another not bad, a third interesting, a fourth surprising, but of which only one is the uniquely right one. It cannot be discovered solely through logical construction and conformity with the rules; it knocks about somewhere in the soul of the composer, and he has to try to find it, and one suitable to it, and the further ones as well.

The combinatory possibilities of those twelve semitones out of which Western music is assembled are exactly calculable in mathematical terms: They are infinite. And out of all these possibilities only the specific one that corresponds to that particular composer who writes it down is right. When Mozart set his quill to paper, he had already completely finished the composition in his head. 331

Beethoven was indisputably a towering musical genius, but we can gather from his drafts, insofar as they are preserved, how tirelessly he worked on the potential continuations of his scores—how he practically worried himself sick over them. In Bach's manuscripts only a few measures are crossed out here and there, but he would still alter his earlier works years later. He rewrote them because better solutions had occurred to him. The original problems had never completely stopped haunting him; secretly he had kept on struggling with them, and with the distance gained he could rethink the old conclusions. Anyone who believes that in writing his compositions he was taking Grigny as a model here, Palestrina there, or Frescobaldi further on has not studied how he used Böhm or Buxtehude as his examples—in fact, not at all. He did not copy them; he absorbed them into himself and made them utterly his own. From the beginning he converted what he had to learn from them into unadulterated Bach. And he did not write *The Well-Tempered Clavier* because Fischer or Mattheson had once composed something similar; it cannot be compared with their works in any way. In the wealth of its demonstrated potentialities, it is something unprecedented up to then.

Yet immersion in the depths and mysteries of musical material made up only one side of his work. The other, to which he was no less strongly compelled, was transmission. At the latest from Mühlhausen on, and then until the end of his life, he had his pupils. He made no secret of his knowledge, his ability, and his insights but willingly expounded everything to others. Along with his Passions, cantatas, concerti, suites, and sonatas, his instructional works were no less important to him. To put it more precisely, they were not merely works for teaching but works through which learners were supposed to teach themselves.

Brecht hoped that it might be said of him that he made suggestions. Until the end of his life, Bach made suggestions, suggestions in music, of course—that was the language in which he could express himself like no one else. As Carl Philipp Emanuel Bach said in his father's obituary, "It is true that our late Bach did not occupy himself with deep theoretical reflections on music, but he was all the more outstanding in the practice of the art." *Keyboard Practice III* was precisely not a "theoretical reflection on a virtually experimental plane"; rather, it was music, and in fact great, melodic, unique music. When in that work Bach presented a prelude with three themes and a fugue with three themes and duets that outgrew tonal bonds, this was certainly never "reflection." On the contrary, it was a groundbreaking departure. Brecht's "experiments" were not a "theoretical reflection on a virtually experimental plane" either, but a fully valid, new kind of theater—theater from which one could learn something if one looked closely. Similarly, Bach's *Keyboard Practice* was music and nothing but music, and yet precisely a music from which one could learn something if one but listened correctly.

Bach's pupils report that a major part of his teaching consisted in playing to them. What matters musically in music can really only be grasped through music. Not only is theoretical reflection never an end in itself, but it is hardly a suitable crutch. No one has learned how to dance on crutches as yet.

Bach created many works in which he was demonstrating something. But he demonstrated by making music, not by employing tones for the elucidation of a theory. That is as true of the *Organ Mass* as it is of the *Goldberg Variations* and as true of the *Musical Offering* as it is of the *Art of Fugue*. The directions for use of all these works are found in the third chapter of the Revelation of John: "He that hath an ear, let him hear what the Spirit saith unto the churches."

There are important connections among Bach's creations of the 1740s. The *Organ Mass*, the *Goldberg Variations*, the twenty-four preludes and fugues of the second *Well-Tempered Clavier*, the B Minor Mass, the *Musical Offering*, and the *Art of Fugue*, considered in their chronological sequence, seem like the *gradus ad Parnassum* of the great Johann Sebastian Bach, his steps toward the summit of his art. At fifty he had long since progressed beyond the time when he

333

would have needed to study the older composers in order to do something of his own again. Rather, the works of this period of his life appear more like Bach's journey into himself, into the depths of his art as it was given to him alone. To manifest those works was one thing; to keep them, to preserve them was another. We also gain the impression that being received by Frederick the Great instilled in Bach a renewed consciousness of the uniqueness of his art. We can draw comparisons between Buxtehude and Telemann—or among Telemann, Albrechtsberger, and Dittersdorf—but the polyphony of Johann Sebastian Bach cannot be compared with anything in its time. We can cite the greatness of Handel, but Handel's style of composing was quite different from Bach's. When Bach applied for admission to Mizler's society, this new realization of his own uniqueness must have been the cause. Membership opened up an opportunity to save his works and present them to his contemporaries and peers. It offered a chance to disseminate his discoveries in the field of polyphony—not as school works but as works of music—to thirteen of those "connoisseurs" he had already addressed in his *Keyboard Practice III*.

"Heading for the end"? Heading for fulfillment!

28

"OLD BACH," OVERTAKEN BY THE "GALLANT STYLE" and "gone out of fashion"? Such claims provoke me to so much head-shaking they make me suspect I suffer from Parkinson's disease.

For there is also the B Minor Mass, the "great Catholic Mass," as Carl Philipp Emanuel called it. It is a puzzling work: No one commissioned it, and it could not even serve a useful purpose. Bach was not of the Catholic faith, and it almost went without saying that the employment of Lutheran music in the Catholic worship service was excluded. (Heinichen, the Protestant court music director of Augustus the Strong, could compose Catholic Masses for the court only because he was backed up by royal authority.) But the decisive reason for the complete impracticality of the work lies in its colossal dimensions. At three full hours, it attains the length of the *St. Matthew Passion;* thus it exceeds the ordinary duration of the Catholic worship service by more than four times, even though it follows the sequence of the order of the Mass.

When Bach sent the first two sections to Dresden along with his application for the title of court composer, he had delivered with the score the written-out parts as well. But separate parts have not turned up for the completed work; apparently, Bach was not contemplating a performance at all. The facts offer no support to the suspicion that he performed sections of it in Leipzig in 1740. Nor did he devise the Mass as a wholly new composition; movements are found in it (produced according to Bach's parody procedure) that he had composed for all sorts of occasions and at many different times. All the same, an academic study on the "breaks in style" in this work has yet to appear, so seamlessly and naturally does everything fit together. This is true even though it was already begun in 1733 and then set aside for fourteen years as a *Missa brevis*—in fact, however, as a torso. Only then did Bach complete the torso as an immense musical construction, without any practical reason and without any prospect of a performance. With regard to a Catholic Mass, there was nothing for him to demonstrate; in this he was an outsider, answerable to no one. If we would grasp the reason for the effort, we must remember that Bruckner dedicated his Ninth Symphony "to the good Lord." In Bach's case there is no dedication, but one such as Bruckner's appears obvious. With pleas, praise, and the profession of faith, the Mass encompasses all the cornerstones of the Christian religion. We can only understand it as Bach's most personal bearing of witness, as the declaration of his belief, for when Bach was working on this composition he cannot have been thinking of any church. Yet his faith had carried him through all the perils of his life and had never deserted him.

The textual content of the Mass is the foundation of both churches; the Nicene Creed Bach set to music is the ecumenical one. To be sure, since the *St. Matthew Passion* and the *Christmas Oratorio* the times had changed a great deal. The *St. John Passion* was virtually the starting point of his official post. He had written the *St. Matthew Passion* to make Leipzigers aware of what kind of music he was capable of creating. The *Christmas Oratorio* was composed at the peak of his Leipzig opportunities. These were all past. The headmaster had turned him out of the school, and his church music had forcibly become a secondary pursuit in which he could contrive nothing truly great. The grandeur of what he had to give in this

Mass he heard while he was still writing it down; he knew that he would never hear it in performance.

And yet he wrote it. He felt within himself the need and the obligation to write it. By subsuming within it pieces he had created earlier he inscribed his life therein as well, and what he was pursuing was once again not simply a "parody procedure." By absorbing earlier compositions into his great Mass, he placed them within a higher relationship, a relationship that was no longer earthly; it was his relationship with God. A Mass bestowed on him the only possible text for this music, the necessary and perfect text. In the light of this Mass, the concept of the "parody procedure" as a mere method of timesaving or expedience collapses. Here we find a new dimension of "lifting" music, in the sense of lifting it up into that higher frame of reference.

By the same token, the theory of the "change in style" also collapses. The integration of the older compositions proves that Bach saw no grounds for distancing himself from them. Of certain passages, he may have thought that in the meantime he could or must write better—but not differently—than he had in earlier years. And as for the claim that in his last years he branched off "into esoteric musical problems," that crumbles utterly to dust. For this Mass, this manifestation of his faith, is nowhere esoteric, nowhere theoretical. It is highly lively throughout, and filled with the greatest expressiveness—all in all very much a music of this world. That fact by no means contradicts the religious origin of the work, since for Bach God was also in this world, not just in the world beyond, despite all the hard blows that fate had dealt to him in the course of his life. He felt compelled to write this Mass, and if he demonstrated something in it besides his relationship with God, it was the tremendous liveliness, the grandiose vitality of his music, which remained unbroken to the end.

With the *Art of Fugue* as well, he proved to the last that his problems were not "esoteric" ones, that he was thinking of the effect of his music up to his final moments. For it is in no way an abstract

337

work; it is a teaching work. No individual parts were written out for the B Minor Mass, but when it came to the *Art of Fugue* nothing was so important to him as immediately engraving the work in copper, publishing it, making it known as the summation of the possibilities he had discovered in his art. And there can be no doubt that this work was not produced for "beginning organists" at all but rather for experts—that from the start it was not conceived "for general education." This is proved by its publication as a score without specific instrumentation; the clarity of the voice leading, not the production of some instrumental sound pattern, was the pressing concern. It was of completely secondary importance to him that such an aural design can be more easily grasped by combining it in two staves—that it can be more readily established with the help of a keyboard.

Certain musicologists apparently assume that tones cannot be perceived without the sound of an instrument. But they are mistaken. Almost everyone can imagine a melody without recourse to an instrument or the idea of a specific instrumental coloring. We do not need a child's voice to imagine the children's song "Fuchs du hast die Gans gestohlen" ("Fox, You Stole the Goose") or a monumental choir to imagine the national anthem. Instruments (the human voice included) merely serve to materialize music; they are not its actual source. We sing as we feel it in our hearts; the music does not come to us only through listening to its notes. The *Art of Fugue* would not have been written for the clavier even if it had been written for the clavier. Carl Philipp Emanuel, who published it as the posthumous work of his father, declared to Forkel quite categorically that it was really music to be read. Certainly, that still does not mean that it constitutes "music for the eyes." After all, we feel the music very clearly in a Goethe poem too, without having to read it out loud. There are poems by Rilke that elude logical comprehension and are nothing but a form of music. The sound of such poems is very difficult to materialize by recitation. Too often the voice cannot rise to the level of their aural expressiveness; the un-

338

voiced sound is the more complete. Similarly, music does not require an instrument for its realization. (We should not forget that the "great Catholic Mass" was not composed with a view to its realization either.)

The claim of certain specialists that the work was written for the keyboard simply because a version for clavier has been found only testifies to their lack of musicality and their insufficient musical education. They obviously do not know what a particell (a partially orchestrated score) is. When an author expresses surprise that an instrumental performance of the composition aroused emotion among the listeners, we must feel surprise in turn. Throughout his life Bach never wrote anything but lively music, even in his boldest constructions; that is just the way Bach was. The *Art of Fugue* is the greatest monothematic work ever composed, but whoever takes it to be only a theoretical teaching exercise has not understood much about it. Bach demonstrates that a theme can be treated in mirror inversion, and backward as well, and even backward and forward at the same time. But though he does all that, it never becomes an abstract construction; again and again he creates marvelous, melody-filled, animated music. That is precisely what no one taught him how to do and what no one has ever copied from him either. His *Art of Fugue* stands alone in music history, inimitable. Yet over and over again, in the most multifarious forms, it has been delivered to its genuine destiny, the world of sound.

Speculators have read the most absurd numeric relationships and the most cryptic symbolism into the work and then read them out of it again. But they are confusing cause and effect. Bach was a stunningly magnificent musical architect. He did not have to invent three themes because he had the urge to depict the Holy Trinity, or make little crosses out of notes because he felt obliged once again to prove his religiousness, or pay homage to the number fourteen here and forty-one there in order to tout his name. Such antics may impel people who are far removed from music to outbursts of enthusiasm. But insofar as they are not purely accidental, they are contained in

339

his music because they correspond to his musical architecture. Even the good Lord did not count up 231 bones and make a human being out of them afterward; rather, a human being comprises exactly 231 bones, along with other things. A devotee of the Cabala may explain to us that in this we can recognize the divine principle of our being, since three is the number of the Trinity, one plus two is three once more, and the sum of the digits is even two times three. But a natural scientist may be permitted to doubt any connection between the Holy Trinity and the number of our bones.

People who believe in the significance of such numeric relationships in music are victims of a fundamental error: that written notes and music are identical. But music obeys a very simple formula: What we do not hear is not music. Certainly the contrapuntal constructions in the *Art of Fugue* are all extremely elaborate. But the real marvel Bach grants us in this work is that he makes a unique and wonderful music ring forth time and again. Among others (not counting the recordings), Hermann Scherchen performed the composition in Lugano in 1965 with the radio orchestra of Italian Switzerland. Although the theoreticians have chiefly propagated intimidation before the extreme complexity of the work, he proved that it embodies music even completely unpracticed listeners deem captivating. Achieving the greatest accessibility with the highest complexity is an accomplishment of Bach's that no one has imitated since (and that many of his interpreters also find rather difficult on occasion).

It has recently been pointed out as quite a new discovery that there is a preliminary form of the *Art of Fugue* from 1740 and thus that the composition as we know it is not a work of the composer's old age. All that means is that at the earlier juncture the project was still so unimportant that it could be left unfinished for the time being. But then, in 1749, after the *Musical Offering* and the great 340 Mass, it suddenly became so significant to Bach that he did not finish writing the score before preparing its publication. While still at work on it, he went to the printers. He must have been virtually possessed by the thought of circulating the piece—that is how meaningful it was to him then.

He was not doing well at that time, either physically or financially. He must have foreseen the absolute failure of this publication; barely 100 purchasers had been found for the *Musical Offering*. Nowadays publishers would hardly be tempted to produce a collector's edition with such a modest sales outlook. A larger circle of prospective customers for this new composition could not be reckoned with—on the contrary, it might even become a smaller one. Bach had much work to do at the time; he had his pupils and a number of extremely pressing tasks. The quantity of fundamental compositions he created from the middle of 1747 to the beginning of 1750 is hardly comprehensible. He could no longer personally see to every christening, every wedding, every funeral. As for his contractual obligations, those did not matter at all anymore, so he had others substitute for him more and more in that sphere as well. The obituary speaks of "his still very lively powers of soul and body," but Detlev Kraneman has discovered that he was diabetic; others think that one can detect some of his frailties in his musical notation. Thus the state of his health was probably not the best— and the same certainly goes for his income. In 1746 he had six organ chorales published by Johann Georg Schübler in Zella, in Thuringia. They are substantially pieced together from earlier cantatas, so it is quite clear this was a work intended for sale. In 1749–1750, besides the *Art of Fugue*, he was also working again on the Eighteen Chorales, undoubtedly because he hoped to derive some urgently needed income from them.

With all this, he could hardly concentrate on his great works alone, on what today we would call "his musical legacy." At the same time, he still had to try to earn some money; he was not very well-to-do. The doctors of Bach's era could neither diagnose nor treat diabetes, a disease that can greatly affect one's eyesight (although Bach's eye ailment does not necessarily have diabetes as a precondition). The Haussmann portrait of 1747 clearly shows his

341

diminished vision. His condition probably involved not only cataracts but a painful deterioration of the retina at the same time. The oculist John Taylor, who operated on Bach twice in 1750, cites this as the reason for the failure of his treatment (although he was also unsuccessful with other patients, Handel among them).

Though the blindness of Bach and Handel is lamented as a sad ending to both their lives, the deafness of Beethoven is generally felt to be a worse fate for a musician. We should not measure one tragedy against the other. Beethoven was able to go on composing even if no tone from the external world got through to him any-more and even if he could never hear his last sonatas any more than Bach could hear his great Mass. But Bach could no longer write down what he heard within himself. It is reported that he dictated his last chorale, "Vor deinen Thron tret' ich hiermit" ("I Step Herewith Before Thy Throne"), to his son-in-law Johann Christoph Altnickol. But you need only try that—not really dictat-ing but simply writing down what you would say if you did dic-tate. Then you will experience the entire misery that must have overcome Bach when he had to describe in sequence what was meant to sound forth in unison.

In the middle of his labors over a few salable chorales, not to mention the supreme, final mysteries of the contrapuntal style, Bach was pierced as by a spear in the most sensitive point of his soul—his music. The insult came at a time when he was tormented (and no doubt frightened too) by increasing pain in his eyes and dangerously deteriorated powers of vision. He was also afflicted at this juncture by a severe attack of weakness (perhaps a stroke).

In May 1749 his pupil Johann Friedrich Doles in Freiberg suf-fered a serious injustice from the headmaster there, Johann Gottlieb Biedermann, who was as hostile to music as he was learned—an ab-solute counterpart to Bach's headmaster Ernesti. Like Bach in the old days, Doles had garnered acclaim and general recognition with his music. And as with Ernesti in Leipzig, it had rubbed Bieder-mann in Freiberg the wrong way that thanks to Doles's ability, music threatened to attain more prestige than erudition. In the school program he issued in May 1749, he gave vent to his wrath and did his best to topple music. He used Terence and Horace as well as ecclesiastical history and aimed his fire not only at Doles but at the whole musical profession.

As a result, reproaches rained down on Biedermann from every side. Mattheson alone composed five essays refuting Biedermann's disquisition. Bach also had to join in the fray, but writing articles was not his cup of tea. In the case of Scheibe's jibes against him, he had requested Master Birnbaum to speak out on his behalf. Here he enlisted his colleague Christoph Gottlieb Schröter in Nord-hausen, who like him was a member of the Musical Society. Though Schröter complied, Bach's health prevented him from see-ing to the publication himself. On his own initiative, the publisher must have spiced the article up considerably, for a conflict over this with Schröter ensued. But this is not nearly as important as the out-come: What befell the pupil was what the teacher himself had ear-lier endured.

To be sure, in Freiberg Biedermann could no longer get away with what Ernesti had pulled off in Leipzig; it took more than two years for the dust to settle after he committed his faux pas. Bach did not live to see that, but he did intervene musically in the affair. He gave a new performance of his eighteen-year-old cantata *Der Streit zwischen Phöbus und Pan.* In addition, on no less than three occasions he presented "O holder Tag, erwünschste Zeit" ("O Lovely Day, Longed-For Time"), set to a text in praise of music and against its censors. His remark that he hoped the author's (Biedermann's) "filthy ear" would be cleaned became notorious; Mattheson in particular upbraided him for the "unrefined" ex-pression. But as a music critic, Mattheson was only indirectly af-fected by the matter, after all, whereas Bach justifiably felt cut to the quick. Lessing's Countess Orsina had the right words to de-scribe the case: "He who does not lose his mind over certain things has none to lose."

Yet this was not the only malicious insult that beset Bach in 1749. Word that he had others substitute for him more frequently and the news of his current weakness had already reached as far as Dresden. In his eventual decease, Count Brühl saw a good opportunity to get rid of his music director, Johann Gottlob Harrer. So he wrote a letter of recommendation for the latter—or to put it more correctly, a request in case of Bach's death to hire Harrer as his successor.

That was on June 2, and already on June 8 Harrer arrived in Leipzig to deliver the letter in person. True, Bach still occupied the post, but the pride of Leipzig citizens before royal thrones was not so unbending after all. The city council bowed to Brühl's suggestion right away, and a musical examination of Harrer was hastily organized at the Three Swans Inn. But this was a pure formality; not one of the gentlemen dared to doubt the perfect qualifications of a man whom the almighty minister had recommended. The matter was agreed on right away, especially since the minister had even called for a "decree" to be issued on the subject. It bespeaks a remarkable tactlessness to designate a successor when the holder of the post is still in service, although Spitta would even like to give the council credit for not firing Bach then and there. Everywhere else the authorities at least waited out of decency until the incumbent was in the ground before seeing about a replacement. But the Leipzig council did not possess even that much decency.

Although the so-called audition was held behind closed doors, Bach surely found out about Harrer's appearance before the council at the Three Swans. Geck even claims that Bach "took part in the public spectacle in a silent role." How he knows that remains a mystery, for the event was by no means public, and there was really no reason any longer for the council to consult Bach. That his skin was being sold while he was still alive was more than hurtful enough for him as it was. Of course, that was of no interest to councilmen who delivered their notifications to him via a subcoroner.

The year 1749 had begun very happily. In January Johann Sebastian Bach was able to celebrate the wedding of one of his children at his own home for the first and only time. His pupil Altnickol had tied the knot with Bach's favorite daughter, Elisabeth ("Liesgen" or "Lizzy"). So that they would have something to live on as a married couple, he had got Altnickol the job of organist in Naumburg. That had been a rosy beginning, but things had not continued in that vein; 1749 became yet another bad year for him.

The following one turned out worse, even if it too started with some good news. Bach was able to find employment for his second youngest son, Johann Christoph Friedrich, in the court orchestra of Bückeburg, even though the boy was not yet eighteen. His old relations with Cöthen had brought that off. His former prince, Leopold, buried for more than twenty years, had wedded Princess Charlotte Friedericke von Nassau-Siegen in his second marriage. She in turn, after Leopold's death, had married Albrecht Wolfgang, count of Schaumburg-Lippe, thus establishing a connection with Bückeburg. That is why the name Bach had an excellent ring to it there even after such a long time. And so at sixty-five, Bach was left with only five more children to provide for at home.

The main problem was that he suffered from increasing pain and could see less and less. Even the town physician, Nagel, was able to diagnose reliably that a clouding of the eye lenses was discernible. He could not help, though it was commonly known what could bring help: a cataract operation. The clouded lenses had to be cut out and tucked under the irises; the missing lenses could be replaced reasonably well afterward by strong glasses, cataract glasses. That sounded logical and even fairly simple. But this operation demanded of the surgeon not only the highest skill but also practice in the technique, and who had that in Leipzig?

Happenstance came to Bach's aid. At the time an oculist (or ophthalmiator, the Greek term he tended to use), the Englishman John Taylor, was traveling through half of Europe. On his tour through Germany, he turned up in Leipzig in the second half of

345

March 1750. He prided himself on his ability to incise cataracts. He boasted of many successes, and this seemed like a unique opportunity for Bach. After all, what alternative was left?

The operating room was located in that very same Three Swans Inn where the notable audition of Bach's successor had taken place. The operation began with the application of hot boiled apples to the eyes in order to soften the cornea. The patient was tied down on a chair. There was no anesthetic of any kind. Dr. Taylor had a strong assistant who clamped the patient's head in the vice of his hands. Sterilizing the instruments was out of the question; no one even knew what that meant. (A hundred years later the physician Semmelweis was still declared foolish by his colleagues because he insisted they should wash their hands before a delivery.)

As small as the wounds were, the operation must have been a good bit nastier than pulling teeth, a procedure that also took place without any anesthetic in those days. But what followed the ordeal itself was even worse, for then the medical treatment in support of the operation came into play. In Bach's case it consisted of repeated bloodletting, in conjunction with laxatives and such poisons as belladonna and aconite "to combat the evil humors."

In the meantime Dr. Taylor traveled to Dresden, and when he returned to Leipzig at the beginning of April he was obliged to recognize that the lenses had moved back into the pupils again. He operated a second time, with the same follow-up treatment, of course.

From the day of the first operation onward, Bach was entirely blind, with bandages and a black blindfold over his eyes. He could make out his surroundings only by touch and had to be led about. He also had to be fed, for he would have to learn anew where the plate was and where to aim the spoon when he directed it to his mouth and even where his mouth was. At the same time the follow-up treatment ensured that he must have felt sicker, weaker, and more wretched as each day passed. Whether he was actually diabetic did not matter anymore. The two horse cures prescribed one after the other would have shattered even a man in the prime of his life, and he was far from his prime anymore—the attack in May of the previous year had made him aware of that.

It was the end of winter when he submitted to the knife. Spring arrived without his seeing anything. The summer came and nothing had changed, except that he was becoming weaker and weaker.

Finally, he could no longer stand the darkness. On July 18 he tore the blindfold from his eyes, and he could see again. So the second operation had succeeded. But the patient did not survive the miracle. The overwhelming strain of the months he had gone through was compounded by his excitement over the outcome. A few hours later a stroke laid him low. He lingered for ten days more with a raging fever. On the evening of July 28, at almost a quarter past eight, he closed his eyes forever, without having regained clear consciousness.

This last half year had been his long path from Gethsemane to Golgotha—without a crucifixion, to be sure, but with a flagellation and a crown of thorns and after many humiliations. And on his tombstone the words from 2 Timothy 4:7 might have been written:

I have fought a good fight,
I have finished my course,
I have kept the faith.

29

BUT THERE WOULD BE NO TOMBSTONE. There was no money for that. Rueger has demonstrated that in Leipzig the Bachs were very well-off people; he calculated this based on Bach's earnings as compared with the local price of beer. (We recall the city council's resolution "that it should be very weak beer and sold cheaply.") If he had converted the scant income of an East German pensioner into streetcar tickets, he would have arrived at the salary of a government minister.

Bach had made no will, so only a third of his estate went to his widow, Anna Magdalena, even though three of the children remained with her after his death: the eldest, Catharina Dorothea, forty-two by then, and the two youngest, Johanna Carolina, thirteen, and Regina Susanna, eight. She herself was not yet fifty at the death of her husband, but the council granted her the guardianship of her children only on the condition that she must not remarry. This meant that in the event she wedded again the children would be taken away from her; in other words, the authorities had prearranged her poverty. In other ways as well the council showed its superiority in arithmetic. Bach's widow should have been entitled to a full half year's salary; that would have come to 50 thalers. But on this occasion it was ascertained that twenty-seven years ago Bach had taken up his post belatedly, and so a corresponding sum was deducted from the widow's portion. Only 21 thalers and 10 groschen were left. A proper council knows how to save and where to start doing so—with the defenseless.

As for cash, Bach had been unable to put aside very much. All of 1,100 thalers remained from his twenty-seven years in Leipzig; that was barely the income from one and a half years of work. Of that, as I have said, only a third went to Anna Magdalena, with her four mouths to feed. The Altnickols took the feeble-minded Gottfried Heinrich home with them to Naumburg, and Carl Philipp Emanuel accepted the fifteen-year-old Johann Christian in Berlin. But though little money was left to her, Anna Magdalena buried her beloved husband in an oak coffin. Very few people could afford such a luxury, but she allowed it to herself anyway, even though there would not be enough for a gravestone. It was the last loving favor she could do for her husband.

She found a place to live in Hayn Street. In fact she received a special compensation for getting out of the choirmaster's lodgings as quickly as possible. The council had also generously granted her a few bushels of grain; that would suffice to quell the initial hunger. But it was inevitable that she soon fell into serious poverty. Her stepsons Wilhelm Friedemann and Carl Philipp Emanuel, though they were both in good circumstances at the time, did nothing to help her. The rift their father's love for the young woman had brought into the family in Cöthen had never healed; for both of them, she had remained an outsider. With a trace of mercy, the council bought a few of her husband's manuscripts by awarding her 40 thalers—"because of her wretchedness, and also because of some musical papers she presented." It is not reported whether they have ever turned up again in the council archives. How Anna Magdalena managed to raise her younger daughters we do not know. She did not find a husband for either, nor were they good catches. At the end of her life, she depended completely on the charity of other people; she died as a "receiver of alms."

A few scholars have gathered from this that she drew a pension from the council, though they cannot cite any examples of other

Leipzig widows doing so in a similar situation. If there were any sources for their claim, Spitta would surely have found them. Besides, had such a provision for widows really existed at that time, Mendelssohn would not have had to set up a fund to provide for the widows of his Gewandhaus musicians in Leipzig 100 years later. This theory as well is built on sand; the only verified payment of the council to Anna Magdalena is that one-time purchase of musical manuscripts.

Of greater concern to scholarship than this pension theory is the problem of where Bach's musicological library ended up. Spitta voices the suspicion that his sons got hold of it while their father was still living, since no such library came to light after his death. True, while preparing Bach's obituary, Carl Philipp Emanuel wrote to Mizler: "The deceased was, like myself and all real musicians, no lover of dry, mathematical stuff." But this remark can have no claim to credibility, since it curbs musicology too much. After all, Bach must have got his contrapuntal tricks from somewhere. For example, what was his recipe book for the *Art of Fugue?*

All the scholars put together will certainly have to search a long time before they find other composers of "Baroque" music who, like Bach, immediately recast a fugue as a *"fuga inversa"* or a *"canone per augmentationem in motu contrario."* They are all victims of a fundamental mistake: They confuse Bach's profound interest in the contrapuntal possibilities of his music with an interest in mere theory. Bach did not have to study this or that system of harmony; when he was not yet twenty, he had already created one that was utterly his own. Nor did Bach first have to read in this or that treatise how a *"canone per augmentationem in motu contrario"* was supposed to be. He simply presented one in praxis—not only because he could do it but because in that way he could make some exciting music.

For this very reason, there can be no doubt that Mizler's endeavor to "raise music completely to the rank of a mathematical science" was dim-witted stuff for Bach. He long since knew about operating with the infinite, and he possessed too many and too varied pupils in order not to recognize that the decisive factor in art is precisely the unlearnable—what is inaccessible to any science.

That is why he did not join Mizler's society for such a long time. Mizler's views on music necessarily had to conflict with his own in the sharpest manner. His erudition did not consist in writing a treatise on the *"canone in motu contrario"* but in presenting one— and not on a "virtually experimental plane" but as tuneful, animated music.

Whoever sees it otherwise has not understood anything about Bach and so falls victim to a host of misconceptions that are not without their comic side. For example, take the notion that when Mizler translated Fux's *Gradus ad Parnassum,* Bach "accompanied" the German version, writing some educational examples to illustrate the instructions of his Vienna colleague. Although people may be able to become professors by disseminating such opinions, they prove that the authors have no clue whatsoever about the creative process of the artist and that they have explored their own special field precious little. In fact we know of Bach that "in composition he started his pupils right away on what was practical, omitting all the dry kinds of counterpoint that are found in Fux and others." So how can a scholar arrive at the claim that Bach composed according to the model of Fux? In the same source the researcher could have also read: "Through his own reflection alone, he became a pure and powerful fugue writer already in his youth."

Unlike the professors, Carl Philipp Emanuel knew quite well that he would not have to hunt for his father's books on musical theory very long, as these quotations demonstrate. In fact, here is another question for those who insinuate that Wilhelm Friedemann and Carl Philipp Emanuel virtually stole their father's musicological library in his dying hours: Why did the books never subsequently turn up in their own estates? By the way, the music theory libraries of Mozart, Handel, Haydn, Beethoven, Brahms, and Wagner have never been located either. The mystery of why Bach alone is thought to have had one remains unsolved to this day.

And something else strikes me as odd. All Bach's sons had received an outstanding musical education from their father, and the two eldest, the primary suspects, had long exercised an extensive and successful musical praxis by this time. So they needed their father's theoretical books about as urgently as a professional driver would need his father's explanations of traffic regulations.

Schleuning, who deals with Bach's life in a thoroughly eccentric fashion in other places as well, goes a stretch further with his assumptions about Bach's theoretical predilections. Mizler had designated Leipzig as the depository for works received by his society. From that Schleuning concludes with astounding logic that the collecting point must have been Bach's house and that Bach served as the lending librarian of Mizler's collection. He is able to give an irrefutable proof of the correctness of his theory: At Bach's death nothing of Mizler's entire collection was discovered in his house. Exactly this, he explains, is the proof. It was all lent out.

Bach's burial took place as a "great funeral" with the participation of the "entire school." Sixteen years later only "a quarter of the school" accompanied Anna Magdalena's coffin; hers was an indigent's burial. In the annual school report for 1750, Headmaster Ernesti did not deign to write a single word about the deceased school choirmaster; he had already finished with the man thirteen years before. As for the church where he had faithfully directed the music for twenty-seven years, achieving a series of unique masterworks, its official farewell stuck to the unavoidable minimum. "The esteemed and highly respected Mr. Johann Sebastian Bach, Court Composer to His Royal Majesty in Poland and Serene Electoral Highness in Saxony, as well as Music Director to the Prince of Anhalt-Cöthen and Choirmaster of the St. Thomas School, here at the Square of St. Thomas, has passed away in God peacefully and blessedly. His lifeless body was committed to the earth today in accordance with Christian usage." 353 The ecclesiastics had nothing more to say about their unloved subordinate.

The city council already began filling Bach's position that same week; it was all settled anyway. Others had applied as well, among them a colleague, a pupil, and a son of the deceased. But that only proves they had no inkling of the audition that had taken place at the Three Swans Inn, otherwise they undoubtedly would not have bothered.

The obituary pronounced by the mayor, Dr. Stieglitz, privy councilor to the war council, is famous: "Mr. Bach was a great musician, to be sure, but he was not a schoolteacher, and so in replacing him in the post as choirmaster of the St. Thomas School, a person should be sought who is skillful in both capacities." Councilman Plaz immediately seconded the thought with his statement: "The choirmaster of the St. Thomas School should be a schoolteacher above all, though he must also understand music."

After this declaration of principle, Plaz put in a plea for Brühl's ousted music director, who had never given a single Latin class in his entire life up to then. But he "wanted to try" and was characterized "by an easygoing disposition." Besides, Brühl stood behind him, when all was said and done.

That is why the motion in favor of Harrer was adopted right away, unanimously, as we can read in the council minutes. Harrer had been the music director at Brühl's home in Dresden for nineteen years. Moritz Fürstenau, who described the Dresden music world exhaustively in his work *History of Music and Theater at the Court in Dresden,* did not even deem Harrer worthy of mention. Brühl must have known why he was pressuring the council to take him. But his musical capacity and the quality of his Latin teaching did not matter to the Leipzig council. Its chief interest was being left to rule in peace. And above all the councilmen were glad they had finally rid themselves of this useless troublemaker Bach. Neither for the rest of the century nor in the following one did the council of Leipzig feel an obligation to honor the fact that Bach had bestowed his magnificent music on the city for twenty-seven years.

Bach had been buried somewhere by the wall of St. John's Church. But just forty years later the exact location had already been completely forgotten. Even when the great Bach renaissance began, the council took no interest in him. There were other people Leipzig could pride itself on when it came to the cultivation of music. For example, a young, talented conductor from Berlin by the name of Felix Mendelssohn-Bartholdy had not only brought the Gewandhaus Orchestra to a high level but also had founded Germany's first conservatory in Leipzig. The important piano pedagogue Wieck lived in the city with his famous daughter Clara; her husband, Robert Schumann, was a gifted composer and published the well-respected *Neue Zeitschrift für Musik (New Journal for Music)*. And at the opera there was a young music director named Lortzing who did not lack talent. So even without Bach, Leipzig was a musical city.

Mendelssohn alone committed himself to Bach without consulting the authorities, just as he had struggled on the composer's behalf in Berlin. At the St. Thomas Church, he performed a series of organ works by Bach. The recitals became an event for the whole music world of Leipzig; Schumann wrote an enthusiastic review about them. From the proceeds of these recitals, Mendelssohn donated the first Bach monument in 1843. The contribution of the city consisted merely in not raising any objections to it.

Still, no one showed any concern for Bach's grave. It would have remained missing if St. John's Church had not undergone an expansion in 1894. During the excavations for the new foundation wall, three oak coffins were found. It was still known that Bach had been buried in an oak coffin, and so his bones were recovered. The sculptor Karl Seffner modeled a head over a plaster cast of the skull that showed a considerable similarity to portraits of Bach. Now at last Bach's mortal remains were buried in honor—not at the St. Thomas Church but at St. John's Church, in a sarcophagus in the crypt, right beside those of Christian Fürchtegott Gellert, which had arrived there somewhat earlier. Bach's bones were not transferred to the St. Thomas Church until 1950. Seffner also created the Bach monument that replaced Mendelssohn's more modest memorial. It was unveiled in 1908 not by the city council but by the New Bach Society.

The councilmen were not the only ones who forgot him, however. The period following Bach's death is often sweepingly portrayed as a time in which Bach temporarily fell into utter oblivion, not coming to light again until Mendelssohn's Berlin performance of the *St. Matthew Passion*. "On the whole, at the end of the eighteenth century it seemed as though Bach were dead forever," writes Schweitzer. Of course, that is just as false as so much else.

Already in his lifetime Bach was not a fashionable musician, and above all he was anything but an easy one. There is one thing that he really was not at all: a composer of generally usable church music. Carl Philipp Emanuel published his father's chorale harmonizations, 371 of them, but they did not generate an organ accompaniment book for congregational singing. Nor was a single such composition by Bach to be found in the hymnbook of the established Protestant churches of Germany for 1995, and that is surely not because of an underestimation of Bach. His harmonizations are simply too independent as artworks to be adaptable to congregational singing. The situation is much the same with regard to his organ chorales and the majority of his chorale preludes. Because of their proportions, many of them go far beyond the possibilities of the worship service; they not only lead up to the congregational singing but virtually sweep it along with them. To be sure, no one could claim that Bach ever exceeded the limits of music, but an organist who wanted to play nothing but Bach in the worship service would certainly gain the disapproval of the congregation. And there is another factor that Bach himself never concealed: Most of his works are difficult. Not only the *Goldberg Variations* but the pieces in his *Well-Tempered Clavier* are appreciably harder to play than the piano sonatas of Haydn or Mozart. So Bach did not win popularity with his compositions in his lifetime, and he almost never worried about that either. If he played them himself, that was something different; then the admiration of his hearers knew no bounds. The problem was to imitate his playing. But he was never forgotten by his fellow experts.

Nor was he ever an "ending." Schweitzer put forward an unfortunate and totally false assertion when he said of Bach that "everything leads to him; nothing comes from him."

Nothing came from him? His pupils have been counted; there were eighty-one, and at least forty-six of them were professional organists. All eighty-one went through his teaching, were instructed in his music, and surely in turned passed on what they had learned. Among them we know of no one who rejected Bach's music as "old-fashioned," with the possible exception of Johann Christian Bach. To have been a pupil of Bach's was more than commendable; it was virtually a seal of quality. Many are even said to have availed themselves of that seal without having earned it, for the name Bach was a letter of recommendation in itself. Forty-six positions as organist in important places were filled by pupils of Bach. There were some very famous musicians among them: Krebs for example, and Kittel, Homilius at the Dresden Kreuzkirche, and Kellner as well. Thirty-four years after his death, Johann Adam Hiller could write: "To this day one still considers it an honor to have enjoyed the instruction of this great man." Nothing came from him?

We should not forget that these pupils went on to have pupils of their own. Kittel, for example, had an organ pupil named Christian Heinrich Rinck, who later earned his doctorate and became a professor. He brought into the nineteenth century a fine contrapuntal organ style in Bach's own manner. Bach's organ works, hardly published and extremely demanding in technique, did not perish any more than did his *Well-Tempered Clavier.* Again and again enthusiasts of those works copied them out because they had to have them for themselves at all costs—and in music, that is a highly unusual form of falling into oblivion.

There was also Johann Philipp Kirnberger, a violinist in the orchestra of Frederick the Great and the music teacher of Princess Amalie in Berlin. That he appreciated his teacher above all else is proved by his extensive collection of Bach's compositions, which later formed the basis of many a printed publication. He himself enjoyed a high reputation. The music theory works he authored were widely disseminated throughout the second half of the eighteenth century, and they made use of what he had learned from his teacher, Johann Sebastian Bach.

It is notoriously difficult for sons to survive in the shadow of a great father. Franz Xaver Mozart, although he was a capable musician, has remained as good as unknown. Siegfried Wagner mastered almost all the stylistic devices of his father, and for that very reason he sank into almost total insignificance. Brachvogel's *Friedemann Bach* draws its fundamental cause for conflict from this idea of the genius in his father's shadow. But Bach had no less than three sons who did not let themselves be eclipsed by him; they showed the same independence as their father and made pioneering contributions to the music of their time. Carl Philipp Emanuel is often portrayed as almost the artistic antithesis of his father, as though he had set up his "new style" in opposition to the supposedly "old" one. Whoever studies him more closely recognizes how much he learned from Bach, how beautifully he understood how to work with the monothematic technique (for example, in his organ concerti). At the same time, however, he was not simply his father's son and nothing more (like Mozart's Franz Xaver). He was his father's son precisely because as a musician he was just as independent as his father had been from the start.

And there is something else I find remarkable. As Carl Philipp Emanuel's own creations prove, he was a thoroughly experienced and self-assured contrapuntalist, taught by his father and fully familiar with his style. It was he who after his father's death saw to the engraving of the *Art of Fugue* in 1751–1752, corrected the proofs, and painstakingly supervised the entire edition. Schleuning even depicts him as a clever advertising man in this instance. Of course, his argument breaks down after only a few sentences. That Carl Philipp Emanuel was unfortunately no such thing is revealed in that he managed to get rid of no more than ten copies, and shortly thereafter he could only sell the copper plates as metal scrap.

358

For such a thrifty man, the whole enterprise must have been a bitter disappointment. His exceptional cleverness in advertising technique, Schleuning tells us, can be recognized in his additional comment to the uncompleted triple fugue that trails off into one voice. "While writing this fugue, where the name B-A-C-H appears in the countersubject, the composer died." Now that is very curious.

Giacomo Puccini also died while finishing his opera *Turandot*. His pupil Franco Alfano completed the work with reverence and stylistic aplomb. Nor did Mozart manage to bring his Requiem to its conclusion. His pupil Süssmayr finished the uncompleted work and, familiar with Mozart's style, finished it in such a way that to this day it is still performed with his ending. As we listen we cannot say precisely where Mozart leaves off and Süssmayr begins. But though Carl Philipp Emanuel was intimately familiar with the working method and style of his father, he did *not* complete the triple fugue. This was because he knew without a doubt that the only one who could have finished this triple fugue was Bach himself. It was a great and respectful decision that we can only note with the deepest admiration. His own development went in other directions. Joseph Haydn later declared that he would not have become Haydn without his knowledge of the work of Carl Philipp Emanuel Bach. But the son had gained his qualifications in music from his father. And Haydn proved that he could write excellent fugues in Bach's manner as well, not only in his Symphony No. 40 but also in his oratorios.

And nothing came from him?

Carl Philipp Emanuel imparted his own qualifications in turn to his youngest brother, Johann Christian. He possessed the same independence as his father and brother, as well as that adventurous, enterprising spirit that marked the life of his eldest brother, Friedemann, and that had been the undoing of his unfortunate brother Bernhard. Johann Christian had in him a happy balance between Friedemann's restlessness and Carl Philipp Emanuel's stability. A pinch of the thoughtlessness of his brother Bernhard enabled him to go to Italy, convert to Catholicism without any misgivings, and become a cathedral organist and opera composer at the same time. At twenty-seven he moved to London, and as the impresario of Bach-Abel Concerts he won a dominant position in London concert life for many years. Whoever knows his symphonies gains an inkling of the lasting influence he must have exercised on the young Mozart during the latter's stay in London. And whoever devotes his attention to the secondary themes of these symphonies discovers an accomplished contrapuntalist. He received his qualifications not only from his brother but also from his father.

And nothing came from him?

Then there was Baron Gottfried van Swieten, who as an Austrian diplomat in Berlin had studied with Marpurg and Bach's pupil Kirnberger and who practically became a Bach fanatic. When he was named prefect of the Vienna court library, he sought out the company of Mozart. Mozart reported that "nothing is played but Handel and Bach" at Swieten's residence every Sunday; not only that, but Mozart took Bach's compositions home with him. When his wife, Constanze, heard them, "she quite fell in love with them," and so in 1782 Mozart began to compose fugues himself under the influence of Bach. His Fantasy and Fugue (K. 394) is nearly a Mozartian paraphrase of Bach's *Chromatic Fantasy and Fugue.*

Swieten introduced Haydn as well to the works of Bach and Handel, which gave him the inspiration for the *Creation* and the *Seasons.* Beethoven also played Bach at Swieten's home. Incidentally, Beethoven already had Bach's *Well-Tempered Clavier* down pat as an eleven-year-old. He had derived his reverence for the composer from his teacher Christian Gottlob Neefe in Bonn, who drew his appreciation of Bach from Johann Adam Hiller. And Hiller had absorbed it from Bach's pupils Homilius and Doles, whose successor he eventually became at the St. Thomas School. The music critic Rochlitz learned his esteem for Bach from Doles as well. His *Allgemeine Musikalische Zeitung (General Musical Newspaper)* was one of the most respected in Germany, and for him Bach surpassed all else. Rochlitz was present when Mozart visited Leipzig. He was at Doles's house when Mozart enthusiastically spread the individual parts of Bach's motets around him and said: "Now here is something we can learn from." It was Mozart's last journey, and he had long been at the height of his powers. Bach inspired him as well, up to the last.

And that is what Schweitzer describes as an "ending"? And he can say that nothing more came from Bach? Apparently he was of the opinion that after Bach all sorts of people would have had to write like Bach from then on. But geniuses cannot be copied, and all truly great talents have never been imitators. It is true that after Bach nobody wrote like Bach anymore. But after Wagner nobody wrote like Wagner, after Strauss nobody wrote like Strauss, and even after Orff nobody wrote like Orff. If certain people were not always trying to prove from whom Bach copied what, they would long since have been able to prove what no one did before Bach. Not only did no one write like Bach after Bach, but no one wrote like Bach before Bach. Nor does it signify anything when he is said merely to have adopted the forms of his time—in fact, he developed them into unique, unprecedented, large-scale forms.

But at no time did Bach's legacy lack expert admirers, and not only in Germany and Austria. The first printed edition of *The Well-Tempered Clavier*, which had circulated for decades only in handwritten copies, appeared in 1799 in London. In England too there was a whole community of enthusiasts for the "old-fashioned, forgotten" Johann Sebastian Bach, so large that it made the printing seem financially viable. The first German edition did not appear until an entire year later, at the Schott publishing house in Mainz.

I have yet to speak of the central figure of the Berlin music world after 1800, Carl Friedrich Zelter, the teacher of Mendelssohn, Meyerbeer, and Otto Nicolai. He was also a close friend of Goethe's. Under Zelter's instruction the very young Mendelssohn learned fugal composition after the example of Bach, and he succeeded in writing superbly crafted fugues. Zelter's admiration for 361 Bach inspired his efforts. Zelter knew what Bach was worth even without having been schooled by one of Bach's pupils. Among the musical treasures at his singing academy (still called Fasch's Singing Association at the time), he kept the score of the *St. Matthew Passion* that captivated Mendelssohn—so much so that already as a sixteen-year-old, all he wanted for Christmas was a copy of it. As a seventeen-year-old, he was absolutely bent on performing the work. Zelter knew its difficulties and was convinced that the young man would founder in the attempt. But Mendelssohn and his friend Devrient kept at him until the old gentleman finally gave in. And so in 1827, under the baton of the eighteen-year-old Mendelssohn, a performance took place that made music history. But an enthusiasm for Bach, as we can see, by no means had to be kindled by this performance; it simply caused the admiration to spread even more widely. Zelter is said to have been a gruff and difficult man; his main objection was supposedly that the whole composition was antiquated. But on closer inspection, that notion is implausible. After all, it was he who had inculcated his pupil with a reverence for Bach, so he did not consider him to be an old-fashioned musician at all. He simply needed a reason to prevent the two young people from failing. He himself, a man of long experience, did not think he was up to the difficulties of performing the work, even though it was now almost 100 years old.

It is not true that Bach was forgotten after his death, and no one who was familiar with his music found it old-fashioned. On the contrary, despite all the changes in style, it was capable of filling connoisseurs and experts with enthusiasm. But it was for them that Bach had written his music anyway, and even in those times when he had supposedly fallen into oblivion, he not only reached them but enraptured them.

Nothing came from him? On the contrary: no great musical figure overlooked him.

30

"WHOEVER MISSES THE FIRST BUTTONHOLE," SAYS GOETHE, "cannot manage to button up." In his first chapter Schweitzer writes: "Bach is among the objective artists. These stand wholly within their time and create only with the forms and ideas that it offers them. They do not criticize the means of artistic expression they find at hand and feel no inner compulsion to break new ground."

We can read more of this passage, but it does not become any more correct. Criticism of "the means of artistic expression" has nothing to do with art itself. "They feel no inner compulsion to break new ground" may apply to this artist or that; toward Bach it testifies to total misunderstanding, just like the famous expression "the culmination and end of Baroque music." That phrase determined the assessment of Bach for almost half a century, until in the middle of the twentieth century the East German president threw the bone "Enlightenment" into the debate out of completely political motives. Although the latter idea is increasingly revealed to have been a mere fabrication of expedience, a chimera, Bach still seems to be as inseparably bound to "Baroque music" as the tree to the ground on which it stands.

But if we look at Bach's musical milieu more closely, the picture goes a bit awry. For it is indisputable—Hasse, Quantz, Telemann, Graupner, Fasch, Vivaldi, Marchand, Daquin, Rameau, Handel,

Tartini, the Scarlattis, the Grauns, Kuhnau, Torelli, Corelli, Franz Xaver Richter, Pergolesi, Couperin, Krieger, Muffat, Böhm, and Buxtehude—none of them wrote like Bach. It is not true that the *St. Matthew Passion* stands in a grove of other Passions, not even true that Handel's *Brockes Passion* or Graun's *Tod Jesu (Death of Jesus)* can be compared with Bach's *St. John Passion*. At most they can be juxtaposed only in a very general way, because in detail the differences become tremendous. Of course Bach *also* wrote like his contemporaries. *Keyboard Practice I* still bears comparison with Handel's harpsichord music; *Keyboard Practice II* already develops very distinctive forms—it is really orchestral music for the clavier. But at the latest from *Keyboard Practice III* onward, Bach has no further parallel. And as an organ composer he is totally unparalleled from much earlier on. The elemental force of such organ toccatas as the D Minor, C Major, or the Dorian or such organ preludes as the D Major, E-flat Major, or G Minor is nowhere to be found in what is generally understood by "Baroque music." A giant musical edifice such as Bach's Passacaglia and Fugue—anything but a "work of old age"—is completely unique in the century. We cannot describe the whale as a fish merely because it swims in the same water with fish. Certainly there is a lot of splendid music by Bach that utterly does correspond to his time. But do the solo Violin Sonatas and Partitas, including the giant Chaconne, also correspond to it? In a great deal of his music, he is ahead of his time by eons. The organ works cited are something as completely new in their musical milieu as the Fifth Symphony of Beethoven, the opening of Wagner's *Dutchman* Overture, or Stravinsky's *Petrushka*.

I choose these works purely at random, and it goes without saying that they cannot be compared with each other; the point is that there is nothing like any of them in their time. In order to set something comparable beside the B Minor Mass, we have to go as far as the *Missa Solemnis* of Beethoven, composed three-quarters of a century later.

When Schweitzer speaks of Bach as one of those artists who "do not feel any inner compulsion to break new ground," I cannot believe that he is really referring to Bach. After all, already in Arnstadt Bach clashed with the authorities precisely *because* he was breaking new ground. And we are not even talking yet of the large-scale musical architect whose formal constructions, whose boldly built periods are not discussed in the specialist literature at all. (Goethe gives an explanation for this. "Everyone sees the material before him, but only someone who treats it finds the content—and for most the form remains a mystery.")

We must at least invoke the revolutionary harmonist who is unparalleled in all of Baroque music and who was ahead of the harmony of his time by at least a century. Leonard Bernstein—who as a musician, not a musicologist, was reporting from a realm in which he was at home—has described this aspect precisely:

> [The] twelve tones of the circle of fifths . . . generate a circle of twelve *keys*. . . . How does music contain this loose, runny chromaticism? By the basic principle of *diatonicism*—that stable relationship of tonics and dominants, subdominants and supertonics, new dominants and new tonics. We can now modulate as freely as we want, as chromatically as we want, and still have complete tonal control. . . . This great system of tonal control was perfected and codified by Johann Sebastian Bach, whose genius was to balance so delicately, and so justly, these two forces of chromaticism and diatonicism, forces that were equally powerful and presumably contradictory in nature. This point of delicate balance is like the still center in the flux of music history—a condition of such stability that it was able to continue without remarkable changes for almost a century, a century which became a Golden Age.

If Johann Sebastian Bach means "the end of Baroque music," then it is because he toppled the barriers of Baroque music and paved the way for the music of the coming century—not as a precursor but as a leader. To be sure, many people still believe that the combination "prelude and fugue" was the predominant form of Baroque music. Yet they are utterly mistaken. It was merely the favorite form of

Johann Sebastian Bach, just as the étude was the favorite form of Chopin and the sonata was the favorite form of Haydn, Mozart, and Beethoven. All these forms are incommensurable with each other, and it does not make much sense to speak of a "higher development" on the way from one to the other. John Cage's *Music for Twelve Radios* is certainly not a higher development of the symphony merely because the idea for it arose in the century after Beethoven.

Enough. Let me put it this way: Johann Sebastian Bach was not at all among those artists who feel no inner compulsion to break new ground. If he signifies the end of Baroque music, then it is only because he overcame it and created compositions that went far beyond the music of his time. Nor was he forgotten after his death. His pupils maintained his memory through their practical effectiveness. There were many of them, and they had students in turn, and they imparted Bach to those students as well.

The oddest thing about all this is that there were so many Bach enthusiasts when the man was supposedly entirely out of fashion. One of the most important, Johann Nikolaus Forkel, was neither a Bach pupil nor the student of one, and yet he was among the greatest of Bach's admirers and propagandists. Like Bach, he acquired his profound musical knowledge as an autodidact, and though he studied law, he became university music director and received an honorary master of arts at Göttingen. Among his students were August Wilhelm Schlegel, Ludwig Tieck, and Wilhelm von Humboldt—truly anything but insignificant minds.

Yet for the preservation of Bach's work, another of his pupils was crucial, though we know precious little about him otherwise. This was Friedrich Konrad Griepenkerl, who from 1820 onward, together with Ferdinand August Roitzsch, twenty-three years his junior, systematically collected Bach's organ compositions wherever they were available, whether in original manuscripts or handwritten copies. In more than twenty years of tireless work on the Leipzig Peters Edition, they brought out such an exemplary edition of Bach's organ works that it is still on the market, unaltered to this day. From

366

Griepenkerl as well, in a letter to Roitzsch from December 30, 1846, we have an explanation that makes the wisdom of certain professors appear somewhat dubious. "The entire 'Art of Fugue,'" he writes, "is not for the organ, and not for the clavier either, but intended for study. . . . What I have just stated is from Forkel's mouth, but Forkel would not say such a thing if he had not heard it from Friedemann or Emanuel Bach. . . . All these pieces sound far better when merely read in the mind than they do when played on some instrument."

Of course we should not confuse Bach's pleasure in extraordinary contrapuntal feats, which came to the fore more and more markedly in the last decade of his life, with a theoretical interest. It is chiefly theoreticians who occupy themselves with theory, and as the above quotation shows, it is as hard to hold down certain theories with facts as it is to hold down balloons. They need time to rise until they burst. (In this regard Jean Paul observed that daring judgments often spare us the effort of deeper insights.)

For Bach, the joy of counterpoint consisted in producing new, beautiful music under more and more difficult requirements, again and again. Keyserlingk may or may not have recognized straight away whether he was hearing a *"canone alla quinta"* or *"alla nona"*— Glenn Gould's listeners assuredly could not. But they did not doubt for a moment that this music was enchanting. Bach's pleasure in his art may most aptly be compared with Schoenberg's exploration of the twelve-tone row. He could hardly expect that his listeners would always count to twelve, but it is unmistakable that he made music in this manner.

All the same, the long-standing professor of musicology at the University of Halle, already cited several times, has identified the true reason behind the genesis of the *Art of Fugue*: Bach's senile stubbornness. He cannot account for this composition otherwise. "It is awful," said Goethe, "when the stupid praise an excellent man."

Between 1732 and 1754 one of the most important works of 367 the century appeared in Leipzig: Johann Heinrich Zedler's *Großes vollständiges Universal-Lexicon aller Wissenschaften und Künste (Great Com-*

plete Universal Lexicon of All Sciences and Arts). In the second supplementary volume, the most important bearers of the name Bach are listed:

1. Bach, ancient noble lineage, eighty-seven lines
2. Bach, Ernst Ludwig, Württemberg priest for fifty years, nine lines
3. Bach, Georg Michael, secondary-school teacher in Halle, four lines
4. Bach, Johann August, doctor of both philosophy and law, associate professor in Leipzig, ninety-four lines
5. Bach, Johann Sebastian, musician, forty-five lines
6. Bach, Salomon, jurist in Danzig, sixty-nine lines

It is remarkable that Johann Sebastian received such a large entry of forty-five lines even though he was neither of the nobility nor an intellectual and had even retired to some extent in recent years. Even more remarkable is the detailed appreciation, more than twice as long, of the associate professor Johann August Bach, especially since at the time of its printing he was just thirty. Did he become one of the most important Leipzig scholars of his time? Not at all. But he was a student of Ernesti's.

And how many lines did Gottsched rate? "Gottsched, Johann, 1667–1704, from Königsberg" received seventeen lines. But that was the father. About the great son, "the spokesman of the Leipzig Enlightenment," Zedler found nothing worthy of mention. His name is also missing in Christian Gottlieb Jöcher's *Allgemeines Gelehrten-Lexicon (General Scholars Lexicon)*, which appeared in Leipzig in 1750. Not until eighteen years after Gottsched's death did the publishers of the lexicon get around to including him in the new edition of 1784. At that time the French Encyclopedists had long since delivered their complete work along with the supplement, and the Enlightenment had become a European movement, virtually a fashion. The entry in that new edition reads as follows:

Gottsched had the merit of calling attention again, after long neglect, to the purity and correctness of the language, however defectively and dully he wrote it himself. He recommended good taste according to the rules of beauty and the example of the ancients, though he himself was scarcely able to follow either. In philosophy, his contribution was insignificant.

This, then, was the state of the Enlightenment in Leipzig in Bach's time.

We do not come closer to Bach's music by detecting—or believing we can prove—that elements from this or that musician are included in it. According to Bernstein, "All composers write their music in the idioms of all the music that preceded theirs. Every art acknowledges the art that has existed or still does." And it is of no use either to claim that theoretical problems were reflected in Bach's music or that it was created because of them. That is reserved for people who think they are being clever when they spin a web of theories around themselves.

Bernstein again, in quite a different passage: "Only artists can make magic understandable. Only in art does nature find its expression. And by the same token, art can only be expressed by art. For that reason there is only one real way to say something about music, and that is by writing music." Bach did not know Bernstein, but he shared his opinions, as his behavior in many cases makes clear. And even if it had been interesting to him that fourteen was his number—or forty-one or seventy—for his music it is totally uninteresting. We do not hear any of that; his music does not become any richer through it or more comprehensible either. Anyway, what kind of music obliges us to count it out on our fingers?

In music the small crosses, crescents, anchors, or stars we may perceive in a score do not signify a thing. Those are little games for people who do not know how to eat bread but roll it into tiny balls 369 instead. Paul Badura-Skoda considered that the *Art of Fugue* was the first composition for piano. As a pianist, he is of course entitled to that impression. But the C Major Prelude from *The Well-Tempered Clavier* also sounds quite superb on the synthesizer, though in all likelihood it was not composed for it. Yet in view of the splendid effect achieved, that detail is of no interest. In the 1960s the Swingle Singers proved that even highly successful pop music can be made with Bach. They were proud that in the process they did not change a single note or a single note value; they merely brought out the rhythm a little more clearly.

The indignation that Bach could become popular was tremendous. In East Germany a certain Professor Goldschmidt saw to it that the Swingle Singers' records were forbidden; people had to buy them under the counter in Czech "culture shops." The professor could never have made Bach popular, but in the mouths of the Swingle Singers he was fascinating.

It is hard to make any sense of this. The huge Bach industry has decked the composer with all kinds of problems, origins, and enigmas, like a Christmas tree suffocated by tinsel and ornaments. Yet in the world at large he is not a puzzle at all but an extremely successful musician. A Christmas without the *Christmas Oratorio*? Inconceivable. If a cantata is performed, it is a Bach cantata; if an organ recital is taking place somewhere, then it almost always includes a work by Bach. A Bach discography would be more extensive than the official list of Bach's works, the *Bach-Werke-Verzeichnis*. And the notion that he could ever have been considered old-fashioned seems simply unbelievable, in fact ridiculous. It is obvious that the predilection for music of the past has advanced to the same degree that the serious music of our time has retreated from its listeners.

How seriously contemporary music need be taken would call for another chapter in another book. But returning to Bach, his music is almost always composed of several voices. It is actually different strains of music at the same time and the presentation of several independent melodies all at once, jointly driven forward by their harmonic development. That is a highly mysterious process; it requires

370

extreme calculation in a person, and yet it eludes mere calculation. Carl Philipp Emanuel knew that he could not complete his father's triple fugue. Only a very few have the listening praxis at their disposal to follow all Bach's voices with perfect clarity. Yet only a very few are able to resist their captivating unity.

On one occasion, when Goethe heard some trio sonatas by Bach, he declared it was "as though the eternal harmony were conversing with itself." The sentence has often been circulated by other writers as the friendly utterance of an elderly gentleman of whose musicality they did not think too much. But if he had not been exceedingly musical he would not have become a poet; poetry is written according to the ear. Above all, Goethe was a thinker of sibylline wisdom and profundity, and he had his own special relationship with the mystery of music. With the first two lines of the prologue to *Faust*, he erects the entire edifice of the resounding universe. The same conception is also found in Shakespeare.

The idea of the sonorous universe is an ancient one. It is common to all kinds of cultures—Japanese, Chinese, Indian. It is embedded in ours since Pythagoras, who found all movement embodied in numbers and sound. He claimed that the numeric interrelationships of sounds were also those of the world and that the harmony of the spheres could be condensed into sounds.

A thousand years later Boethius, at first the all-powerful minister and later the prisoner of Theoderic the Great, defined music as a trinity. In the accord of the spheres, it made up the *one* music that exists and of which the human *musica instrumentalis* is the reflection.

All this may strike us as myth, as something unreal. But moving forward another 1,000 years, we come to Johannes Kepler, the mathematician and astronomer who discovered the laws of the orbits of the planets. As a scientist, he was anything but a mystic with his head in the clouds, and yet he asserted: "Give air to the heavens, and music will really and truly resound. There is a *concentus intellectu-* 371 *alis*, a mental harmony, from which purely spiritual beings—and in a certain way, God Himself—experience no less pleasure and delight than man does with his ears from musical chords." And in another passage: "That is why we must not really be surprised that the beautiful, useful sequence of tones in the musical scales was discovered by humans. In this they did nothing other than imitate God's work, in order to play downward to earth, so to speak, the showpiece of that heavenly image of movement." This is what inspired Paul Hindemith to compose his opera and symphony *The Harmony of the World*.

"As though the eternal harmony were conversing with itself"— Goethe's categorization of Bach's music is not to be understood in any lesser context than that evoked by Kepler. In the meantime we have learned that these are not ideas that should be taken no more literally than the story of Creation; rather, the scientific findings of our time bear them out. Musical interrelationships actually do reflect those that govern the orbits of the planets. There is a rhythm in the cosmos, and "the deep structure of music" really is "identical with the deep structure of all things," as Joachim Ernst Berendt proved in his radio series *The World Is Sound*.

Here biology also offers some curious findings. The American scientists Peter Tompkins and Christopher Byrd have seen themselves obliged to conclude that plants are musical. Also in the United States, when Professor Rathelag exposed pumpkin sprouts to the music of Johann Sebastian Bach, the young shoots grew toward the speakers. (With rock music they grew in the opposite direction.)

It is no fantasy: There is a link between Bach's music and the harmony of the world. In that respect I quote the great musician Bernstein once again: "Bach was a man, after all, not a god; but he was a man *of* God, and his godliness informs his music from first to last."

Truly, Bach links us with the universe.

WORKS CITED

Aland, Kurt, and Erhard Peschke, eds. *Texte zur Geschichte des Pietismus*. Berlin, 1972.

Allgemeine Deutsche Biographie. Leipzig and Munich, 1877ff.

Allgemeine Encyklopädie der Wissenschaften und Künste. Leipzig, 1842.

Bach-Archiv Leipzig. *Bach-Dokumente*. Leipzig, 1963, 1969.

———. *Kalendarium zur Lebensgeschichte J. S. Bachs*. Leipzig, 1970.

Bach-Komitee der DDR. *Bach-Gedenkschrift 1950*. Leipzig, 1950.

———. *Festschrift zum III. Internationalen Bachfest*. Leipzig, 1975.

Bartha, Dénes. *Johann Sebastian Bach*. Budapest, 1960.

Barz, Paul. *Bach, Händel, Schütz*. Würzburg, 1984.

Berendt, Joachim Ernst. *Nada Brahma—die Welt ist Klang*. Frankfurt am Main, 1987.

Bernstein, Leonard. *The Infinite Variety of Music*. New York, 1967.

———. *The Joy of Music*. New York, 1959.

———. *The Unanswered Question*. Cambridge, 1976.

———. *Worte wie Musik*. Freiburg, 1992.

———. *Young People's Concerts*. New York, 1992.

Besseler, Heinrich. *Bach als Wegbereiter*. Kassel, 1950.

———. ed. *Bach in Thüringen*. Weimar, 1950.

———. *Bachs Meisterzeit in Weimar*. Weimar, 1950.

Blankenburg, Walter, ed. *Johann Sebastian Bach*. Darmstadt, 1970.

Bojanowski, Paul von. *Das Weimar Johann Sebastian Bachs*. Weimar, n.d.

Brecht, Bertolt. *Leben des Galilei*. Berlin, 1955.

Brockhaus-Riemann Musiklexikon. Wiesbaden, 1979.

Dessau, Paul. *Notizen zu Musik und Musikern*. Leipzig, 1978.

Du Bouchet, Paule. *Johann Sebastian Bach. Musik zur Ehre Gottes*. Ravensburg, 1992.

Elste, Martin. "Probleme der historischen Aufführungspraxis." *Fono Forum*, September 1996.

Engelbert, Ernst. *Die Karl-Marx-Universität Leipzig 1409 bis 1959.* Leipzig, 1959.

Engels, Friedrich. "Deutsche Zustände." In Karl Marx and Friedrich Engels, *Werke*, vol. 2: 1844–1846. Berlin, 1975.

————. *Notizen über Deutschland.* Berlin, [1873] 1975.

Foerster, Friedrich. *Friedrich August II, König von Polen, und seine Zeit.* Potsdam, 1839.

Forkel, Johann Nikolaus. *Über Johann Sebastian Bachs Leben, Kunst und Kunstwerke.* Leipzig, 1802.

Fürstenau, Moritz. *Geschichte der Musik und des Theaters am Hofe zu Dresden.* Dresden, 1861–1862.

Fürstlich sächsische Landes-Ordnung des Herrn Ernsten, Hertzogen zu Sachsen, Jülich, Cleve u. Berg etc. Gotha, 1695.

Galletti, J.G.A. *Gallettiana.* Leipzig, 1968.

Geck, Martin. *Johann Sebastian Bach.* Reinbek, 1993.

Geiringer, Karl. *Johann Sebastian Bach.* Munich, 1971.

————. *Die Musikerfamilie Bach.* Munich, 1974.

————. *Spruchweisheit, Sprüche in Prosa.* Leipzig, 1951.

Gottsched, Johann Christoph. *Gesammelte Werke.* Leipzig, 1908ff.

Gurlitt, Wilibald. *August der Starke und seine Zeit.* Dresden, 1928.

Haacke, Franz. *Geschichte Augusts des Starken.* Leipzig, 1924.

Herrmann, Rudolf. *Thüringische Kirchengeschichte.* Jena, 1947.

Hess, Ulrich. *Geheimer Rat und Kabinett in den Ernestinischen Staaten Thüringens.* Weimar, 1962.

Jean Paul. *Weg der Verklärung. Aphorismen.* Berlin, n.d.

Jöcher, Christian Gottlieb. *Jöchers Allgemeines Gelehrten-Lexikon.* Leipzig, 1750, 1784.

Kaiser, Joachim. "Was wortlose Musik zur Sprache bringt." *Süddeutsche Zeitung*, March 16–17, 1985.

Keller, Hermann. *Die Klavierwerke Johann Sebastian Bachs.* Leipzig, 1950.

Kluke, Paul. *Das Recht des Widerstands gegen die Staatsgewalt in der Sicht des Historikers.* Hannover, 1957.

Küster, Konrad. *Der junge Bach.* Stuttgart, 1996.

Landeskirchenrat Thüringen, ed. *Bach in Thüringen.* Jena, n.d.

Leipzig City Council. City records, 1720–1753.

Leipziger Neuen Bach-Gesellschaft. *Bach-Jahrbücher.* 1902–1992.

Lichtenberg, Georg Christoph. *Die Sudelbücher.* Munich, 1974.

Machiavelli, Niccolò. *The Prince.* Florence, 1931.

374

Maurois, André. *Voltaire*. Paris, 1935.

Menge, Wolfgang. *So lebten sie alle Tage. Berichte aus dem alten Preußen*. Berlin, 1982.

Mentz, Georg. *Weimarische Staats- und Regentengeschichte*. Jena, 1936.

Metzger, Heinz-Klaus. "Blutige Himmelsschlüsselblumen." *Frankfurter Allgemeine Zeitung*, March 27, 1997.

Meyer, Ernst Hermann. *Musik der Renaissance, Musik der Aufklärung*. Leipzig, 1979.

Meyers Handlexikon. Leipzig, 1873.

Mittenzwey, Ingrid. *Friedrich II. von Preußen*. Berlin, 1979.

Neumann, Werner. *Das kleine Bach-Buch*. Salzburg, 1971.

Ottenberg, Hans-Günter. *Carl Philipp Emanuel Bach*. Leipzig, 1982.

Otterbach, Friedemann. *Johann Sebastian Bach*. Stuttgart, 1982.

Petzoldt, Martin, ed. *Bach als Ausleger der Bibel*. Berlin, 1985.

Petzoldt, Martin, and Joachim Petri. *Ehre sei dir, Gott, gesungen. Bilder und Texte zu Bachs Leben als Christ und sein Wirken für die Kirche*. Leipzig, 1975.

Philosophisches Wörterbuch. Leipzig, 1970.

Pieck, Wilhelm. *Rede zur Bach-Feier 1950*. Leipzig, 1975.

Pirro, André. *Les Clavecinistes*. Paris, 1924.

_____. *Louis Marchand*. Paris, 1904–1905.

Pischner, Hans. "Johann Sebastian Bach heute." *Musik und Gesellschaft*, July 1975.

Raffalt, Reinhard. "Johann Sebastian Bach." Presentation on Bavarian Radio.

_____. "Musik jenseits der Töne." Presentation on Bavarian Radio.

Reumuth, Karl. *Heimatgeschichte für Leipzig und den Leipziger Kreis*. Leipzig, 1927.

Richter, Klaus Peter. *J. S. Bach, Leben und Werk*. Frankfurt am Main, 1985.

Riemanns Musiklexikon. Berlin, 1922; Mainz, 1959–1961.

Rueger, Christoph. *Soli Deo Gloria Johann Sebastian Bach*. Berlin, 1985.

Salmen, Walter, ed. *Der Sozialstatus des Berufsmusikers vom 17. bis 19. Jahrhundert*. Kassel, 1971.

Schering, Arnold. *J. S. Bach und das Musikleben Leipzigs*. Leipzig, 1941.

Schleuning, Peter. *Johann Sebastian Bachs "Kunst der Fuge."* Kassel, 1993.

Schönberg, Arnold. *Gesammelte Schriften*. Frankfurt am Main, 1976.

Schopenhauer, Arthur. *Über die vierfache Wurzel des Satzes vom zureichenden Grunde*. Zürich, 1991.

_____. *Vom Genie / Zur Metaphysik der Musik*. In *Die Welt als Wille und Vorstellung*, vol. 2. Zürich, 1991.

Schweitzer, Albert. *Johann Sebastian Bach*. Leipzig, 1905.

Seeger, Horst. *Musiklexikon*. Leipzig, 1966.

Siegmund-Schultze, Walther. *Johann Sebastian Bach*. Leipzig, 1976.

Smend, Friedrich. *Bach in Köthen*. Berlin, 1951.

Spitta, Philipp. *Johann Sebastian Bach*. 2 vols. Leipzig, 1873–1880.

Sturmhoefel, Konrad. *Illustrierte Geschichte der sächsischen Lande und ihrer Herrscher*. Leipzig, 1898–1908.

Szeskus, Reinhard, ed. *Johann Sebastian Bach und die Aufklärung. Symposium*. Leipzig, 1982.

Terry, Charles Sanford. *Johann Sebastian Bach*. London, 1928.

Theophili nötiger und nützlicher Unterricht von der Pflicht und Schuld der Untertanen. Berlin, 1723.

Urner, Hans. *Der Pietismus*. Berlin, 1961.

Vetter, Walter. *Der Kapellmeister Bach*. Potsdam, 1950.

Wallmann, Johannes. *Der Pietismus*. Göttingen, 1990.

Walther, Johann Gottfried. *Musicalisches Lexicon*. Leipzig, 1731.

Wette, Gottfried Albin. *Historische Nachrichten von der berühmten Residenzstadt Weimar*. Weimar, 1737.

Wolff, Christoph. *Johann Sebastian Bach: A Learned Musician*. New York, 2000.

Zedlers Großes Vollständiges Universal-Lexikon aller Wissenschaften und Künste. Leipzig, 1732–1751.

Ziller, Martin. "40 Jahre unter großen Dirigenten."

NOTES

Why do you distance yourself
From all of us and our opinions?
I do not write to please you,
I write to teach you something.

                                       —*Goethe*

INTRODUCTION

XII   *as a personal offense:* For example, the Berlin professor Georg Knepler, in his indignation over the film *Amadeus*, gathered his colleagues together to condemn it. The play by Peter Schaffer that formed the basis of the film was unknown to him.

XIII   *built according to Karl Straube's intentions:* The present organ of the St. Thomas Church was built in 1889-1895 by the Sauer Company in Frankfurt an der Oder, which also constructed the great organ in the Berlin cathedral.

CHAPTER I

8   *"ob defect. hospitios":* The delicate point in this matter is that in the *Bach-Dokumente (Bach Documents)* of 1969 as well, *"ob defectum hospitiorum"* is printed in full, although an *"-orum"* cannot be gathered at all from the handwritten Ohrdruf original, not even by assuming an abbreviation; thus this is a freewheeling completion. Meanwhile, at the expense of considerable erudition, more recent Bach researchers have discovered that *"defectum hospitiorum"* meant the cancellation of free lunches, from which we would have to conclude that either social conditions had considerably worsened in Ohrdruf (for which a reason

is admittedly lacking) or that the boy Sebastian was helping himself to several free lunches (why else the plural?). At any rate, we would have to accept that Sebastian was driven out of Ohrdruf by hunger; in the opinion of all these researchers, he got nothing to eat from his brother's farm.

10   *"had voluntarily given him to learn":* The Freiburg professor Konrad Küster concludes from this that Johann Christoph might have taught Sebastian something willingly. Incidentally, he praises the big brother for apparently not having asked for any money for the lessons and insinuates that he probably appropriated Sebastian's portion of the inheritance as a fee.

11   *Geck is of the opinion:* In his Bach biography, published by Rowohlt in 1993.

Chapter 2

15   *the language they used among themselves was French:* In his Bach book, Otterbach claims that therefore Bach learned French at the school. But that he did not master it or only insufficiently so is revealed by his never using it anywhere and that he had the French dedication of his *Brandenburg Concerti* translated for a fee.

16   *it lay at a certain distance:* Since Spitta did not point this out, all his successors have adopted his phrase "neighboring city" for Celle without double-checking it.

16   *driving on the roads of the time was not much faster:* Wolfgang Menge proved this in detail in his book *That Is How They Lived Every Day* (Berlin, 1984).

Chapter 3

29   *Bach was already counting on the organist post in Arnstadt:* Werner Felix in Leipzig and others hold this view.

29   *though it was not yet completed, had already been in use for some time:* This is technically possible without any problem; an organ can be played even if the pipes for only some registers have been installed.

31   *was related to the mayor of Arnstadt through his mother:* Again a comment by Werner Felix, which others agree with as well. It does not gain any credibility because of that, as the later events of the story prove. In none of Bach's Arnstadt disagreements did his relatives manifest themselves.

378

32   *a man of childlike piety serving his church at last:* Terry would have us believe this.

CHAPTER 4

46   *the impression of being the weaker fugue:* According to Geck. Hermann Keller is of this opinion too. Both fail to notice the magnificent intensification to which Bach leads the theme. The initial withdrawal is nothing but architectonic consistency. In accord with the view of these two critics, Bach should have piled one huge structure on top of another unnecessarily. But he was not that foolish.

46   *he lacks practical experience:* If he had explored the history of music more thoroughly, Geck would have ascertained that as early as the sixteenth century the four-voiced rather than the three-voiced composition was seen as the epitome of technical perfection.

46   *handle chorale preludes in the same manner:* Schweitzer even declares that no other possibility exists at all.

52   *"easily provoked to temper, and prone to outbreaks":* This is claimed by all sorts of people over and over again, yet statements to this effect from Bach's own time are not to be found.

CHAPTER 5

65   *to make a Pietist:* Geck has devoted intensive attention to demonstrating Pietistic influences in the texts of the church cantatas of Buxtehude. That is not really difficult, mind you, since Pietism is above all a spiritual attitude, not a self-contained theology. Pietism never abandoned its grounding in Lutheran Protestantism, though it did thoroughly embrace the exuberance of the literary Baroque in religious poetry. Thus "Pietistic influences" would not be hard to detect in the cantatas Bach performed in Leipzig, where they surely would not have been tolerated as such. Yet it can be asserted with certainty that the church-music praxis of Buxtehude remained completely untouched by the attitude of Pietism toward sacred music. How stark the contrasts between Pietists and the Orthodox really were can be gauged from the fate of the Protestant Advent chorale "Macht hoch die Tür, die Tor' macht weit" ("Open the Door, Throw Wide the Gates"). Since it originated in Halle in 1707, it was regarded as Pietistic. As a result there is not a single contemporary chorale prelude to this hymn. The Pietists did not want any preludes, and the Orthodox did not sing any Pietistic chorales.

68   *"the Pietistic movement strongly appealed":* Other authors as well have adopted this supposition indiscriminately, without weighing its likelihood.

68   *had to intervene once again:* Küster, who refers to his detailed research of primary sources again and again, has no clue about this. He simply claims that it was all exaggerated and that nothing took place.

CHAPTER 6

73   *we know where he gets it from:* This method of indiscriminately adopting quotations (which occurs elsewhere on occasion) has two indisputable advantages: It relieves authors of doing research of their own and garners them the goodwill of those they honor through their transcriptions.

CHAPTER 7

84   *an opulent banquet:* Terry has shared the menu with us: "A piece of beef à la mode—pike with anchovy butter sauce—smoked ham—a dish of peas—a dish of potatoes—two dishes of spinach and *Zerzigen*—a quarter of roast mutton—boiled pumpkin-fritters—candied lemon peel—cherry preserves—warm asparagus salad—lettuce—radishes—fresh butter—roast veal." That this menu was preserved in detail shows that such a sumptuous meal constituted a great exception in this period.

85   *"as a composer, [Bach] possessed no great name":* An assertion by the Leipzig musicologist Hans-Joachim Schulze. He fails to notice that assessments among colleagues very rarely find expression in writing. But already in 1717 Bach's reputation extended from Weimar to Hamburg, Dresden, and Kassel. Mattheson wrote at that time: "I have seen things . . . by the *famous* organist in Weimar." This proves that Bach's compositions were already being copied out by colleagues, which is all the more remarkable when we consider that only a small number of his organ compositions were suitable for use in the worship service.

86   *something he calls "character theme":* Besseler has expounded in detail his idea of the "character theme" without mentioning, of course, the composers named below.

89   *structure of this text is illogical:* According to the Czech musicologist Kamil Slapák, commenting on the Supraphon recording of the cantata.

90   *"wandering off into the dramatic":* Slapák speaks of a "foreign dramatic element."

CHAPTER 8

93   *with exemplary thoroughness:* Jauernig's work is found in the anthology *Bach in Thuringia* (Weimar, 1950).

CHAPTER 9

104   *and splendid court after Versailles:* Voltaire described it as "the most brilliant in Europe."

106   *spirit of a German underling:* Spitta's unique achievement in elucidating Bach's life cannot be overestimated. Nevertheless, his example shows that even the most careful collection of facts does not always lead to correct conclusions. Peter Hacks in his book *The Stipulations of Art* (Berlin, 1978) and Mark Twain in his story "How the Jungle Animals Went on an Expedition" have aptly portrayed this phenomenon. Küster produces a number of fine specimens in his book *The Young Bach* (Stuttgart, 1998).

108   *Marchand was fully his equal in reputation:* In his *Dictionnaire des artistes* (Paris, n.d.), the Abbé de Fontenai wrote about him: "Hardly had he placed his hands on the clavier when he astonished all the listeners."

109   *famous for the bravura of his harmonic modulations:* André Pirro praises Marchand's "audacious novelties" and writes in his book *Les Clavecinistes* (Paris, 1848): "Incidentally, he did not hesitate to use the diminished seventh chord." His great French contemporary the composer and theoretician Rameau esteemed and admired him.

110   *occasional impurities:* An assessment of the Freiberg cathedral choirmaster Hans Otto, which was repeatedly confirmed during the discussion about the restoration of the Silbermann organ at the Dresden Church of Our Lady.

110   *required it for his composing:* How much Bach was impelled to course through the keys is shown quite beautifully by the C Major Prelude in *The Well-Tempered Clavier I*, which includes seventh chords on the third (E minor) and seventh (B minor) and indeed even on the third of D major (F-sharp minor), and all these as well as other chords are harmonically ambiguous. Except at the end, this C Major Prelude truly offers pure C major chords in only four out of thirty-five bars. Although in eight bars the note C is missing, it nonetheless occurs exactly 100 times altogether (with only a tiny bit of fudging). From this feature, mystical numerologists will probably conclude that Bach composed the entire piece simply in order to strike C 100 times, and that C appears no less than three times in the final chord as his homage to the Holy Trinity.

111   *had remained closed to Marchand until then:* In Marchand's *Livres d'orgue* we find no key signatures at the beginnings of the staves other than a # or a ♭. Whoever compares the three volumes of his organ composi-

tions with those of Bach from the Weimar period will grasp right away that immediate, secret flight was the only alternative for Marchand.

112   *to study the Vivaldi concerti in the music library:* We can see that this claim is untenable because Bach wrote all his Vivaldi arrangements *before* his Dresden journey; no stimulus whatsoever from his trip in that regard can be proved. Geck could have found the confirmation of Marchand's Dresden stay not only in such sources as Marpurg and Adlung but also in the biography that André Pirro placed at the beginning of the new edition of Marchand's organ works (Paris, 1842). We may shake our heads at such a careless musicology, but according to the information from his publishing house he is "a competent author, as attested by his musicological publications."

113   *important trump card:* Bach retained as well the high esteem of his successor, the all-powerful Count Brühl.

CHAPTER 10

123   *there were court orchestras elsewhere:* The court orchestra of Frederick the Great would become particularly well known, but in 1717 he was just five years old. His uncle, the margrave of Brandenburg, only had a sextet.

126   *"exceeded the limits of the artistically possible":* On the contrary, the solo partitas demonstrate a quite unusual familiarity with the instrument. Such breathtaking passages could not possibly have occurred to a less competent violinist, if only because such technical difficulties would have lain outside his capacity to reproduce them. In the B Minor Partita (BWV 1002), Bach accomplishes the compositional feat of immediately presenting the same piece of music again in the *Doubles* so precisely that one can play both simultaneously. No less an authority than Yehudi Menuhin has pointed out that the six keys of these six compositions are the most favorable for the violin and that the most difficult pieces are written with at most a single sharp or flat in the key signature. He cites this as proof that Bach knew the particularities of the violin to a quite exceptional degree.

131   *he improvised for half an hour:* The organ is generally considered to be an instrument that especially stimulates improvising. That is true, though among experts the results are also infamous as "organist doodles." Bach's improvising in Hamburg, however, may be imagined as similar to Beethoven's on the piano. When a listener once lamented that

all these melodies were born for but a passing moment, Beethoven repeated what he had just played note for note; for him the spontaneous invention had immediately taken on a definite form. Bach's fugal improvisations at Sanssouci may be conceived this way as well.

Chapter 11

134 *using goose quills alone:* The best way to get an idea of this achievement is to try it out for ourselves. With a properly trimmed goose quill, one can write fairly well, but in addition to a good penknife the process requires some dexterity, and the need to trim frequently holds up the writing.

137 *the field of musical tuning:* Extremely noteworthy on this point is the article "Bachs Klangwerkstatt" ("Bach's Sound Studio") by Martin Elste in *Fono Forum* of September 1996.

138 *as did the Canadian pianist Glenn Gould:* It is true that Gould's interpretation of *The Well-Tempered Clavier* is characterized by great transparence, but he does not manifest a cantabile, or "singing," performance such as Bach demanded of his pupils, one of the cornerstones of his teaching. His son Carl Philipp Emanuel similarly insisted on the ability to "sing on the clavier" as the basis of musical performance style. And on occasion Gould treats Bach's score rather high-handedly.

139 *eagerly pursued by others as well:* Hertha Kluge-Kahn provides an almost incredible example of this in her study *J. S. Bach: die verschlüsselten theologischen Aussagen in seinem Spätwerk (J. S. Bach: The Encoded Theological Messages in His Late Works)*, mentioned in Paule du Bouchet's book. The advocates of such theories could gain important insights if they attempted to compose something themselves according to the method they have discovered, by which one would not connect notes with tones but rather see in them a kind of hieroglyphics. Although tones can be derived from those signs, their real and deeper meaning lies in their arrangement. If that were so, we could infer the content of a newspaper from its layout. Many people may consider this sort of thing to be scholarship, but it has nothing to do with music. It is remarkable that Bach did not share something of this technique with his sons even in passing and that no confirmation of Bach's number manipulations is found anywhere else either. On this subject Walter Kolneder comments in *J. S. Bach—Life, Work, and Lasting Influence, in Contemporary Documents* (Wilhelmshaven, 1991): "Bach's supposed number manipulations are a pure invention of recent decades, averred

and seemingly proved by half- and non-musicians, to whom the tonal world of a work by Bach hardly means a thing."

141 *"before playing a five-finger exercise":* Terry certainly does not reveal to us how he knows this, but technical dexterity on the clavier cannot really be improved through piety.

CHAPTER 12

155 *the Tübingen professor Ulrich Siegele:* In the *Bach-Jahrbuch* of 1983, 1984, and 1986 as "Bachs Stellung in der Leipziger Kulturpolitik seiner Zeit" (Bach's Position in the Leipzig Cultural Policy of his Time).

CHAPTER 13

163 *"freed music from the bonds of medieval scholasticism":* All quotations from Wilhelm Pieck's Bach celebration address of 1950 are from the reprint by the New Bach Society in 1975. The society thus still identified itself with Pieck's theories twenty-five years later, long after the conclusion of the Stalin era.

164 *Hans Pischner, director at that time of the Berlin State Opera:* Pischner also became well known for his numerous harpsichord recordings.

CHAPTER 14

169 *"called to Leipzig as Cantor Figuralis":* It is remarkable that the name Bach, which after all enjoyed a considerable reputation among experts—and not only in Hamburg and Dresden—does not appear at all in this notice. The man's name clearly did not matter to Leipzig.

175 *Leipzig council records:* The following facts are drawn from them but have not been included in any Bach biography up to now.

176 *a princess from the electoral house:* The stubbornness with which the New Bach Society has denied Augustus the Strong his Polish royal dignity—legitimately acquired—is admirable. Even its edition of Bach's complete works entitles the relevant pieces merely "compositions for the electoral house."

CHAPTER 15

181 *at the university church:* The Leipzig university church, a fully intact architectural monument that also housed a valuable organ, was demolished on May 30, 1968, by order of the East German government to make room for a massive university building constructed of concrete.

182 *unanimous resolution:* The resolution appears in the university records of 1724.

186   *commissioned Bach for the job:* Walter Blankenburg describes this as a "coincidence" (see the collection of articles edited by Martin Petzoldt, *Bach as Interpreter of the Bible* [Berlin, 1985]).

Chapter 16

199   *"powerful forces of the Enlightenment":* The notion of "powerful forces of the Enlightenment" in Leipzig was originally adopted from Spitta. In writings about Bach, Leipzig authors naturally attached particular importance to the idea, without proving it in detail.

Chapter 17

204   *respected musicologists:* About Mozart: the Vienna musicologist Walter Engelsmann. About Haydn: the Berlin musicologist Gert Schönfelder. About Beethoven: the Berlin musicologist Georg Knepler. These are the views of serious scholars, exactly as in the case of Martin Geck, Peter Schleuning, Christoph Wolff, and Walther Siegmund-Schultze.

204   *"Early German Enlightenment":* A discovery of the Halle musicologist Walther Siegmund-Schultze.

204   *Lutheran Orthodox father confessors:* An idea of the Leipzig theologian Martin Petzoldt.

207   *his character the painter Conti:* In the first act of Lessing's *Emilia Galotti.*

208   *Schopenhauer:* In *The World as Will and Idea,* volume 2, chapter 35.

208   *feels obliged to worship at its altar:* Nevertheless, a certain kind of scholarship is always discovering new character traits in Bach. For example, the music theoretician and aesthetician Heinz-Klaus Metzger claimed (in the *Frankfurter Allgemeine Zeitung,* March 27, 1997) that the realism with which Bach set the "Crucify Him!" chorus to music in the *St. Matthew Passion* demonstrates his Lutheran anti-Semitism.

Chapter 18

211   *two organs at the St. Thomas Church:* These were not just small organs. The larger one, with three manuals and thirty-five stops, was built in 1489 and so had been in service for 240 years at that time. The other one, dating from 1693, was equipped with two manuals and twenty-one stops; after only thirty-six years of use, it was still almost new. In 1742, however, the council had it demolished without even asking the opinion of the *director musices,* Bach, who was both in charge of the music at this church and an organ expert.

217   *addressed a petition to the council:* Nothing whatever can be read about a single one of Bach's petitions in the council records. The council simply ignored them all, a fact that none of Bach's biographers points out.

219   *the American Joshua Rifkin:* As to Rifkin's theory, Paule du Bouchet cites an interview with Rifkin on this subject in her book *Johann Sebastian Bach. Musik zur Ehre Gottes (Johann Sebastian Bach: Music for the Glory of God)* (Ravensburg, 1992).

219   *who ever reads petitions?* In regard to Joshua Rifkin's theory, everyone ignored Bach's own statements on the topic in his petition.

221   *Bach's enormous creative achievement:* People always fail to notice that Bach was not a composer by profession like Mozart, Beethoven, Schubert, or Brahms but a city employee caught up in diverse tasks as well as a music practitioner. In fact he created his colossal oeuvre in Leipzig exclusively in his free time.

222   *"amid almost constant vexation, envy, and persecution":* For over 125 years, all his biographers have read through this shattering statement of Bach's without being moved.

224   *Esther Meynell:* Known for *The Little Chronicle of Anna Magdalena Bach* in her *Little Bach Book.*

Chapter 19

231   *"and Arion twenty times over":* There are people who conclude from this description ("though he himself is performing the most difficult part") that Bach directed his musicians from the organ. They should try to warn somebody with a finger or stamp their foot while playing the organ; they would be surprised at the effect.

234   *comparison between the careers of Gesner and Ernesti:* The careers of Gesner and Ernesti are described in detail in the *Allgemeine Deutsche Biographie (General German Biography)* (Leipzig, 1875ff.).

Chapter 20

240   *Gesner's insights and influence:* It is all the more astounding that Gesner's importance for Bach's working and living conditions was suppressed with such consistency by the New Bach Society.

241   *woman who for many years exercised considerable power:* Joanna Rudolph, a journalist. She asserted her views not only in the main publication of the state party, *Neues Deutschland (New Germany),* which governed political speech, but also at length in the notes to the recording of the *Christmas Oratorio* by the Dresden Kreuzchor (produced by Eterna in East Germany).

CHAPTER 21

248   *two great pioneers of the Enlightenment:* Such is the opinion of Felix, among others. It is noteworthy in this regard that Zedler's *Universal-Lexicon aller Wissenschaften und Künste (Universal Lexicon of All Sciences and Arts)* (Leipzig, 1732-1754) does not even mention Gottsched.

CHAPTER 22

267   *"one does not recognize among them any principal part":* Scheibe's remark is not only a proof of his inferior musical gifts but also a valuable insight into the performance of Bach's organ chorales "for two keyboards and pedal." Organists usually play them by particularly emphasizing the chorale melody through a striking register or stop. Scheibe's carping shows that when Bach played them, all voices were treated equally; the parts that did not carry the tune were not subordinate at all. Whoever attempts to do likewise will be surprised by the power of expression achieved and the overflowing wealth of Bach's creation (and will also comprehend that Scheibe was unable to cope with it all).

268   *Scheibe's criticism completely justified:* This is the opinion of Bach's admirers Geck, Siegmund-Schultze, and Otterbach, among others. Although considerable importance is attributed to Scheibe in various Bach biographies, he never comes to the fore in music history again otherwise. His notorious criticism makes him similar to Herostratos, who attained immortality only by setting fire to the Temple of Artemis.

268   *"a poverty of invention":* Siegmund-Schultze nevertheless describes Scheibe as a "leading musician" (which he was not at all, even in his own time).

272   *also been declared "Protestant":* Volume II/2 of the New Bach edition (Kassel: Bärenreiter, 1978) entitles them *Lutheran Masses.* But one of Luther's fundamental acts in the Reformation consisted precisely of replacing Church Latin in the worship services with German that everyone could understand. Leipzig was a bastion of Lutheran Orthodoxy. For this reason as well, the idea that Bach composed his brief Latin Masses for the Thomas Church is not plausible. No Masses in Latin by his Lutheran predecessors or his Lutheran contemporaries have come down to us.

CHAPTER 23

279   *stile antico:* In his *Tractatus compositionis augmentatus* of 1660, Christian Bernhard distinguishes between *contrapunctus stylus praxis,* or *antiquus,* the strict compositional style of Palestrina, on the one hand; and *contrapunctus stylus luxurians* or *modernus*—on the other. The theories of affects

and musical-rhetorical figures are assigned to the latter style. In his doctoral dissertation Christoph Wolff has endeavored to prove in detail that Bach occupied himself intensively with the *stylus antiquus* after the fiftieth year of his life—thus not until his late creative phase. In their melodic handling, harmony, and rhythm, Bach's compositions from this period do not suggest parallels at all with Palestrina's compositions, such as the *Missa Papae Marcelli* or the *Missa aeterna Christi munera*. Moreover, whenever Bach used a certain style he always explicitly named it (as with the *French* and *English Suites*, the *Concerto in the Italian Style*, the notation *"in stilo francese"* in the *Art of Fugue*), but the expression *in stilo antico* is found nowhere in his works. For that matter, it is not found in Johann Gottfried Walther's music lexicon of 1732 either, even though Walther holds forth on musical styles for two full pages. The *Universal-Lexikon der Tonkunst (Universal Lexicon of Music)* (Stuttgart, 1838) does not mention the concept, nor does Donner's *Musikalisches Lexikon (Musical Lexicon)* (Heidelberg, 1865). Reimann's *Handbuch der Musikgeschichte (Music History Handbook)* (Leipzig, 1920) and *The International Cyclopedia of Music and Musicians* (New York, 1956) still do not include it. So we may be fairly sure that the *stile antico* was utterly irrelevant for the whole eighteenth century and even the nineteenth century. Quite certainly, it was irrelevant for Bach, if he knew the concept at all. (The apocryphal motet "Amen, Lob, Ehre, und Weisheit" ["Amen, Praise, Glory, and Wisdom"; BWV-Anh. 160] differs from Bach's compositional style so widely that its classification seems more than questionable.) It is Wolff's contribution to have demonstrated Bach's preoccupation with a stylistic concept that did not exist in his century. As a supplement to this, Geck has put forward the claim that the composition of the B Minor Mass only became possible at all for Bach through his study of Palestrina. To be sure, both authorities conceal from us how Bach, in Protestant Leipzig, could have got hold of the scores of a Catholic Italian who had died 135 years earlier. In any case they were not found in his estate, according to Spitta's inventory. In addition, it is characteristic of the first half of the eighteenth century that there was generally no interest in historical styles. That is proved by the paintings of the period as well as the buildings (the renovation of Catholic churches in contemporary style that was taking place just at this time). It is also revealed by the universally anachronistic theater costumes and decorations for the many "Roman plays."

280 *advent of the "gallant style":* At most one may point out that in Mannheim a new musical style, that of the Mannheim School, had developed. Franz Xaver Richter, Johann Stamitz, Ignaz Holzbauer, and Christian Cannabich were Bach's contemporaries. But as the term "Mannheim School" implies, they were all from Mannheim. Nor is Arnold Schering able to report in his *Music History of Leipzig* that their works were ever played in Leipzig in Bach's time.

281 *he did have his public:* That Bach was able to continue the café concerts with his Collegium Musicum students until 1744 or probably 1746—that is, until his health gave him trouble—is overlooked with remarkable consistency by those who claim he went out of fashion toward the end of his life. These writers conceal from us as well what other musicians' works Leipzig's citizens might have appreciated instead of Bach's.

284 *"Count von Keyserlingk Variations":* Hermann Carl, imperial count von Keyserlingk, 1676-1764. Spitta and Terry spell it "Keyserlinck"; my spelling follows that of the *Deutsche Biographie*.

Chapter 24

292 *a programmatic meaning into his work:* Reinhard Raffalt has written an extraordinarily learned work, *On the Problematic Nature of Program Music,* in which he proves with painstaking scholarship that one cannot get a handle on program music through scholarship.

292 *That does not mean any renunciation of their spiritual content:* Unfortunately, it does often mean an inevitable renunciation of their use in the worship service. But clearly, the latter was not Bach's concern in these compositions either.

294 *impute a change in style:* Like the preoccupation with the *stile antico,* this is something that escaped the notice of Bach's admirers for 200 years and that Christoph Wolff alone has discovered.

296 *assimilating other people's works:* The discovery of Wolff and Schleuning.

297 *"macrostructures," "sound grids," and the like:* The study by Michael-Christian Winkler in Martin Petzoldt, ed., *Bach as Interpreter of the Bible* (Berlin, 1985) shows what grotesque things are possible along these lines. None of these experts has dealt with the following question: Why should Johann Sebastian Bach, of all people, have constantly imitated art that left almost completely untapped his own innate talent?

296   *the nimbus of a specialized superiority:* Of course, one reason for that lies in the belief of their listeners, who think that when the authorities claim something, they have also taken the trouble to prove it. Thus they trustingly receive mere hypotheses as facts as well. For example, when Schweitzer asserts that Bach wrote the Trio Sonatas for Organ in 1724 as études for his son Friedemann, no one doubts it. Yet Friedemann was only thirteen at the time, and the intellectual and technical demands of the composition go far beyond those of a teaching work. Similar things occur elsewhere. For instance, it has been averred that the Overture (BWV 1067) with flute obligato may have been written in 1738 as a farewell present from Bach to his son Carl Philipp Emanuel. But he had left home four years earlier and did not play the flute at all.

298   *or exclusively because of the Cabala:* The most remarkable thing about this theory is that there are no grounds whatever for believing that Bach even knew the Cabala, much less that he ever devoted his attention to it.

298   *specialized theological literature on his harmony:* The book cited above, *Bach as Interpreter of the Bible,* edited by the theologian Martin Petzoldt, is full of this kind of thing, but similar material abounds elsewhere. The Russian musicologist Marina Lobanowa, for example, claims that Bach incorporated "Baroque emblematics" into his compositions, actually imitating the visual arts—with which Bach never occupied himself. She also sees in a slowly ascending bass the outstretched arm of Jesus Christ, and so on. (See *Das Orchester,* April 1997.)

298   *"also an expression of personal involvement with the text":* This truly astounding discovery, as well as what follows, is presented with the highest scholarly seriousness in *Bach as Interpreter of the Bible.*

CHAPTER 25

303   *only in Leipzig at the end of the 1730s:* See Wolff as well as Geck and Schleuning, who largely adopt Wolff's findings.

303   *Gradus ad Parnassum of Fux:* This idea also comes from Schleuning and can be found in his book on the *Art of Fugue* (Kassel, 1993).

304   *the same harmony as a Mr. X:* Since it has been alleged that the *Eight Little Preludes and Fugues* for organ are not by Bach, it would be excellent to discover at last what other master was able to create gems of such imagination and perfection. Incidentally, in a television presentation of West German Broadcasting (on June 22, 1997), the Arnstadt church music director, Gottfried Preller, explained that Bach did not

in fact compose his D Minor Toccata either but merely copied it. Unfortunately, he could not tell us from whom.

305   *as though they would have had anything to tell him:* The recent discovery that Bach copied ancient rhetoric in his compositions is also myth. It grotesquely confuses cause and effect. Bach's music does not copy rhetorical formulas; rather, the formulas of rhetoric copy musical structures. Their effect is based on them to begin with. (His written documents show that rhetoric was utterly alien to Bach.)

306   *"he conquered the field of keyboard music according to plan":* If Geck's claim were correct, this would not have happened until between 1725 and 1742, after Bach had long since composed the bulk of his organ and clavier works.

306   *a fugue from the last years of Bach's life:* This and the following remarks were made by Schleuning.

309   *the greatest melodists in musical history:* According to a statement by Martin Ziller.

CHAPTER 26

312   *the important father of his harpsichordist:* In fact, Frederick had no less than three Bach pupils in his orchestra. Besides Carl Philipp Emanuel, there were the second harpsichordist, Christoph Nichelmann, and the violinist Johann Philipp Kirnberger (whom I mention again later).

319   *at number fourteen it was "his turn":* Geck and Rueger came up with this idea.

319   *character pieces as well:* Schweitzer already brings this to the attention of those who believe that in playing Bach's fugues they must above all present his technical feats of composition.

CHAPTER 27

323   *even recommended Fux to others:* Hans Werner Henze still recommends Fux's work to this day.

324   *owe only to Mattheson:* This and the following are all ideas of Wolff's that no theoretician has yet contradicted.

326   *all the curious findings:* The list of all those involved would be quite long, hence at this point I can only offer the assurance that everything cited here can be verified by naming the authors.

326   *"a rather mechanical development":* Scholarly assessment by Geck.

327   *reproaches Bach for his parallel fifths:* Schleuning.

327   *Bach's thoroughbass rules:* In "Instructions for His Students in Music for the Four-Part Playing of the Thoroughbass or Accompaniment, by the Royal Court Composer etc. Mr. Johann Sebastian Bach of Leipzig, 1738." The quotation is from the copy by Peter Kellner, as communicated by Schweitzer (p. 165).

327   *third scholar:* Heinrich Besseler.

328   *"Enlightenment ideas"* . . . "stile antico": Schleuning claims the former, whereas Wolff asserts the opposite.

328   *"At universities, young people learn to believe":* A particularly macabre proof of the justifiability of this theory was furnished in the defunct East Germany by university teachers of political economy, who with supreme learning taught their listeners to believe in the absolute superiority of an economic system that subsequently led to economic collapse in all nations of the Eastern bloc. But they do not stand alone.

329   *"It is granted to the genius":* See section 34 of Lessing's *Hamburg Dramaturgy.*

330   *he never attended a lecture on acoustics:* In a similarly brilliant fashion, Richard Wagner knew exactly how ideal acoustics could be obtained at his Bayreuth Festival Theater without any consideration of all the other theater buildings in the world—and he was right.

331   *wholly new harmonic combinations:* Forkel gives an analogous account of his quite unusual tone combinations on the organ ("His way of combining the stops was so uncommon that many organ builders and organists were frightened by it"). The extremely sparing stop indications in his organ compositions confirm this: They amaze us and achieve remarkable effects (an example: the chorale prelude BWV 720, "Ein feste Burg ist unser Gott" ["A Mighty Fortress Is Our God"]).

CHAPTER 28

338   *written for clavier:* Geck and Schleuning announce this as a completely new realization. Since there are composition sketches by Richard Wagner as well for two staves, we could derive the analogous claim that *Tristan* was not originally intended for orchestra either. The assertion that the *Art of Fugue* was primarily intended for the clavier is

392   implausible anyway, because the clavier is the least suitable instrument for making the development of the voices transparent (which was what mattered in the end).

339   *aroused emotion among the listeners:* The passage is found in Schleuning. It does not exactly show a great understanding of music. On the thoroughbass, we possess Bach's theoretical explanations. But on the *Art of Fugue* he did not write a teaching manual at all—as a matter of fact, he composed lively music.

340   *could be left unfinished for the time being:* Bach began many different things and set them aside for the time being, still unfinished. That he composed something in 1740 that could then be expanded in 1749 into the *Art of Fugue* is no proof that he already had the plan for this work in mind at that earlier juncture.

343   *"has none to lose":* In *Emilia Galotti.*

346   *operating room:* Helmut Zeraschi depicts the whole procedure thoroughly and precisely in the article "Bach and Taylor the Oculist" in the *Bach-Jahrbuch* of 1956.

CHAPTER 29

351   *really existed at that time:* Such care had been accorded to widows and orphans of the court musicians under Augustus the Strong in Dresden since 1712. Yet proof of provisions for widows by the Leipzig council during Bach's time has not come to light. Anna Magdalena first had to go to the trouble of lodging an explicit petition (on August 15, 1750) even for the (reduced) one-time mercy payment. Not until 1837 did Mendelssohn institute a benefits fund for widows and orphans of his Gewandhaus Orchestra, evidence that such a thing did not exist in Leipzig up to then.

354   *music director at Brühl's home:* Johann Gottlob Harrer was born in Görlitz in 1703 and died in Karlsbad in 1755. From 1731 he was music director of Count Brühl's private orchestra, and in August 1750, less than three weeks after Bach's death, he became the Thomas choirmaster.

356   *exceeded the limits of music:* Schweitzer repeatedly makes this incomprehensible claim.

357   *Johann Philipp Kirnberger:* Moses Mendelssohn, the grandfather of Felix, took lessons from him; so did Felix's mother, née Salomon. The Bach school had a definite place in the Berlin music world of that time.

360   *to the works of Bach and Handel:* Haydn, Mozart, Beethoven, Neefe,   393
Hiller, Homilius, Kirnberger, Doles, Rochlitz, Zelter, Neumeister, Swieten, Forkel (and who else can there be?)—we should bear in

mind that all these people honored their enthusiasm for Bach at a time when neither his organ works nor his *Well-Tempered Clavier* were printed and available for purchase. His Passions, cantatas, and motets were equally inaccessible. Whoever wanted to own something by Bach had to copy it by hand—and that is what everyone did. Haydn possessed a copy of the B Minor Mass. The score from which the young Beethoven played *The Well-Tempered Clavier* at Neefe's was a handwritten copy. Mendelssohn was already familiar with copies of Bach's works from childhood on, since his great-aunt Sara Levy "had a considerable number of them" (as Eric Werner recounts in his biography of Mendelssohn). That is how fully Bach was "forgotten" after his death and how fully the "gallant style" had "superseded" him.

361   *Carl Friedrich Zelter:* Incidentally, as early as 1794 he performed a Bach motet with the Berlin Singakademie (Vocal Academy) on one occasion.

362   *difficulties of performing the work:* That is not quite correct. Zelter did conduct the second repetition of the *St. Matthew Passion* all the same. His copy of the score was also a handwritten one, and Mendelssohn's was a handwritten copy of that. (The complete course of events is described in detail in the memoirs of Eduard Devrient.)

CHAPTER 30

364   *none of them wrote like Bach:* The Psalm compositions of Bach's famous Italian contemporary Benedetto Marcello can hardly be classified as typical Baroque music either, nor do they embody a "gallant style."

365   *by at least a century:* Johann Friedrich Reichardt wrote in October 1782, more than thirty years after Bach's death, in his *Musikalisches Kunstmagazin (Musical Art Magazine)*:

> Never did a composer, not even the best and deepest of the Italians, so fully exhaust all the possibilities of our harmony as J. S. Bach. There is almost no possible harmonic combination that he did not bring to bear. He made use of every proper harmonic art and every improper harmonic artifice a thousand times over, in earnest and in jest, with such boldness and idiosyncrasy that the greatest harmonist, if he were expected to furnish a missing measure in one of his greatest works, could not be fully certain of having completed it as Bach had done.

371   *"as though the eternal harmony were conversing with itself":* The complete quotation is as follows: "I said to myself: it is as though the eternal harmony were conversing with itself, as it may have done in the bosom

of God just before the creation of the world. In the same way, it moved within my soul. And it seemed to me as though I neither possessed nor needed ears, nor any other sense—least of all the eyes" (letter to Zelter, June 21, 1827).

371   *also found in Shakespeare:* "Look how the floor of heaven / Is thick inlaid with patines of bright gold: / There's not the smallest orb which thou behold'st / But in his motion like an angel sings" (*The Merchant of Venice,* act 5, scene I).

372   *the harmony of the world:* Leibniz explained that the term "harmony" derives from mathematics and that the concept already existed in mathematics before the idea of the "harmonic" in music came into being—it is "a hidden arithmetic movement." Jean-Philippe Rameau speaks in this connection of a "science of tones." The French musicologist Jules Combarieu defined music as "the science of thinking in tones."

INDEX

The Abuse of the Free Arts, Especially Music (G. Vockerodt), 66
Academic Festival Overture (Brahms), 296
Adlung, Jakob, 21, 382
"Age of Sentimentalism," 320
Ahle, Johann Georg, 56, 61, 65
Ahle, Johann Rudolf, 56, 61
Albinoni, Tommaso, 85, 125, 320
Albrechtsberger, Johann Georg, 334
Alfano, Franco, 359
Allgemeine Musikalische Zeitung (Rochlitz), 360
Allgemeines Gelehrten-Lexicon (Jöcher), 368
Altnickol, Elisabeth. *See* Bach, Elisabeth
Altnickol, Johann Christoph, 342, 345, 350
Amadeus, 377
Amalie, Princess, 357
"Amen, Praise, Glory, and Wisdom," 388
"A Mighty Fortress Is Our God," 392
Anfangsgründe des Generalbasses, nach mathematischer Lehrart abgehandelt (Mizler), 295
Anhalt-Cöthen, 121
Anhalt-Zerbst, 142
Anna Iwanowna, Czarina, 260, 284
Ansbach, 227
Anti-Semitism, 385
Anton Günther II, 74–75

Ariadne Musica (Fischer), 137, 300
Arndt, Johann, 64
Arnold, Johann Heinrich, 9
Arnstadt, xiv, 28–29, 67
  Bach in, 4, 29–41
Arnstadt Castle, 30
Arnstadt Latin School, 51
Art of Dexterity (Czerny), 138
Art of Fugue (Bach), xvii, 16, 43, 81, 241, 279, 294, 306, 307, 316–318, 321, 324, 325, 327–328, 333, 337–340, 351, 358, 369–370, 388, 390, 392, 393
  publication of, 338
Atheism, 163
Atonal music, 296–297
Augustus II. *See* Augustus the Strong
Augustus III, 104, 241, 245, 246
Augustus the Strong, 90, 102, 104, 105, 124, 165, 176, 184, 245, 335, 384, 393
Austria, 247
"Awake, the Voice Calls Us!" (Bach), 88

Bach, Anna Magdalena (née Wilcke, Wilcken, or Wülcken), 142–145, 159, 212, 214, 226, 241, 349–351, 353, 393

Bach, Barbara Margarethe, 6

Bach, Bernhard, 128, 133, 140, 237–238, 266, 269, 359

Bach, Carl Philipp Emanuel, 1–2, 27, 81, 97, 109, 112, 132, 133, 140, 143, 237, 279, 283, 295, 305–306, 311, 313–314, 316–317, 332–333, 335, 338, 350, 351, 352, 356, 358–359, 367, 371, 383, 390, 391

Bach, Catharina Dorothea, 72, 81, 133, 140, 237, 349

Bach, Christoph, 2

Bach, Elisabeth (née Lämmerhirt), 4, 5, 345, 350

Bach, Ernst Ludwig, 368

Bach, Georg Michael, 368

Bach, Gottfried Heinrich, 237, 350

Bach, Heinrich, 2

Bach, Johanna Carolina, 349

Bach, Johann Ambrosius, 3–6

Bach, Johann August, 368

Bach, Johann Bernhard, 2, 97

Bach, Johann Christian, 300, 350, 357, 359–360

Bach, Johann Christoph, 2, 6–8, 9, 10, 14, 25, 378

Bach, Johann Christoph (Arnstadt branch), 6

Bach, Johann Christoph Friedrich, 345

Bach, Johann Elias, 269, 283, 284, 285

Bach, Johann Ernst, 8, 21, 48, 57

Bach, Johann Jacob, 5, 8, 25, 39

Bach, Johann Lorenz, 2

Bach, Johann Michael, 2, 51, 56

Bach, Johann Sebastian
  in Arnstadt, 4, 29–41
  and Baroque music, 364–366
  Bible, 196–197
  burial, 353–354
  children, 72, 81, 128, 133–134, 140, 142–143, 229, 237, 240–241, 266, 269, 282, 283, 345, 349–351. *See also particular children*
  children's godparents, 72, 81, 102, 128, 197, 240–241, 282
  in Cöthen, 117–128, 131–132, 133–145
  death, 347, 349–350
  deteriorating health, 341–342, 345–347
  in Eisenach, 3–6, 20
  eye ailment, 341–342, 345–347
  family musical talent, 2–3
  family portraits, 140–141
  family tree, 1–2
  first marriage, 59–60. *See also* Bach, Maria Barbara
  grave, 355–356
  household management, 134
  humor of, 41, 285
  individuality of, 304–305
  legacy, 356–362
  in Leipzig, 4, 37–38, 47, 55, 136, 147–157, 159–167
  library, 351–353
  in Lüneburg, 8–14, 15–24
  mathematical talent of, 318–319, 351–352
  monument, 355–356
  in Mühlhausen, 56–58, 59–69
  as musician of Enlightenment, 163–167, 328. *See also* Enlightenment
  obituary, 341, 351, 354
  in Ohrdruf, 7–9
  pension, 349–351
  pupils, 357–362, 366–367
  and religion, 195–197, 225
  residence, at St. Thomas School, 229
  salary, at St. Thomas School, 174–175, 229
  salary, in Cöthen, 122
  salary, in Leipzig, 122, 152, 183
  salary, in Weimar, 80–81
  second marriage, 119, 142–145. *See also* Bach, Anna Magdalena
  and "self-ordained retirement," 278–280
  temperament of, 48
  in Weimar, 27–29, 54, 71–82, 83–91, 93–102, 112–115
  works, publications of, 338, 356, 361, 366–367. *See also* Printing, of compositions

Bach, Maria Barbara, 51, 55–56, 59–60, 72, 81, 100, 113, 122
  death, 128–130, 133–134, 140–141
Bach, Nikolaus, 8
Bach, Regina Susanna, 349
Bach, Salomon, 368
Bach, Viet, 1, 140
Bach, Wilhelm Friedemann, 2, 81, 87, 97, 113, 133, 137, 140–141, 143, 161, 212, 213, 237, 245–246, 283, 284, 313, 350, 352, 359, 367, 390
Bach-Abel Concerts, 360
"Bach and the Enlightenment" (Leipzig symposium, 1976), 248
"Bach and the Enlightenment" (Schneiderheinze), 233
Bach as Pathfinder (Besseler), 86–87
Bach Festival, 163
Bach in Thuringia, 380
Bach-Jahrbuch, xviii, 155, 273, 329, 393
Bach literature, 298
Bach Society, 104, 176. *See also* New Bach Society
Bach the Music Director (Vetter), 159
Bach-Werke-Verzeichnis, 370
Badura-Skoda, Paul, 369–370
Bako of Verulam, 328
"Banter" (Bach), 161
Baroque music, 394
  Bach as end of, 364–366
Barz, Paul, 119–120
Bayreuth Festival Theater, 392
Beatles, 303
Beethoven, Ludwig van, xi, 11, 47, 87, 126, 136, 162, 268, 296, 300, 302, 319, 320, 322, 342, 352, 364, 366, 382–383, 385, 386, 393
Beiche, Johann Siegmund 282
Benardi, Angelo, 324
Berendt, Joachim Ernst, 372
Berlin, 105, 145, 312
Berlin cathedral
  organ in, 377
Berlin Singakademie, 394
Berlin Singing Academy, 214
Berlin State Opera, 164, 384

Bernays, Michael, 188
Bernhard, Christian, 387–388
Bernstein, Leonard, xiii, 88, 162, 297, 302, 329, 365, 369, 372
Besseler, Heinrich, xvii, 33, 81, 86–87, 88, 91, 162, 249, 380, 392
Bible, Bach's, 196–197
Biblical Sonatas (Kuhnau), 40–41, 304
Biedermann, Johann Gottlieb, 342–343
Bienengräber, Andreas Gottlieb, 275
Biographies, Bach, xii
Birnbaum, Johann Abraham, 270, 271, 343
Blankenburg, Walter, 385
Boethius, Anicius Manlius Severinus, 371
Böhm, Georg, 20–21, 22, 24, 46–47, 65, 308, 322, 364
Böhmer, Georg Wilhelm, 101
Boléro (Ravel), xiii
Bordoni, Faustina
Bormann, Theodor Benedict, 114
Born, Jacob, 156
Börner, Christian Friedrich, 29–31
Borrowings, 45
Bose, Georg, 197
Brachvogel, Albert Emil, 2, 358
Brahms, Johannes, 126, 296, 300, 303, 352, 386
Brandenburg, margrave of, 125, 126, 382
Brandenburg Concerti (Bach), 124–126, 134, 144, 145, 159, 325, 328–329, 378
Brecht, Bertolt, 47, 322, 328, 332–333
Brockes Passion (Handel), 215, 364
Brockhaus-Riemann, 321
Bruckner, Anton, 2, 86, 268, 300, 301, 336
Brühl, Heinrich Reichsgraf von, 245, 246, 260, 285, 344, 354, 382, 393
Bruhns, Nicolaus, 13
Bückeburg orchestra, 345
Bühnau, 226
Buxtehude, Anna Margareta, 50
Buxtehude, Dietrich, 13, 44, 46–50, 55, 65, 87, 191, 293, 304, 322, 334, 364, 379
Byrd, Christopher, 372
"By the Waters of Babylon" (Bach), 131

Cabala, 139, 298, 318–319, 331, 340, 390
Cage, John, 366
Calvin, Johannes, 119, 120–121
Calvinism, 23, 121
Cannabich, Christian, 389
Canonic Variations (Bach), 327, 329
Cantatas, 39, 216, 283, 293–294, 394
  in Leipzig, 173, 180–181, 191,
    204–206, 221
  in Mühlhausen, 60
  in Weimar, 88–91, 97
  See also Homage cantatas
*Capriccio on the Departure of His Much Beloved
  Brother* (Bach), 39–41, 138, 304
Capriccios, 39–40
Carl, Hermann, 389
Carlsbad, 123, 128, 1225
Carnival Farce from Vienna (Schumann), 289
Casanova, memoirs of, 139
Cathedral of Nevers, 106
Catherine the Great, 284
Catholic Church, 121
Catholic hymnbook, 67
Catholicism, 23
Catholic Mass, 324, 335, 336
Cavaliers Academy, 15, 123, 144
Celle, 22, 24
  French Orchestra in, 15–17, 24
Cello, 145
Chamber music
  in Leipzig, 273
Chamber orchestra, 126
Charles V, 102
Charlotte Friedericke von Nassau-Siegen,
  345
Choice of Hercules, 241–242, 243–244
Chopin, Frédéric, 322, 323
Chorale harmonizations
  publications of, 356
Chorale preludes
  in Arnstadt, 47–48
  See also Organ chorales
Chorale settings, 301–302
Choral partitas
  in Arnstadt, 47
Choral singing, 24

Chorus symphoniacus
  and Lüneburg Latin School, 10, 15, 22
Christiane Eberhardine von Ansbach-
    Bayreuth, 184–185
  funeral service for, 185–187
Christian of Saxe-Weissenfels, 96
Christmas Oratorio (Bach), 41, 206,
    241–245, 261, 293, 336, 370, 386
Chromatic Fantasy and Fugue (Bach), 111,
    134–135, 203, 360
Chromaticism, 365
Chronicon Helveticum (Tschudi), 2
Church cantatas, 293–294. *See also* Cantatas
Church music, 66. *See also* Sacred music
Church of Our Lady, 83
  organ at, 260, 381
Circle of fifths, 365
Clavier, 10, 127
Cleopatra (Mattheson), 36
Clio (Fischer), 138
Cockatoo Variations (Beethoven), 47
Coffee Cantata (Bach), 41, 161, 206, 286
Collection of Edifying Thoughts (Henrici), 271
Collegium Musicum, 130, 153, 179, 181,
    211, 221, 223, 250, 251, 270, 273,
    274, 277, 279, 282, 389
Colloquii corderi, 228
Combarieu, Jules, 395
Compendium locorum theologicorum (Hutter), 22
Complete Music Director (Mattheson), 324
Composition, music
  in Arnstadt, 39–43, 47–48
  in Mühlhausen, 60–61, 62
  printing of, 84–85, 136. *See also*
    Publications
Concerti, 85
  in Leipzig, 273
Concerti grossi, 125
Concerto for Three Harpsichords in D minor
    (Bach), xiii
Contrapuntal music, 13, 387–388. *See also*
    Counterpoint
Copies, handwritten, 84
Corelli, Arcangelo, 28–29, 125, 364
Corresponding Society of Musical
    Sciences, 294–295

Cosel, Anna Constanze Gräfin von, 2, 102
Cöthen, 205, 273
    Bach in, 117–128, 131–132, 133–145
    organ in, 119
    salary in, Bach's, 122
Counterpoint, 86, 285, 307–308, 351,
        367. *See also* Contrapuntal music
Counter-Reformation, 23
Couperin, François, 14, 40, 45, 320,
        364
Court musician
    status of, 72
Court orchestra
    in Weimar, 88
Cracow, 324
Cramer, Wilhelm, 80
Critica musica (Mattheson), 89
Cross, the, 138–140. *See also* Symbolism
Cruciform. *See* Cross, the
"'Cuckoo, Cuckoo' Rings out from the
        Woods," 138
Czerny, Carl, 138, 322, 329

Dante Alighieri, 201
Daquin, Louis Claude, 364–365
"Dearest Jesus, We Are Here," 56
The Death of Jesus (Graun), 215, 364
Debussy, Claude, 303
Defense of the Orchestra (Mattheson),
        84–85
De institutione oratoria (Quintilian),
        230–231
Der Streit zwischen Phöbus und Pan (Bach), 343
Descartes, René, 201, 203
Dessau, Paul, 329
Detailed Rhetoric (Gottsched), 203
"Deutsche Zustände" (Engels), 177
Devout Wishes (Spener), 64
Devrient, Eduard, 362, 394
Deyling, Salomo, 171, 193, 195, 221,
        234–236, 258, 261, 264
Diabelli, Anton, 296
Diabelli Variations (Beethoven), 296
Diatonicism, 365
Dicta scripturae sacrae, 22
Dieskau, Carl Heinrich von, 286, 287–288

Dietel, Johann Ludwig, 213, 238
Dieupart, François, 14, 45
Dittersdorf, Karl Ditters von, 320, 334
Doles, Johann Friedrich, 342–343,
        360–361, 393
Donner, 388
Dorian toccata (Bach), 364
Double Concerto (Brahms), 126
Dresden, 103–112, 229, 239–240,
        244–246, 274–275, 324,
        354
Dresden Kreuzchor, 386
Dresden orchestra, 105, 107–108
Drese, Adam, 78
Drese, Samuel, 67, 80, 97, 98
Drese, Wilhelm, 78, 98
Dresig, Siegmund Friedrich, 191, 254, 264
Du Bouchet, Paule, 37, 383, 386
Dürer, Albrecht, 306
Dutchman Overture (Wagner), 364
Dutch music, 22

East Germany, 163
Ecclesiastical modes, 303
Eckstein, Friedrich August, 249–250
Effler, Johann, 28, 30, 71
Eighteen Chorales (Bach), 293–294, 342
Eight Little Preludes and Fugues (Bach), 390
Eilmar, Georg Christian, 67, 68–69, 72,
        118
Einstein, Albert, 163
Eisenach, 23, 67
    Bach in, 3–6, 20
Eisenach school, 4
Eleonore Wilhelmine of Saxe-Merseburg,
        96
Elephant Hotel, 101
Elste, Martin, 383
Encyclopedists, 164–165, 368
Engels, Friedrich, 177, 262
Engelsmann, Walter, 385
English Revolution, 64
English Suites (Bach), 161, 301, 388
Enlightenment, xvii, xviii, 66, 77, 118,
        163–167, 201–204, 233, 328, 364,
        368–369, 385, 387, 392

Ensemble director, 127
Ensemble music
    in Mühlhausen, 61
Equal-tempered tuning, 110. *See also* Tuning
Erdmann, Georg, 9, 11, 25, 222, 223
Ernesti, Johann August, 234–236, 238,
        240–241, 244, 247–262, 263–264,
        269, 277–278, 283–284, 342, 353,
        368, 386
Ernesti, Johann Heinrich, 174, 180,
        198–199, 217, 226, 233
    funeral service for, 187
Ernst August, 28, 72, 74, 78–79, 93–96,
        101, 102
Essay on a Critical Art of Poetry for the Germans
        (Gottsched), 203
Esterházy, Prince, 99
Études, 322, 323, 366, 390
Exercises, 322

Falckner, Johann, 197
Fantasy and Fugue (K. 394) (Mozart), 360
Fantasy in G major (Bach), 46, 47
Fasch, Johann Friedrich, 148, 153, 179,
        181, 364–365
Fasch's Singing Association, 362
Faust (Goethe), 371
Feldhaus, Martin, 36
Felix, Werner, 189, 202–203, 378, 387
Fifth Symphony (Beethoven), 87, 364
Figural music, 13
    at Arnstadt, 33–38
Finger Language (Mattheson), 325, 329
Fischer, Deacon, 30, 56
Fischer, Johann Caspar Ferdinand, 13, 87,
        137–138, 300, 322
Flemming, Jakob Heinrich von, 102, 105,
        112, 113, 245
Flemming Palace, 108, 111–112
Flute sonatas, 312
Fontenai, Abbé de, 381
Forkel, Johann Nikolaus, 2, 27, 54, 106,
        108, 112, 313, 330, 366, 367, 392,
        393
Four Duets (Bach), 296
Fourth Symphony (Brahms), 303

Fourth Symphony (Sibelius), 303
Franck, Hans, 2
Franck, Salomo, 77, 89, 97, 98, 226
Francke, August Hermann, 165
Franz I, 245
Franz Joseph, Emperor, 247
Frauenplan, the, 4
Frederick II, 311–319
Frederick the Great, 105, 122, 202, 245,
        284, 311, 324, 334, 382
Free organ music, 292–293
    in Arnstadt, 47
Free place
    and Lüneburg Latin School, 9
Freischütz (Weber), 320
Freistelle
    and Lüneburg Latin School, 9–10, 15
French lute music, 45
French music, 22, 107–108, 388
    and Lüneburg Latin School, 15–17
French orchestra, 15–17, 24
French Revolution, 204
French Suites (Bach), 161, 294, *301,* 388
Frescobaldi, Girolamo, 14, 303, 322, 329
Freytag, Gustav, 302–303
Friedemann Bach (Brachvogel), 358
Friederike Henrietta, 143–145, 169–170
Friedrich, 391
Friedrich August, Prince, 103
Friedrich I, 104
Friedrich II, 104
Friedrich Wilhelm I, 90–91, 102, 104,
        105, 123, 125, 144–145, 187
Friese, Heinrich, 129
Froberger, Johann Jacob, 10, 13, 44
Frohne, Johann Adolph, 64, 66, 67, 147,
        225
"From Heaven on High" (Luther), 293
Fugue in C-sharp minor (Bach), 138, 140
Fugue in F minor (Bach), 296–297
Fugues, 39, 43, 44–45, 46, 86–87, 268,
        327
Fürstenau, Moritz, 354
Fürtwangler, Wilhelm, 162, 214–215, 309
Fux, Johann Joseph, 271, 303, 322, 352,
        390

Galetti, Professor, 324
Galileo, Galileo, 201
Gallant style, 40, 280, 320, 389, 394
Gatz, Felix Maria, 162
Gaudlitz, Gottlieb, 195, 197–199, 221, 256
Gay, John, 47
Geck, Martin, xvii, 3, 11, 46, 86–87, 112, 233, 305, 344, 378, 379, 382, 385, 387, 388, 390, 391, 392
Geiringer, Karl, xvii, 2, 20, 112, 278
Gellert, Christian Fürchtegott, 206, 355
Geminiani, Francesco, 125
General German Biography (Eckstein), 250, 267–268, 271
Gerber, Christian, *239*
Gerhardt, Paul, 65, 121
Gerlach, Carl Gotthelf, 274, 277, 282
German Biography (Bernays), 188
German Democratic Republic, 164
German Enlightenment, xvii. *See also* Enlightenment
German hymns, 23
German music, 22
German Socialist Unity Party, 164
Gesner, Johann Matthias, 78, 97, 98, 127, 150, 226–235, 237, 239–240, 248, 250, 251, 264, 294, 313, 386
Gewandhaus Orchestra, 355, 393
Geyersbach, Johann Heinrich, 35–37, 38
"Glory Alone to God in the Highest" (Bach), 53, 304
"Glory Be to God on High Alone" (Bach), 298
"God Is My King" (Bach), 62
Godparents. *See* Bach, Johann Sebastian, children's godparents
Goethe, Johann Wolfgang von, xviii, 73, 77, 166–167, 249, 292, 298, 338, 361, 363, 365, 367, 371, 372
Goldberg, Johann Gottlieb, 285
Goldberg Variations (Bach), 41, 161, 284, 285, 289, *291*, 294, 307, 308, 321, 324, 325, 333, 356
Goldoni, Carlo, 269
Goldschmidt, Harry, 370

Görner, Johann Gottlieb, 161, 180, 181–183, 185–186, 211, 212, 214, 215, 274, 277, 279
Göttingen, 232
Gottsched, Johann, 368–369
Gottsched, Johann Christoph, 165, 187–190, 202–203, 206, 208, 234–236, 235, 268, 305–306
Gottsched, Louise, 282
Gottsched Society, 189
Gould, Glenn, 138, 331, 367, 383
Gradus ad Parnassum (Fux), 271, 303, 322, 352, 390
Gräffenhayn, Gottfried Christoph, 27, 28
Graun, 215, 267
Graun, Carl Heinrich, 295, 312, 364
Graun, Johann Gottlieb, 312, 364
Graupner, Christoph, 148, 149–150, 153, 154, 156, 157, 160, 179, 364–365
Great Concern, 279
Greiff, 227
Griepenkerl, Friedrich Konrad, 366–367
Grigny, Nicolas de, 14, 45, 303, 322
Großes vollständiges Universal-Lexicon aller Wissenschaften und Künste (Zedler), 367–368
Guido of Arezzo, 201

Hacks, Peter, 381
Halle, 22, 83–84, 96, 118, 202
organ at, 84
Hamburg, 21–22, 24, 128–132, 133, 152
Hamburg Opera, 22
Handel, George Frideric, 2, 10, 11, 22, 36, 43, 50, 57, 83, 87, 97, 104, 125, 167, 215, 295, 304, 320, 325, 334, 342, 352, 360, 364–365, 393
Hanff, Johann Nicolaus, 46–47
Hanover, prince of, 232
Hanslick, 268
Harmony, 308, 351
The Harmony of the World (Hindemith), 372
Harpsichord, 24, 29, 85, 108, 127
at St. Nicholas Church, 192–193
Harrer, Johann Gottlob, 344, 354, 393

Harz Mountains, 49

Hasse, Johann Adolf, 320, 364–365

Haussmann, Elias Gottlob, 341–342

Haydn, Joseph, xi, 80, 99, 126, 204, 243, 280, 352, 356, 359, 360, 366, 385, 393

Hebenstreit, Pantaleon, 103, 176

Heinichen, Johann David, 103, 124, 126, 335, 1125

Heitmann, Johann Joachim, 131, 152

Held, Johann Balthasar, 20, 22, 26, 30

Henlein, Peter, xiii

Hennicke, Johann Christian von, 281–282, 286–287

Henrici, Christian Friedrich (pseud. Picander), 188, 197, 206, 209, 244, 271, 282, 287, 288

Henry IV, 184–185

Henze, Hans Werner, 391

Herda, Elias, 9, 12

Herder, Johann Gottfried von, 66–67

Hiller, Johann Adam, 86, 357, 360, 393

Hindemith, Paul, 216–217, 372

History of Music and Theater at the Court in Dresden (Fürstenau), 354

History of the Enlightenment in Germany, 165

History of the Leipzig Schools (Köhler), 247–248

Hoffman, 35–37, 38

Hohenlohe, Count von, 7

Holstein Correspondent, 169, 170

Holy Roman Empire, 105

Holzbauer, Ignaz, 389

Homage cantatas, 281–282, 286–287. *See also* Cantatas

Homilius, Gottfried August, 357, 360, 393

Horace, 343

"How Beautifully Shines the Morning Star," 65

Humboldt, Wilhelm von, 366

Hummel, Johann Nepomuk, 320

Humor, of Bach, 41, 285

Hungarian Rhapsody (Liszt), 303

Hunt Cantata (Bach), 90–91, 96

Hurlebusch, 283

Hutten, Ulrich von, 65

Hutter, Leonhard, 22

"I Had Much Distress" (Bach), 89–90, 294

Ihle, Johann Jacob, 128

Imitation, musical, 40–41, 303

The Immortal Heart, xiii

Improvisation, musical, 45, 47–48, 382–383

Individuality, of Bach, 304–305

"Innsbruck, I Have to Leave You," 293

Institutiones jurisprudentiae divinae (Thomasius), 101

Inventions (Bach), 81, 137, 159

"I Step Herewith Before Thy Throne" (Bach), 342

Italian Concerto (Bach), 85, 326

Italian music, 22, 107–108, 388

Jansenists, 64

Jauernig, Reinhold, 93, 380

"Jesus, Lead the Way on the Path of Life" (Drese), 78

"Jesus Took unto Him the Twelve" (Bach), 149

Jewish numerology, 318. *See also* Cabala; Number symbolism

Job, Johann, 156

Jöcher, Christian Gottlieb, 368

Johann Ernst, 100

Johann Ernst, Duke of Saxe-Weimar, 27, 33

Johann Ernst, Prince, 89

Johann Ernst II, Duke of Saxe-Weimar, 28–29, 31, 72–74, 78

Johann Ernst III, 28, 85

Johann Georg, Duke of Saxe-Weissenfels, 27

Johann Sebastian Bach, the Poet-Musician (Schweitzer), xvi

Johann Sebastian Bach (Spitta), xvi

Joseph II, 76

Journalists (Freytag), 302–303

Kaiser, Joachim, 46

Kant, Immanuel, 66, 77, 162–163, 201

Kassel, 229–230
Kastner, 253
Keiser, Reinhard, 22
Keller, Hermann, 44, 138, 140, 296, 379
Kellner, Johann Christoph, 357
Kellner, Peter, 392
Kepler, Johannes, 371, 372
Kerll, Johann Kaspar von, 10, 13, 44
Keul, Barbara Margarethe. *See* Bach, Barbara
    Margarethe
Keyboard instruments, 10
Keyboard practice, 322, 323
Keyboard Practice I (Bach), 81, 321, 364
Keyboard Practice II (Bach), 81, 321, 364
Keyboard Practice III (Bach), 81, 283, 291,
    292, 295, 296, 301, 303, 305–306,
    321, 324, 333, 334, 364
Keyboard Practice IV (Bach), 81, 284, 291,
    321
Keyserlingk, Imperial Count von, 260, 311,
    312–313, 324, 367, 389
Keyserlingk, Dietrich von, 284–285, 311
Kirchbach, Hans Carl von, 185–186,
    188–189
Kirnberger, Johann Philipp, 309, 357–358,
    360, 391, 393
Kittel, Johann Christian, 357
Kittler, Samuel, 257
Klein-Zschocher, 289, 2887–288
Kluge-Kahn, Hertha, 383
Knepler, Georg, 377, 385
Kobelius, Augustin, 28
Köhler, Johann Friedrich, 247–248, 263
Kolneder, Walter, 383–384
Kortte, Gottlieb, 182, 216
Kozeluch, Leopold, 2, 268
Kraneman, Detlev, 341
Kraszewski, Józef Ignacy, 2
Krause, Gottfried Theodor, 238
Krause, Gottlieb Theodor, 247, 250,
    252–254, 255–256, 257, 259
Krause, Johann Gottlob, 255–258, 275
Krebs, Johann Ludwig, 213, 238, 259,
    283, 357
Kreuzstab Cantata (Bach), 139
Krieger, Johann Philipp, 44, 364

Kuhnau, Johann, 40–41, 84, 124, 138,
    147, 149, 151, 152, 154, 173, 174,
    180, 181, 182, 183, 193, 199, 217,
    280, 293, 304, 322, 364
Kunstbuch (Theile), 315
Küster, Konrad, 378, 380, 381

Lairitz, Johann Georg, 94
Lämmerhirt, Elisabeth. *See* Bach, Elisabeth
Lämmerhirt, Valentin, 4
Lange, Gottfried, 150, 179
Lasso, Orlando di, 14
Latin Masses (Bach), 387
Latin School of Schulpforta, 235
Latin study
    and Lüneburg Latin School, 22
Legrenzi, Giovanni, 87
Lehmann, Gottfried Conrad, 171
Leibniz, Gottfried Wilhelm, 165, 188, 395
Leipzig, xii, xiii
    Bach in, 4, 37–38, 47, 55, 136,
        147–157, 159–167
    salary in, Bach's, 122, 152, 183
    See also St. Thomas School; University of
        Leipzig
Leipzig Bach Festival, 163
Leipzig Bach researchers, 233–234
Leipzig consistory, 274
    vs. Leipzig council, 171–172, 191–199
    Leipzig council, 265, 274–275, 280,
        384, 386
    and Gesner, Johann Matthias, 226–235
    records, 175–177
    and *St. Matthew Passion*, 219–224
    vs. Leipzig consistory, 171–172,
        191–199
    vs. University of Leipzig, 179–190, 240
Leipzig Enlightenment, 202–204, 248. *See
    also* Enlightenment
Leipzig research, 163–164
Leipzig Society for the Cultivation of
    German, 188
Leopold, Prince, 96, 101, 112, 113, 119,
    120, 121–122, 122–124, 128, 131,
    143–145, 169–170, 345
    funeral service for, 212–213

Lessing, Gotthold Ephraim, 207, 329, 343, 385, 392

Leszczyński , Stanislas, 246

Leupold, Anton Wilhelm, 241–242

Levy, Sara, 394

Lichtenberg, Georg Christoph, 66, 317

Lincke, Paul, 3

Liszt, Franz von, 303

Literature, Bach, xii

Little Music Book (Bach), 140

A Little Night Music (Mozart), 138

Little Organ Book (Bach), 81, 87–88, 113, 119, 292, 297, 302, 306

Livre d'orgue (Grigny), 14

Lobanowa, Marina, 390

London, 104, 105

London symphonies (Haydn), 80

Lortzing, Albert, 355

Louis XIV, 16

Löwe, Johann Heinrich, 20–21, 22

Lübeck, 48–51

Lübeck, Vincent, 21–22

Ludwig II, 184–185

Lully, Jean-Baptiste, 16–17, 107, 320

Lüneburg
    Bach in, 8–14, 15–24

Lüneburg Cloister School, *17*

Lüneburg Latin School, 8–9, 15–24
    studies at, 23–24

Lute, 127

Luther, Martin, 22, 23, 64, 120–121, 293, 301

Lutheran Church, 22–23, 119–121

Lutheran Latin School, 23

Lutheran Orthodox, 23, 64, 65, 67, 77, 120, 165, 166–167, 204, 379, 387

Lutheran Protestantism, 379

Lutherans, 64

Luther Street, 4

Machiavelli, Niccolò, 307

Macrostructures, 297. *See also* Symbolism

Madrid, 104, 105

The Magic Flute (Mozart), 203–204

Magnificat (Bach), 191, 192, 221

Manebach, 35–37, 38

Mann, Thomas, 299

Mannheim School, 389

Marcello, Benedetto, 394

Marchand, Louis, 14, 45, 105–112, 245, 304, 364–365, 381–382

Maria Theresa, 76, 245

Mark Twain, 381

Marpurg, Friedrich Wilhelm, 360, 382

Marxism, 163

Marxist musicology, 164–165

Mass in B minor (Bach), 43, 139, 239, 279, 294, 324, 333, 335–341, 364, 388, 394

Masses (Bach), 272–273

Mathematical talent, of Bach, 318–319, 351–352

Matins choir
    and Lüneburg Latin School, 10

Mattheson, Johann, 22, 36, 50, 55, 57, 84–85, 89, 93, 130, 131, 267, 322, 324, 325, 329, 343, 380

Maupertius, Pierre-Louis Moreau de, 202

Meck, Joseph, 85

Meckbach, Friedemann, 102

Meditations (Descartes), 203

Melanchthon, Philipp, 22

Melody, 309

Mencke, Johann Burckhard, 187

Mendelssohn, Lea (née Salomon), 393

Mendelssohn, Moses, 393

Mendelssohn-Bartholdy, Felix, xii, 11, 85–86, 136, 293, 351, 355, 356, 361–362, 393, 394

Menge, Wolfgang, 378

Mense, Carl Friedrich, 171

Mentz, Georg, 78

Mersenne, Marin, 110

Metzger, Heinz-Klaus, 385

Meyer, Ernst Hermann, 164

Meyerbeer, Giacomo, 361

Meynell, Esther, 224, 386

Miesner, Heinrich, 312–313

"A Mighty Fortress Is Our God," 191

Missa aeterna Christi munera (Palestrina), 388

Missae breves (Bach), 283

Missa Papae Marcelli (Palestrina), 388

Missa Solemnis (Beethoven), 364
Mizler, Lorenz Christoph, 268, 294–295,
    305, 318–319, 322, 334, 351–352,
    352
Mizler Society, 25
Modernistic style, 304
Monothematic variations, 307
"Morning Splendor of Eternity,"
    56
Motets, 394
Mozart, Constanze, 360
Mozart, Franz Xaver, 358
Mozart, Wolfgang Amadeus, xi, xii, 11, 43,
    88, 136, 138, 203–204, 218, 280,
    300, 331, 352, 356, 359, 360–361,
    366, 385, 386, 393
Muffat, Gottlieb, 44, 47, 364
Mühlhausen, 332
    Bach in, 56–58, 59–69
Müller, Wenzel, 47, 320
Music, practice of
    and Lüneburg Latin School, 22
Music, sacred vs. secular, 118–119,
    291–293
Musical Offering (Bach), 293–294, 313–319,
    324, 333, 340–341
Musical Parnassus (Fischer), 138
Musica mechanica organoedi (Adlung), 21
Music for Twelve Radios (Cage), 366
Musicology, 162, 204
    Marxist, 164–165
Music theory, 29
Müthel, Johann Gottfried, 279–280
"My Heart Is Full of Yearning," 293
Nagel, 345
Neefe, Christian Gottlob, 360, 393,
    394
Nelson, Horatio Viscount, 204
Neuber, Caroline, 203
Neuber troupe, 215
Neue Zeitschrift für Musik, 355
Neumann, Werner, xvii, 77, 132, 142, 286,
    287, 288
Neumeister, Erdmann, 129, 130, 131,
    132, 152, 216, 393
Neumeister collection, 88

New Bach Society, xvii, 154, 164, 190,
    199, 233, 384, 386. *See also* Bach
    Society
New Church, 154, 172
Newton, Isaac, 207
Nichelmann, Christoph, 391
Nicolai, Otto, 361
Nicolai, Philipp, 64, 65
Nicolet, Aurèle, 315
Nienburg Palace, 96
Ninth Symphony (Beethoven), 320
Ninth Symphony (Bruckner), 336
Nocturnes (Debussy), 303
Northern War, 145
Notes on School History (Köhler), 263
"Now We're Going Where the Bagpipes
    Drone in Our Tavern," 288
Number symbolism, 297, 318–319,
    327–328, 339–340. *See also*
    Symbolism

Observationes sacre (Deyling), 195
Occasional compositions, 41, 43, 283,
    288–289
Offenbach, Jacques, xiii–xiv
"Of Genius" (Schopenhauer), 208
Ohrdruf, 20, 23
    Bach in, 7–9
Ohrdruf Latin School, 7, 9–10, 24
Olearius, Johann Gottfried, 51, 67
"O Lovely Day, Longed-For Time," 343
On the Imitation of Greek Artworks
    (Winckelmann), 325
"Open the Door, Throw Wide the Gates,"
    379
Opera, 97
Orchestral music
    in Arnstadt, 33
Orchestral Suites (Bach), 134, 145,
    161
Orff, Carl, 361
Organ, 10, 18–22, 29, 127
    at Arnstadt, 44
    in Berlin cathedral, 377
    at Church of Our Lady, 381
    at Sophia Church, 246

at St. Blasius Church, 63
at St. Boniface Church, 29–33
at St. Catharine's Church, 21
at St. George's Church, 20
at St. John Church, 20–21
at St. Michael's Church, 20
at St. Nicholas Church, 21–22,
192–195
at St. Paul's Church, 124
at St. Thomas Church, 385
Organ building, 22, 24, 26, 30–31, 44
in Weimar, 82
Organ chorales, 292–293, 387
at Arnstadt, 53
See also Chorale preludes
Organ compositions, 43, 110
in Mühlhausen, 61
Organ construction, 127
Organ inspection, 30–32, 43
Organ Mass (Bach), 279, 283, 291,
292–293, 333
Organ Prelude in G major (Bach), 61
Orthodoxy, 64. See also Lutheran Orthodox
Otterbach, Friedemann, xvii, 45, 52, 59,
73, 141, 387
Otto, Hans, 381
Overtures
in Leipzig, 273

Pachelbel, Johann, 6–7, 10, 13, 44, 46–47,
49
Paer, Ferdinando, 2
Paganini, Niccolò, 127
Palestrina, Giovanni Pierluigi da, 318, 322,
324, 387–388
Parallel fifths, 327
Partita in B minor (Bach), 382
Partitas, 126–127
Passacaglia and Fugue (Bach), 364
Passion music, 205–209, 261, 275, 394
Passion Music According to John (Bach), 191
Pathétique (Tchaikovsky), 329
Peace of Westphalia, 23
Peasant Cantata (Bach), 41, 161, 206,
286–287, 288, 291
Pergolesi, Giovanni Battista, 14, 364

Peter III, 284
Petrushka (Stravinsky), 364
Petzoldt, Martin, 65–66, 118, 385, 389,
390
Piano concerti (Mozart), 321
Picander. See Henrici, Christian Friedrich,
271, 282
Picasso, Pablo, 269
Pieck, Wilhelm, 233, 248, 384
Pietism, 23, 64, 65–69, 120, 165, 379
Pietistic chorales, 379
Pietsch, Johann Valentin, 188
Pirro, André, 381, 382
Pischner, Hans, 164, 249, 384
Plaz, Abraham Christoph, 154, 155–156,
176, 354
Pleisenburg Castle, 260
Pleyel, Ignaz, 320
Pochette, 15
Poland, 104–105
Polyphony, 13, 127, 319, 331, 334
Pop music, 370
Porpora, Nicola, 87
Possible Encounter (Barz), 119–120
Potsdam, 324
Praetorius, Friedrich Emanuel, 13
Prefects war, 246, 247–262, 269, 273–274
Preller, Gottfried, 390–391
Prelude and fugue, 365–366
Prelude and Fugue in A minor (Bach), 117
Prelude in C major (Bach), 370, 381
Prelude in D major (Bach), 364
Prelude in E flat (Bach), 364
Prelude in G minor (Bach), 364
Prelude No. 1 (Bach), 136, 138
Preludes, 46, 364, 379
The Prince (Machiavelli), 307
Printing, of compositions, 84–85, 136. See
also Publications
Program music, 40, 292, 389
Protestantism, 23
Protestant Lutheran schools, 22
Protestant schools, 22–23
Prussia, 104, 145
Prussia, king of
and Gesner, Johann Matthias, 232

Publications
  of Bach works, 338, 356, 361,
    366–367. *See also* Printing, of
    compositions
Puccini, Giacomo, 359
Pufendorf, Baron Samuel von, 101
Purcell, Henry, 320
Pure research, 43
Pure tuning, 110. *See also* Tuning
Puritans, 64
Pythagoras, 109, 371

Quantz, Johann Joachim, 312, 364–365
The Quarrel Between Phoebus and Pan (Bach),
    286
Questenberg, Johannes Adam von, 271, 273
Quintilian, 230–231

Raffalt, Reinhard, 213, 389
Raison, André, 14, 45
Rambach, Johann Andreas, 54
Rameau, Jean-Philippe, 320, 364–365,
    381, 395
Raphael, 208
Rath, Gisela Agnes von, 123–124
Rathelag, 372
Ravel, Maurice, xiii
*Reasonable Thoughts About Human Action and
    Inaction* (Wolff), 203
Red Palace, 28–29, 78, 79, 94, 95=96
Reformation, 22, 23, 64, 112
Reformation Symphony (Mendelssohn), 293
Reformed Church, 119, 120–121
Reformers, 23
Reger, Max, 293
Reichardt, Johann Friedrich, 394
Reiche, Gottfried, 173
Reinken, Johann Adam, 21, 22, 24, 44,
    129, 216
Religion
  and Bach, 195–197, 225
Religious studies
  and Lüneburg Latin School, 22
Requiem (Mozart), 43
Revelation of St. John, 333
Rheingold (Wagner), 139–140

Richter, Franz Xaver, 364, 389
Richter, Klaus Peter, 16, 139
Riemann, Hugo, 137, 388
Riemann's Music Lexicon, 321
Rifkin, Joshua, 219, 386
Rilke, Rainer Maria, 338
Rinck, Christian Heinrich, 320, 357
Rochlitz, Friedrich, 360–361, 393
Roitzsch, Ferdinand August, 366–367
Rolle, Heinrich, 84
Rossini, Gioachino, 88, 320
Roux, Gaspard le, 14, 45
Royal Academy of Arts (Berlin), xvi
Royal Academy of Music, 16
"Royal fugal theme," 313–319
Royal Prussian Academy of Sciences, 202
Rudolph, Joanna, 386
Rueger, Christoph, xvii, 2, 29, 55, 57, 117,
    126, 141, 145, 244, 291, 315, 349,
    391
Russell, Bertrand, 188

Sacred music, 85
  vs. secular music, 118–119, 291–293
Salary
  Bach's, at St. Thomas School, 174–175,
    229
  Bach's, in Cöthen, 122
  Bach's, in Leipzig, 122, 152, 183
  Bach's, in Weimar, 80–81
Salieri, Antonio, 320
Salomon, Lea. *See* Mendelssohn, Lea
Sangerhausen, 27, 266
Sanssouci, 383
Sanssouci Palace, 313
Sauer Company, 377
Saxony, 105
Scarlatti, Alessandro, 325, 364
Scarlatti, Domenico, 364
Schaffer, Peter, 377
Scheibe, Johann, 124
Scheibe, Johann Adolph, 266–269,
    270–271, 281, 282, 305–306, 308,
    343, 387
Scheidemann, Heinrich, 13
Scheidt, Samuel, 13, 303, 329

Schelle, Johann, 180, 293

Schemelli, Georg Christian, 238

Scherchen, Hermann, 340

Schering, Arnold, 389

Schiller, Friedrich von, 2, 73, 77

Schilling, 282

Schindler, Anton, 319

Schlegel, August Wilhelm, 366

Schleuning, Peter, xvii, 241, 273, 278, 279, 294, 303–304, 305, 307, 312, 316–317, 322–323, 325, 353, 358–359, 385, 389, 390, 391, 392, 393

Schmitt, Johann Gottfried, 103

Schneiderheinze, Armin, 202–203, 233

Schoenberg, Arnold, 316–317, 367

Schönbrunn Palace, 104

Schönfelder, Gert, 385

School attendance, compulsory, 75, 133

Schopenhauer, Arthur, 208, 328, 385

Schotte, Georg Balthasar, 149, 154, 157, 211

Schröter, Christoph Gottlieb, 343

Schubert, Franz, xi, 26, 112, 300, 320, 386

Schubert, Johann Martin, 81

Schübler, Johann Georg, 342

Schübler Chorales (Bach), 293–294

Schulze, Hans-Joachim, 380

Schumann, Clara (née Wieck), 355

Schumann, Robert, xi, 36, 136, 289, 300, 355

Schüttewürfel, Johann Freidrich, 35–37, 38

Schütz, Heinrich, 20–21, 315

Schwarzburg, Imperial Count von (Anton Günther II), 30, 59, 114

Schweitzer, Albert, xi, xvi–xvii, xviii, 37, 38, 46, 47, 52, 57, 59, 62–63, 72, 80, 85, 87, 109, 112, 118, 120, 121, 126, 132, 135, 154, 173, 204, 221, 224, 241, 242, 244, 249, 263–264, 280, 291, 292, 296, 297–298, 356, 361, 363, 364–365, 379, 390, 391, 392, 393

Sechter, Simon, 86, 319

Secondary School
in Weimar, 77–78

Secular music
vs. sacred music, 118–119, 291–293

Seffner, Karl, 355–356

Selle, Thomas de la, 15–16

Semmelweis, Ignaz Phillipp, 346

Serbia, 247

Serfdom, 101

Seven Years' War, 105

Shakespeare, William, 306, 371, 395

Shostakovich, Dmitri, 135

Sibelius, Jean, 303

Siegele, Ulrich, 155, 175, 259, 384

Siegmund-Schultze, Walther, xvii, 16, 61, 67, 73, 117, 123, 129, 139, 141, 144, 148, 385, 387

Silbermann, Gottfried, 110

"Silent Night," 293

Silesia, 311

Silesian Wars, 245

Singability, 309

Sixth Symphony (Sibelius), 303

Slapák, Kamil, 380

Smend, Friedrich, xii, 128, 139, 159–160

Society of Musical Sciences, 294, 318

Socrates, 201

Sonatas, 126–127, 366, 371
in Leipzig, 273

Sophia Church, 237, 284
organ at, 246

"Sound, Ye Drums," 241

Sound grids, 297. See also Symbolism

Soviet Union, 162–163

Spener, Philipp Jakob, 64, 66

Speth, Johann, 44

Spinoza, Baruch de, 201–202, 204

Spitta, Friedrich, xvi

Spitta, Karl Johann Philipp, xvi

Spitta, Philipp, xii, xvi, xvii, 1, 9, 28–29, 38, 51, 54, 55, 59, 67, 73, 93, 97, 103, 106, 107, 109, 115, 121, 128–129, 137, 141, 145, 154, 162, 173, 174–175, 183, 214–215, 216, 224, 247–248, 249, 259, 260–261, 274, 278, 283, 286, 288–289, 344, 351, 378, 381, 385, 389

Spontini, Gaspare, 2

Sporck, Franz Anton Graf, 271, 272–273

St. Andrew's cross, 138

St. Anne Fugue. See Trinity Fugue

St. Blasius Church, 56, 60, 61, 64, 66, 67, 238

  organ at, 63

St. Boniface Church, 27

  organ at, 29–33

St. Catharine's Church

  organ at, 21

St. Francis of Assisi, 67

St. George's Church, 27

  organ at, 20

St. James Church, 129, 131

St. John Church, 13, 355

  organ at, 20–21

St. John Passion (Bach), 160, 191–192, 220, 221, 275, 278, 280, 336, 364

St. John the Apostle, 79, 333

St. Mark Passion (Bach), *239*

St. Mary's Church, 50, 60, 62, 67, 238, 266

St. Matthew Passion (Bach), 71, 86, 144, 206–209, 238–239, 250, 293, 294, 329, 335, 336, 356, 362, 364, 385, 394

  at St. Thomas Church, 211–224

St. Michael's Church

  organ at, 20

St. Michael's Cloister, 15

St. Nicholas Church, 20, 121, 172, 181

  harpsichord at, 192–193

  organ at, 21–22, 192–195

St. Nicholas School, 150

St. Paul's Church, 153, 172, 179, 181

  organ at, 124

St. Paul the Apostle, 55

St. Peter Church, 172

St. Petersburg, 104, 105

St. Peter's Gate, 219

St. Thomas choir, 174, 212

  and *St. Matthew Passion*, 216–218

St. Thomas Church, xiii, 84, 124, 160, 172, 192–195, 355, 377, 387

  choosing of hymns at, 197–199

  organs at, 385

  St. Matthew Passion at, 211–224

St. Thomas School, 37, 124, 147–157, 169–174, 179, 181, 211, 238, 249, 277

  Bach residence at, 229

  choirmaster doctrinal test, 170–171

  choirmaster inauguration, 171–172

  curriculum, 174, 228, 229

  and Ernesti, Johann August, 247–262, 263–264

  and Gesner, Johann Matthias, 227–231

  official duties at, 172–174

  and prefects war, 247–262

  renovations at, 227–231

  salaries at, 174–175, 229

Stalinism, 163

Stamitz, Johann, 389

Stauber, Lorenz, 59–60

Steger, Adrian, 156, 221

Stein, Leo, 280

Stieglitz, Christian Ludwig, 221, 234–236, 240, 354

Stifter, Adalbert, 322

Stile antico, 283, 297, 318, 328, 330, 388, 389, 392

"A Stranger I Arrived, and a Stranger I Leave" (Schubert), 26

Straube, Karl, xiii, 377

Strauss, Richard, 292, 361

Stravinsky, Igor, 364

Stützhaus, 35–37, 38

Style Brisé, 45

Style theories, 291–300, 301–309, 311–322, 323–334, 335–347

Superstition, 318–319

Süssmayr, Franz Xaver, 359

Sweelinck, Jan Pieterszoon, 13

Swieten, Gottfried van, 360, 393

Swingle Singers, 370

Symbolism, 138–140, 291–292, 297, 339–340

  and the cross, 138–140

  See also Number symbolism

Symphony No. 40 (Haydn), 359

Tartini, Giuseppe, 28–29, 320, 364

Taylor, John, 342, 345–346

Tchaikovsky, Pyotr Ilich, 329

Telemann, Georg Philipp, 43, 81, 85, 88, 97–98, 132, 148, 149, 150, 152, 153, 154, 156, 157, 179, 191, 216, 267, 295, 304, 334, 364–365

Temperament, of Bach, 48, 52, 54, 214–215, 325

Tempered tuning. See Tuning

Ten-tone series, 139

Terence, 343

Terry, Charles Sanford, xvi, 8, 14, 16, 27, 38, 52, 59, 73, 93, 99–100, 106, 107, 117–118, 121, 122, 126, 129, 132, 135–136, 159, 162, 224, 278, 378, 380, 384, 389

Teuner, D., 94–95

Theatrical poetry, 97

Theile, Johann, 315

Theoderic the Great, 371

Theological Institute of the Kaiser Wilhelm University, xvi

Theoretical reflections, 333

Theory, 351

"These Are the Holy Ten Commandments" (Bach), 139

Third International Bach Celebration, 233

Thirty Years' War, 22–23, 60, 64

Thomasius, Christian, 101, 165

Thoroughbass, 160–161, 392

Three-part inventions (Bach), 81, 137, 159

Three-Penny Opera (Brecht), 47

Three Swans Inn, 344, 346

Thuringia, 1–2, 20, 26, 73

Tieck, Ludwig, 366

Till Eulenspiegel's Merry Pranks (Strauss), 292

Toccata and Fugue (Franck), 2

Toccata in C major (Bach), 364

Toccata in D minor (Bach), xiii, xiv, 43–47, 364, 391

Toccatas, 44–45, 364

Tompkins, Peter, 372

Tone language, 297–298

Tone painting, 40

Torelli, Giuseppe, 85, 125, 364

Toscanomo, Arturo, 214–215

Town bands, 3

Trassdorf, 35–37, 38

Treiber, Johann Friedrich, 33–34, 51

Trinity Fugue (Bach), 291–292

Trio Sonatas for Organ (Bach), 390

Triple Concerto (Beethoven), 126

Triple fugue (Bach), 296, 359

Tristan (Wagner), 214, 329, 392

Tschudi, Aegidius, 2

Tuning, 53, 109–111, 127, 134–136, 309

Turandot (Puccini), 359

2 Chronicles, 196

Two-part inventions (Bach), 81, 137, 159

Unfinished Symphony (Schubert), 320

Unigenitus, 64

University of Frankfurt, 311

University of Göttingen, 233

University of Halle, 165, 367

University of Königsberg, 187, 188

University of Leipzig, 152, 157, 165–166, 235, 384

   and Gesner, Johann Matthias, 231, 234

   vs. Leipzig council, 179–190, 240

University of Wittenberg, 235

Unrecognized Sins (Gerber), 239

Unwed mothers, 76–77

Uthe, Master, 55

Verdi, Giuseppe, 309

Versailles, 104, 105–107, 111

Vetter, Walter, xii, 159

Victoria, Queen, 214

Vienna, 104, 105

Vienna Court Opera, 214

Vienna School, 126, 320

Viola, 28, 29, 127

Viola pomposa, 127

Violin, 10, 24, 28, 29, 126–127, 127, 145

Virgil, 232

Virtuosity, 127

Vitali, Giovanni Battista, 315

Vivaldi, Antonio, 28–29, 79, 85, 112, 125, 304, 320, 364–365, 382

Vocal compositions
  in Mühlhausen, 62
Vockerodt, Gottfried, 66
Vockerodt, Sebastian, 66
Voltaire, 75–76, 107, 120, 166–167, 202,
  381
Volumier. *See* Woulmyer, Jean Baptiste

Wagner, Gottfried, 156
Wagner, Richard, 136, 139–140, 214,
  268, 300, 329, 352, 361, 364, 392
Wagner, Siegfried, 358
Walther, Johann Gottfried, 78–79, 85, 87,
  88, 114, 270, 324, 388
Wars of Religion, 23
Weber, Carl Maria von, 320
Wedemann, Regina, 56, 59–60
Weimar, 20, 67
  Bach in, 27–29, 54, 71–82, 83–91,
    93–102
  dismissal from, Bach's, 112–115
  imprisonment in, Bach's, 113–114
  resignation from, 99–100
  salary in, Bach's, 80–81
Weisse, Christian, 118, 148–149, 152,
  157, 171, 197
Weissenfels, 27, 90–91, 96, 205
The Well-Tempered Clavier (Bach), xiii, 134,
  135–138, 159, 164, 203, 279,
  296–297, 297–298, 315, 321, 332,
  356, 357, 360, 370, 381, 383, 394
  publication of, 361
The Well-Tempered Clavier II (Bach), 284, 315,
  333
Well-tempered tuning, 109–111, 127,
  134–136, 309.
  See also Tuning
Wender, Gottlieb, 29–32, 56, 63
Werckmeister, Andreas, 110, 309
Werner, Eric, 394
Westhoff, Paul, 126
Wette, Gottfried Albin, 114
Wettiners, 104–105, 114
"What Pleases Me Is Only the Merry
  Hunt," 96

Wieck, Clara. *See* Schumann, Clara
Wieck, Friedrich, 355
Wilcke (Wilcken, Wülcken), Anna
  Magdalena. *See* Bach, Anna Magdalena
Wilhelm, Duke of Saxe-Weimar, 72
Wilhelm, Emperor, 247
Wilhelm Castle, 79, 90, 95
Wilhelm Ernst, 28, 31, 71, 72–80, 90,
  93–102, 112–115, 115, 117, 120,
  227
Wilhelm I, 214
William Tell (Rossini), 88
Winckelmann, Johann Joachim, 325
Winkler, Michael-Christian, 389
Witch burnings, 202
"With You, with You to the Featherbed,
  with You, with You to the Straw"
  (Bach), 289
Wolff, Christian von, 165, 188, 202, 203,
  204,
Wolff, Christoph, xviii, 265, 273, 278,
  279, 295, 302, 305, 324, 385, 388,
  389, 390, 391, 392
Wolfgang, Albrecht, 345
Works, Bach
  publications of, 338, 356, 361,
    366–367. *See also* Printing, of
    compositions
The World Is Sound (Berendt), 372
World War I, 247
Woulmyer, Jean Baptiste, 103, 108
Wülcken (Wilcke, Wilcken), Anna
  Magdalena. *See* Bach, Anna Magdalena

"The Youthful Hothead" (Du Bouchet), 37
Zachau, Friedrich Wilhelm, 10, 83, 87, 88
Zedler, Johann Heinrich, 367–368, 387
Zehmisch, Gottlieb Benedict, 279
Zelter, Carl Friedrich, 214, 361–362, 393,
  394
Zeraschi, Helmut, 393
Ziegler, Christiane von, 197
Ziller, Martin, 391
Zimmermann's Café, 212, 280–281
Zwingli, Ulrich, 119